THE HANDBOOK OF
COUNTRY RISK
2003

A Guide to International Business and Trade

THE HANDBOOK OF
COUNTRY RISK
2003

A Guide to International Business and Trade

coface

KOGAN
PAGE

Publisher's note
Every possible effort has been made to ensure
that the information contained in this book is
accurate at the time of going to press, and the
publishers cannot accept responsibility for
any errors or omissions, however caused.
No responsibility for loss or damage occasioned
to any person acting or refraining from action,
as a result of the material in this publication,
can be accepted by the editor, the publisher or
any of the authors.

First published in 1999 by Kogan Page Limited.
This (Fifth) edition published 2003

120 Pentonville Road   22883 Quicksilver Drive
London N1 9JN   Sterling VA 20166-2012
www.kogan-page.co.uk   USA

British Library Cataloguing-in-Publication Data

A CIP record for this book is available from the British Library

ISBN 0 7494 3978 5 HB
ISBN 0 7494 4044 9 PB
ISSN 1478-6293

Library of Congress Cataloguing-in-Publication Data

Typeset by Kingswood Steele Ltd, London EC2
Printed and bound in Great Britain by Cambrian Printers Ltd., Aberystwyth, Wales

Contents

■ THE AMERICAS

The US Economy 118

Experts from Oxford Analytica, London

The range of country @ratings in the Americas 122

Sylvia Greisman and Olivier Oechslin,
Coface Country Risk and Economic
Studies Department, Paris

■ ASIA

The outlook for South and South-East Asia 182

Experts from Oxford Analytica, London

The range of country @ratings in Asia. 187

Sylvia Greisman and Pierre Paganelli
Coface Country Risk and Economic
Studies Department, Paris

Acknowledgements

The publisher is most grateful to the Oxford Analytica and Coface country risk and short-term experts (Nathalie Ballage, Jean-Louis Daudier, Dominique Fruchter, Laura Gastellier, Catherine Monteil, Bernard Lignereux, Olivier Oechslin, Pierre Paganelli, Jean-François Rondest, Yves Zlotowski). Without their valuable input *The Handbook of Country Risk 2003* would not have been possible.

Our thanks also to Govind Bhinder of FEAT (Financial and Economic Authors & Translators), Stanley Glick of Lingua Franca and to Coface's Communication department.

FOREWORD

2003, A Transition Year

François David, *Chairman and Chief Executive, Coface*

Will 2003 be a year of recovery that finally allows us to emerge from the slowdown of the last two-and-a-half years? If we are to believe the statistics, and particularly past trends of short-term company payment behaviour, it appears that each cycle lasts about ten years, with eight growth years followed by two years of contraction. Optimism would therefore be in order. However, the skittishness of operators, aggravated by political uncertainties, prompts a more circumspect stance.

As an upturn began taking shape in the first quarter last year, notably in the United States, the scepticism that progressively overcame entrepreneurs only intensified throughout the year. The succession of financial scandals that compounded doubts about the growth's solidity heightened investor wariness and led to a stock market collapse that created financing difficulties for companies and impeded an investment recovery. Moreover, the conflict in Iraq, with its consequences for energy prices and household purchasing power, has prolonged the wait-and-see stance taken by entrepreneurs.

Provided geopolitical uncertainties can be rapidly dissipated, a number of conditions now appear ripe for an economic trend reversal. Company profitability has been improving in many sectors. Moreover, the monetary policies adopted by industrial countries have pushed interest rates to historic lows. Prospective enlargement of the European Union to admit new countries paves the way for significant development opportunities, as does WTO admission of countries constituting large markets. International financial institutions are primed to avoid a new emerging-country crisis.

Recovery will nonetheless substantially depend on a return of confidence. Otherwise, recovery prospects will continue to be postponed from quarter to quarter. The most optimistic forecasts now see recovery coming by mid-year – providing there is no new postponement.

In this context, a company's capacity to identify risks appears crucial. This book, as well as the @rating Solution with its latest tool, the @rating Score – which measures the likelihood of a company failing within a year – will, I hope, allow you to develop your sales activities while maintaining sound accounts receivable.

INTRODUCTION

The Outlook for 2003-04

Jonathan Reuvid, *Consultant Editor, Global Market Briefings,*
Kogan Page

By the time this edition is in print the second Gulf War will probably be in progress or even over. Misquoting from Winston Churchill (1942), this will mark 'not even the beginning of the end, but, perhaps, the end of the beginning' in the campaign against weapons of mass destruction and global terrorism on which the United States of America under President George W Bush has embarked. The consequences of an invasion of Iraq, assuming a relatively short and decisive war resulting in regime change are uncertain. Much will depend on post-war US foreign policy within the region and elsewhere and the reactions of Islamic fundamentalists including possible further acts of terrorism by extremists. Progress in reaching a lasting settlement of the Palestinian–Israeli conflict and the defusing of the nuclear threat posed by North Korea under Kim Jong II are the foremost urgent tasks.

The prospect of Middle East conflict which we characterised as the 'wild card' in our economic prognosis a year ago evolved into reality in the final quarter of 2002 with the unanimous United Nations Security Council resolution 1441. It remains to be seen whether America, Great Britain and their allies will go to war against Iraq with or without a further United Nations resolution and, if a resolution is put, which permanent members of the Security Council exercise their vetoes or abstain in the voting. The alternative of a peaceful solution in the form of proactive compliance by Iraq in total disarmament, the abdication of Saddam Hussein or his overthrow by coup d'etat are discounted in the analysis which follows.

In surveying regional economics we review the United States first as the mainspring for interaction between the world's economies, followed by the remaining Americas; then, in line with the contents of the book, Europe, followed by Asia, North Africa, the Middle East and lastly Sub-Saharan Africa. Drawing distinctions between the interwoven economic and political issues is particularly difficult this time having regard to the possible impact of a Gulf war on relationships between the United States and its traditional trade partners and political allies. The credibility of the United Nations as the legitimate global arbiter of international relations is at stake. Within Europe, too, progress towards this unpopular war has exposed unwelcome cracks between EU member states with the risk of more permanent disaffection which could delay the movement towards a more cohesive Community.

■ THE UNITED STATES

Both optimists and pessimists among the economic commentators were confounded by the erratic progress of the US economy in 2002. There was no V-shaped or saucer-shaped recovery, in spite of promising first quarter GDP year-on-year growth of 5 per cent, nor double-dip recession when the economy remained positive in the fourth quarter with year-on-year growth at 0.7 per cent. Instead, growth fluctuated between spurts in the first and third quarters and relapses in the second and final quarters. Consumer spending which had powered the economy in the first nine months fell back to just 1 per cent in the fourth quarter and is reported to have declined by 0.3 per cent in January 2003. Inflation had risen to 2.6 per cent at the end of January 2003 compared with just over 1 per cent a year earlier and was matched by an average earnings increase of 2.7 per cent while unemployment was steady at 5.7 per cent. GDP growth for 2003 may be expected to remain close to the overall 2002 level at around 2.5 per cent. However, so long as productivity continues to grow at the 2.5 per cent annual average rate of the past seven years, overall GDP growth of more than 3.5 per cent is required to curtail rising excess capacity and downward pressures on wages and profitability. This level of growth may be possible in 2004.

Business investment was slack throughout 2002 and actually fell in the final quarter for the first time in twelve months as inventories were run down. Government spending offset much of the fall in business investment, rising 4.6 per cent overall with both state and local expenditures being maintained at higher levels than the weak condition of states' finances had led economists to expect. Trade figures released in January 2003 revealed a further widening in the trade deficit as domestic demand was satisfied more by imports than increased production; the trade gap for 2002 was a massive US$484 billion.

A more significant factor in the trade gap has been the unaccustomed weakness of the dollar whose trade-weighted fall of 10 per cent in 2002 was the largest since 1987. In the second week of January 2003, the US currency slumped to its lowest level against the euro since November 1999, although GDP growth for the year as a whole was more than three times that of the eurozone and compared with a GDP fall in Japan. The recent US$674 billion fiscal package resulting from the abolition of double taxation on dividends has apparently failed to stimulate the dollar exchange rate, down to US$1.10 to the euro in the first week of March, and it seems that the US currency is in for another difficult year in 2003.

A part of the problem appears to reside in the nature of recent growth. From 1995 to 2000 business investment in the US, fuelled by strong overseas investment, rose at an average of 8.6 per cent a year compared with 3.6 per cent in the eurozone and was the driver of economic growth. As a consequence, and despite a rising current account deficit, the trade-weighted value of the dollar over the same period rose by 29 per cent. With business investment down 3.2 per cent in 2002 and improvement in 2003 likely to be minimal, any impetus for growth can only come from consumption and government spending. If the American economy continues to grow faster than other leading economies, which seems likely in the case of Western Europe and Japan, the US current account deficit may be expected to swell further to the level of US$550 billion. But this time around the foreign investment necessary to counterbalance the increase is less likely to be attracted and the dollar may have to fall further in order to entice foreign investors to re-engage in the US. However, the dollar remains underpinned by the holdings of foreign central banks which rose US$122.2 billion in 2002, of which about US$100 billion is attributable to Asian central banks keen to head off rises of their own currencies against the dollar which would snuff out their own export growth. Further falls in the dollar during 2003 into 2004 will be dampened by the large current account surpluses of China and Hong Kong the currencies of which are pegged to the dollar, and which automatically accumulate US currency.

Weak corporate investment and slackening consumer demand have not responded to the continuing low level of interest rates. The US three month money market rate of interest has fallen from 1.78 to 1.24 per cent in the year to 1 March 2003 while the equivalent eurozone rate has reduced from 3.37 to 2.55 per cent over the same period. The Federal Reserve has also cut the rate on ten year Treasury bonds to 3.75 per cent over the past year, the lowest rate for more than 40 years. No doubt monetary policy has played its part in preventing double-dip recession.

The President's recent tax cut may be more effective in bringing back private investors to equity markets, particularly those who have run out of available tax shelters, and a stock market recovery would help to mop up the deficits of those pension funds which remain invested in equities. However, the tax cut together with increased defence expenditure will certainly add to the Federal budget deficit.

The present lack of US budgetary discipline gives cause for concern to those European countries with lower growth economies which are struggling rather more successfully to contain their budget deficits and to maintain trade surpluses. The US current account deficit of approximately 5 per cent and budget deficit which the OECD has estimated at 3.1 per cent of GDP for 2002 compare unfavourably with the Euro area which maintained a current account surplus of US$60 billion in 2002 and a budget deficit at 2.2 per cent of GDP. The current year forecast for the US budget deficit in 2003 is 5.3 per cent, falling back to 4.0 per cent in 2004 on the assumption of a 3.5 per cent GDP increase. In effect, the US financial position is becoming increasingly exposed and, in the absence of an identifiable programme to restore the budget balance over the coming years, is damaging international investor confidence by posing sustainability risks.

Turning from macroeconomics to the financial markets, corporate America has shown remarkable resilience in the face of a profusion of financial scandals which have called into question the regulatory controls and ethical standards of modern capitalism. The overhang from the burst technology and telecoms bubbles ensured that stock markets remained depressed in the opening months of 2002, but the general bear market gloom was soon overtaken by the Enron scandal arising from falsely inflated profits with the compliance of its auditors, Arthur Andersen, whose North American audit practice rapidly disintegrated in the resultant crisis of confidence. It soon became apparent that Enron was not an isolated case of corporate malfeasance; other major corporations and their chief executives were identified as the perpetrators of similar practices and their auditors from the remaining world-class practices were subjected to the same finger of suspicion.

Meanwhile, the previously little known New York state's attorney-general, Eliot Spitzer, was laying siege to the pillars of Wall Street's banking establishment, alleging misdeeds by research analysts in puffing shares that their colleagues were discarding from investment portfolios. At the blast of Spitzer's trumpet the so-called 'Chinese walls' of investment banking propriety soon fell down and the banks have been scrambling to negotiate settlements in the form of fines to limit their exposure to civil suits. By December 2002, an initial settlement, worth US$1.4 billion, with Wall Street firms had been announced but the ongoing

investigation continues to unravel further instances of likely fraud involving blue-chip investment banks which are likely to keep financial malpractice in the headlines.

Inevitably, the mistrust generated by these revelations has impeded investment recovery from the three year bear market and may continue to do so. At the end of December the Dow Jones index had fallen 17 per cent year-on-year, the worst performance for 28 years, and the technology-weighted NASDAQ was down 22 per cent. By the end of February 2003 the decline steepened with the Dow Jones down 22 per cent and the NASDAQ 33 per cent from end of 2001 levels. No doubt the further deterioration reflects of anxieties concerning the impending war in Iraq.

As we shall see, the slump in securities values is as steep or steeper in Tokyo and European markets. The delayed recovery in markets has exposed companies with under-funded pension plans in America as well as Europe.

■ THE AMERICAS

The prompt actions of the US authorities in introducing monetary and fiscal policies designed to boost demand and revive investment have also benefited its NAFTA partners' economies, albeit to a lesser extent.

Canada

Throughout 2001 and 2002 Canada appeared to be defying infection from the wobbling US economy. GDP growth was the strongest among G7 countries in 2002 at 3.3 per cent 2002 (2001 – 1.5 per cent) and both its current account on foreign trade and budget have remained in surplus. With some risk of inflation, the Bank of Canada raised interest rates three times in 2002 and the three-month market rate stands currently at 2.87 per cent. One reason for the more comfortable performance of the economy than that of its neighbour is the lower dependence on the reeling technology and telecom sectors. Other factors in Canada's favour have been Ontario's buoyant automobile industry and the benefit of higher prices for Alberta's oil and gas producers. However, the self-styled 'Northern tiger' has seemed to be losing its immunity since the beginning of 2003 with housing starts down in January, factory orders in decline and inventories rising for five months, the longest downturn for three years. In fact, Canada's dependence on the US economy has grown rather than diminished since 1988 when the two countries first entered into their free trade agreement; over this period America's share of Canada's exports has risen from 73 per cent to 85 per cent. The target of 3.1 per cent GDP growth for 2003 looks optimistic.

Mexico

In 2002 the Mexican economy returned to growth after a slight recession in 2001, registering a 1.9 per cent year-on-year increase in GDP in the final quarter. Depreciation of the peso against the dollar by 21 per cent over the year to end-February 2003 has aided exports and the 12 month current account deficit was reduced from US$16.1 billion at the end of the third quarter 2002 to US$8.6 billion at the end of January 2003. However, the short-term interest rate remains high at 9.3 per cent and the health of the economy will continue to depend on that of the USA. In dollar terms the decline in stock market values mirrors Wall Street markets.

Argentina

Argentina represents the foremost intensive care patient in the IMF hospital. The saga of crises afflicting the economy can be traced back to Argentina's ill-chosen decision to peg its currency to the dollar in 1991 which resulted in the massive US$40 billion aid package granted in December 2000 during the Fernando de la Rua presidency. In spite of drastic reductions in its credit ratings in July 2001, the IMF managing director agreed to recommend a US$8 billion increase in Argentina's US$14 billion stand-by loan agreement the following month. When Argentines withdrew US$1.3 billion from their bank accounts in November 2001, the International Monetary Fund (IMF) retaliated by freezing an equivalent sum in aid pushing Argentina to the brink of default, resulting in the resignation of President de la Rua. Throughout 2002 the Fund remained entangled in negotiations and in November Argentina defaulted on a US$805 million debt repayment to the World Bank. Not surprisingly, the IMF management recommendation to allow Argentina to roll over US$6 billion in debt in January 2003, coincidentally

within hours before the Argentines agreed to repay US$1 billion to the IMF, has been criticized by its members as a sell-out which damages the Fund's credibility. With inflation at nearly 40 per cent and a last recorded year-on-year fall in GDP of 10.1 per cent (2002 Q3), the only bright spots in the economic scene are a continuing positive trade balance and rising industrial output in January 2003 of 10.1 per cent. In the past year the currency has depreciated 50 per cent.

Brazil

The election of Luiz Ignacio Lula da Silva, of the leftwing Workers Party in October 2002 has brought fresh hope that Brazil may achieve the difficult of task of providing change while maintaining the stabilising fiscal policies of the outgoing centrist president Fernando Henrique Cardoso. Mr Lula da Silva is focusing on the elimination of hunger from the impoverished north-east and the cities and in addressing the social imbalance between the extremes of wealth and poverty. He has also pledged to support and stimulate business, in particular SMEs. In order to succeed, the new president must also address the problems of endemic corruption and crime. In 2002 Brazil avoided debt default after the IMF stepped in with a US$30 billion loan in August but the public debt burden which had doubled in the previous eight years to 56 per cent of GDP has plainly become unsustainable. Consumer price inflation stood at 14.5 per cent in January 2003 but industrial production was 5.5 per cent up on a year before while the current account deficit was US$6.3 billion. With short-term interest rates at a punitive 26.25 per cent and weak growth in GDP forecast for 2003, the economy stands at a cross-roads. The real has depreciated by 50 per cent over the past year making companies with heavy external dollar debts or those utilising imported materials and components in their production particularly vulnerable.

Chile

Chile suffered several setbacks in 2002 following the collapse of copper prices and a contraction of its export markets. However, the current account deficit in the fourth quarter was only US$0.6 billion against 2002 year-end foreign reserves of US$16.4 billion. An upturn in GDP growth is forecast for 2003 from the modest growth achieved in 2002 (Q3 – 1.8 per cent). Inflation is relatively low at 3.0 per cent with interest rates at a comfortable 2.64 per cent and industrial production growing at 7.2 per cent year-on-year at 2002 year-end.

Other Latin American countries

Economic activity in Colombia was at a low level even before the recent resurgence of political violence with GDP growth below 2 per cent, minimal growth in industrial production and the current account deficit beginning to climb. There is a growing external debt and short-term interest rates are rather high at 7.69 per cent. Contrary to general global experience the Colombian stockmarket on 1 March, 2003 was 15.3 per cent up in dollar terms on end-2001.

Another Latin American economy where the financial situation is relatively healthy is Peru. Currency depreciation in the 12 months to end-February 2003 was minimal and the stockmarket, in dollar terms, stood at 28.6 per cent above its value at 2001 year-end. Peru ended 2002 with GDP growth of 6.3 per cent in December and industrial product-ion up 11.7 per cent, thanks to exploitation of the Antamina copper and zinc mine. The trade balance was just positive at 2002 year-end and inflation and interest rates are modest. A knock-on effect from the successful minerals exploitation is needed to maintain the high growth rate through 2003.

For Venezuela total collapse of the day to day economy is looming. After the failed coup in April 2002 to dislodge the left-leaning president Chavez it was hoped that the devastating opposition-led strike of 30,000 employees at the state oil company might finally dislodge him. Supported by the poorest elements of the population, Mr Chavez's response of declaring a state of emergency and sacking almost 10,000 of the strikers has saved his office but done nothing for the economy. The oil-dependent economy shrank by 16.7 per cent in the fourth quarter of 2002 (8 per cent over the full year) and is expected to decline further by up to 30 per cent in 2003. With consumer price inflation at 38.7 per cent over the 12 months ended February 2003 and interest rates also in excess of 30 per cent, the only redeeming feature of the economy is the oil-driven current account surplus – still US$7.6 billion in the fourth quarter of 2002. Before the strike reduced oil production to a trickle of 200,000 barrels a day, Venezuela was the world's fifth largest producer. The economic collapse is judged locally to be the worst since the country's 19th century civil wars. The crisis of confidence is total.

Of the remaining South American economies, Uraguay and Ecuador deserve comment. Previously classed as a good debtor, Uraguay, with its tiny population of 3.5 million people, has suffered severely from the economic collapse of neighbouring Argentina. The loss of tourism and, more importantly, the withdrawal of funds by Argentines caused the peso to fall and four local banks to collapse reducing foreign reserves by 4200 million. Uraguay struggled to continue servicing its debts and, finally, in August 2002 the IMF came to the rescue with a US$3.8 billion loan. Since then the peso, which lost half its value in the first six months of 2002, has stabilised and funds have begun to be redeposited with the banks. The IMF intervention came too late to contain general damage to the economy; the burden of foreign debt, all in dollars, doubled in 2002 and is forecast to climb to 120 per cent of GDP by the end of 2003. At the same time, unemployment rose to 20 per cent and GDP withered by 10.5 per cent in 2002. In an effort to avoid default President Jorge Batlle's government has tried to impose a fiscal squeeze. However, on 21 February 2003 the government announced agreement with the IMF on a softer target of a primary fiscal surplus (before interest) of 3.3 per cent of GDP. Uraguay will also seek a 'voluntary' restructuring of some of its debt in due course. By contrast Ecuador's new president Lucio Gutierrez, who gained power on a left-wing platform, has risked political rejection by a series of centre-right measures taken within his first month of office in order to capture an IMF deal which will release US$500 million in multilateral loans. Faced with a 2003 budget deficit estimated at 8 per cent of GDP and a probable debt default, Mr Gutierrez has increased the price of petrol by one third, frozen public sector wages for a year, announced a gradual rise in electricity tariffs and talked of introducing new taxes in order to achieve a budget surplus of US$250 million in 2003.

It is anticipated that the president will have a

previously by the division of power with the former Socialist primer minister, is now deploying the extensive powers of France's presidential system to pursue a more assertive foreign policy. However, both he and Mr Raffarin are mindful of their party's unexpected 1997 defeat that followed a failure to honour election promises and are approaching with caution the task of restructuring the public sector pensions system. Negotiations with the trades union confederations are sure to be hampered by the rising unemployment and concerns about private pension funding which France shares with other OECD economies.

Germany

While France may be able to defer a restructure of its public sector spending on social security, cutting the costs of Germany's expensive statutory health and pension scheme has become a priority. These costs, averaging over 40 per cent of gross wages, have long been recognised as one of the most damaging structural rigidities in the German economy which succeeding CDU and SPD coalition governments have lacked the resolution to tackle. The promising start which Chancellor Gerhard Schroder's first government made by restructuring corporate taxation was not carried through and Germany has suffered the consequences of a relaxed fiscal policy in the period of global economic downturn up to the end of 2002. In the final quarter of 2002 the German economy stagnated bring GDP growth for the year down to a bare 0.2 per cent and, in December, unemployment reached a four-year record level of 4,197 million with an average unemployment rate for the year of 9.8 per cent. GDP growth for 2003 is forecast at 0.5 per cent with the prospect of a return to 1.9 per cent in 2004 if the more decisive government measures now under discussion are introduced. Consumer price inflation in February was just 1.3 per cent against the current 2.7 per cent level of wage increases.

Although the issue of Germany's budget deficit at 3.7 per cent for 2002 has received the most attention within the EU there are other major causes for concern. The banking sector has come under increasing pressure with a surge in corporate failures resulting in record bad loan charges being taken by the Big Four universal banks as well as the publicly-owned landesbanken and sparkassen which hold some 50 per cent of Germany's corporate loans. Hopefully, the banks have absorbed the worst of their losses and talk of emergency measures along the lines of the plan adopted for the Swedish banks in the early 1990's to transfer the banks' bad debts to a government-owned 'bad bank' is premature but a structural reform of the banking system seems increasingly likely. Like the life assurers in other leading markets, the German life groups have announced reduced bonuses for 2003 and are registering massive write-downs as a result of tumbling equity prices. Capital markets have suffered too with the DAX stockmarket index falling 52.5 per cent in local currency between the end of 2001 and the end of February 2003, nearly twice the fall experienced on New York stock markets. The Deutsche Borse's woes were highlighted by its decision to close its junior Neuer Markt in 2003 following a fall in its Nemax 50 index of 95 per cent between March 2000 and September 2002 amid a series of failures and inadequate regulation.

Inevitably the Mittelstand, the backbone of privately-owned German industry, has come under pressure from the tighter banking environment. Compared with the small and medium-sized sectors of private industry in other eurozone member states, there is a significantly lower share of own capital in the total balance sheets of the smaller companies and this sub-sector has been hit both by the tougher times and by the new Basle II rules governing bank loans. One of the few positive factors in the current situation has been the initiatives of Mr Wolfgang Clement, head of the newly-formed federal economics and employment ministry and premier of North Rhine-Westphalia, to stimulate public loans, encourage regional banks and savings institutions to provide continuing finance, introduce labour market reforms and provide tax breaks for start-ups and small-scale enterprises. The stronger euro will hardly help Germany in 2003 to stimulate its export sales. In 2002 there was a positive balance on current account of US$50.4 billion, representing 2.1 per cent of GDP; for 2003 the surplus to GDP ratio is expected to be no more than 1.7 per cent.

The political strength of Chancellor Schroder has been severely diminished, first by the parliamentary election last September when the SDP and its allies scraped home, and then by the heavy defeats suffered in two regional elections at the end of January 2003 at the hand of the CDU which strengthened its control of the upper house. Perversely, this weakening of the government may help Mr Schroder to carry through the much-needed structural reforms through programmes agreed with the opposition, although this will involve confronting the left-wing of his own party, and the trade unions hostile to change with whom he negotiated an outline public sector pay deal of 4.4 per cent spread over 27 months before the regional elections. On 14 March 2003 the government is due to unveil a radical package of labour-market and welfare reforms to the Bundestag which seems certain to be construed by union leaders as a dismantling of the welfare state.

Other European countries

The slowdown in Italy's economy has been deteriorating towards stagnation. For 2002 GDP growth was a meagre 0.4 per cent and no better than 1.2 per cent is predicted for 2003 rising to 2.2 per cent in 2004 if recovery has set in. Unemployment was running at 8.9 per cent in October 2002 and no improvement is believed to have occurred since. Although industrial output fell 0.6 per cent in December 2002, it had increased by 2.1 per cent year on year which was a marked improvement on the 4.2 per cent decline registered for 2001. Italy ran a current account deficit of US$6.4 billion in 2002, representing only 0.2 per cent of GDP, which is expected to be much the same in 2003 and 2004. The budget deficit was 2.3 per cent in 2002 and is expected to remain sound through 2003. Public investment has remained solid and, with inflation expected to remain modest at around 2.3 per cent in 2003, the recent tax breaks to those with low and middle class incomes could encourage consumption.

Spain's rapid growth of recent years has faded to commonplace levels with GDP growth in 2002 limited to 2.0 per cent. Although industrial production continued to grow in December 2002 at 2.5 per cent, unemployment stood at 12 per cent in December 2002 and the slackening labour market is eroding real wages. Industrial investment has declined and activity is reported as strong only in residential housing and public infrastructure expenditure. The collapse of export markets and reduced revenue from tourism resulted in a current account deficit of US$15.3 billion for the 12 months to November 2002, representing a deficit of 2 per cent on GDP.

The Belgian and Dutch economies are superficially in rather better shape than those of their larger eurozone neighbours, France and Germany. GDP growth in Belgium was 0.7 per cent in 2002 and improvements to 1.3 per cent and 2.3 per cent are forecast for 2003-04. There was a budget balance in 2002 and a current account surplus in 2002 of US$18 billion representing 5.2 per cent of GDP is forecast to fall to 4.9 per cent in 2003. Inflation at 1.7 per cent is not expected to rise in 2003-04. However, consumer spending is weak with retail sales down 4.8 per cent last December. In the Netherlands, GDP growth in 2002 was 0.2 per cent but is expected to recover to 0.8 per cent in 2003 and 2.2 per cent in 2004. The budget deficit in 2002 was a modest 0.8 per cent of GDP and a current account surplus of US$9.1 billion was recorded, representing 3.1 per cent of GDP which is forecast to be maintained through 2003-04. However, retail sales volume in the Netherlands also took a tumble of 2.5 per cent and industrial production was down 6.8 per cent. Nevertheless, it is doubtful whether either economy is sufficiently robust to withstand severe downturns in their major partners' economies.

Austria is in a somewhat different category since its economy is more integrated with those of the neighbouring CEE states scheduled to join the EU in May 2004. At 0.8 per cent GDP growth in 2002 was in line with the euro area average but an improvement in growth to 1.2 per cent in 2003 and 2 per cent in 2004 is currently forecast. The budget deficit ran at 1.6 per cent of GDP in 2002 but is forecast to improve to 0.7 per cent this year. Disappointingly, the current account on foreign trade was barely in balance in 2002 and is expected to be in deficit in 2003 at 0.7 per cent of GDP rising to 1.4 per cent in 2004 and reflecting an expected increase in imports from the new EU members. Consumer price inflation remains steady at 1.8 per cent and unemployment at 4.2 per cent compares favourably with the major EU economies. The parliamentary election of September 2002 has left Chancellor Wolfgang Schussel's centre-right People's Party in power in coalition again with the Freedom Party. The difference this time is that the People's Party share of votes has risen to 42 per cent while the Freedom Party's share has sunk from 27 to 10 per cent. This may give Mr Schussel the opportunity to lighten Austrians' heavy tax burden by restructuring the current expensive pension and health-care systems.

The United Kingdom

It is becoming likely that 2003 will be a watershed year for the UK, economically as well as politically. Up to the end of 2002 it seemed that the UK had escaped the worst effects of the global slowdown experienced by the larger mainland European economies although the pound sterling's strength had continued to handicap exports before its recent decline. In 2002 there was a decline of 10.1 per cent in company investment as lower utilisation of production capacity was recorded, the sharpest decline since records began in 1965, but until the final months of the year household spending remained the growth engine of the economy. GDP growth for 2002 was revised down to 1.6 per cent but the final quarter ratio of 1.3 per cent year-on-year compared with 2.1 per cent a year earlier. The brunt of the investment slump fell on manufacturing where investment reached its lowest point since 1984; in the last quarter of 2002 it declined 17.7 per cent year on year. Non-manufacturing investment in the same period was broadly flat. The high sterling exchange rate may have been a factor in the dearth of investment, but the main cause was lack of competitiveness against alternative investment locations, particularly eastern EU accession states and China. Although the unemployment rate has been held so far to 5.1 per cent, it is expected to rise and current forecasts of GDP growth in 2003 in excess of 2.2 per cent may be optimistic. Meantime, Bank of England interest rates stand at 3.75 per cent. In foreign trade the 2002 current account deficit of US$20.5 billion represented 1.6 per cent of GDP; the deficit is forecast to rise to 1.8 per cent in 2003.

At the beginning of March 2003 the IMF endorsed the Bank Governor's warning to Chancellor Gordon Brown that the Treasury estimates of tax revenues may be optimistic and that government borrowing is more likely to stabilise at over 2 per cent than the 1.5 per cent projected. Accordingly, he was urged to increase taxes or lower spending to cut the budget deficit by up to 1.25 per cent. The electorate is already braced for increased local taxes and higher national insurance contributions in the April Budget; further tax increases are now possible at a time when manufacturing industry is pressing for taxation relief.

The government's problems have been compounded by consumer dissatisfaction with the slow rate of improvement in healthcare, education and transport where the bulk of increased public spending has been channelled. The threat to individual wealth posed by pension and endowment assurance shortfalls which have followed the free fall in stockmarket equity prices (down 41.5 per cent since 2001 year-end up to end-February 2003) have also increased the pressure for pension reform. In this climate of growing disillusion with the government, Mr Blair's main electoral asset may be the weakness of the Conservative opposition which supports his foreign policy and still has little credibility as an alternative government.

Other EU member states

Denmark and Sweden both registered GDP growth for 2002 at more than twice the Euro area average, although in Denmark's case GDP fell sharply in the final quarter on a year-over-year basis. Both countries are forecast to achieve slightly higher GDP growth at the 1.8 per cent level in 2003 rising to perhaps 2.4 per cent in 2004. Unemployment in both countries is less than 5.5 per cent and consumer price inflation is running at slightly more than 2 per cent. In 2002 both countries achieved surpluses on foreign trading current account representing 2.2 per cent and 3.5 per cent respectively which they expect to maintain in 2003. The picture of stability is completed by the budgets of both countries being in surplus during 2002 and forecasts that they will each continue to run a surplus in 2003 at just under 2 per cent of GDP.

EU Accession states

The foremost three CEE states awaiting EU entry, Czech Republic, Hungary and Poland all achieved positive GDP growth above the eurozone average, although in Poland's case growth was a bare 1 per cent. In 2003 all three economies are forecast to grow at 3 per cent or more. The Czech Republic and Poland both contained consumer price inflation below 2 per cent in 2002 but inflation is rising in Poland. Hungary's inflation rate exceeded 5 per cent in 2002 but is forecast to decline in 2003.

Unemployment remains a problem in Poland at 17.8 per cent in 2002 with little relief expected in 2003. In the Czech Republic unemployment is approaching 10 per cent but Hungary has contained its unemployment below 6 per cent. All three countries run budget deficits representing 8.9 per cent of GDP in the case of the Czech Republic and at the 6 per cent level for the other two. Among the remaining CEE entrants, only Slovakia runs a budget deficit exceeding 3 per cent of GDP and all of their economies are growing in excess of 3 per cent with unemployment at 10 per cent or more. Gross foreign debt is a problem for all three leading entrants, approaching 60 per cent of GDP in the case of Hungary and at 43.2 per cent and 32 per cent respectively for the Czech Republic and Poland. However, all three foreign debt/GDP ratios are expected to decline through 2004 as current account surpluses on foreign trade increase.

Russia

The Russian economy continued to power ahead driven by expanding private consumption and supported by a strong foreign trade current account balance thanks to oil revenues and firm oil prices. The rest of the economy is slowing down and GDP growth, at 3.7 per cent in 2002, will require a strong performance from the energy sector to be sustained. The slowdown in investment, excepting the recent announcement of BP's US$675 billion injection, is a reflection of an overvalued rouble; the banking system remains flawed. Both consumer price inflation at 14.3 per cent and short-term interest rates at 18.0 per cent betray economic weakness and are further deterrents to inward investment. The IMF proposal for the creation of a stabilisation fund to ring-fence windfall profits from high oil prices may not be heeded.

■ ASIA

China

The year 2002 was very much a year of fulfilment for China. In December the WTO completed its first post-entry review of China's trade policy, reporting that in the first twelve months of membership China had enacted and amended a large number of new laws in compliance with its WTO obligations. China has also adopted new standards of transparency and acceptance of competition which have removed many of the former barriers to investment and trade. Although tariffs and quantitative controls have been reduced across the board and restrictions on engagement in foreign trade by private enterprise are being removed, it is no surprise that the first fruits of a more open market economy have been a marked increase in China's exports. A further surge in foreign direct investment is being experienced as international business positions itself to take advantage of the relaxed conditions for foreign ownership of private industry in China and Chinese manufacturing competitiveness. In 2002, a 21.8 per cent increase in foreign trade registered a new high of US$620.8 billion and advanced China's position in world trade to fifth. Foreign reserves excluding gold stood at £269.9 billion in October 2002. Also in 2002, China's absorption of foreign investment reached a new record of US$82.8 billion in contract value and US$52.7 billion in utilised value, increases of 19.6 per cent and 12.5 per cent over 2001.

The domestic economy had a good year too with GDP growth topping 8 per cent, minimal inflation and industrial production running more than 14 per cent up year-on-year. Not unexpectedly, the transfer of government to China's fourth generation of leaders was effected seamlessly with Mr Hu Jintao succeeding Jiang Zemin and Mr Wen Jiabao assuming the mantle of Mr Zhu Rongji as Prime Minister. However, there is still much to be done. The pump-priming of public expenditure which kept China's economy on track during the Asian financial crisis, and has sustained continuing growth at 7-8 per cent per year since, has been at the price of increasing China's budget deficit projected to rise in 2003 to 3.2 per cent of GDP. Other longstanding problems persist such as the unresolved weakness of the state-owned banking sector, non-performing loans to other state-owned industries and the chronic imbalance between the prosperous, industrially developing eastern seaboard and its hinterland with the underdeveloped agricultural economy of western China.

Nevertheless, the leadership has set itself ambitious targets of continuing to grow GDP by 7 per cent annually so as to quadruple GDP and raise foreign trade to US$2 trillion by the year 2020 under the umbrella objective of 'full engagement in the building of a well-off society'. Whether the new leadership also takes tentative steps towards a more democratic form of government remains to be seen.

Japan

The contrast between the continuing stagnation of the Japanese economy and the dynamism of China, now playing a more active role in the global economy, is even more marked than a year ago. High hopes of Junichiro Koizumi as a reforming Prime Minister when he took office in April 2001 have faded with his failure to translate policy goals into action. The opportunity characterised by Mr Koizumi 'to fight deflation aggressively' with the appointment of a new Bank of Japan governor in March 2003 may have been missed with the nomination of Mr Toshihiko Fukui, a central banker of 40 years experience and a conventional 'safe pair of hands', when what is needed are a reflationary monetary policy and a fiscal policy that begins to haul back the public debt burden which has risen to 140 per cent of GDP. In addition, the endless banking crisis and continued propping up of bankrupt companies demands banking and structural reform which identifies non-performing loans and nationalises the weakest banks, while closing down bankrupt entities and re-privatizing sound assets. Meanwhile, GDP growth for 2003-04 is projected at no more than 0.6 per cent, while deflation continues at an annualized rate of 0.4 per cent or more. Domestic consumption remains depressed by declining wages and fears of unemployment and pension under-funding. So far, unemployment has been held at 5.5 per cent up to January 2003.

The current account surplus on foreign trade was at 2.8 per cent of GDP for 2002 but was shown to be shrinking at 1.4 per cent year-on-year in the December trade figures. The 2002 budget deficit at 7.9 per cent of GDP was the highest among developed countries, being more than 2.5 times that of the USA and approaching four times that of the euro area. It can no longer be claimed that Japan is an engine of regional growth.

South Korea

The second most successful economy in Asia in 2002, South Korea's GDP growth of 6.1 per cent which the OECD expects to be maintained at the level of 5.7 per cent through 2003-04, has been driven by continued domestic consumption and rising exports to China which have offset lower sales of electronic equipment to North America and Western European markets. Consumer price inflation in February 2003 was at 3.9 per cent with short-term interest rates at just above 4.5 per cent. The foreign trade current account remains positive and the economy's finances are sound with recovery in the banking sector. South Korea's new president, Mr Roh Moo-hyun still has the problem of restructuring some of the chaebols financially but he will be pre-occupied in the short-term brokering a deal to dismantle North Korea's nuclear programmes.

Hong Kong, Singapore and Taiwan

Economic recovery in the three other more mature Asian economies will continue to depend more on revival of the sluggish demand for their manufactures from North America and Western Europe. In the meantime, Hong Kong, Singapore and Taiwan are all maintaining growth and strong current account surpluses in foreign trade.

The Hong Kong economy is under deflationary pressure but has resumed modest growth, forecast at 3 per cent for 2003, and the administration is focused on its repositioning in the service sectors to avoid marginalization by post-WTO entry China and the strong competitive threat of Shanghai as greater China's premier financial centre. Hong Kong based manufacturers which have failed to delocalize to the mainland are severely weakened. The Hong Kong stockmarket, although hardly buoyant, has suffered less than its North American and European counterparts; between end-December 2001 and end-February 2003 prices fell 20 per cent.

The record budget deficit of 2002-03 is being funded by increases in personal and corporate income taxes.

Singapore's predominant electronics sector has been impacted by reduced demand from Europe and North America but the economy has undergone a modest recovery.

The government is attempting to focus on services and is forging closer ties with China. High taxes and wages are making Singapore increasingly uncompetitive. Over the fourteen month period to the end of February 2003, Singaporean stockmarket prices also fell by about 20 per cent.

Admitted to the WTO immediately following China at the end of 2001, Taiwan has benefited from a slight recovery in external demand but remains vulnerable to the condition of the US economy. Constructive engagement with China has also resulted in delocation of manufacturing to China which is expected to improve corporate profits. Again, falls in stockmarket prices over the fourteen months to end-February 2003 were contained at 20 per cent.

India

The continuing risks of domestic sectarian conflict and confrontation with Pakistan ensure that the political situation remains tense. Although third quarter GDP growth of 5.8 per cent was recorded in 2002 with a foreign trade surplus on current account and consumer price inflation was maintained at 3.2 per cent in December, the economy remains weak with growing public debt and budget deficit.

Emerging countries of south-east Asia

Indonesia, Malaysia, the Philippines, Thailand and Vietnam are all in growth mode with GDP growth varying from Indonesia's 3.8 per cent to Thailand's 6 per cent. All of them are maintaining positive trade balances with current account surpluses.

Consumer price inflation was highest in Indonesia at 7.3 per cent (February 2003) and lowest in Malaysia at 1.7 per cent (January) where both domestic demand and exports have picked up. In Indonesia the renewed IMF assistance programme has boosted prospects for the economy together with external debt rescheduling agreements, but the Bali terrorist attack in October 2002 has depressed tourism. However, structural reforms in Indonesia and company restructuring in Malaysia are lagging. Thailand's economy is under threat

from increased public debt and needs to upgrade to more value-added manufacturing in response to Chinese competition. In the Philippines, although household demand is strong, domestic savings and foreign direct investment are insufficient to support deteriorating public finances and the economy has become over-dependent on external debt capital. Vietnam continues to enjoy strong growth supported by strong domestic demand, a dynamic private sector and the benefical effects of a trade agreement with the USA. Implementation of the programme agreed with the IMF in 2001 to restructure the banking and industrial public sectors has generated economic reforms.

Australia

The Australian economy continues to thrive. GDP grew by 3.7 per cent in 2002 having fallen back to 1.5 per cent at an annualised rate in the fourth quarter. Currently, GDP is forecast to grow at about 3.1 per cent in 2003 rising to 3.4 per cent in 2004. A delayed global recovery will dampen any recovery in exports which could also be affected by the strengthening Australian dollar which has risen so far in 2003 by 8 per cent against the US currency. The current account deficit inflated to 6.2 per cent of GDP in the fourth quarter of 2002 but is expected to fall back to 4.3 per cent for 2003 and, perhaps 3.8 per cent in 2004. In 2002 there was a small budget surplus which should be maintainable in 2003. The IMF advocates a simplification of the taxation system to narrow the gap between the top personal tax rate of 48.5 per cent and 30 per cent rate for companies.

■ NORTH AFRICA AND THE MIDDLE EAST

The political uncertainty regarding the likely invasion of Iraq makes informed comment on the Middle East region almost impossible so that the summaries which follow are predicated by the caveat that war in Iraq is likely to affect growth in non-oil countries adversely whereas oil-exporting countries, particularly Saudi Arabia, could benefit from escalating crude oil prices in the event that the Iraqi oilfields are put out of commission for any length of time.

Of the Gulf States, Qatar has bright prospects as a result of its cautious economic liberalization and some political opening but it remains vulnerable to a reversal of the oil situation. Likewise, oil and gas remain the stabilizing factor in Saudi Arabia's economy whose continued improvement in 2003 after two years of slowdown is subject to the strength of the rebound in US growth. The fiscal deficit is at present controlled by steady oil prices.

For Iran, disregarding the impact of war in Iraq, the economic and financial situation is favourable. Moderation of the external debt depends on the oil sector. In an economy where the public sector predominates and the political context is complex, the structural reform programme needed to consolidate the foundations of growth and contain unemployment will be difficult to implement.

Turkey's pivotal geographical and cultural position between Europe and the Muslim world contributes to its political and economic volatility. The ruling Development Party's leader, Tayyip Erdogan, finished 2002 strongly having wrung a commitment from the EU to open negotiations on Turkey's entry in December 2004, subject to continued internal progress. However, his standing with the EU has not been improved by failure to bring together the leaders of the Turkish-Cypriot and Greek-Cypriot factions into agreement for a united Cyprus which would have entered the Community as a single nation in May 2004. In economic terms recovery has been faster than expected with third quarter 2002 GDP growth at 7.9 per cent although inflation remained at an uncomfortably high 27 per cent in February 2003. The trade balance in December was in deficit by US$15.7 billion but IMF aid should permit avoidance of a further financial crisis in 2003. However, the financial outlook dipped on 1 March 2003 when parliament voted not to allow US troops to use Turkey as a base from which to attack Iraq, thereby putting US$30 billion of promised US financial assistance in doubt.

Israel, of course, is also in a separate category. The Israel-Palestine conflict continues to take its toll on the economy. Economic activity is declining, although year-on-year growth of 1.3 per cent was mustered in the final quarter of 2002. Consumer price inflation was at 5.6 per cent in January 2003 and interest rates are at the level of 6 per cent. A current account deficit was registered in the third quarter of 2002. Not unexpectedly, tourism, transportation, farming and construction have all been affected adversely by the intifada and the downturn in the USA, Israel's predominant export market, has contributed to the decline. With fiscal revenues down and defence expenditure up, the present austerity budget necessary to address a budget deficit, already at US$1.1 billion after two months and equivalent to 6 per cent of GDP, is also a constriction on recovery. Prime Minister Ariel Sharon's general election triumph in January has enabled him to form a new right-wing cabinet with a tighter control of government than almost all his predecessors. Under this new regime the only flicker of hope for Middle East peace and an end to the slaughter resides in Mr Yasser Arafat's February announcement that he would appoint a prime minister for the Palestinian Authority.

Moving down the Mediterranean, Egypt's economy experienced GDP growth of 3.1 per cent with industrial production rising 4.2 per cent in the year ended June 2002. In December consumer price inflation was 3 per cent and the trade balance for the 12 months ending November 2002 was in deficit by US$7.8 billion. The current account is roughly in balance and short term interest rates are at 7.5 per cent. Investment has been discouraged by the regional tensions and the fall-out from 11 September has affected, tourism and oil and Suez canal revenues.

Along the rim of Africa, Tunisia has benefited from political stability to continue privatisation and structural reforms which should attract additional external financing. The outlook for 2003 is more positive after the economy deteriorated in 2002 due to a decline in tourism, weak export demand from Europe and drought. Steady oil prices have helped Algeria to regain macroeconomic equilibrium with external debt declining and a strong financial situation. Growth remains weak and is wholly insufficient to raise the general standard of living. Indeed the imbalance between the oil sector and the remainder of the economy emphasises the need for structural reforms. Finally in Morocco, although the economy remains vulnerable to exogenous factors affecting tourism revenues and farm produce, the pace of economic activity is expected to remain high. However, the 2002 European slowdown has impacted Morocco's export sectors and products such as textiles, clothing, leather, fruit and vegetables now face competition from the CEE and Asia.

■ SUB-SAHARAN AFRICA

In 2002 the entire Sub-Saharan African region, including the Republic of South Africa, experienced GDP growth of 3 per cent or less. Prices for primary products such as coffee or cotton fell while the surplus resources generated by firm oil prices were not dispersed evenly across the region. Recourse to international aid to coveer financing needs is commonplace.

The sub-continent remains chronically vulnerable to political, social and ethnic tensions. In particular, conflict in the Ivory Coast, West Africa's second leading economic centre, has paralysed the country's northern region. Meanwhile, the systematic repression in Zimbabwe by Robert Mugabe's ruling ZANU-PF party has almost destroyed what was formerly one of East Africa's most prosperous economies.

There have been some positive developments in the region. The creation of the New Partnership for Africa's Development (NEPAD) and regional economic development policies are intended to provide the foundations for a growth environment. Peace agreements to end conflicts in Angola, the great Lakes region, the Democratic Republic of Congo and Burundi are positive developments. The organisation of African Unity became the African Union in 2002 with the aspiration of evolving along European Union lines. At another time, not overshadowed by the Middle East crisis and the global threat of terrorism, these events might evoke more encouragement and support from the developed economies. As matters stand, neither the Group of Seven nor a wider grouping of OECD countries are likely to focus on Africa and its problems in 2003.

Southern Africa

The economies of South Africa, Botswana, Namibia and Mozambique have all enjoyed a relatively problem free 2002. The South African economy remains buoyant after fourth quarter 2002 GDP growth of 3 per cent with consumer price inflation running at 13.7 per cent in January 2003 matched by short-term interest rates at the same level. The trade balance for the 12 months ended January 2003 was positive.

Broadly speaking, South Africa's macro-economic framework is favourable with moderate external debt and relative political stability. However, economic growth is insufficient to combat unemployment, poverty and inequality and the foreign exchange rate is still over-dependent on raw material price trends. Capital markets, remain a potential source of weakness. In the fourteen month period to the end of February 2003 Johannesburg stockmarket prices fell 20.7 per cent. The continuing challenge of attracting foreign direct investment to South Africa persists.

■ THE NEW ORDER

For better or for worse, the events of 11 September 2001 triggered a major change in the world political order. The United States of America finally took on the job of global policeman, a role which it had previously avoided. As the world's one remaining military super-power it is appropriate that it should do so. However, policemen are seldom popular and it is understandable that allies of longstanding, and former ancient enemies too, should be uncomfortable with America's hegemony in foreign policy. In the coming months it will be important to remember that the long term imperative to combat global terrorism and eliminate weapons of mass destruction is common ground among all members of the UN Security Council although opinions may differ as to priorities and the timing of events. Many Europeans would attach a greater priority to reaching a peaceful settlement between Israel and Palestine or addressing the threat of Mr Kim Jong II's nuclear poker game than to the early neutering of Saddam Hussein. Our security may not be less than a year ago but, at the end of the day, we live in a safer world with a policeman on the beat than in the post-1945 age of cold war confrontation.

March 2003

The @rating System

In 2000 Coface introduced the first worldwide insurable company rating scheme. The @rating system assesses the ability of a company to meet its short-term business obligations vis-à-vis customers and suppliers. International businesses can now log on to www.cofacerating.com or any of the national websites (eg www.cofacerating.fr) and access the three following rating systems.

@rating credit opinion indicates the recommended credit exposure for a company using a very simple assessment scale (1 @ = €20,000, 2 @ = €50,000, 3 @ = €100,000, etc). Credit exposure arising from BtoB credit transactions is insurable by Coface. An @rating credit opinion is assigned to some 44 million companies worldwide (including French firms), reflecting Coface's dual expertise in corporate information and credit insurance.

@rating score, which was launched in October 2002 by Coface and Coface Scrl, measures a company's default risk over one year. It comprehensively and accurately rates 4.5 million large, medium and small-sized French companies. @rating score is used not only by different sized companies but also by financial institutions looking to develop a rating system that complies with new banking regulations (McDonough ratio). Measuring credit risk among companies is an important exercise when addressing not only traditional needs (bank loans to firms, BtoB credit and market credit) but also emerging needs created by new instruments such as loan securitisations and new banking solvency regulations (McDonough ratio). The need for companies and banks to have reliable tools is a matter of great urgency today against a background of rising credit risk and growing scepticism over corporate accounting practices.

Country @rating, Coface's key achievement, allows people and businesses engaged in international trade to strengthen the security of their transactions. It continuously tracks a series of indicators for 141 countries, evaluating political factors, the risk of currency shortage, the ability of a government to meet its international obligations, the risk of devaluation following massive capital withdrawals, the risk of a systemic crisis in the banking sector and payment behaviour for short-term transactions. An aggregate rating is assigned to each of the 141 countries monitored on the basis of seven risk categories. As in the approach used by rating agencies, there are seven different rating grades from A1 to A4 for investment-grade risks and B, C, D for 'speculative' risks. This classification is used for each of the countries covered by this guide.

Country @rating Definition

Economic liberalization has led to a boom in BtoB trade, with 70 per cent of accounts being settled by short-term instruments. It is therefore vital to assess the risk associated with such transactions. Country @rating addresses this need by evaluating the extent to which a firm's financial commitments in a given country are influenced by that country's economic, financial and political prospects. Log on to www.cofacerating.com to access country @rating, the supplement to company @rating.

A1 The highly stable political and economic situation has a favourable effect on corporate payment behaviour, which is generally good. The likelihood of default is very low.

A2 The likelihood of default is low, even if the country's economic and political environment or corporate payment behaviour is somewhat shakier than in countries rated A1.

A3 Payment behaviour in these countries – generally less satisfactory than in A1 and A2 countries – could be affected by shifts in the economic and political climate, although defaults remain unlikely.

A4 Payment behaviour is often rather mediocre and could be affected by an economic downturn or deteriorating political climate, although the risk of default remains acceptable.

B The uncertain economic and political environment is likely to affect corporate payment behaviour, which is often mediocre.

C The highly uncertain economic and political environment could worsen the payment behaviour of companies that already often have a bad track record.

D The economic and political environment represents a very high risk that could worsen corporate payment behaviour, which is generally deplorable.

Country Operating Definition

Sectoral Panorama

Sylvia Greisman and Dominique Fruchter
Coface Country Risk and Economic Studies Department, Paris

After several months of price and inventory decline, a cyclical upturn in some economic sectors could provide the basis for more sustained recovery in 2003. That favourable hypothesis will nonetheless remain dependent on an investment recovery, itself reliant on industrialist expectations and company financial stabilization.

Meanwhile both macro- and microeconomic uncertainties have continued to undermine the timid recovery registered in the most cyclical sectors and dampen the dynamism of economic sectors less exposed to fluctuations in economic conditions:

- Pharmaceuticals and mass distribution, two sectors relatively untouched by cyclical fluctuations, have continued to trend upward overall despite increasing pressure on margins.
- Recovery in more cyclical sectors such as electronics, chemicals, paper, or even mechanical engineering should develop progressively and will remain dependent on recovery of investment and, more broadly, of world demand.
- The outlook is less bright in the car industry and construction, whose markets are suffering from a glut.
- Prospects have remained gloomy for tourism, still affected by fears of terrorist attacks, and for textiles and steel, which have to contend with structural imbalances.

In this context, deterioration of company solvency has resulted in worsening payment-incident indicators in many sectors. Although stabilizing and, in some cases, perceptibly improving in the last months of 2002, levels of risk have remained high.

1. Pharmaceuticals and mass distribution, two sectors relatively untouched by cyclical fluctuations, have continued to trend upward overall despite increasing pressure on margins.

Pharmaceutical product sales have continued to grow strongly in most world regions although declining in South America and stagnating in Japan. The outlook remains bright for 2003.

The sector has been benefiting from ageing industrial-country populations and expanded access to health care in emerging countries. Despite government policies aimed at limiting public health spending the market has remained buoyant and laboratory profitability globally enviable. However, margin growth slowed markedly in 2002.

Besides increasing price control exercised by health authorities, pressure from generic drug manufacturers, currently benefiting from the expiration of many patents, has compelled industrialists to lower prices on their own to remain competitive. While drugs that had been very profitable until now have been falling into the public domain, there has been a concomitant dearth of new drug introductions. In such conditions sector companies continue to seek alliances to achieve economies of scale in their research and development programmes and replenish their range of exclusive products.

Payment incidents have stabilized at a relatively low level with accidents remaining nonetheless possible. Sudden compulsory withdrawal of a drug could thus weaken a small or medium-size laboratory. Similarly, the rapid opening up of the Japanese market to foreign manufacturers and generics could also spell

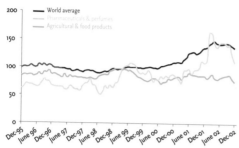

trouble for small and medium-size domestic laboratories just when health authorities have been imposing price reductions.

Excluding the extreme Argentina case, mass distribution has withstood the consumption slowdown relatively well overall. However, reduced household demand has increased price pressure and strengthened the position of discounters at the expense of other chains. Department stores, meanwhile, have been suffering from weaker demand.

In the United States, household consumption continued to trend upward in 2002. Amid economic uncertainty, however, consumers have been giving preference to brands offering the most attractive prices, which has permitted Wal-Mart to increase its lead. Specialized clothing stores have also been suffering from that competition as well as from languishing brands. The upsurge of bankruptcies and closings recorded in 2001 and early 2002 should ease in 2003 provided consumption remains firm. However, Wal-Mart will continue to exert pressure, which could spell more trouble for department stores and clothing store chains.

In Japan, retailer earnings have been suffering from prolonged consumption sluggishness and severe price pressure in a deflationary context. Department stores have lost both their competitive edge and their lead over discounters, with several of them going into bankruptcy. Supermarkets and discounters will have to contend with the new alliance between Seiyu and Wal-Mart. Restructuring should continue in 2003 in a still sluggish context.

In Western Europe, retailers have generally performed well despite the consumption slowdown and setbacks suffered by their subsidiaries, notably in Argentina. However, some German players have been undergoing difficulties due to the domestic market's persistent sluggishness with consumers giving preference to the least expensive items. Discounters such as Aldi and Lidl & Schwarz have thus continued to increase their market share at the expense of traditional supermarkets or even the newcomer, Wal-Mart.

In emerging countries, mass distribution performance (including in the food segment) is more closely tied to economic conditions than it is elsewhere. That explains the setbacks suffered by retailers in Argentina and the marked slowdown of their business in, for example, in Poland.

Overall, mass distribution players will be able to cope with less buoyant demand in 2003. The average probability of a payment incident occurring has remained low. However, the more vulnerable players and those least able to withstand the heightened price competition could encounter difficulties that force them into bankruptcy.

2. Recovery in more cyclical sectors such as electronics, chemicals, paper, or even mechanical engineering should develop progressively and will remain dependent on recovery of investment and, more broadly, of world demand.

● The IT equipment market shed another 1 per cent in 2002 amid the sharp contraction of sales of servers, printers and photocopiers affected by a market glut. Personal computer sales have managed to grow weakly (about 2 per cent), due particularly to the booming Chinese market. They are nonetheless far from duplicating the dizzy growth of past years. Sales performance has also varied greatly by region.

The booming Chinese market is in stark contrast with the stagnation of traditional Western European, North American and Japanese markets and severe contraction registered in South America. In 2003, the world equipment market should gain 5 per cent, thanks notably to an upturn in personal computer purchases buoyed by the company investment recovery. This should concern all regions, except Japan, where the upturn should be more moderate. The company financial situation should improve in consequence, the persistence of strong price pressure notwithstanding.

● The telecommunications equipment market has continued to suffer from the sharp depreciation of assets and failure of many operators. Fixed-network equipment is fairly recent and largely sufficient to handle traffic that has remained stagnant. Mobile networks, meanwhile, are currently sufficient due to the repeated postponements of third-generation implementation and takeovers of networks of failed operators. The only sources of growth thus derive from emerging countries that are developing their networks and mobile hand-set sales that gained 2 per cent last year thanks notably to the Chinese market's expansion.

In 2003, telecommunications-related spending worldwide could accelerate and reach 8 per cent. Two factors underlie that forecast: growth of the Chinese market and inevitable replacement of mobile hand-sets currently in operation in Europe, many of which are already three or four years old. The arrival of new functionalities such as imaging and colour screens could spur equipment renewals by users. However, the windfall should not entirely benefit traditional manufacturers. They will be facing brands launched by operators through alliances with Asian manufacturers, who will also be the main beneficiaries of the growing Asian market. This should encourage traditional manufacturers to rely increasingly on Asian subcontractors, which already supply 20 per cent of the market.

In this context, the level of risk has remained high in this business sector. Despite financial stabilization efforts the newest and most indebted operators have remained very vulnerable, which affects their suppliers' financial situation in turn.

After dropping 32 per cent in 2001, world electronic component sales gained 2 per cent in 2002. This improvement particularly concerned components for pocket computers, digital cameras and mobile telephones, like flash memories, whose prices have increased sharply. Conversely, components intended for traditional computers, which represent 40 per cent of market outlets (DRAM memories) have continued to stagnate. Most of the improvement has concerned Asia, with other world regions stagnating or declining. Many manufacturers registered losses accentuated by strong competition from emerging Asian countries. Some have even decided to withdraw from the market.

In 2003, the recovery should firm up (gaining 12 per cent). All regions should be involved and the sector could benefit from increased office – computer production. The consolidation process will nonetheless continue in the sector due to the scale of investments needed to remain competitive.

Unlike the end of previous cyclical downward phases, the wood pulp market's improvement appears moderate and uncertain. Prices have remained at levels

that barely permit covering production costs as economic uncertainties have been preventing the interplay of inventory levels and expectations from having a favourable influence. Increased exports from emerging countries, buoyed by declines in their exchange rates, have exacerbated the difficulties.

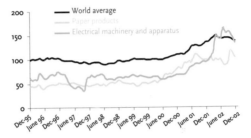

Further downstream, **paper – cardboard** manufacturers have been benefiting from continued low pulp prices and better control of their sales prices. Company restructuring in the United States paved the way for higher paper prices late last year despite contraction of the market. Factory closings resulting from bankruptcies and mergers should thus lead to improved earnings for the remaining companies starting this year.

In West Europe, production and consumption growth resumed tentatively in 2002. Although shaky, that trend should continue in 2003 for three reasons: per capita paper product consumption is apt to rise, euro-dollar parity has remained favourable to exports, and a relatively concentrated industrial fabric affords good control over prices.

In Japan, demand has remained weak. As in the United States, however, profits should improve due to beneficial effects of company restructuring on prices.

In South America, the situation of paper and cardboard producers (mainly Brazilian) has remained constrained by the unfavourable regional economic environment. In Russia and East Asia (excluding Japan), demand has been trending strongly up and it should continue to do so in 2003.

Activity in the chemical industry improved in 2002. That trend should continue and gain momentum in 2003.

In the United States, the sector has benefited from a significant intermediate-product restocking process by industrialists and from a more favourable final-demand trend. In this context companies have been able to improve their profitability, which had deteriorated in prior years. However, that improvement has remained limited due to price pressure stemming from overcapacity and imports. The improvement should continue and intensify in 2003 with production growing this time by nearly 4 per cent, provided the recovery of industrial activity firms up.

In Europe, the renewal of activity has essentially concerned basic chemistry. Resulting from an intermediate-product restocking process, however, the upturn has not been sustained by an increase in demand. Price increases have not been sufficient to cover higher raw material prices and offset the deterioration of margins that occurred in 2001. In 2003, production should rise slowly and register a 2.5 per cent growth rate.

In Japan, business declined in 2002 but less markedly than in the past. The sluggishness of domestic demand again overbalanced the dynamism of demand from regional countries. Substantial overcapacity along with competition from Europe and increasingly from China has continued to weigh on prices while raw material prices have been rising. In 2003, an upturn should finally develop in fine chemicals. Already-completed restructuring should permit regaining some control over pricing and improving margins.

The mechanical engineering sector has continued to suffer from sluggish industrial investment in the United States, Japan and, to a lesser extent, in Western Europe (notably Germany and the United Kingdom). South American market outlets have shrunk further. Only shipments to Central and Eastern Europe and to emerging Asian countries have shown any dynamism. However, the order book trend, moderately up since spring last year, could augur improved production in 2003.

That merely relative improvement should be viewed with caution considering the uncertainties surrounding the investment recovery scenario and low production – capacity utilization rates in the United States and Asia.

Payment incidents have remained relatively rare. That does not exclude occasional payment defaults, notably in the United Kingdom where the manufacturing industry is particularly affected. A company's staying power will particularly depend on its market positioning in terms of destinations and user sectors. Those offering very sophisticated products are less sensitive to economic conditions and monetary fluctuations.

3. The outlook is less bright in the car industry and construction, whose markets are suffering from a glut.

The slight production and sales decline registered in the world car industry in 2002 should persist this year. After four years of euphoric sales the North American market, confronted with saturation, will continue to lose ground (a decline of 4 per cent in 2003 after a decline of 2 per cent last year) while remaining at satisfactory levels. Continuation of promotional offers, recovery of vehicle purchases by companies and renters, and Canadian and Mexican market firmness will not suffice to reverse that trend. The profitability of US carmakers and their subcontractors will remain constrained by the promotional campaigns and growing foreign competition across the entire range. The South American market's dizzy downward spiral could ease before stabilizing at a low level. The decline of local foreign exchange rates has caused imported spare part prices to soar, considerably raising the price of vehicles sold locally. However, that situation could spur increased local production and export development.

The Western European market should continue to shrink (a decline of 3 per cent in 2003 after a decline of 4 per cent in 2002) while remaining at a satisfactory level. Local manufacturers should be able to compensate for setbacks endured in the South American market and the sluggishness of their own market by expanding sales to other world regions.

The Japanese market should remain stable at a low level. Local carmakers will nonetheless continue to register good financial results thanks to excellent performance on external markets and the major restructuring undertaken in recent years.

The other Asian markets, strongly driven by the unrelenting sales boom in the Chinese market and the recovery of Korean sales, should continue to grow.

In construction, meanwhile, business conditions and company financial health continue to depend primarily on the local or regional environment.

In the United States, although housing construction remained very dynamic in 2002, it should begin to sag slightly this year due to progressive saturation of the market and the interest rate rise expected in the second half. Similarly, public construction should decline in 2003 due to deterioration of public accounts. Conversely, private non-residential construction, after continuing to decline in 2002, should begin to recover in 2003 with supply more in balance with demand.

In Japan, the construction market contracted again in 2002. In the housing segment, income deterioration and the employment situation have had a negative influence while tighter fiscal policy has limited infrastructure spending and government contracts. Competition has increased and has been affecting company profitability. Many companies have failed (Aoki, Sato Kogyo and Dai-Nihon Doboku) and more will fail in this sector despite backing granted by banks. The decline should continue this year.

The construction sector should register a slight decline overall in Western Europe while continuing to expand in Mediterranean countries and remaining at a low level in Germany. German companies, which are also contending with structural difficulties, should therefore remain particularly weak and subject to payment defaults.

4. Prospects have remained gloomy for tourism, still affected by fears of terrorist attacks, and for textiles and steel, which have to contend with structural imbalances

Although tourism has won back much of the ground lost after the September 2001 attacks, a complete return to the prior situation is not yet feasible. New attacks at major tourist sites (Bali, Kenya), persistent terrorist threats worldwide, and prospects of conflict in the Near East have continued to prompt tourists to choose nearby destinations where they feel more secure.

In this difficult context sector companies traditionally very active in long-distance travel have continued to register poor performance. Realignment towards nearby tourism will take time. Meanwhile the pace of mergers in the sector will accelerate. The situation has thus remained particularly shaky in the cruise segment where the recurrence of viral epidemics on several Caribbean cruise ships has again destabilized the largely US clientele.

Similarly, the textile industry has remained in a precarious situation in industrialized countries.

In Western Europe, it is suffering from competition from imports of products manufactured in Asia, North Africa and Eastern Europe using thread and fabric manufactured in those regions. Sagging domestic demand has also hampered the sector, with sales of clothing, cars and housing – major market outlets for textiles – having lost some dynamism. Company profitability has been affected not only by declining volumes but also by the impossibility of raising prices substantially while wool prices and, to a lesser extent, cotton and artificial fibre prices have markedly increased. The situation will be unlikely to improve before late 2003 due to the persistence of negative factors.

In the United States, the situation has improved slightly since last summer due notably to an increase in orders, higher prices and improved profitability. That situation has been benefiting US production all the more with pressure from Asian imports easing due to strong demand from Asian consumers.

Payment default frequency has remained high overall throughout the branch, especially in the clothing segment. The household consumption slowdown could thus cause a new deterioration of payment behaviour in 2003.

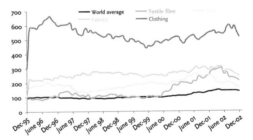

Finally, the steel industry benefited from higher prices in 2002. However, that brighter interlude resulted more from reduced supply than from buoyant demand.

In the **United States**, the protectionist measures adopted by the Bush Administration have triggered rapid price rises. Scarcity has developed for some products. Steelmakers – with many benefiting from Chapter XI protection – have thus seen their operating accounts improve.

In 2003, the upturn should progressively gain momentum thanks this time to increased demand from industry, where an upturn is likely during the year. However, the brighter period could again lead to postponement of restructuring that is all the more necessary with the pension and social benefit problems remaining unresolved.

In Western Europe, despite demand stagnation in most user sectors, the prices of many products rose – although to a lesser extent than in North America. This is attributable to a reduction of supply stemming partly from control over production and partly from the institution of dissuasive customs duties. Company financial performance improved sharply in 2002. Continuation of that improvement in 2003 will depend on renewed growth.

In Japan, steelmakers increased production moderately last year thanks to booming sales to Asia, which more than offset sluggish domestic demand. Profitability has nonetheless remained inadequate, despite the restructuring already accomplished (merger of NKK and Kawasaki Steel, alliance between Kobe Steel, Sumitomo Metal Industries and Nippon Steel). Production in other Asian countries rose strongly in 2002, buoyed by consumption growth (up 25 per cent in China where needs are considerable). The trend was also very favourable in Korea and Taiwan. The 2003 outlook is bright.

In South America, production grew in 2002, not only in Brazil and Venezuela but also in Argentina, driven by an export boom stemming from the sharp decline of local currencies.

Overall, continued improvement in steel product prices should permit progressive reduction of payment incidents, which have increased substantially in recent years. However, the lack of restructuring and sluggishness of world demand gives this upturn a particularly artificial character.

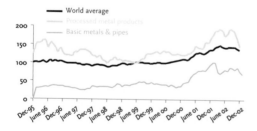

The Outlook for the Global Economy and World Trade

Experts from the Oxford Analytica, London

The growth of the global economy will continue to disappoint in 2003 amid higher international imbalances and geopolitical uncertainty. Illiberal policy regimes will become more pronounced during the course of the year. Combined with looser monetary policy these are likely to forestall macroeconomic adjustments until the medium term.

World trade growth should return to a trend growth of around 6 per cent in 2003 after only marginal expansion in 2002. If this figure is achieved it will help an already faltering economic recovery. However, trade relations will be dominated by crucial deadlines for the Doha negotiations and continuing emphasis on new regional and bilateral trade agreements.

The weakness of recovery since global growth stalled in 2001 is clarifying the unique character of the current global business cycle: burdened by legacies of a two-decade growth spurt and a record-breaking financial bubble. The impact of previous corporate debt expansion on balance sheets in the developed economies provides limited ability to invest, while overcapacity provides little incentive. This, combined with manufacturing expansion in the developing world, suggests below-potential GDP growth into the mid-to-late part of this decade. In 2003 global GDP, with the benefit of East Asian growth, led by China, is likely to grow between 2 and 3 per cent at market exchange rates.

According to the OECD the combined output gap (the amount by which actual GDP falls short of potential GDP) of the developed world will equal 1.7 per cent of potential GDP in 2003, up from 0.5 per cent in 2001, when stagnating demand began to leave productive capacity disused. Capacity utilization in the United States has fallen enough to meet Japan's rate, of about 8 per cent below 1990s' average capacity utilization. Euro-area capacity utilization has yet to fall significantly below 1990s' averages, indicating the amount by which developed – world spare capacity could increase if Euro-area demand falters. Sustained output gaps erode pricing power, which depresses profitability and inflation. Japan points the way, with a corporate sector unable to service loans and deflation in excess of 1 per cent. In the United States, the GDP price deflator (the broadest measure of inflation) fell to 1.0 per cent in the third quarter of 2002.

Possible 'double-dip' scenario

Key stimuli, which sustained global growth in 2002, face limits in 2003. As a result the global economy could suffer a second phase of deterioration (the first phase being 2001), although illiberal policy regimes seem likely to forestall harsher currency and asset-price adjustments until the medium term. Policy boosts in the United States, with second-order effects on Asia, are the most likely to stall in 2003, although other long-expected constraints could also materialise:

1. **Fiscal impulse.** The OECD estimates that US budget deterioration (moving from surplus to substantial deficit) contributed almost all of the global fiscal impulse in 2002, equal to 1 per cent of potential US GDP. It predicts that fiscal consolidation will remove all global fiscal stimuli in 2003.

2. **'Zero bound' constraint.** The US Federal Reserve will reach the limit of conventional monetary policy with just 125 more basis points left to cut. Note that 500 basis points

were pared in the preceding two years. Fed officials have begun to emphasize the variety of unconventional means potentially at their disposal to reflate the economy should they reach this 'zero bound' constraint.

3. **Renewed dependence.** East Asian vulnerability to a slowdown in the US growth engine is higher in 2003 than a year previously. Expansionary fiscal policies in Malaysia, Thailand and the Philippines have been replaced with external demand as the main source of growth, due to creeping fiscal constraints. The need to engineer a 'soft landing' in the South Korean economy has accentuated reliance on the external sector. A contraction in domestic demand in the third quarter (the first since 2000) was more than offset by a rise in net exports.

4. **Imbalances.** The global economic slowdown was expected to correct two key US imbalances built up during the 1990s boom. One of these adjustments is, to a limited extent, under way and could become more pronounced in 2003, constituting a global growth constraint:

- **Household savings.** The six-month moving average of US personal savings as a per cent of disposable income rose from 2.2 per cent in March 2002 to 4.0 per cent in October, the highest since March 1999. Further increases in this rate, perhaps likely given the still significant deviation from the post-1960 average of 8.0 per cent, would hinder global GDP growth significantly.

- **US external deficit.** International imbalances are set to deepen significantly in 2003. The US current account deficit of 4.9 per cent of GDP in 2002 exceeded most previous estimates by as much as a percentage point. It is forecast to reach 5.1 per cent in 2003 and 5.3 per cent in 2004. In the experience of most industrialized countries a 5 per cent of GDP deficit triggers a correction, although the dollar's status as the central global currency could make the US deficit more tenable.

Illiberal policies

Even a sharp weakening of the US economy will produce at most a gradual depreciation in the dollar. The reaction function of Asian central banks to dollar weakness, easily identifiable in changes to foreign exchange reserve positions, provides an automatic support mechanism for the dollar. At the recent troughs of dollar weakness (September 2001 and July 2002), central bank dollar reserve purchases reached US$15 and US$24 billion respectively. Japan and China were prominent buyers in the September 2001 dollar purchase peak, but were joined in the latter peak by (in order of magnitude) Taiwan, the ASEAN countries, Western Europe, South Korea, India and Russia. Renewed Asian reliance on external demand suggests deeper aversion to market-determined exchange rates, and hence less prospect of a sharp correction in the dollar until the medium term.

Other asset price adjustments are similarly likely to be forestalled into the medium term. Despite higher US government borrowing, US Treasury bond prices will probably rally due to the aforementioned Asian official flows, combined with 'flight to safety' flows seeking shelter not only from emerging markets but from the developed world's corporate sector.

Outlook

While European investors might flee dollar assets on fears of dollar depreciation and/or US economic stagnation, these outcomes would motivate higher purchases of dollar securities by Asian central banks, wishing to brake their currencies' appreciation. This has systematically interrupted an orderly depreciation of the dollar, which is a precondition for correction of the US external imbalance. The longer the dollar remains overvalued the deeper the imbalance. Sustained overvaluation of the dollar also erodes the US manufacturing base (with unpredictable but adverse political – economy implications) and pushes inflation close to or beyond zero.

Buoyant inflows into US government securities also produce low long-term US interest rates, which in turn support expansion of the US mortgage market. In the near term this has been helpful in sustaining the US and global economy. However, from a medium-term global perspective it exacerbates US household indebtedness and the US negative net international investment position. The deeper and more prolonged each of these negative positions become the more harsh the eventual adjustment and the greater the risk of a crisis-driven adjustment in US asset prices.

Trade prospects

Forecasts for world trade growth in 2002 have been regularly revised downwards. The WTO now expects an increase of just 1 per cent in volume and 2 per cent in value over 2001 (when volume actually fell by 1.5 per cent). Prospects of significant economic recovery before mid-2003 are poor. The IMF's current (and cautious) forecast of 6.1 per cent trade growth in 2003 depends heavily on continuing strong US demand for imports, and on avoidance of serious shocks to the world economy. However, the chances of a renewed downturn in global growth, led by a falloff in US demand, remain. If the IMF's forecast trade growth rate is achieved trade will have returned to its traditional role as a stimulating factor in world economic growth.

Little new trade liberalization is in the pipeline in 2003 or 2004. China, now a full and active WTO member, will continue the gradual opening of its booming market. Russia and Saudi Arabia, the remaining major applicants, are unlikely to gain membership in 2003. Liberalizations agreed in the past are largely in effect, apart from the removal of remaining US, EU and Canadian restrictions on imports of textiles and clothing from developing countries, which will not happen until January 2005. Prospects for further multilateral opening of world markets therefore depends on progress in the current negotiations launched by the WTO's Doha meeting in November 2001.

Doha round

The Doha round got off to a fairly good start in January 2002, and has since moved forward without major difficulties. However, WTO members have only laid out their initial negotiating positions, with little or no attempt to accommodate the views and positions of others. This is particularly true of the talks on agriculture, which are key to the success or failure of the negotiations as a whole. The year ended with tense negotiations, with a December 31 deadline on two matters of great concern to developing countries: whether they may override patents in order to import generic drugs to meet public health emergencies such as the AIDS crisis; and whether the industrialized countries will concede ground on some 80 separate claims by developing countries that WTO agreements have not been fairly applied to them.

1. **Deadlines.** The year 2003 will be far more testing, with major deadlines already looming and a crucial WTO ministerial meeting in Cancun, Mexico in September:

- Agriculture. Agriculture negotiators are pledged to reach agreement by March 2003 on the ground rules or 'modalities' for each participant's offers to cut import duties, domestic support and export subsidies. The offers themselves should be submitted by the Cancun meeting. Positions remain far apart, with the major exporters calling for far-reaching liberalization while the Europeans, Japan and South Korea have defended their present policies and have made no clear counter-proposals. A crisis in March 2003 seems inescapable. On 31 December 2003 the temporary 'peace clause' shielding some agricultural subsidies against challenge in the WTO will expire.

- Services. Services negotiations are going better than agriculture negotiations, but also face a March 2003 deadline for submitting offers in response to requests made earlier this year.

- Market access. Proposals for tariff cuts on non-agricultural goods are now in, including an ambitious US proposal (for total phase-out of duties) that will not be accepted as it stands. The deadline for agreement on tariff-cutting objectives is 31 May. Talks on possible changes in rules on trade remedies (including anti-dumping action) are moving, but have not got far.

Other Doha issues facing 2003 deadlines include changes in dispute settlement rules (May); whether new rules should govern registration of geographical names of wines and spirits (September in Cancun); and whether negotiations should go ahead on competition and investment issues, on transparency in government procurement and on easing border formalities (Cancun).

2. **Cancun 2003** The Cancun meeting will be a trial of strength. The 18 Cairns Group[1] countries will block any agreement that does not promise substantial agricultural liberalization and reform. Many developing countries are unenthusiastic. The EU has little room for manoeuvre. The United States wants reform in some areas but not in others. Failure of the meeting might, as in the past, provide the catalyst for necessary re-examination of negotiating positions, but would probably extinguish hopes of completing the negotiations by the formal deadline of end-2004.

3. **Disputes** Seventeen WTO members launched a total of 33 new formal complaints against other members' trade practices during 2002. Of the 18 complaints directed against the United States, 9 form an unprecedented joint assault on 'safeguard' measures for steel approved by US President George Bush, and 3 more also concern protection for steel products. Other disputes include complaints by Australia and Brazil against EU sugar subsidies and several that pit one developing country against another. All will carry over into 2003, along with the threat of retaliatory trade measures of up to US$4 billion by the EU against the United States for corporate tax subsidies.

Regional and bilateral developments

In parallel, and perhaps in competition with these multilateral developments, expansion and proliferation of the 250-odd existing regional and bilateral free trade agreements (FTAs) appear certain:

1. **Europe and North America** The EU signed an association agreement with Chile in November, and seeks an agreement with Mercosur (the trade bloc composed of Argentina, Brazil, Paraguay and Uruguay). The imminent entry of ten new members into the EU will happen only in 2004 but is already a major factor in the WTO agriculture negotiations. The United States, which until recently had FTAs only with its immediate neighbours and Israel, has added one with Jordan, and will soon sign with Chile and Singapore. It will negotiate with Australia, Morocco, the Southern African Customs Union and several more ASEAN countries; has renewed its drive for agreement by 2005 on a continent-wide Free Trade Area of the Americas (FTAA); and will pursue FTAs with individual Latin American countries if the FTAA talks fail. Canada too is negotiating with Latin American countries.

2. **Asia Japan's first FTA**, with Singapore, took effect on 30 November 2002. Its next FTA will probably be with Mexico; others may follow with South Korea, the Philippines and Thailand. South Korea has signed an FTA with Chile, and contemplates others with Japan, Mexico and Singapore. Singapore has also signed FTA agreements with a bloc comprising Iceland, Norway, Switzerland and Liechtenstein; and with New Zealand. Chile may join the Singapore – New Zealand FTA. China will start negotiations in 2003 on an FTA with ASEAN, which faces a deadline under its own trade agreement, AFTA, for phasing in preferences for some products still currently excluded. India is also interested in a possible FTA with ASEAN.

While views currently differ as to whether these developments are building blocks or stumbling blocks for the wider efforts in the WTO to open world trade, the answer may become clearer in 2003. What is clear is that challenges to multilateral, regional and bilateral trade policy in 2003 will test the ability of governments to put trade itself, after two lacklustre years, back on track as a locomotive for world economic growth.

[1] Group within the OMC that comprises Argentina, Australia, Bolivia, Brazil, Canada, Chile, Columbia, Costa Rica, Fiji, Guatemala, Indonesia, Malaysia, New Zealand, Paraguay, Philippines, South Africa, Thailand and Uruguay.

Oxford Analytica

Our mission: *to serve as the information industry standard for strategic analysis of geopolitical, macroeconomic and social developments.*

Founded in 1975, *Oxford Analytica* is an international consulting firm that provides business and political leaders with timely analysis of worldwide political, economic and social developments.

Oxford Analytica acts as a bridge between the world of ideas and the world of enterprise. One of its major assets is an extensive international network that draws on the scholarship and expertise of over 1,000 senior members at Oxford and other leading universities around the world, as well as think tanks and institutes of international standing.

Clients of *Oxford Analytica* are able to integrate the judgements drawn from this unparalleled resource into their own decision-making process. Clients include multinational corporations, major banks, national governments and international institutions in more than 30 countries.

Strategic analysis for professionals

Europe

1

The Outlook for The Euro Area Economy and for the Economies of Central Europe and the Baltic States

Experts from Oxford Analytica, London

The weak economic cycle in the euro area economy continues to disappoint expectations. With little prospect of a marked recovery of global production and trade, the export-dependent euro area is unlikely to generate sufficient endogenous demand to escape further low levels of economic growth and a continued deterioration in employment.

◼ THE EURO AREA ECONOMY

The decision by the ECB to lower its main refinancing rate by a full 50 basis points on December 5 indicated a belated acknowledgement of the deteriorating fortunes of the euro area economy. The subsequent strengthening of the euro against both the dollar and sterling in turn has suggested that financial markets may believe that the interest-rate move will help to stimulate consumption, investment and growth within the euro area in the medium term and that the fear of deflation, stagnation and unemployment outweighs any residual fear of inflation.

Modest growth

While the economic fundamentals of the euro area economy are healthier than those of the United States – with sound trade, payments and capital balances, and higher savings ratios – the weak performance of domestic demand and the correspondingly higher dependence on exports for maintaining even modest rates of growth look set to continue:

- The growth of private consumption, which had been healthy in the first two years of the euro area, averaging 3 per cent, slowed markedly in 2001 to 1.8 per cent and is set to be a mere 0.6 per cent in 2002.
- Government consumption has stayed steady at 1.9 per cent growth but, according to Stability Programme commitments for 2003, is set to grow by only 1.2 per cent.
- Investment, which had already fallen by 0.7 per cent in 2001, declined both year-on-year and on a quarterly basis throughout 2002 and is set to end up some 2.5 per cent lower than 2001. Low investment mirrors the recession in euro area industrial production in early 2001 and in the first two quarters of 2002 and the fall in capacity utilisation from the cyclical peak of 84.4 per cent in 2000 to 81 per cent in July 2002. The improvement to 81.5 per cent in October 2002 is insufficient to suggest any prospect of an investment-led recovery in 2003.
- After the record export performance of 2000 (up 12.7 per cent), followed by 2.6 per cent in 2001, the slump in global trade growth was reflected in a decline in exports averaging 2.9 per cent in the winter quarters of 2001-02. There has been a modest recovery in both exports and export order books, but these again will be insufficient to prevent the current deceleration of growth.

As a result, aggregate real GDP is set to grow by just 0.8 per cent in 2002, with worsening prospects for 2003. The ECB on December 12 issued its staff projections for 2003 GDP, which are sharply down from the last projections in June: a range of 1.1-2.1 per cent from 2.1-3.1 per cent previously. Indeed, the unpredictability of both economic and political affairs worldwide means that a persistence of low growth and rising unemployment in the medium term cannot be ruled out. Accordingly, business confidence – as measured by the European Commission's surveys, by the Reuters Purchasing Managers' Index (PMI) and Germany's monthly IFO surveys – has deteriorated over the last two years, most notably in relation to the retail and services sectors in the euro area. While there have been recent signs of improvement in the PMI, it still remains below 50, indicating continued contraction.

Healthy external balances

In contrast to the serious external deficits of both the United States and the United Kingdom, the euro area enjoys a very strong balance in traded goods, and a modest surplus in services and in the capital balance. With the overall decline in global merger and acquisition activity, direct investment flows have fallen significantly, but the euro area's normal net deficit in direct investment flows was turned into a slight surplus in August, driven both by the relative solidity of the euro and by concerns over potential volatility in the US economy. The growing attractiveness of euro-denominated assets is a mixed blessing in that it will put upward pressure on the exchange rate and reduce the competitiveness of euro area exports.

Labour market

Since employment growth in 1999 and 2000 was driven primarily by the retail trade and other services, the prospects for the labour market are not promising:

- Unemployment, having fallen from the peak of 13.9 million in 1997 to 10.9 million in the second quarter of 2001, rose to around 11.5 million in October 2002, or 8.4 per cent of a total labour force of some 133 million.
- The ratio of job vacancies to labour force has fallen markedly to an average of around 1 per cent (the Netherlands is an exception with 2.5 per cent) – full employment is assumed to exist

when the vacancy ratio exceeds the unemployment rate.

- The growth level required for employment to increase is currently over 2 per cent. With growth probably unlikely to exceed 1.5 per cent in 2003, unemployment is therefore set to rise, albeit tempered by the increase in part-time employment across the euro area.
- Within the common trend of deteriorating labour market prospects, there are distinct national variations. Ireland, Portugal, Luxembourg, Austria and the Netherlands have relatively low rates of unemployment, while the larger core economies have rates at or above the average: Germany 9.4 per cent, France 8.8 per cent, Italy approximately 9.5 per cent.
- Nominal hourly wage costs rose faster in 2002 than in 2001, averaging 3.85 per cent growth year-on-year in the first two quarters of 2002. With a fall in labour productivity growth in the downturn, unit labour cost growth has also risen slightly to just under 3 per cent in 2002 (1.2 per cent in 2000)

Policy framework

The overall policy architecture of the euro area is characterised by a single institution, the ECB, pursuing monetary pragmatism, supported by separate national finance ministries bound together in a commitment to reduce state borrowing through the Stability and Growth Pact (SGP). The current cyclical slowdown is revealing some difficulties with that architecture, which may become more evident as the slowdown persists:

- ECB dilemmas. During its first two years of unitary control of the new currency, the ECB pursued a policy of benign neglect which allowed the external value of the euro to fall without countervailing rises in interest rates, in order to boost the euro area's rate of growth via exports. However, in contrast to the US Federal Reserve, it has been very slow to react to the political and economic crises of 2001/02, since its main focus has been on price rises and the growth of M3. Both the latter continue to exceed their respective 'reference values' and, if

3

inflation remains sticky, the ECB may feel that its mandate prevents it from acting further. Furthermore, the fact that the ECB rate cut renders real interest rates negative in some euro area countries but positive in low-inflation countries compounds the general problem of a one-size-fits-all monetary policy and the specific dilemma of how best to help the area's core economy, Germany, escape from recession.

- SGP rules. The SGP, committing all euro area states to budgets close to balance in the medium term (currently defined as a limit of 2006), was designed partly to remove the danger of the state 'crowding out' corporate borrowers from capital markets and to reduce upward market pressure on interest rates. This can be effective in periods of strong growth, but in the current cyclical downturn, the resistance of both corporations and the state to borrowing is arguably having a pro-cyclical effect in parts of the euro area: it is reinforcing the downturn and making recovery more difficult. Above all, it is easier for states to cut back on investment programmes than on recurrent expenditure: this in turn reinforces the pro-cyclical nature of the SGP, since state investments have markedly better multiplier effects.

The centrality of Germany as the original architect of the SGP, as currently its main victim and as the most important economy in both the euro area and Europe more widely, makes greater SGP flexibility an urgent priority for euro area governments and finance ministers. A Commission proposal to this effect will be considered in the run-up to the spring European Council.

It is clear, then, that despite relatively strong economic fundamentals, 2003 is likely to see a continuation of the stagnation of the euro area economy. The current slowdown highlights difficulties in the euro area policy architecture, relating most notably to the ECB's mandate and room for manoeuvre and the design of the Stability and Growth Pact.

■ CENTRAL EUROPE AND THE BALTIC STATES

The states of Central Europe and the Baltic (CEB) (Hungary, Poland, the Czech Republic, Slovakia, Estonia, Latvia and Lithuania) were expected at the end of 2002 to conclude negotiations for accession to the EU in 2003, with the expectation of becoming full members in 2004. This will require them to balance the objectives of preserving macroeconomic stability in order to prepare for entry to the European monetary system, maintaining growth to reduce the income gap between themselves and the EU, and modernising production to withstand competitive pressures in the EU market. This will have to be achieved against the background of a continuing difficult global economic climate and the possibility of international instability.

General outlook

Growth in CEB slowed to an estimated 2.1-2.2 per cent in 2002, the lowest level since economic recovery began in the region in 1994, as growth in the EU, the major market for the region's exports, slowed to 0.7 per cent. The impact of slow growth in the EU on exports is also having an indirect effect on domestic demand, as policymakers are being forced to pursue more restrictive fiscal and monetary policies to prevent a major deterioration in current account deficits prior to EU accession. Euro area growth is expected to pick up only slowly in 2003, to around 1.5 per cent, as economic recovery in the United States remains sluggish. Recovery in Germany, the most important market for the CEB economies, will be slower than the EU average, with growth only expected to pick up from 0.3 per cent in 2002 to about 1.0 per cent in 2003. The modest recovery in EU growth will help exports from CEB and allow some macroeconomic easing, which will contribute to a modest acceleration in the region's growth rate to around 3.3-3.5 per cent in 2003. Growth in CEB will therefore remain slower than in south-east Europe and the European CIS states, but will be faster than the OECD average. The economic performance in 2003 will also be affected by the damage caused by the floods in the summer of 2002.

Although a modest improvement in the growth rate in CEB states will help to narrow the income gap with the EU, the gap will remain significant when they become full members in 2004. Anti-inflationary policy in CEB will involve a modest real appreciation of exchange rates, which will help to narrow the income gap, measured in euros, but will also have a negative impact on competitiveness. However, this will be partly modified by the continued strength of the euro against the dollar, which will help to preserve the region's competitiveness in EU markets, while slowing inflationary effects arising from commodity prices that are linked to the dollar.

The major threats to modest economic recovery in the region in 2003 are external. The most important of these is the possibility of a large and sustained rise in oil prices as a result of instability in the Middle East and the possibility of a prolonged war in Iraq. This would have a severe negative impact on growth in the region – both directly (all economies are substantial net oil importers and would face an immediate inflationary impact and deterioration in the current account), and indirectly through its effect on EU growth. However, investors are becoming more selective in their assessments of emerging market economies and it is anticipated that CEB economies will not be badly affected by any deterioration in the economic performance of Latin America, and Brazil in particular.

Country prospects.

Individually, the countries in the region are expected to perform as follows:

1. Poland. The growth rate for CEB as a whole will continue to be affected by the relatively flat performance of Poland, the region's largest economy. Growth in the country slowed to an expected 1.2 per cent in 2002 – mainly as a result of slow growth in domestic demand and investment. This mostly resulted from a combination of tight monetary policy and lax fiscal policy, which drove up interest rates. The large domestic economy means that the country is less dependent on the EU market than is the case for other Central European states (exports to the EU account for about 14 per cent of GDP), and a more favourable monetary environment in 2003 should allow growth to increase to over 3 per cent. Nevertheless, weak demand in Italy, which is a major importer of Polish-produced Fiat cars, could slow the recovery.

2. Hungary. Growth in 2003 is expected to be the highest in Central Europe at 4.5-5.5 per cent. The consolidated fiscal deficit is expected to reach 6 per cent of GDP and the resulting pressure to contain money-supply growth has forced up interest rates and pushed the forint to the top of the 15 per cent band against the euro. This will continue to affect export competitiveness in 2003. However, the country has substantially improved its export structure, and exports to the EU now compete on quality grounds and are expected to hold up well. It avoided the worst of the flood damage in Central Europe in 2002.

3. Czech Republic. The Czech Republic suffered the worst economic damage from the floods in the summer of 2002. Prague, which is a major source of tourist income, was particularly badly affected, as were other areas in Bohemia that are important for foreign direct investment (FDI) and form much of the productive base of the Czech economy. Flood repair costs have driven the fiscal deficit to over 9 per cent of GDP in 2002, and necessitated cuts in government expenditure. The country is also highly dependent on EU demand, which accounts for over 30 per cent of GDP. These factors contributed to a fall in growth from 3.3 per cent in 2001 to an expected 2.5 per cent in 2002. However, the impact of adverse factors should diminish in 2003, allowing growth to rise to 3.5-4 per cent

4. Slovakia. Slovakia has been the only Central European economy to experience an increase

in the growth rate in 2002, from 3.3 per cent in 2001 to an expected 3.5-3.8 per cent. This was accompanied by a current account deficit of an estimated 7.7 per cent of GDP, which has been largely financed by high inflows of FDI. Inflation at 3 per cent is under control for the moment, and growth is expected to rise to 4 per cent in 2003, provided that the external deficit continues to be financed by FDI inflows.

5. Baltic States. These have experienced faster economic growth than the Central European economies in 2002, with Latvia's economy growing by an estimated 4.5 per cent, Estonia's by over 5 per cent, and Lithuania's by 5.2 per cent. However, this represents a fall from the levels recorded in 2000 and 2001 during the recovery from the impact of the Russian crisis of 1998. Inflation has remained relatively low in Latvia and Lithuania, while Estonia has continued to benefit from high FDI inflows. Growth rates are expected to rise by 0.5-1 per cent across the region in 2003, but this performance could be affected by a downturn in Scandinavia, particularly in Sweden and Finland, which are highly important markets for the Baltic states.

In conclusion, economic growth is expected to improve across the region in 2003 from mildly repressed 2002 levels as the EU starts to recover. However, this will depend on international factors and would be vulnerable to any further slowdown in the EU and to oil price increases resulting from instability in the Middle East.

The Range of Country @ratings in Europe

Sylvia Greisman, Jean-Louis Daudier, Dominique Fruchter and Yves Zlotowski

Coface Country Risk and Economic Studies Department, Paris

1

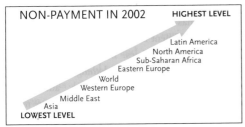

This country @rating scale measures the average level of short-term non-payment risk presented by companies in a particular country. It reflects the extent to which a country's economic, financial and political outlook influences financial commitments of local companies.

It is thus complementary to @rating Credit Opinions on companies (*cf. article page XXVI-XXVII*).

In 2002 the growth slowdown continued in both Western and Eastern Europe but affected eurozone countries the most.

Sluggish exports, in a less than buoyant international climate, exacerbated domestic difficulties in the major eurozone economies. The euro-transition euphoria that had largely sustained household consumption has given way to anxiety about employment and questions about the future of pension systems. The progressive weakening of consumption, depressed international demand, and public spending constrained by fiscal discipline have had a negative impact on industrialists' outlooks. Meanwhile the stock market slump and excessive debt burden of many companies have limited their financing capacity. In consequence, investment has significantly declined and the major eurozone economies have undergone a marked slowdown that

nonetheless varied in intensity by country.

The recovery expected in 2003 should prove moderate considering the authorities' lack of room for manoeuvre in fiscal policy terms and the scale of structural problems hampering the German economy, the region's principal economic engine.

Central European economies have been steadier than expected amid weak Western European growth. With the notable exception of Poland domestic demand has been buoyant. The currencies have withstood the crisis of confidence that buffeted emerging markets last summer, supported by the near-term prospect of European Union admission.

However, the scale of public finance imbalances has remained a weakness for most neighbouring countries. Farther East, the Russian economy has also been trending up supported by firm oil prices and expanding household consumption. An investment slowdown nonetheless reflects the weaknesses of the country's economic situation, linked to the overvalued rouble.

The less than favourable business environment has caused deterioration of company payment behaviour in most West European countries, particularly Germany. Despite recent stabilization risk levels remain high. Payment-incident indices have improved in Eastern Europe while remaining higher than indices for Western European companies. They largely reflect the numerous payment defaults recorded in Poland, which underscores the work still needed on company streamlining and restructuring.

Increasing payment incidents in conjunction with a less than bright growth outlook have

remained limited thanks to expansionary fiscal policy. This nonetheless resulted in a notable increase in the public deficit, while increased imports have widened the current account deficit. However, buoyed by the improved quality of exports and progressive recovery of external demand, the country's sales abroad should again become its main economic engine. Meanwhile the authorities should give priority to more disciplined management of public accounts. Hungarian companies have registered stable payment indices that reflect a level of risk below the world average.

Countries rated A3

Company payment behaviour is generally less good than in the preceding categories and could be affected by a change in the country's economic and political environment, although the likelihood of that leading to large-scale payment defaults remains relatively low.

In the Czech Republic, the international environment's deterioration and the floods of last August have weighed on economic activity. The Czech koruna's strength and worsening public finance situation could hamper growth. Nonetheless European Union admission will open the door to vast opportunities. Economic activity should thus recover in 2003, spurred by increased investment.

After deteriorating slightly in early 2002 payment behaviour has stabilized at a level below the world average. However some sectors have been experiencing greater difficulties, including textiles, leather, furniture, metals, wood, and transportation. Moreover, the floods have had a greater effect on small and medium-size companies.

Countries rated A4

These countries often present fairly mediocre payment behaviour that could be affected by an economic downturn, although the probability of that causing a large number of payment defaults remains moderate.

In Poland, although company solvency still gives rise to fears, the worst seems to be over. Growth actually registered a modest third-quarter upturn last year thanks to improved domestic demand. However risks continue to surround growth. A new currency appreciation and depressed foreign demand could hamper recovery. Conversely, a strong depreciation, stemming from erosion of foreign investor confidence, would cause new payment difficulties for companies carrying heavy foreign currency debt.

In this context the relative improvement of company payment behaviour has remained shaky while several important sectors such as construction,

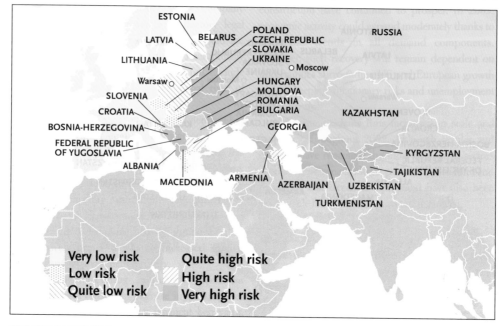

ESTONIA
POLAND
RUSSIA
LATVIA BELARUS
CZECH REPUBLIC
SLOVAKIA
LITHUANIA UKRAINE
o Moscow
Warsaw o
HUNGARY
MOLDOVA
SLOVENIA
ROMANIA
CROATIA BULGARIA
BOSNIA-HERZEGOVINA GEORGIA KAZAKHSTAN
FEDERAL REPUBLIC
OF YUGOSLAVIA KYRGYZSTAN
ALBANIA TAJIKISTAN
MACEDONIA ARMENIA
AZERBAIJAN UZBEKISTAN
TURKMENISTAN

Very low risk   **Quite high risk**
Low risk   **High risk**
Quite low risk   **Very high risk**

shipyards, chemicals and steel have been undergoing a marked business slowdown. Uncertainties continue to surround recovery in 2003.

Countries rated B

A precarious economic environment could affect company payment behaviour, which is often mediocre.

In Russia, growth has remained firm thanks to steady household consumption and high oil prices. However, the investment slowdown constitutes a warning signal: the real exchange rate appreciation has been hurting company competitiveness. Sustaining strong growth will thus increasingly depend on the energy sector.

Moreover, microeconomic problems have persisted with progress on creditor and property legal rights slow to percolate through actual business practices. Meanwhile the banking system has remained the Russian economy's Achilles heel.

In this nonetheless favourable environment payment arrears by companies canvassed by the Russian National Committee on Statistics stopped declining in 2002. They remain strongly vulnerable to a possible economic downturn. Moreover, the lack of reliable information on companies justifies caution.

Romania has performed well in growth terms amid cautious monetary policy, steady exports, higher productivity and easing inflation. The authorities should continue to pursue their reform programme with the prospect of European Union admission in 2007. The country must notably restructure its public sector, particularly concerning energy, which has been suffering heavy losses.

In a more favourable business environment company payment behaviour has improved, although the level of risk is still high. Payment times have remained long and incidents frequent, although often resulting in collection. Often weakly capitalized, companies still encounter difficulties in coping with their recent development.

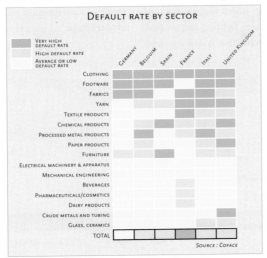

DEFAULT RATE BY SECTOR

Very high default rate / High default rate / Average or low default rate

Clothing, Footware, Fabrics, Yarn, Textile products, Chemical products, Processed metal products, Paper products, Furniture, Electrical machinery & apparatus, Mechanical engineering, Beverages, Pharmaceuticals/cosmetics, Dairy products, Crude metals and tubing, Glass, ceramics, Total

Germany, Belgium, Spain, France, Italy, United Kingdom

Source : Coface

Commentary

The manufacturing and distribution of clothing articles remains the sectors most exposed to non-payment risk and should suffer even more in a context of slowing consumption. Moreover, the difficulties have tended to spread to weaving and spinning in the face of competition from low-wage countries via finished-article imports.

Industrial production's lack of dynamism has spurred modern deterioration of payment behaviour in chemicals and paper. The steel industry, benfitting from price rises triggered by North American protectionist measures, has remained steady in Western Europe, except in the United Kingdom where the strong pound sterling has been severely handicapping local industry. Amid sluggish demand industrialists have reduced their investments, which has in turn affected payment timeliness in the metal processing industry: tools, machines, tanks, boilers, etc.

The food, glass and pharmaceutical industries, which continue to benefit from buoyant demand, present relatively little risk.

Albania

Coface analysis

Short-term: **D**

Medium-term:
Very high risk

RISK ASSESSMENT

Albania could achieve at least 7 per cent growth in 2003, provided economic activity is not beset with electricity supply problems, as was the case last year.

After three successive governments in 2002 political stability is essential to reducing the budget deficit. The government must find a way of improving tax collection and fighting tax evasion and corruption. This consolidation is also required to attract privatization-related foreign investment and so cover the chronically high external financing needs. The country remains dependent mainly on multilateral finance and could receive assistance from the European Union, with which it is due to negotiate a stabilization and association agreement

Albania, which remains one of Europe's poorest countries, must redouble efforts to improve infrastructure, education and healthcare.

KEY ECONOMIC INDICATORS

US$ million	1998	1999	2000	2001	2002 (e)	2003 (f)
Economic growth (%)	8	7.3	7.8	6.5	6	7
Inflation (%)	21.9	0.4	0	3.1	5.3	3
Public-sector balance/GDP (%)	−10.4	−11.4	−9.1	−8.5	−8	−7.2
Exports	205	275	255	305	342	391
Imports	826	1121	1076	1332	1414	1507
Trade balance	−621	−846	−821	−1027	−1072	−1116
Current account balance	−187	−270	−270	−258	−372	−357
Current account balance/GDP (%)	−6.1	−7.4	−7.2	−6.3	−8.1	−7.1
Foreign debt	970	1078	1130	1157	1067	1187
Debt service/Exports (%)	3.1	2.2	2.1	2.1	4.1	3.4
Reserves (import months)	4.7	4.5	4.8	4.9	4.7	4.9

e = estimated, f = forecast

Armenia

Coface analysis

Short-term: **D**

Medium-term:
Very high risk

RISK ASSESSMENT

The performance of the Armenian economy is improving thanks to the support of international organizations and fairly buoyant exports of mainly precious and semi-precious stones to Belgium and Israel.

However, the country's financial position remains fragile. The current account and budget deficits, though down on the previous year, are responsible for the country's high financing needs, which are mainly covered by multilateral organizations and private transfers (including grants and remittances from Armenian expatriate workers). The debt for equity swap agreement concluded with Russia in 2002 has substantially eased Armenia's foreign debt burden and extends the strategic alliance between the two countries from the military to the financial field.

The country remains hamstrung by organizational problems arising from lack of restructuring and delays in fiscal reform. In addition, the political situation is not fully stable, because of the unresolved dispute over the province of Karabakh. As a result foreign investment is weak and inflows from non-resident Armenians remain way below expectations.

KEY ECONOMIC INDICATORS						
US$ million	1998	1999	2000	2001	2002 (e)	2003 (f)
Economic growth (%)	7.3	3.3	6	9.6	7.5	6
Inflation (%)	−1.3	2.1	0.4	3	3	3
Public-sector balance/GDP (%)	−4.8	−7.2	−6.4	−4	−2.1	−3
Exports	229	247	310	353	458	516
Imports	806	721	773	773	847	913
Trade balance	−577	−474	−463	−420	−389	−397
Current account balance/GDP (%)	−21.2	−16.6	−14.6	−9.5	−8.7	−8.7
Foreign debt	787	855	862	862	905	1105
Debt service/Exports (%)	19	14.3	10.6	9.7	10.5	13.3
Reserves (import months)	3.4	4	3.9	4	4.1	4.1

e = estimated, f = forecast

Austria

Coface analysis   Short-term: **A1**

RISK ASSESSMENT

Following the recession at the end of 2001 the economy stabilised in 2002 but remained sluggish as a result of the unfavourable international economic situation and weak domestic demand. Exports have stagnated due to the downturn in foreign markets and household spending has been reined in due to the increase in pension contributions and the abolition of tax cuts in the aftermath of the floods. Investment has continued to shrink in both capital goods and construction.

The economy should pick up somewhat this year, bolstered by the recovery in exports. Consumption should get stronger on the back of rising real disposable incomes spurred by an increase in family allowances and substantial wage rises. Against a background of more favourable trading conditions investments in equipment and machine tools should pick up. Finally, faster growth and continued cuts in public spending should help to restore budgetary equilibrium.

Despite the sluggish economy the number of bankruptcies rose only very slightly in 2002. The default ratio observed by Coface remains below the Western European average. However, sectors such as construction, publishing, printing, furniture and the new technologies appear to be at greater risk than others.

KEY ECONOMIC INDICATORS

%	1998	1999	2000	2001	2002 (e)	2003 (f)
Economic growth	3.5	2.8	3	1	0.9	2.1
Consumer spending (% change)	2.8	2.7	2.5	1.3	1.1	2.0
Investment (% change)	3.4	1.5	5.1	−1.5	−2.9	2.6
Inflation	0.5	0.7	1.5	2.3	1.7	1.7
Unemployment	5.7	5.3	4.7	4.9	5.3	5
Short-term interest rate	3.6	3	4.4	4.2	3.3	3
Public-sector balance/GDP	−2.5	−2.4	−1.7	−0.1	−1	−0.5
National debt/GDP	63.9	64.9	63.6	61.7	60	57
Exports (% change)	7.9	8.7	12.2	5.5	3.2	5
Imports (% change)	5.9	8.8	11.1	3.6	0.3	5
Current account balance/GDP	−2.5	−3.2	−2.8	−2.3	−1.7	−1.8

e = estimated, f = forecast

PAYMENT AND COLLECTION PRACTICES

Payment

Bills of exchange and cheques are not widely used and are not recommended in so far as they are not always the most efficient means of payment.

To be valid, bills of exchange must meet strict criteria. This deters business people from using them. Cheques need not be backed by funds at the date of issue but must be provisioned at the date of presentation. Banks generally return bad cheques to their issuers, who may also stop payment on their own without fear of criminal proceedings for misuse of this facility.

Bills of exchange and cheques are more commonly used for repayments agreed between counterparties.

Conversely, SWIFT transfers are widely used for domestic and international transactions and offer a cost-effective, rapid and secure means of payment.

Debt collection

As a rule the collection process begins with the issue of a final notice of payment to the debtor by registered mail. This entails reminding the debtor of his obligation to pay the outstanding sum plus any default interest as may have been agreed between the parties. In the absence of a benchmark rate the applicable rate of interest from 1 August 2002 is the Bank of Austria's refinancing rate marked up by eight basis points.

Where a claim is certain, liquid and uncontested, plaintiffs may seek a court injunction (Mahnverfahren) upon completing a printed application.

This entitles plaintiffs to a fast-track procedure for dealing with claims of up to 10,000 euros (previously 130,000 Austrian Schillings). The judge then serves the debtor with an order to pay the outstanding amount, plus legal costs. If the debtor does not appeal against the injunction, it is enforceable in a relatively short timeframe.

A special procedure (Wechselmandantverfahren) exists for unpaid bills of exchange. This entails obtaining an enforcement order from the court that gives the debtor two weeks in which to pay. Alternatively, if a claim is contested, the creditor must litigate through the ordinary court system.

Where no settlement can be reached, or where a claim is contested, the last remaining alternative is to file an ordinary action (Klage) before the district court (Bezirksgericht) or the court of first instance (Landesgericht) depending on the amount of the claim. A specific commercial court (Handelsgericht) exists in the district of Vienna to hear commercial cases (commercial disputes, bankruptcy procedures, etc.).

During the preliminary stage of proceedings the parties must make written submissions of evidence and file their respective claims. The court decides on the facts of the case presented to it and does not investigate cases on its own initiative. At the main hearing the judge examines the evidence submitted and hears the parties' arguments as well as their witnesses' testimonies.

Generally an enforcement order can be obtained in first instance within ten months.

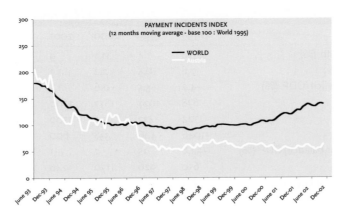

PAYMENT INCIDENTS INDEX
(12 months moving average - base 100 : World 1995)

— WORLD
— Austria

Azerbaijan

Short-term: **C**

Medium-term:
High risk

Coface analysis

RISK ASSESSMENT

Growth remains buoyant thanks to increased investment in the oil sector. The new oil pipeline linking Baku to the Mediterranean Sea should drive up crude oil exports to Europe. The bulk of investment focuses on the energy and ancillary sectors (construction, communications). The declining competitiveness of the non-oil sectors looms and threatens overall economic performance because of the economy's over-exposure to energy prices.

The country's public finances, though notably sound, are increasingly dependent on oil revenues. The seemingly high financing need is more than covered by direct foreign investments, which have helped prevent the country from running up a massive debt.

Azerbaijan's economic performance is dependent on its ability to attract and retain foreign investment. Investors can be discouraged by the high costs of off-shore oil production and oil transportation. Moreover, the political and social environment appears unstable. The problem of President Aleev's succession has not been resolved and social tensions are exacerbated by the fact that the country's development only benefits a small section of the population.

KEY ECONOMIC INDICATORS

US$ million	1998	1999	2000	2001	2002 (e)	2003 (f)
Economic growth (%)	10	7.4	11.1	9	8.5	7.5
Inflation (%)	−7.6	−0.5	2.2	1.3	3	3.5
Public-sector deficit/GDP (%)	−4.2	−5.5	−0.6	1.5	−0.5	−1
Exports	678	1027	1877	2100	2200	2300
Imports	1724	1433	1539	1500	1800	2300
Trade balance	−1046	−406	338	600	400	0
Current account balance/GDP (%)	−32.6	−15	−2	−1	−5	−8.5
Foreign debt	650	926	1170	1246	1425	1540
Debt service/Exports (%)	8.2	5	4.5	5.3	7.1	8.2
Reserves (import months)	2.2	4.1	3.5	3.4	2.9	2.4

e = estimated, f = forecast

Belarus

Short-term: **D**

Medium-term:
Coface analysis   **Very high risk**

RISK ASSESSMENT

The country's economic stability is more apparent than real, with falling growth and extremely high inflation. The Belarus economy is still characterized by lack of structural reforms, massive industrial and price subsidies for basic commodities and unwillingness to liberalize trade. This has hit the country's economic performance. The economy is also highly dependent on its Russian neighbour, with whom a large proportion of trade is carried out through barter.

Russian economic and financial assistance is therefore vital for Belarus, which is gradually falling out of favour with the international community as demonstrated by the increasing hostility of the United States and the European Union. Even Russia, with which a monetary union is due to be concluded in 2007, is increasingly embarrassed by the government. The Kremlin is unsure about how to deal with its unreliable partner, reintegration with which would be costly, but across whose territory stretches a vital gas and oil transit route. The fact remains that President Loukashenko, weakened by his international ostracism, rules the country with an iron hand and enjoys some popular support.

KEY ECONOMIC INDICATORS						
US$ million	1998	1999	2000	2001	2002 (e)	2003 (f)
Economic growth (%)	8.4	3.4	5.9	4	3	2
Inflation (%)	72.9	293.7	168.6	61	65	85
Public-sector balance/GDP (%)	−0.3	−2.2	−0.6	−1.8	−0.7	−3
Exports	7138	5949	6986	7314	7525	7816
Imports	8488	6700	7824	7694	8197.1	8565
Trade balance	−1350	−751	−838	−380	−672.1	−749
Current account balance	−865	−700	−161.9	192.8	−53	1
Current account balance/GDP (%)	−6.1	−1.6	−1.3	−1.6	−1.8	−1.8
Foreign debt	2483	2395	2298.6	2251.4	2209.5	2209.5
Debt service/Exports (%)	2.5	3.5	1.7	2.5	2.4	2.4
Reserves (import months)	0.4	0.5	0.5	0.5	0.5	0.5

e = estimated, f = forecast

Belgium

STRENGTHS

- Located in the centre of Europe's business heartland.
- Hub of road, water and rail transport.
- Multicultural and multilingual identity, promoted by proximity to various countries and presence of European and international institutions, boosts foreign corporate presence and trade.
- Continued progress towards balanced budget gives government freer hand in economic management.

WEAKNESSES

- Open economy based on narrow domestic market exposes country to external influences and Belgian groups to foreign takeovers.
- Declining public debt remains one of the highest in Europe and is big drain on budget.
- Low degree of involvement in development of new technologies.
- Complex political organisation interferes with operation of economy and maintains regional disparities.

RISK ASSESSMENT

The economy continued to perform sluggishly in 2002 due to stagnant domestic and external demand. Consumer spending remained weak. The favourable impact of wage indexing and income tax cuts was negated by the worsening job market and the stock market slump. In the face of uncertainty over the future of the markets and their dwindling profitability businesses preferred to curb investment in an attempt to cut the overcapacity accumulated in recent years. Exports continued to suffer on account of the downturn in neighbouring markets and shrinking market share.

In 2003 growth should gradually pick up as exports get firmer and domestic demand recovers. Additional income tax reductions and the rebound of the job market will no doubt encourage consumer spending. Corporate investment should pick up as uncertainties about the markets fade, production capacity is better utilized and businesses stabilize their financial position. Fiscal policy will remain neutral, but cuts in defence spending in particular should promote fiscal balance despite tax relief for individuals and businesses.

Corporate payment behaviour remains satisfactory despite the sharp economic slowdown. The number of corporate bankruptcies recorded by the national statistics office were slightly up, while the number of defaults noted by Coface remained below the European average.

KEY ECONOMIC INDICATORS

%	1998	1999	2000	2001	2002 (e)	2003 (f)
Economic growth	2.1	3.2	3.7	0.8	0.7	1.8
Consumer spending (% change)	2.9	2.1	3.3	0.9	0.8	1.7
Investment (% change)	4.3	3.3	2.6	2.7	-4	2.2
Inflation	1.2	1	2.2	2.4	1.6	1.5
Unemployment	9.5	8.8	7	6.6	6.9	7
Short-term interest rate	3.6	3	4.4	4.2	3.3	3
Public-sector balance/GDP	-0.8	-0.6	0.1	0.3	-0.1	0.1
National debt/GDP	119.8	116.4	110.8	108	104	101
Exports (% change)	4.4	5	9.7	1.1	-1.6	2.5
Imports (% change)	6.5	4.1	9.7	0.8	-1.9	3
Current account balance/GDP	5.1	4.8	3.8	3.8	4.5	5.2

e = estimated, f = forecast

MAIN ECONOMIC SECTORS

Paper and cardboard

The year 2002 was a gloomy one for the paper industry, despite a rise in demand for certain products. The newsprint segment in particular was severely affected. Exports, which traditionally account for 70 per cent of Belgian output, continued to slacken due to declining consumption in neighbouring countries, especially Germany. Nevertheless papermakers have made or are planning sizeable investments to cope with the growth in demand over the next few years. If the planned investments go through the Belgian paper industry should see an estimated 70 per cent growth by 2010.

Chemicals

Belgium is an important player in the European chemicals industry, accounting for 8.2 per cent of European sales and 14 per cent of European exports. As well as large groups such as Solvay, Belgium has many small, dynamic chemical firms that should rapidly take advantage of any recovery in world markets. Belgian chemical production consists mainly of base chemicals and pharmaceuticals, which account for 31 per cent and 22 per cent of total output respectively.

Retail

The relatively small Belgian market has made it difficult for retail groups to maintain the profitability of their buying centres. This, together with the fact that many shops are run as franchises, explains why supplies are increasingly being contracted directly between shops and suppliers. There is also a growing demand for medium-sized stores (town-centre supermarkets) and small neighbourhood shops offering extended opening hours and located in busy areas such as train stations, hospitals and petrol stations. Given the fairly large market share held by independent retailers, retail groups still have plenty of room for expansion. This was reflected in the arrival of foreign groups such as Carrefour and Metro. In the non-food retail segment specialist groups have posted particularly sharp growth.

Textiles

The first five months of 2002 were marked by a mild recovery. This was followed by another slump in the summer and a small rebound in autumn. Short-term prospects for the sector remain mediocre, although firms have adopted radical measures to adjust to difficult market conditions, including delocalization and the setting up of own-brand stores to the detriment of independent multibrand outlets.

19

■ Construction

Trading conditions in this sector remain poor. Office, warehouse and factory construction has been hit by weak corporate investment and slack manufacturing demand. Housebuilding has been affected by sluggish consumer spending, upon which low mortgage rates seem to have had little influence. Public works have been hit by cuts in public spending resulting from fiscal tightening, even though local authorities appear to have been more spendthrift than the federal government and the Walloon, Flemish and Brussels regions. A significant upturn is not expected until the second half of 2003

PAYMENT AND COLLECTION PRACTICES

■ Payment

Bills of exchange are a common mode of payment in Belgium. In case of default a protest may be drawn up by a bailiff within two days of the due date, thus permitting bearers to initiate proceedings against the bill's endorsers.

Moreover the National Bank of Belgium publishes a list of protests that anyone can consult at the clerk's office of the commercial court and in some economic and financial newspapers (Journal des protêts, Echo de la Bourse). The list acts as an effective means of pressuring debtors to settle disputes to avoid being refused credit by banks and suppliers.

Cheques are also commonly used, though less so than bills of exchange.

Issuing bad cheques is a criminal offence. The Belgian public prosecutor's office is frequently willing to file criminal charges for claims over about 5000 euros (formerly about 200,000 Belgian francs). Bad cheques (like protested drafts) are probative documents equivalent to an acknowledgement of debt and permit obtaining, when needed, a security attachment.

Although bank transfers are the fastest mode of payment thanks to the SWIFT system used by major Belgian banks, settlement is not fully guaranteed since making payment by transfer depends on buyer good faith. Possessing background financial information on buyers is thus necessary before accepting this mode of payment.

■ Debt collection

Out-of-court collection begins with formal notice addressed to the debtor by registered letter inviting him to settle the outstanding principal increased by past-due interest or application of a penalty clause conforming to the terms and conditions of sale.

In the absence of a prior contractual agreement, interest on an invoice remaining unpaid will automatically run from the due date and be calculated based on the European Central Bank's refinancing rate, increased by seven basis points (2 August 2002 law that went into effect on 7 August 2002).

Summary proceedings for injunction to pay, intended for claims under 1,860 euros (formerly 75,000 Belgian francs) – falling exclusively within the competence of a justice of the peace – and materialized by a document written by the debtor that permits supposing the claim is undisputed, are little used due to their formalism. Moreover, such proceedings require a lawyer's signature.

Where debtors refuse to settle disputes amicably or fail to respond to formal notice to pay, creditors may summon them to appear before the competent commercial court via ordinary proceedings. For undisputed claims, rulings may be delivered either immediately from the bench or within the month following the court proceedings. For disputed claims, proceedings may take up to two years (notably in case of appeal). However some provisions of the Belgian Code of Civil Procedure allow parties to request that the judge set a rigid schedule for submission of arguments and evidence.

Since the 8 August 1997 Bankruptcy Law (amended by the 4 September 2002 law) and 17

July 1997 Composition Law went into effect on 1 January 1998 retention of property rights is recognised, albeit under specific conditions. In particular, an action for recovery of property will only be admissible if initiated before the registered list of admitted debts is drawn up (procès-verbal de vérification de créances).

Another safeguard for creditors is the right granted to them in respect of debtors' movable property stipulated under article 20-5 of the mortgage law – this concerns all durable equipment employed directly in an industrial, commercial or craft activity and generally considered as 'real estate' by incorporation or economic destination. A creditor may act on this right during a five-year period, a debtor's bankruptcy notwithstanding, provided he has registered certified true copies of invoices with the clerk's office of the commercial court within 15 days of delivery of the goods.

1

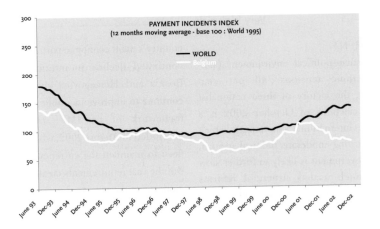

PAYMENT INCIDENTS INDEX
(12 months moving average - base 100 : World 1995)

— WORLD
— Belgium

Bosnia and Herzegovina

Coface analysis

Short-term: **D**

Medium-term:
Very high risk

RISK ASSESSMENT

In a difficult socio-political environment (simmering inter-ethnic tensions, 40 per cent unemployment), the victory of three nationalist parties in the elections of October 2002 is a reversal for the international community, which has been supporting moderate political groups. The coalition government is likely to further slow the pace of much-needed structural reforms (especially telecommunications and electricity privatization and banking sector restructuring), perpetuating Bosnia and Herzegovina's de facto administration by the United Nations High Representative.

Growth could be hampered by the downturn in the European Union, especially Germany, the country's main economic partner, as well as by the continued decline in international assistance. Bosnia and Herzegovina should, nevertheless, continue to improve its public finances within the framework of an IMF stand-by agreement concluded in August 2002, which also stresses the need to maintain the currency's peg to the euro. But the vast requirements created by the country's modernization are driving large deficits in the external account. As a result the country remains at the mercy of declining international financial assistance and weak direct foreign investment. The daunting challenges facing the country will be around for some time yet.

KEY ECONOMIC INDICATORS

US$ million	1998	1999	2000	2001	2002 (e)	2003 (f)
Economic growth (%)	9.9	10.6	4.5	2.3	2.3	4.1
Inflation (%)	5.2	−0.7	1.9	1.7	1.5	1.6
Public-sector balance/GDP (%)	−20.1	−22.4	−20	−14	−12	−7
Exports	702	744	903	1002	1165	1388
Imports	2583	2542	2558	2670	2764	2904
Trade balance	−1881	−1798	−1655	−1668	−1599	−1516
Current account balance/GDP (%)	−16.2	−19	−20.7	−23.3	−20.9	−17
Foreign debt	2839	3260	2993	2499	2931	3354
Debt service/Exports (%)	6.1	6.4	7.1	4.2	6.6	7.9
Reserves (import months)	0.7	1.9	2.1	5.1	6.2	6.1

e = estimated, f = forecast

Bulgaria

Coface analysis

Short-term: **B**

Medium-term:
Quite high risk

STRENGTHS

- Skilled manpower.
- Enjoys support of multilateral institutions and is actively involved in EU accession talks.
- Cautious economic policy and implementation of reforms have improved economic position and reduced burden of public sector debt.

WEAKNESSES

- Major external imbalances caused by rising imports to meet needs of transition economy.
- Poor level of economic development and inadequate savings. High unemployment.
- Slow progress in key areas of reform: energy sector restructuring, completion of large-scale privatizations, business climate improvement, banking sector development.
- Special efforts required to promote foreign investment not linked to privatization programme.

RISK ASSESSMENT

Growth remained fairly buoyant despite the world economic slowdown and continued to be driven by investment. Inflation is controlled. The budget deficit has been brought under control, giving the country favourable access to the capital markets. The public sector debt, though large, is steadily contracting.

Against a background of a swelling current account deficit and falling direct foreign investment repatriations by non-residents and lower debt amortization have boosted foreign exchange reserves. While the increase in reserves supports the currency board system for the time being, generating regular capital inflows to maintain the system over the medium term will require further fiscal discipline and reform.

The prospects of EU membership by 2007 should encourage the government in this direction. But the social costs of reform have led to a decline in the government's popularity, with rifts appearing within the ruling coalition and complicating the business of government.

KEY ECONOMIC INDICATORS						
US$ million	1998	1999	2000	2001	2002(e)	2003(f)
Economic Growth (%)	4	2.3	5.4	4	3.5	4.3
Inflation (%)	39.9	2.6	10.3	7.3	5.9	4.7
Public-sector balance/GDP(%)	0.9	−0.9	−1	−0.9	−0.8	−0.7
Unemployment (%)	12.2	16	16.4	19.5	n/a	n/a
Exports	4193	4006	4825	5107	5290	5980
Imports	4574	5087	6000	6674	7000	7780
Trade balance	−381	−1081	−1176	−1568	−1710	−1800
Current account balance	−61	−654	−677	−828	−1010	−1100
Current account balance/GDP (%)	−0.5	−5.0	−5.4	−6.1	−6.4	−6.1
Foreign debt	10892	10914	11202	10616	11291	11797
Debt service/Export (%)	20.9	16.2	17	19.2	13.9	12.4
Reserves (import months)	5.2	5.3	4.8	4.4	5	4.7

e = estimated, f = forecast

CONDITIONS OF ACCESS TO THE MARKET

■ Means of entry

Bulgaria is determined to continue with its structural reforms policy of the last five years. In 2003 tenders will be invited in monopoly sectors such as energy, railways and water treatment and supply. The government has already adopted legislative amendments to enhance the effectiveness and transparency of its privatization programme. The privatization law has been revised, and the preferences awarded to employee and management-owned companies have been abolished along with the system of direct bargaining with potential buyers. All privatization deals now are solely handled by the privatization agency.

■ Attitude towards Foreign Investors

The new government is clearly focusing on improving the investment climate so as to attract more direct foreign investment into the country. There are few overall restrictions on foreign investment and those that remain concern property ownership, residence permits and VAT refund.

It should be noted that there are no restrictions on the transfer of profits and dividends arising from commercial and industrial activities, only on income derived from financial speculation. Foreign companies have no problems with capital transfers.

OPPORTUNITY SCOPE

- Population   8.2 million inhabitants
- GDP   11,995 million US dollars

Breakdown of internal demand (GDP + imports) %
- Private consumption   43
- Public spending   11
- Investment   10

Exports: 58% of GDP → ← Imports: 64% of GDP

1

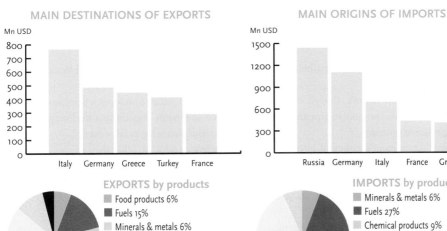

MAIN DESTINATIONS OF EXPORTS

Mn USD

Italy   Germany   Greece   Turkey   France

MAIN ORIGINS OF IMPORTS

Mn USD

Russia   Germany   Italy   France   Greece

EXPORTS by products
- Food products 6%
- Fuels 15%
- Minerals & metals 6%
- Chemical products 12%
- Other manufactured products 47%
- Transport & capital goods 10%
- Miscellaneous 4%

IMPORTS by products
- Minerals & metals 6%
- Fuels 27%
- Chemical products 9%
- Other manufactured products 26%
- Transport & capital goods 25%
- Miscellaneous 7%

STANDARD OF LIVING / PURCHASING POWER

Indicators	Bulgaria	Regional average	DC average
GNP per capita (PPP dollars)	5560	7936	6548
GNP per capita	1520	3052	3565
Human development index	0.779	0.796	0.702
Wealthiest 10% share of national income	23	26	32
Urban population percentage	70	61	60
Percentage under 15 years old	16	20	32
Number of telephones per 1000 inhabitants	350	273	157
Number of computers per 1000 inhabitants	44	98	64

Croatia

Coface analysis

Short-term: **A4**

Medium-term:
Quite high risk

STRENGTHS

- Reforms have helped to strengthen market confidence.
- Foreign investment inflows, though declining, have led to partial economic restructuring.
- Strong tourism potential.
- Coalition government's policy of international openness is well received by international community and brings country closer to EU (conclusion of stabilization and association agreement in 2001).

WEAKNESSES

- Rising public sector debt could threaten long-term macroeconomic stability.
- Increased reliance on foreign borrowings in the face of foreign investment's declining share of external financing needs cover.
- Delays in reforms, other than privatization and pension reform.
- Infighting within coalition government against a background of rising popularity of nationalist parties and soaring unemployment.

RISK ASSESSMENT

Buoyant domestic demand drove growth while inflation was brought under control. To maintain growth, however, the government will have to speed up reforms, in particular those aimed at reducing the budget deficit, which remains the black hole of the economy, and improving the legal and administrative environment for business.

The country's external financing needs have grown under the dual impact of a swelling current account deficit and higher debt amortization. At the same time direct investment has shrunk as privatization-related inflows dry up. However, asset repatriation by banks and favourable terms for government borrowings on the international capital market for the moment enable the borrowing requirement to be met without major difficulties.

On the political front, cracks have begun to appear within the coalition government in the face of the rise of nationalist parties, high unemployment and a low standard of living.

KEY ECONOMIC INDICATORS

US$ million	1998	1999	2000	2001	2002 (e)	2003 (f)
Economic growth (%)	2.5	−0.3	3.7	4.1	3.8	4
Inflation (%)	5.7	4.1	6.2	4.9	2.6	3.2
Public-sector balance/GDP (%)	−3.5	−8.2	−6.3	−6.6	−6.5	−6.3
Unemployment	18.6	20.8	22.6	23.1	n/a	n/a
Exports	4604	4395	4567	4752	5100	6010
Imports	8752	7693	7771	8764	9790	11240
Trade balance	−4147	−3299	−3204	−4012	−4690	−5230
Current account balance	−1512	−1365	−412	−490	−770	−820
Current account balance/GDP (%)	−7	−6.8	−2.2	−2.4	−3.4	−3.1
Foreign debt	9639	9872	11002	11189	13132	13829
Debt service/Exports (%)	12.1	18.2	19	19.1	18.6	15.3
Reserves (import months)	3	3.5	4.1	4.8	5.9	5.7

e = estimated, f = forecast

CONDITIONS OF ACCESS TO THE MARKET

■ Market overview

Of an estimated population of 4.38 million inhabitants, 1.36 million are employed. The average rate of unemployment, which was 21.8 per cent at the end of 2002, masks sharp regional disparities. The estimated take-home wage in July 2001 was 3757 kunas (501 euros). Of the total population ten per cent live below the poverty line.

As a rule imports, which are rising sharply, do not require prior authorization, except for products governed by international agreements (arms, gold, works of art, and so on) or subject to public health restrictions (food products, livestock, etc). Under the most-favoured nation system, applicable since Croatia's WTO membership, customs duties are being cut. The stabilization and association agreement concluded with the European Union, and applicable since 1 January 2002, provides for duty free access for the vast majority of products. The country has signed free trade agreements with almost all its trading partners and is preparing for membership of EFTA. Under the various agreements Croatia has undertaken to introduce import quotas for some products (beef, pork, wheat, sugar, chocolate), and to levy below-average customs duties on them within set quotas. The average tariff for industrial products is due to be cut to 5 per cent by 2005, while that for agri-foodstuffs will be gradually reduced to 16.4 per cent by the same date. All means of payment are used in Croatia. Given the country's widespread debt cash payments are in great demand and carry a 10 per cent discount. Credit cards are also being used more widely.

For business transactions the most widespread means of payment are bank transfers, bank guarantees confirmed by a foreign bank and cheques drawn on a recognized local bank. Documentary credit is hardly used and drafts are not recommended.

■ Attitudes towards foreign investors

While Croatian law guarantees foreign investors equality of treatment with locals, a number of stumbling blocks remain. The uncertainty surrounding land and property rights creates a climate of insecurity that the judicial system does not always address satisfactorily (lengthy court procedures, non-enforcement of court orders, lack of independence of the judiciary). Between 1993 and the second quarter of 2002 direct foreign investment amounted to US$7.3 billion. During this period the three leading investors were Austria (28.6 per cent), Germany (24.07 per cent) and the United States (15 per cent). Of US$578 million in overseas investment during the first six months of 2002, Austria accounted for almost 50 per cent, Italy 27.3 per cent and Germany 11.5 per cent. France's share of foreign investment over the 1993–2002 period was 2.19 per cent and 7.28 per cent

27

during the first six months of 2002 (fourth largest overseas investor).

■ Foreign exchange regulations

The national currency, the kuna, is not convertible outside the country. Foreign companies must open a foreign exchange account and a kuna account to do business in the country.

The central bank (HNB) has adopted a floating exchange rate band for the kuna, outside which it intervenes on the currency market. The kuna is slightly overvalued and at 25 October traded at 7.399 kunas to the euro.

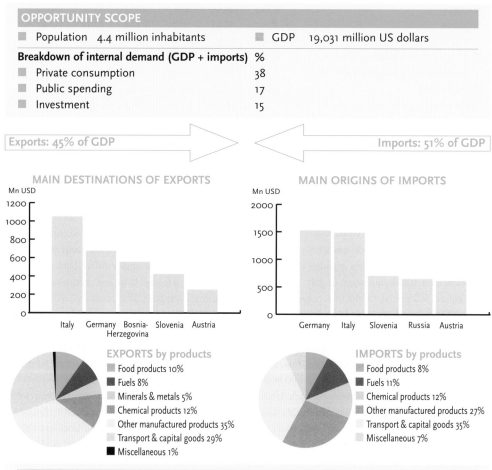

OPPORTUNITY SCOPE

■ Population   4.4 million inhabitants   ■ GDP   19,031 million US dollars

Breakdown of internal demand (GDP + imports)	%
■ Private consumption	38
■ Public spending	17
■ Investment	15

Exports: 45% of GDP   Imports: 51% of GDP

MAIN DESTINATIONS OF EXPORTS
Mn USD — Italy, Germany, Bosnia-Herzegovina, Slovenia, Austria

MAIN ORIGINS OF IMPORTS
Mn USD — Germany, Italy, Slovenia, Russia, Austria

EXPORTS by products
- ■ Food products 10%
- ■ Fuels 8%
- ■ Minerals & metals 5%
- ■ Chemical products 12%
- ■ Other manufactured products 35%
- ■ Transport & capital goods 29%
- ■ Miscellaneous 1%

IMPORTS by products
- ■ Food products 8%
- ■ Fuels 11%
- ■ Chemical products 12%
- ■ Other manufactured products 27%
- ■ Transport & capital goods 35%
- ■ Miscellaneous 7%

STANDARD OF LIVING / PURCHASING POWER

Indicators	Croatia	Regional average	DC average
GNP per capita (PPP dollars)	7960	7936	6548
GNP per capita	4620	3052	3565
Human development index	0.809	0.796	0.702
Wealthiest 10% share of national income	23	26	32
Urban population percentage	58	61	60
Percentage under 15 years old	18	20	32
Number of telephones per 1000 inhabitants	365	273	157
Number of computers per 1000 inhabitants	81	98	64

Czech Republic

Coface analysis

Short-term: **A3**

Medium-term:
Low risk

STRENGTHS

- Strong manufacturing potential.
- Export competitiveness enhanced by modernisation, restructuring and rising investment.
- Moderate foreign debt.
- Political and economic continuity and stability bolstered by EU membership in 2004.

WEAKNESSES

- Public sector deficit, widened by banking sector restructuring programme and likely to worsen with welfare spending, could become unsustainable.
- Economy highly dependent on economic situation of main trading partners, in particular Germany.
- Reform, especially of country's public finances, hampered by dissensions within Social Democrat-led coalition.

RISK ASSESSMENT

The international economic downturn and the floods in August 2002 dampened growth, which should pick up in 2003 on the back of growing investment and foreign demand. While EU membership opens up big opportunities the strength of the koruna and the worsening state of the country's finances are likely to hamper growth in the medium term.

The country's external solvency gives little cause for concern due to its moderate external financing needs and manageable burden of foreign debt. The needs are largely covered by foreign direct investment, while foreign exchange reserves are sharply up.

Finally, given the fragility of the coalition government, there is little likelihood of major progress in structural reforms.

CONDITIONS OF ACCESS TO THE MARKET

■ Market overview

The economy slowed in 2001 but weathered the downturn in the European Union thanks to the high degree of market openness. In the first half of 2002 growth continued to slow.

■ Means of entry

There are no quotas or tariff restrictions on imports of industrial products from the European Union. Talks with the European Commission aimed at establishing mutual concessions for farm products have been under way since March 2000.

Most transactions between regular business partners are settled by SWIFT transfers. This is a

KEY ECONOMIC INDICATORS

US$ billion	1998	1999	2000	2001	2002 (e)	2003 (f)
Economic growth (%)	−1.3	0.5	3.3	3.3	2.4	3.3
Inflation (%)	10.7	2.1	3.9	4.7	1.9	0.9
Public-sector balance/GDP (%)	−2.9	−3.4	−4.6	−5.4	−10.2	−9
Unemployment (%)	6.1	8.6	9	8.5	9	n/a
Exports	26.4	26.3	29.1	33.4	35.3	40.1
Imports	28.9	28.2	32.2	36.5	37.4	42.8
Trade balance	−2.6	−1.9	−3.1	−3.1	−2.1	−2.7
Current account balance	−1.3	−1.6	−2.7	−2.6	−2.6	−3.6
Current account balance/GDP (%)	−2.3	−2.9	−5.4	−4.7	−3.8	−4.5
Foreign debt	24	22.6	21.4	21.7	25.3	26.2
Debt service/Exports (%)	16.6	13.7	13.2	9.3	9.5	6.4
Reserves (import months)	4.1	4.2	3.8	3.8	5.4	6.2

e = estimated, f = forecast

problem-free means of payment. However, for first-time transactions or large contracts documentary credit is recommended. Payments are generally made within the standard time limit of 30 days.

■ Attitude towards foreign investors

The government has adopted a proactive policy of promoting foreign investment, mainly via the investment promotion agency, CzechInvest. Local and foreign investors receive identical treatment. A new investment incentive law came into force in May 2000. Formerly limited to start-ups, it now also applies to companies engaged in expanding or modernizing existing facilities. To qualify for incentives the minimum investment is 350 million koruna (10.2 million euros), and 175 million koruna (5.1 million euros) in high-unemployment regions. Newly formed entities pay no corporation tax for ten years, while existing entities are granted a partial five-year tax exemption. The new law also provides for other forms of support, including job creation subsidies, training allowances and infrastructure development grants.

Companies investing in the strategic services and technology sectors (computer software, NICT, e-solutions, high-tech, audit and consultancy) are eligible for additional government incentives if they invest a minimum of 50 million koruna (1.5 million euros), create 50 new jobs over three years and generate half their turnover abroad.

The gradual modernization of business law and the adoption of an auction law offer creditors more effective safeguards. However there is room for improvement in the enforcement of these measures. Moreover, bankruptcy proceedings can be lengthy.

Ownership of land and other property by foreigners is prohibited, except in the case of inheritance. Since January 2002 property ownership, formerly the exclusive preserve of Czech companies, has been opened up to Czech-based branches and subsidiaries of foreign companies, which may now acquire property and land, with the exception of farm and forest land.

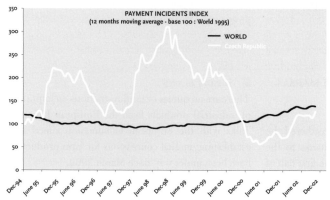

PAYMENT INCIDENTS INDEX
(12 months moving average - base 100 : World 1995)

The standard working week is 40 hours. There is a minimum of four weeks annual paid leave.

The Czech crown is fully convertible. The current exchange rate system is a dirty (or managed) float.

PAYMENT AND COLLECTION PRACTICES

■ Payment

The bill of exchange and the cheque are not so commonplace as they must be issued in accordance with certain criteria to be valid.

For unpaid and protested bills of exchange (*směnka cizí*), promissory notes (*směnka vlastní*) and cheques, creditors benefit from a fast-track procedure for ordering payment under which, if the judge admits the plaintiff's application, the debtor has only three days in which to contest the order against him.

Bank transfers are by far the most widely used means of payment. Leading Czech banks – after an initial phase of privatization and a second phase of concentration – are now linked to the SWIFT system, which is an easier, quicker and more cost-effective method of handling domestic and international payments.

■ Debt collection

It is advisable, as far as possible, not to initiate recovery proceedings locally because of the country's cumbersome legal system, the high cost of legal action and the lengthy court procedures – it takes almost three years to obtain a writ of execution due to a lack of judges adequately trained in the rules of the market economy and to insufficient equipment.

Following the issue of a final notice, accompanied by proof of debt, it is advisable to seek an out-of-court settlement based on a schedule of payment, preferably set up by a Public Notary, accompanied by an *enforcement formula* that allows creditors, in the event of default by the debtor, to go directly to the enforcement proceedings, provided the binding nature of this document is admitted by the courts.

Where creditors have significant proof of their claim (unpaid bills of exchange or cheques, acknowledgement of debt, etc) they may obtain an injunction to pay (*platební rozkaz*), under a fast-track procedure – which can take anything from one month to one year depending on the workload of the courts – but that does not necessitate a hearing as long as the claim is sufficiently well founded.

Where a debtor contests this injunction, the parties are summoned to a hearing in which they are required to produce evidence on the basis of which the judge decides whether to throw out the plaintiff's application or to order the debtor to pay principal and costs.

The written part of ordinary proceedings consists in the filing of submissions by the parties and supporting case documents, whereas the oral part involves a hearing of the parties and their witnesses on the main hearing date.

Any settlement reached between the parties during these proceedings and ratified by the court is tantamount to a writ of execution, in the event of non-compliance at a later date.

Commercial disputes are heard by civil courts (district courts and regional courts) since the abolition, in January 2001, of regional commercial courts, which only existed in Prague, Brno and Ostrava.

To speed up enforcement of court orders (there were more than 400,000 cases awaiting enforcement at the end of June 2002), a new body of bailiffs (*soudní exekutor*), with less formal enforcement powers, was established in May 2001.

1

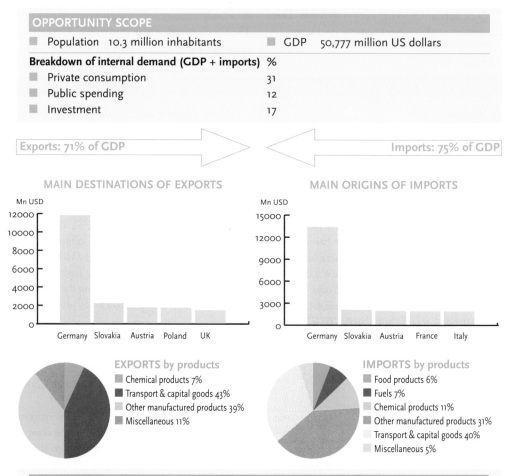

OPPORTUNITY SCOPE

■ Population 10.3 million inhabitants   ■ GDP 50,777 million US dollars

Breakdown of internal demand (GDP + imports) %
■ Private consumption   31
■ Public spending   12
■ Investment   17

Exports: 71% of GDP   Imports: 75% of GDP

MAIN DESTINATIONS OF EXPORTS

Mn USD

Germany Slovakia Austria Poland UK

MAIN ORIGINS OF IMPORTS

Mn USD

Germany Slovakia Austria France Italy

EXPORTS by products
■ Chemical products 7%
■ Transport & capital goods 43%
■ Other manufactured products 39%
■ Miscellaneous 11%

IMPORTS by products
■ Food products 6%
■ Fuels 7%
■ Chemical products 11%
■ Other manufactured products 31%
■ Transport & capital goods 40%
■ Miscellaneous 5%

STANDARD OF LIVING / PURCHASING POWER

Indicators	Czech Republic	Regional average	DC average
GNP per capita (PPP dollars)	13,780	7936	6548
GNP per capita	5250	3052	3565
Human development index	0.849	0.796	0.702
Wealthiest 10% share of national income	22	26	32
Urban population percentage	75	61	60
Percentage under 15 years old	17	20	32
Number of telephones per 1000 inhabitants	378	273	157
Number of computers per 1000 inhabitants	122	98	64

Denmark

Coface analysis   Short-term: **A1**

RISK ASSESSMENT

The economy grew moderately in 2002 largely on the back of stronger domestic demand. Investment picked up, as did household consumption. The increase in consumer spending has largely benefited the automobile sector pending changes in European legislation. Consumer spending was buoyed by higher disposable incomes resulting from lower taxes and fairly sizeable wage increases. However, as these were only partially offset by productivity gains, rising inflationary pressures depressed exports.

The economy should continue to grow in 2003, spurred by firm consumer spending and the continued upturn in industrial investment. Despite a fall in competitiveness caused by the maintenance of the strong krone and a fresh round of wage increases exports in general – and industrial exports in particular – are expected to recover. The year should also see a moderate tightening of monetary policy in order to ward off inflationary pressures.

Corporate bankruptcies continued to rise between 2001 and 2002. The number of defaults remains below the world average despite a slight deterioration year on year.

KEY ECONOMIC INDICATORS						
%	1998	1999	2000	2001	2002 (e)	2003 (f)
Economic growth	2.5	2.3	3	0.9	1.7	2.3
Consumer spending (% change)	2.3	0.2	−0.4	0.6	2	2.2
Investment (% change)	10.1	1	10.7	0	2.1	3.7
Inflation	1.3	2.6	3	2.1	2.3	2
Unemployment	4.9	4.8	4.4	4.3	4.7	4.4
Short–term interest rate	4.1	3.3	4.9	4.6	3.7	3.8
Public–sector balance/GDP	1.1	3.2	2.5	2.8	2.1	2.3
Foreign debt/GDP	59.7	54.9	50.1	46.4	44	41
Exports (% change)	4.3	10.8	11.5	3.1	3.2	4
Imports (% change)	8.9	3.3	11.2	3.8	3.3	4.5
Current account balance/GDP	−0.9	1.7	1.6	2.5	2.4	2.3

e = estimated, f = forecast

PAYMENT AND COLLECTION PRACTICES

■ Payment

Like cheques, bills of exchange are relatively infrequently used in Denmark. Both payment instruments are deemed to constitute above all materializations and acknowledgements of debt.

However, where bills or cheques have been accepted but remain unpaid they are considered as legally enforceable instruments and thus discharge creditors from the need to obtain a court judgment. In this event, a judge–bailiff (*Fogedret*) is appointed to oversee compulsory execution and, as the first stage in the recovery process, the debtor is summonsed to declare his financial situation and determine his ability to repay the debt. It should be noted that the debtor's criminal responsibility may be engaged if he erroneously declares himself insolvent.

Bank transfers are the most commonly used means of payment. All of the larger Danish banks are connected to the SWIFT network, which offers a rapid and efficient method for settling international transactions.

■ Debt collection

The recovery process starts with the issuing of a final notice to pay. This may be transmitted by registered or ordinary mail and sent by either the creditor or his legal counsel, thus giving the debtor ten days in which to settle the principal amount together with – unless otherwise agreed by the parties – interest penalties equivalent to the Danish bank rate plus five basis points.

It should also be noted that any settlements or acknowledgements of debt negotiated at this stage in the recovery process may be directly enforced, where the due date for payment is not complied with, on condition that an executory clause has been duly included in the agreement or deed.

In the event where claims are disputed, the most common alternative is for creditors to engage a lawyer to defend their interests, even though Danish law allows plaintiffs and defendants to represent their interests directly in court. Unlike other countries the Danish legal system does not have a variety of professional categories (eg notaries, barristers, bailiffs–at–law, etc) but only has a single type of legal representative, ie the lawyer.

Where debtors fail to respond to requests for payment, or in the absence of a serious dispute, the creditor may instigate proceedings, generally taking some three months and involving an adversarial hearing or a judgment by default, in order to obtain a ruling ordering the debtor to settle, within 14 days, both the principal amount and the costs of the proceedings as well as a contribution to the creditor's legal expenses.

For more complex or disputed claims, which concern amounts of less than 1 million Danish krone, cases are heard by the court of first instance (*Byret*) in proceedings that are predominately based on oral evidence rather than written submissions. For claims above this amount cases are heard by one of the two regional courts: the *Vestre Landsret* in Viborg or the *Østre Landsret* in Copenhagen. This entails preliminary hearings, in which the parties submit their various conclusions and written proofs, as well as a plenary hearing in which the court hears witness testimonies and the parties' arguments.

Except in the Copenhagen area, which has a maritime and commercial court (*Sø– og Handelsretten*), Denmark does not have a system of commercial courts. The *Sø– og Handelsretten* is presided over by a panel of professional and non–professional judges who have jurisdiction over winding up cases as well as commercial and maritime disputes.

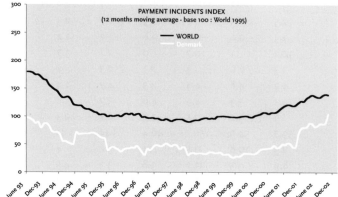

PAYMENT INCIDENTS INDEX
(12 months moving average - base 100 : World 1995)

— WORLD
— Denmark

Estonia

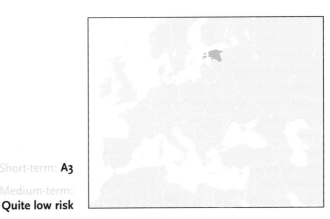

Short-term: **A3**

Medium-term:
Quite low risk

Coface analysis

1

STRENGTHS

- More advanced than other Baltic states in terms of convergence with EU.
- Strong export capacity to EU has followed moves to strengthen foreign trade with Nordic countries.
- Successful transition to market economy has allowed country to establish strong foothold in growing service sector.

WEAKNESSES

- Volatile growth because of country's small size and open economy.
- Vast current account deficit weakens external financial position.
- Low household savings.
- High unemployment.
- High dependency for energy on Russia.

RISK ASSESSMENT

The downturn in Estonia's main export markets (Nordic countries) and in the electronics and telecommunications sectors slowed growth. The economy has nevertheless weathered the slowdown thanks to strong domestic demand, which should continue to drive growth pending a gradual recovery in Europe.

The main thrust of reform continues to be the gradual harmonization of the country's economy with that of the European Union. The present currency board system obliges the government to pursue a tight fiscal policy, which should not undergo significant alteration in the run-up to the parliamentary elections in March 2003.

Economic growth, however, has been accompanied by a deteriorating external account. In spite of the maintenance of a satisfactory services account surplus (transit trade, tourism), the current account deficit has widened significantly due to rising imports and declining exports of machinery and equipment. Foreign direct investment covers a large part of the country's external financing needs, but is showing signs of slowing as the local market saturates.

CONDITIONS OF ACCESS TO THE MARKET

■ Market overview

At purchasing power parity, per capita GDP in 2001 was 8,925 euros, the highest among Baltic states. In early 2002 the average wage was 384 euros.

■ Means of entry

Estonia's ultra-liberal trade policy is the cornerstone of its programme to develop a market economy. EU membership is a government priority as the country prepares itself for accession.

Until 2000 Estonia applied no import duties.

KEY ECONOMIC INDICATORS						
US$ million	1998	1999	2000	2001	2002 (e)	2003 (f)
Economic growth (%)	4.6	−0.6	7.1	5.0	4.8	5.2
Inflation (%)	8.1	3.3	4	5.8	3.6	3.3
Public-sector balance/GDP (%)	−0.3	−4.6	−0.7	0.4	−0.4	n/a
Unemployment	9.9	12.3	13.7	12.6	n/a	n/a
Exports	2690	2453	3311	3338	3509	3883
Imports	3805	3331	4080	4125	4582	5054
Trade balance	−1115	−878	−768	−787	−1073	−1171
Current account balance	−478	−295	−294	−339	−641	−704
Current account balance/GDP(%)	−9.2	−5.7	−5.8	−6.3	−10.1	−9.1
Foreign debt	2785	3052	2991	3309	3717	3996
Debt service/Exports (%)	7.7	7	6.5	6.5	7.5	7.6
Reserves (import months)	2	2.3	2.1	1.7	1.8	1.8

e = estimated, f = forecast

From 1 January 2000 a customs tariff was established for agricultural products and foodstuffs imported from third countries in keeping with Estonia's WTO commitments. From 1 July 2002 Estonia introduced the EU's common external tariff for non-EU goods. Trade with EU countries is exempt from customs duties under the terms of the Association Agreement. Excise duties are levied on certain products without distinction between domestic and imported goods. The duty applied to each import or export transaction for the purposes of self-financing customs procedures has been cut by half to 100 crowns (6.4 euros).

Estonia administers a system of non-tariff barriers based on automatic licensing for some products (wines and spirits, lubricants, medicines). The same licensing rules apply to domestically produced goods. There are no ceilings.

The veterinarian authorities are over cautious about issuing certificates and accordingly have banned imports of beef and pork from France.

The country's standard legislation does not contain any restrictions of note that might serve to protect local industry. Most of the 5000 European standards have already been incorporated into local legislation.

Although down payments are advisable for initial business transactions 30 or 60-day credit is increasingly commonplace. Credit cover is advisable. The Estonian banking industry is perfectly sound. The two leading banks, which are owned by Swedish banks, account for 85 per cent of the country's banking assets.

■ Attitude towards foreign investors

In September 1991 Estonia passed a foreign investment law providing for simple and non-discriminatory company registration procedures.

A foreign company may hold a 100 per cent stake in a local company. No specific promotional programme is in force and a non-discrimination principle applies to direct taxation. There are no restrictions on the repatriation of profits after tax, dividends or proceeds from the sale or liquidation of an investment.

Estonia has concluded a reciprocal investment promotion and protection agreement and a dual taxation agreement with France. Both agreements are still in force.

Income tax and corporation tax are levied at a flat rate of 26 per cent. Profits reinvested by companies have been exempt from tax since 1 January 2000.

One of the most attractive features for foreign investors is the country's highly qualified yet cheap labour.

Social security contributions, borne entirely by employers, amount to 33 per cent of wages, including 13 per cent for health insurance and 20 per cent for pensions. An unemployment contribution – 0.5 per cent of an employee's wage borne by the employer and 1 per cent by the employee – was introduced on 1 January 2002. The second pillar of the country's pension system, a pension fund, was established on 1 April 2002.

■ Foreign exchange regulations

Introduced in June 1992, with a parity unchanged to this day of 8 crowns to the Deutschmark, the Estonian currency is freely convertible and consequently enjoys de facto parity with the euro. Estonia has abolished exchange controls and local banks accept accounts in either local or foreign currency.

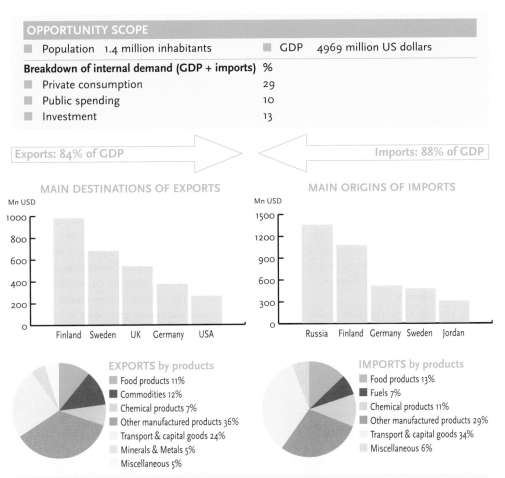

OPPORTUNITY SCOPE

■ Population 1.4 million inhabitants		■ GDP 4969 million US dollars

Breakdown of internal demand (GDP + imports) %
- ■ Private consumption — 29
- ■ Public spending — 10
- ■ Investment — 13

Exports: 84% of GDP   Imports: 88% of GDP

MAIN DESTINATIONS OF EXPORTS
Mn USD

Finland, Sweden, UK, Germany, USA

MAIN ORIGINS OF IMPORTS
Mn USD

Russia, Finland, Germany, Sweden, Jordan

EXPORTS by products
- ■ Food products 11%
- ■ Commodities 12%
- ■ Chemical products 7%
- ■ Other manufactured products 36%
- ■ Transport & capital goods 24%
- ■ Minerals & Metals 5%
- ■ Miscellaneous 5%

IMPORTS by products
- ■ Food products 13%
- ■ Fuels 7%
- ■ Chemical products 11%
- ■ Other manufactured products 29%
- ■ Transport & capital goods 34%
- ■ Miscellaneous 6%

STANDARD OF LIVING / PURCHASING POWER

Indicators	Estonia	Regional average	DC average
GNP per capita (PPP dollars)	9340	7936	6548
GNP per capita	3580	3052	3565
Human development index	0.826	0.796	0.702
Wealthiest 10% share of national income	30	26	32
Urban population percentage	69	61	60
Percentage under 15 years old	18	20	32
Number of telephones per 1000 inhabitants	363	273	157
Number of computers per 1000 inhabitants	153	98	64

Finland

Coface analysis　　　　Short-term: **A1**

RISK ASSESSMENT

The economy grew only slightly in 2002 as the unfavourable global economic situation continued to depress IT exports. Household consumption, on the other hand, benefited from continued growth in real household incomes on the back of tax cuts, lower inflation and low interest rates. The vast budget surplus enabled the government to cut taxes and social security contributions. However, investment fell due to under utilization of existing production capacities.

The pick up in world trade in 2003 should provide a spur to the timber and IT industries and enable the country to achieve faster growth. Investment in mainly machinery and equipment should improve as industrial activity recovers in line with expectations. Consumption should benefit from moderate wage increases and surprisingly high consumer confidence.

The economic slowdown has not jeopardized corporate solvency. Defaults remain rare, although sectors such as electronics, process metallurgy, mechanical engineering and wood processing have been harder hit than others by the world economic slowdown. After plummeting for several years the number of bankruptcies grew slightly in the first half of 2002.

KEY ECONOMIC INDICATORS

%	1998	1999	2000	2001	2002 (e)	2003 (f)
Economic growth	5.3	4.1	6	0.7	1.2	2.9
Consumer spending (% change)	5.1	4	2.5	1.2	2.1	2.5
Investment (% change)	9.3	3	4.8	2.1	−2.2	3.2
Inflation	1.7	1	3.9	2.7	1.8	2
Unemployment	11.4	10.3	9.8	9.1	9.2	9
Short-term interest rate	3.6	3	4.4	4.2	3.3	3
Public-sector balance/GDP	1.3	1.9	7	4.9	3.4	3.3
Foreign debt/GDP	48.8	46.8	44	43.6	43	41
Exports (% change)	8.9	6.8	18.2	−0.7	2.5	5.9
Imports (% change)	8.5	4	16.2	−1	0.6	6.2
Current account balance/GDP	5.6	6	7.4	6.5	5.9	6

e = estimated, f = forecast

PAYMENT AND COLLECTION PRACTICES

■ Payment

Bills of exchange are not commonly used in Finland since, as in Germany, they are considered to reflect a supplier's lack of trust in buyers. A bill of exchange notably substantiates a claim and constitutes a valid acknowledgment of debt.

Cheques, also little used for domestic and international transactions, only represent an acknowledgment of debt. However, cheques not covered when issued can expose issuers to criminal penalties. The timeframe for cashing cheques is particularly long in Finland (20 days for domestic and European cheques, 70 days for cheques outside Europe).

Conversely, SWIFT bank transfers are used increasingly to settle commercial transactions. Finns are familiar with this effective mode of payment although it still depends on buyer good faith. Sellers are advised to provide full and accurate bank account details to facilitate timely payment.

■ Debt collection

An amicable collection process begins with formal notice sent by registered or ordinary mail demanding the debtor to pay the outstanding principal together with any contractually agreed past-due interest. In the absence of prior contractual agreement, interest will automatically accrue from the due date of the invoice remaining unpaid and be calculated based on the European Central Bank's refinancing rate, increased by seven basis points (according to the amended law on interest, effective since 1 July 2002).

The 20 August 1982 law on interest (*Korkolaki*) already stipulated that debtors must make payments within contractually agreed timeframes or fall liable to interest penalties.

For documented and undisputed claims creditors may resort to summary proceedings for injunction to pay (*Suppea haastehakemus*). This is a simple written procedure based on submission of whatever documents substantiate the claim (invoice, bill of exchange, acknowledgement of debt, and so on). Creditors do not need a lawyer to instigate such actions.

Since the 1 December 1993 reform of civil proceedings the plaintiff must attach all supporting documents and evidence substantiating a claim. The court will then invite the debtor to submit a written response elucidating his position.

During the preliminary hearing the court will base its deliberations on the parties' written submissions and supporting case documents. Thereafter, it hears the litigants' arguments.

Where the dispute remains unresolved after this preliminary hearing plenary proceedings are held before the court of first instance (*Käräjäoikeus*), with one or three presiding judges depending on the case's complexity. During this hearing the judges examine the various probative documents and hear the parties' witnesses before rapidly delivering their verdict.

The average timeframe for obtaining an executory judgment is ten months.

Commercial disputes are generally heard by civil law courts. However, a 'Market and Competition Court' (*Markkinatuomioistuin*) located in Helsinki has been established as a single entity since 1 March 2002. It is competent to assess fraudulent business practices, denounce unfair trading, investigate concentrations of commercial companies, deliver injunctions prohibiting such practices and impose fines on offenders.

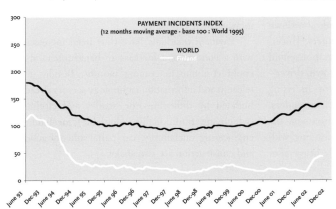

PAYMENT INCIDENTS INDEX
(12 months moving average - base 100 : World 1995)

— WORLD
— Finland

France

Coface analysis   Short-term: **A1**

STRENGTHS

- Inflation is considered to be under solid control by all economic players.
- Despite a recent jump in unemployment, increased purchasing power linked to tax breaks and persistently low inflation continue to spur household spending.
- Greater hiring flexibility – reduced payroll taxes on low-wage jobs and wage restraint – has been driving the job market.
- Industrial productivity is good.

WEAKNESSES

- Public accounts remain structurally in the red.
- Tax reform remains on the back burner with the division of responsibilities between national and local authorities on revenues and spending remaining unclear.
- Employment continues to suffer from the combined effects of practices entrenched during crisis years, high unskilled labour costs and job market rigidity.
- With the projected decline of the working population in coming decades, retirement funding is inadequate and the pension fund is not growing fast enough.

RISK ASSESSMENT

Hopes for economic recovery in the second half of 2002 met with disappointment. Although household spending only slowed slightly in recent months corporate investment declined. Exports have not recovered due to the economic slowdown buffeting France's main trading partners. Uncertainty has been affecting trends in household spending – which has been the sole growth driver – as French consumers start to factor in rising unemployment and the wage restraint it engenders.

In this largely unfavourable environment the situation of companies has been deteriorating, with their debt burden appearing relatively heavy after several years of vigorous growth. Indeed, with French companies relying much less on financial markets than on banks, they are relatively shielded from market turmoil. Facing increasing risks, French banks are also becoming reluctant to increase their exposure.

Payment incidents have thus been increasing with a concomitant increase in bankruptcies that could continue in coming months. Besides the telecom and information technology sectors already buffeted by difficulties, or textiles and clothing (which are traditionally vulnerable) mechanical engineering, metallurgy, car parts subcontracting and construction are also shaky.

KEY ECONOMIC INDICATORS

%	1998	1999	2000	2001	2002 (e)	2003 (f)
Economic growth	3.5	3.2	4.2	1.9	0.9	2
Consumer spending (% change)	3.6	3.5	2.9	2.9	1.6	2
Investment (% change)	7.2	6.2	6.2	2.8	−0.6	1.1
Inflation	0.6	0.2	1.2	1.2	1.8	1.8
Unemployment	11.5	10.8	9.4	8.7	9	9.2
Short-term interest rate	3.6	3	4.4	4.2	3.3	3
Public-sector balance/GDP	−2.7	−1.6	−1.4	−1.4	−2.8	−2.6
National debt/GDP	65	64.6	64.1	64.8	66	67
Exports (% change)	8.2	3.9	13.3	1.1	0.8	3
Imports (% change)	11.9	4.2	15.4	−0.2	1.8	5
Current account balance/GDP	2.7	2.9	1.5	1.8	1.9	2.1

e = estimated, f = forecast

MAIN ECONOMIC SECTORS

Steel

In 2002 the car industry alone sustained its level of real steel consumption. However, apparent consumption benefited from the start of a restocking process, which resulted in price increases and moderate output growth for certain products. The 2003 outlook remains bleak. An increase in orders from the arms industry will not suffice to offset the expected automobile sector decline. Price increases, while providing a much-needed boost, may prove unsustainable.

Chemicals

The sector posted a mild recovery in 2002. However, the industry reorganisation achieved through business sell-offs and refocusing on specialities, particularly in pharmaceuticals and agrochemicals (deemed more profitable than basic chemicals) was not enough to offset the energy shock's impact on earnings. The possibility of a surge in oil prices in 2003 triggered by conflict in Iraq could erode any gains generated by the expected upturn.

Construction and public works

Since early 2002 construction sales have fallen by an estimated 0.9 per cent in volume terms. The downturn has affected new group and detached housing as well as non-residential construction. Renovation, meanwhile, continues to grow but at a slower pace. Public works construction has remained stable. The downturn should persist and even gain momentum in 2003.

Textiles and clothing

After an upturn earlier in 2002 growth stabilized in the second half. The trend will be down in 2003 due to lower household spending domestically and in France's main foreign markets. Moreover, the sector will remain exposed to strong international competition. Garment retailers, meanwhile, suffer from fierce domestic competition and increasingly fast-changing fashions. The top-end lingerie and children's apparel segments have been outperforming.

Mechanical engineering

With sales shedding an estimated 1 to 2 per cent, 2002 was not a good year for the sector, as reflected in the wait-and-see stance of companies on investment decisions. Exports to Eastern Europe and Russia fared somewhat better than sales to Western Europe and the United States. The approximately 2 per cent growth rate projected for 2003 until recently seems increasingly uncertain. Corporate bankruptcies, hitherto uncommon, could rise.

Car and parts makers

Despite a 5 per cent decline in registrations 2002 is shaped up to being a good year. The recessive trend should continue into 2003 with the reluctance of households to spend spreading throughout Europe. Parts manufacturers benefited from the good performance of all French carmakers despite the strong downward pressure they put on prices. Their sales will register a full-year rise of 2 per cent in value terms for 2002. Although continuing in 2003, carmaker pressure on prices should ease somewhat. However, possible bankruptcies will continue to buffet parts manufacturers, dealers and distributors in particular.

PAYMENT AND COLLECTION PRACTICES

Payment

The cheque remains the most widely used payment instrument in France, representing 43.5 per cent of payments in value terms, or about 1835.5 billion euros in 2001.

For cheques remaining unpaid over 30 days from the date they were first presented for payment, a creditor may immediately obtain an enforcement order (without need of further procedural act or cost) based on a certificate of non-payment provided by his banker after a second unsuccessful presentation of the cheque for payment and where the debtor has not provided proof of payment within 15 days of formal notice to pay served by a bailiff (article L 131-73 of the monetary and financial code).

Bills of exchange, a much less frequently used mode of payment than cheques, have been in virtually constant decline, although total volume remained steady in value terms year on year in 2001 at an estimated 453.6 billion euros[1].

Bills of exchange are attractive for companies in so far as they may be discounted or transferred, thus providing a valuable source of short-term financing. Moreover they allow creditors to bring legal recourse in respect of exchange law (*droit cambiaire*) and are particularly suitable for successive instalment payments.

Although lagging behind cheques, the number of common bank transfer operations has continued to rise every year, increasing 4.9 per cent year on year in 2001. Concurrently, however, volume declined 10 per cent in value terms to 1367 billion euros[1].

Bank transfers can be made within France or internationally via the SWIFT network, which offers a reliable platform for timely payment subject to mutual trust and confidence between suppliers and their customers.

Debt collection

Since the new economic regulations law of 15 May 2001, commercial debts automatically bear interest from the day after the payment due date shown on the invoice. Unless the terms and conditions of sale stipulate interest rates and conditions of application the applicable rate will be the European Central Bank's refinancing rate, increased by seven basis points.

Formal notice to pay nonetheless remains a precondition for creditors to instigate any legal action.

Where a debt results from a contractual undertaking and is undisputed, creditors may obtain an injunction to pay (*injonction de payer*). This relatively straightforward system does not require creditors to argue their case before the appropriate commercial court (the court having jurisdiction in the district where the debtor's registered offices are located) and enables them to rapidly obtain a court order to be served thereafter by a bailiff.

Summary proceedings (*Référé-provision*) offer a rapid and effective means of debt collection, even in routine cases, provided the claims are not subject to dispute. However, the presence of an attorney is required at the proceedings to represent the creditor in court.

If a claim proves to be litigious the judge competent to rule on special urgency summary proceedings (*juge des référés*) evaluates whether the

[1] Source: Conseil national du credit et du titre.

claim is well founded. As appropriate, the judge may then declare himself incompetent and invite the plaintiff to seek a ruling on the substance of the case through the formal court process.

Formal procedures of this kind permit having the validity of a claim recognized by the court, a relatively lengthy process lasting about a year or more owing to the numerous procedural phases involved in the French legal system and the emphasis placed on the adversarial nature of proceedings.

If justified by a claim's size and the uncertain solvency of the debtor, legal action may include a petition to obtain an attachment order on available assets and thereby protect the plaintiff's interests pending completion of the proceedings and enforcement of the court's final verdict.

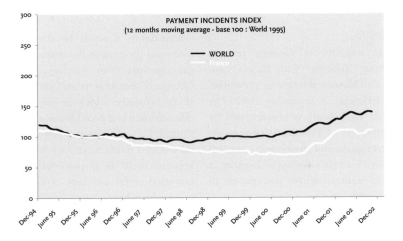

Source: Conseil national du credit et du titre

Georgia

Short-term: **D**

Coface analysis

Medium-term:
Very high risk

RISK ASSESSMENT

The political situation in Georgia remains extremely tense. Relations with Russia have deteriorated, with Moscow threatening 'preventive' strikes against Georgia in September 2002. The situation inside the country is characterised by mounting opposition to President Chevernadze, widespread corruption and deteriorating law and order. Moreover Georgia's territorial integrity is threatened by independence movements in Abkhazia and South Ossetia.

Economic growth has been satisfactory, but its sustainability depends in the long term on continued progress in the construction of oil and gas pipelines from Azerbaijan to Turkey via Georgia. These projects are vital for the country's shaky economy, which is plagued by lack of diversification and poor infrastructure. Exports are sluggish because there is a preponderance of low value-added products and tax revenues are small because there is a powerful grey economy, estimated at 60 per cent of GDP. Finally, the country has a huge current account deficit financed by multilateral aid on which it is totally dependent.

KEY ECONOMIC INDICATORS						
US$ million	1998	1999	2000	2001	2002 (e)	2003 (f)
Economic growth (%)	2.9	3	1.9	4.5	5	5.5
Inflation (%)	7.2	10.9	7	5.5	4	6
Public-sector balance/GDP (%)	−5.4	−6.7	−4	−2	−2.5	−1
Exports	478	477	528	496	511	543
Imports	1164	1026	937	954	986	1085
Trade balance	−685	−549	−409	−458	−475	−542
Current account balance/GDP (%)	−10.7	−8.5	−5.4	−6.7	−6.2	−8
Foreign debt	1629.4	1701.3	1612.7	1704.1	1830.5	1943.7
Debt service/Exports (%)	8.1	9.6	9.2	6.5	10.3	15.1
Reserves (import months)	0.9	1.2	0.9	1.4	2	2

e = estimated, f = forecast

Germany

Coface analysis Short-term: **A2**

STRENGTHS

- Strategically located to take advantage of strong growth potential of the Central and Eastern European countries.
- German industry remains competitive on world markets.
- Large companies with majority family shareholdings give priority to medium-term investment strategies over immediate financial returns.
- Well represented trade unions and co-management of companies promote social cohesion, even if it means slower decision–making at times.

WEAKNESSES

- Economic backwardness of Eastern regions painstakingly slow to overcome.
- Ageing population is restricting growth.
- Inadequate spending on research, particularly in all-important small and medium-sized enterprise sector.
- Low profitability encourages banks to adopt increasingly selective credit policies and call into question their industrial interests, penalizing numerous companies that have traditionally counted on financial institutions.
- Public finances remain structurally in the red.

RISK ASSESSMENT

Despite a slight upturn in exports growth in 2002 remained one of the lowest in Europe. The outlook for 2003 is hardly more encouraging. A lack of confidence continues to weigh on consumer spending. Investment continues to be hit by a sluggish construction market and the slump in industrial production. Fiscal constraints have led to the indefinite postponement of planned tax relief for 2003, and will result in even higher taxation. Finally the banking sector, faced with addressing the problem of inadequate profitability, is less than enthusiastic about maintaining the support it provided in the past for companies.

The increasing number of corporate bankruptcies and defaults, therefore, comes as no surprise. Long known for timely payment and honouring commitments to suppliers, German companies now present a growing level of risk approaching the European average. The only bright spot in this worrying picture is the new government's declared policy of assistance for businesses. However, government support does not provide a guarantee against bankruptcy and may well be scaled down as part of fiscal tightening. One can therefore reasonably expect a new wave of bankruptcies and bad debts in 2003.

The Eastern regions are especially sensitive. In addition to the geographical aspects, the malaise has hit numerous other sectors including weaving, apparel, metals, paper trade, construction, telecommunications and retail.

KEY ECONOMIC INDICATORS

(%)	1998	1999	2000	2001	2002 (e)	2003 (f)
Economic growth	2	2	2.9	0.6	0.3	1.5
Consumer spending (% change)	1.8	3.7	1.4	1.5	−0.2	1.1
Investment (% change)	3	4.2	2.3	−5.8	−4	2
Inflation	1.1	0.4	1.5	1.9	1.5	1.5
Unemployment	8.9	8.2	7.5	7.5	8.2	8.4
Short-term interest rate	3.5	3	4.4	4.2	3.3	3
Public sector deficit/GDP	−2.2	−1.6	1.2	−2.7	−3.4	−3
National debt/GDP	63.2	60.9	60.8	60.3	61	61
Exports (% change)	6.8	5.6	13.2	4.7	2.9	3.1
Imports (% change)	8.9	8.5	10	0.1	−1.3	2.9
Current account balance/GDP	−0.3	−0.9	−1.1	0.1	1.8	2.1

e = estimated, f = forecast

MAIN ECONOMIC SECTORS

Retail

Turnover for the retail industry fell in 2002. Household spending was hit by scepticism of the euro, higher prices for everyday consumer products and services, and the deteriorating economic climate. In the food sector, supermarkets and independent stores again lost market share to discount stores. This trend looks set to continue against a background of unfavourable market conditions, mainly characterized by fierce price competition. Some of the players in this sector will therefore remain in an awkward position.

Telecommunications and IT

The sector's performance for the year 2002 should at worst be stagnant and at best show a slight improvement. The telecommunications sector was hit by the postponement of UMTS operations and, more generally, by collapsing investment of operators, who have run up soaring debts and operate in a saturated mobile phone market. The IT sector has not fared any better. Sales were flat in 2002 and did not offset a slump in demand in 2001. Sales to both individuals and businesses were hit. Apart from certain segments, such as screens, German companies bemoan the over-capacity and fierce price competition in the industry.

In 2003 output from these sectors should increase on the back of better focused demand. However, prices will continue to fall in the face of strong competition.

Mechanical engineering

In 2002 sector output fell by almost 4 per cent. Stable export sales did not offset the sharp decline in domestic orders, which account for 40 per cent of sales. Although an upturn is expected in 2003 it will be slow and gradual.

Automobiles

In the first 10 months of 2002 passenger car production fell by 5 per cent, while domestic and foreign orders declined by 4 per cent. Commercial vehicles were even harder hit. Although a revival is expected in 2003 sub contracting will remain hit by manufacturers' downward pressure on prices, higher debt and tougher regulations for sub-contractors' product warranties.

Construction

The sector fared worse in 2002, in both the old and new provinces (Länder), with the number of bankruptcies rising yet again. The fall in the number of building permits issued in 2002 does not point to a fast recovery. Office property, factory construction and group housing have been hit particularly hard and public works is feeling the turmoil in public finances. In contrast, there was a slight rally in detached housing. No upturn is expected in 2003.

Wood pulp and paper

In 2002 the sector enjoyed a moderate upturn from an already satisfactory level on the back of higher exports and stock replacements by customers. Cardboard posted the sharpest improvement, while paper for graphic arts had a sluggish year. The environment should remain favourable in 2003.

PAYMENT AND COLLECTION PRACTICES

Payment

Standard payment instruments such as the bill of exchange and cheque are not widespread in Germany.

For Germans, bills of exchange imply a precarious financial position or a sign of distrust by the supplier.

Cheques are not considered as payment but as a 'payment attempt'; the issuer always has the possibility of cancelling payment for any reason whatsoever, as the concept of cheques backed by funds is not applied in German law. Bad cheques are therefore relatively frequent.

Bills of exchange and cheques do not therefore seem to be effective means of payment.

In contrast, bankers' transfers (*Überweisung*) remain the most prevalent means of payment. Large German banks are connected to the SWIFT network, which guarantees speedy and efficient processing.

Debt collection

As the first step in the recovery process creditors must issue final notice to pay, via ordinary or registered mail.

A legal reform in force since 1 May 2000 states that, as long as the due date is not specified in the conditions of sale, the debtor is deemed delinquent where payment is not received within 30 days of receipt of the invoice and his debt automatically incurs interest. The reference rate applied is the discount rate of the Bundesbank, plus five basis points.

If no settlement or out-of-court transaction occurs despite this approach, the creditor must instigate proceedings before the courts. If the amount is not contested, the creditor may obtain an injunction to pay (*Mahnbescheid*, a simple and inexpensive procedure that rapidly leads to an executive ruling), by means of pre-printed forms.

The request can be submitted by any foreign creditor in Berlin, at Schöneberg court, which issues the payment summons.

The debtor has two weeks to pay or to contest the summons.

The formal legal procedure is dominated by oral evidence rather than by written submissions. The judge bases his decision on the arguments made by both parties present at court. In the event of a dispute the judge hears the litigants and their lawyers and asks them to submit any evidence considered necessary by himself because he has sole power of decision. The adverse parties are also requested to submit a pleading memorandum outlining their claims.

Once the claim has been investigated a public hearing is held, during which the court renders its reasoned judgment.

In January 2002 the government introduced a reform to the civil justice system with the objective of giving German citizens easier and more efficient access to the law.

The reform has introduced a requirement that parties must first attempt mediation before instigating proceedings and has given more power to district courts (*Amtsgerichte*). In the majority of cases claims must be settled in the first instance either by a settlement out of court or by a court order, since the role of the appeal courts is only to verify the lower court's assessment of the facts at issue and the correct application of the law.

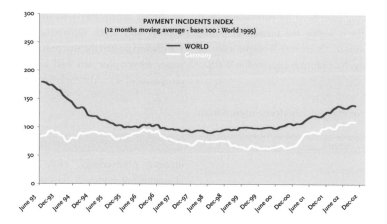

Greece

Coface analysis   Short-term: **A2**

RISK ASSESSMENT

Despite a slowdown in 2002 Greek economic growth was one of the most robust in the euro area thanks to European subsidies and the prospect of the country hosting the Olympic Games in Athens in 2004. Public and private sector investment mainly in infrastructure and capital goods was the driving force behind growth.

Consumer spending continued to be boosted by wage increases, even though these were eroded somewhat by inflation. However, the privatization programme suffered delays due to the unfavourable stock market environment, which upset plans to reduce the extremely large public debt.

The year 2003 should see some growth as exports pick up. Consumer spending and investment should continue to be buoyant as the Olympic Games draw nearer. European subsidies and falling unemployment should also have a positive impact. The upturn will nevertheless generate inflationary pressures, the successful management of which will depend on the reforms undertaken after the elections due to be held at the end of the year.

Against a favourable macroeconomic background corporate payment behaviour remains satisfactory. However, greater vigilance will be called for from the end of 2003 as the spin–offs from the Olympic Games gradually disappear and European subsidies are cut.

KEY ECONOMIC INDICATORS

%	1998	1999	2000	2001	2002 (e)	2003 (f)
Economic growth	3.4	3.6	4.1	4.1	3.5	3.8
Consumer spending (% change)	3.5	2.9	2.7	3.2	2.9	3.1
Investment (% change)	10.6	6.2	7.8	7.4	8	8.7
Inflation	4.5	2.1	3.1	3.1	3.3	3.5
Unemployment	11.1	12	11.4	10.5	10.3	9.8
Short–term interest rate	10.4	11.6	8.9	6.1	3.3	3
Public–sector balance/GDP	−2.4	−1.7	−1.8	−1.2	−1	−0.5
National debt/GDP	104.9	103.8	106.2	107	104	102
Exports (% change)	5.3	8.1	18.9	-1.3	0	5
Imports (% change)	9.2	3.6	15	1.9	1	6.5
Current account balance/GDP	−3.1	−4.2	−6.7	−6.2	−5.5	−4.8

e = estimated, f = forecast

49

PAYMENT AND COLLECTION PRACTICES

■ Payment

Bills of exchange are widely used by Greek companies for domestic and international transactions and, as is the case for promissory notes, are no longer subject to a stamp duty as of 1 January 2002.

Where a bill of exchange remains unpaid a protest is set up by a Public Notary within two working days from the mature date, thus certifying the dishonoured bill.

Cheques are less frequently used for international transactions, whereas for domestic transactions the practice is to use cheques as a credit rather than a payment instrument. Post-dated cheques that have been endorsed by several creditors are quite widespread.

Criminal proceedings may be instigated against issuers of bad cheques where a complaint has been filed.

'Promissory letters' are another payment method that is widely used by Greek companies in international transactions. They are a written acknowledgement of a payment obligation and are issued to the creditor by means of the customer's bank which, in turn, undertakes to pay the letter within a contractually agreed timeframe.

Although promissory letters are adequately efficient in so far as they constitute a legal acknowledgement of debt, they are not considered as commercial instruments and are thus not subject for application of exchange law (*droit cambiaire*).

Lastly, SWIFT bank transfers are used to settle a growing proportion of transactions and offer a fairly rapid and secure method to effect payments.

■ Debt collection

The recovery process commences with the issuing of a final notice to pay by registered mail in which debtors are reminded of their payment obligations together with any contractually agreed interest penalties or, failing this, the legally fixed rate of interest.

Creditors may engage a lawyer to request an injunction to pay through the court. This is a relatively fast procedure, generally taking one month from the date on which petitions are lodged, and enables creditors to obtain immediate execution (provided that the claim is not disputed) of the court order, which generally does not have a suspensory effect.

To obtain such an immediate enforceable ruling creditors must hold a probative document equivalent to an acknowledgement of debt or a commercial instrument. Typically the kind of documents agreed include: an accepted banker's draft, unpaid and protested; an unpaid promissory note or an unpaid promissory letter; an acknowledgement of debt established as a private deed; an original invoice that indicates the goods sold along with a receipt of delivery which has been signed by the buyer.

Cases are heard by a 'justice of the peace'(Eirinodikeio) for claims of up to 5900 euros (previously 2 million drachmas) and are examined by a court of first instance presided over by a single judge (Monomeles Protodikeio) for claims of up to 44,000 euros (previously 15,000,000 drachmas). Claims over this amount are handled by a panel of three judges (Polymeles Protodikeio).

Where creditors do not have a written acknowledgement signed by the debtor, or where the claim is disputed, the only remaining alternative is to initiate proceedings by issuing a formal summons.

Such cases generally take more than a year, or even two years, depending on case backlogs in each jurisdiction. Similarly more complex cases, requiring extensive evidence (such as all of the documents related to a commercial transaction) or multiple witness testimonies, are likely to require longer litigation timeframes.

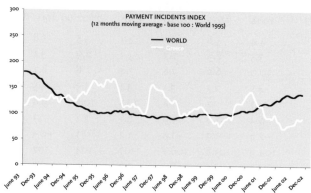

PAYMENT INCIDENTS INDEX
(12 months moving average - base 100 : World 1995)

— WORLD
— Greece

Hungary

Short-term: **A2**

Medium-term:
Coface analysis   **Low risk**

STRENGTHS

- Reforms bear fruit and encourage foreign investment.
- One of the most advanced financial systems in Central Europe.
- Political and economic stability strengthened by prospects of EU membership in 2004.

WEAKNESSES

- Open economy exposed to economic developments in EU member states, country's main trading partners.
- Budget deterioration due to expansionary policies adopted in connection with 2002 parliamentary elections.
- Problems stemming from trade deficit, largely caused by heavy imports of products for re-export, and fairly high level debt to GDP ratio.

RISK ASSESSMENT

Election expenditure, both before and after the parliamentary elections in April 2002, helped contain the economic slowdown, but has left a big hole in the country's finances. Moreover rising imports, coupled with falling tourist revenues, have significantly widened the current account deficit, causing the country's external financing needs to grow. While foreign investment has remained steady, it covers only a small proportion of these needs. Both government and private sector companies made fewer foreign borrowings and foreign exchange reserves fell slightly.

In 2003–04, exports should drive growth as foreign demand is likely to firm. During the same period the new centre-left government should reduce public spending, as it has vowed to do. However, failure to realign the budget would have serious repercussions, including a strengthening of external constraints, a likely tightening of monetary policy, potential pressures on the exchange rate and a delay in the country's entry into the eurozone.

KEY ECONOMIC INDICATORS

US$ billion	1998	1999	2000	2001	2002 (e)	2003 (f)
Economic growth (%)	4.9	4.2	5.2	3.8	3.2	4.0
Inflation (%)	14.2	10.0	9.8	9.1	5.3	4.9
Public-sector balance/GDP (%) (1)	n/a	n/a	−3.0	−4.0	−8.7	−4.5
Unemployment (%)	7.8	7.0	6.0	5.5	5.5	n/a
Exports	20.7	21.8	25.7	28.0	31.1	36.2
Imports	23.1	24.0	27.5	30.1	34.4	39.2
Trade balance	−2.4	−2.2	−1.8	−2.0	−3.3	−3.0
Current account balance	−2.1	−2.0	−1.1	−0.8	−2.9	−2.6
Current account balance/GDP (%)	−4.5	−4.3	−2.3	−1.5	−4.5	−3.5
Foreign debt	27.3	29.1	30.5	32.9	35.6	36.7
Debt service/Exports (%)	17.7	15.7	16.3	14.5	13.7	15.8
Reserves (import months)	3.7	4.2	3.9	3.4	2.8	2.5

(1) According to the European system of integrated economic accounts (ESA-95)   e = estimated, f = forecast

CONDITIONS OF ACCESS TO THE MARKET

■ Means of entry

High rates of customs duty remain in force for food products, but these are gradually being lifted under the farm section of the Association Agreement pending their abolition when Hungary joins the EU. Trade barriers, in the form of long and costly certification procedures, remain in force, especially for consumer goods. Government procurement contracts often prompt complaints. The national preference rule will be abolished upon EU accession.

■ Attitude towards foreign investors

There are no restrictions on foreign investment in Hungary, with regard to either sources of funding or foreign shareholdings.

Since 1998 tax incentives have been granted to investments above a certain level, with additional incentives for investments in the Eastern regions.

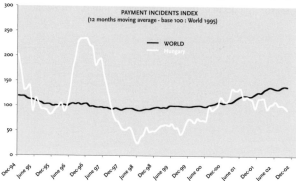

PAYMENT INCIDENTS INDEX
(12 months moving average - base 100 : World 1995)

WORLD
Hungary

There are ten-year tax and duty exemptions for investments exceeding 10 billion forints, or 3 billion forints in under privileged areas. Hungary has set up free zones that offer export-oriented companies a number of benefits, including total relief from customs duties, exemption from VAT and freedom from customs formalities. However, the European Union has asked for the phasing out of these zones.

Defence and property are governed by special regulations. The acquisition of property by foreigners is subject to the approval of the municipal government. On the other hand, any Hungarian-registered company, whatever its ownership structure, may freely acquire property. But only Hungarian nationals are entitled to purchase farmland.

Tax, health and environmental authorities at the central and local levels tend to be over-zealous when enforcing regulations against foreign-held companies. The cost of obtaining work permits is borne by employers, who must prove that Hungarians can not meet the job requirements. Work permit applications have to be dealt with within 60 days and usually lead to the award of a work permit.

Where a foreign-owned company employs an expatriate in Hungary whose salary is paid in his native country the employee is not covered by Hungarian labour law. Hungarian social security legislation does not provide cover for expatriates, who are nevertheless required to contribute to an unemployment solidarity fund (1.5 per cent of gross wages).

■ Foreign exchange regulations

The Hungarian government widened the forint's fluctuation band from +/- 2.25 per cent to +/-15 per cent in May 2001. In June of the same year it abolished all exchange controls, making the forint freely convertible. It has also discontinued the currency's monthly depreciation. From 1 October 2001 the forint has been pegged to the euro at the central rate of 276.1 forints to the euro within a +/-15 per cent crawl band. The currency has appreciated by over 10 per cent since May 2001.

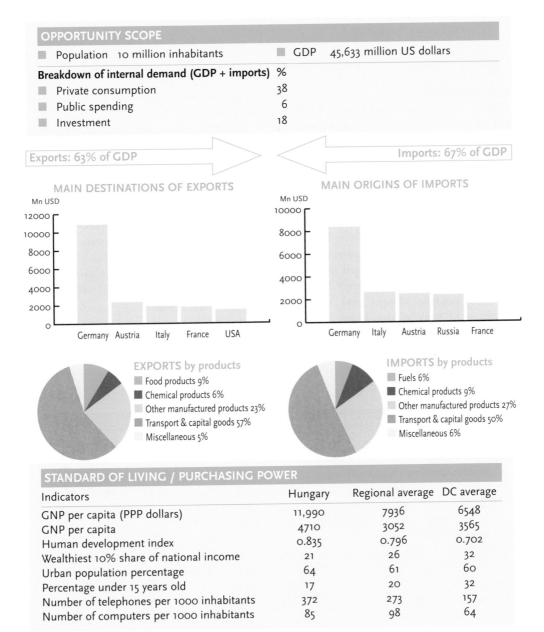

OPPORTUNITY SCOPE

■ Population   10 million inhabitants   ■ GDP   45,633 million US dollars

Breakdown of internal demand (GDP + imports) %
■ Private consumption   38
■ Public spending   6
■ Investment   18

Exports: 63% of GDP   Imports: 67% of GDP

MAIN DESTINATIONS OF EXPORTS

Mn USD

Germany   Austria   Italy   France   USA

MAIN ORIGINS OF IMPORTS

Mn USD

Germany   Italy   Austria   Russia   France

EXPORTS by products
■ Food products 9%
■ Chemical products 6%
■ Other manufactured products 23%
■ Transport & capital goods 57%
■ Miscellaneous 5%

IMPORTS by products
■ Fuels 6%
■ Chemical products 9%
■ Other manufactured products 27%
■ Transport & capital goods 50%
■ Miscellaneous 6%

STANDARD OF LIVING / PURCHASING POWER

Indicators	Hungary	Regional average	DC average
GNP per capita (PPP dollars)	11,990	7936	6548
GNP per capita	4710	3052	3565
Human development index	0.835	0.796	0.702
Wealthiest 10% share of national income	21	26	32
Urban population percentage	64	61	60
Percentage under 15 years old	17	20	32
Number of telephones per 1000 inhabitants	372	273	157
Number of computers per 1000 inhabitants	85	98	64

Iceland

Coface analysis   Short-term: **A1**

RISK ASSESSMENT

Iceland's economy overheated between 1998 and mid-2001, leading the central bank to introduce extremely high interest rates in an attempt to deter all economic players. The economy continued to lose momentum in 2002. Highly indebted consumers and businesses felt the squeeze as soaring interest rates took their toll on domestic demand, causing it to contract sharply. Only the buoyancy of fish exports, which benefited from firmer fish prices, helped stave off a recession. The appreciation of the króna, underpinned by high interest rates, helped reduce the current account deficit by making imported products cheaper and create the conditions for lower inflation, fuelled by renewed upward pressure on wages stemming from a narrow labour market.

In 2003 the economy should return to growth as consumer spending picks up slightly on the back of falling inflation, investment underpinned by cuts in corporation tax, and a joint venture between the State and Alcoa, designed to boost the aluminium industry, is launched. Interest rate cuts should also have a positive impact, although monetary and budgetary policies will remain cautious to prevent the economy from overheating again.

There were numerous bankruptcies in 2002, but the situation should improve in 2003 with the return of better trading conditions.

KEY ECONOMIC INDICATORS

%	1998	1999	2000	2001	2002 (e)	2003 (f)
Economic growth	5.7	3.7	5.5	3.6	0	1.7
Consumer spending (% change)	10.4	7.2	4.2	−2.9	−1.2	1.3
Investment (% change)	32.9	−3.7	14.9	−4.2	−14	4
Inflation	0.9	2.7	4.6	8	5.5	3
Unemployment	2.8	1.9	2.1	2.2	2.6	2.6
Short-term interest rate	7.4	8.6	11.2	11	7.8	5.9
Public-sector balance/GDP	0.5	2.4	2.5	0.5	0.3	0
National debt/GDP	49.2	44.4	41.8	45	43	40
Exports (% change)	2.1	4.8	6	7.7	5.5	4.5
Imports (% change)	23.3	5.5	8.7	−8.5	−3	4
Current account balance/GDP	−7	−7	−10.1	−4.6	−0.1	−0.4

e = estimated, f = forecast

Ireland

Coface analysis   Short-term: **A1**

RISK ASSESSMENT

In 2002 economic growth slumped to its lowest level in ten years, although it was still twice the European average. The unfavourable international economic situation continued to depress ICT exports and tourism. With no prospect of improvement companies barely increased investment. The rise in public spending, accompanied by a drop in tax revenues, wiped out any budget surplus. While consumer spending and investment may not have enjoyed the double-digit growth of the previous decade, they remained buoyant. Consumer spending was bolstered by low interest rates, tax cuts and substantial wage increases, which were only partially eroded by continued strong inflation.

Economic performance should be more or less identical in 2003 in the absence of a notable improvement in demand, as should growth in consumption and exports. Investment, on the other hand, should increase due to improved sales prospects for companies.

Despite a slight deterioration in 2002 corporate payment behaviour does not give any cause for alarm as defaults are in line with the European average. Although agriculture was hit by food scares tourism and technology remain the most exposed sectors. The former has been hit by the fall in US visitors, and the latter by the poor performance of US high-tech companies.

MAJOR ECONOMIC INDICATORS						
%	1998	1999	2000	2001	2002 (e)	2003 (f)
Economic growth	8.6	10.8	11.5	6.1	3.4	3.8
Consumer spending (% change)	7.3	8.3	10	4.8	3.9	4.1
Investment (% change)	15.7	13.5	7.3	0.9	2.1	4
Inflation	3.5	3.3	4.6	5.9	4.8	4.2
Unemployment	7.6	5.6	4.3	3.9	4.5	4.6
Short-term interest rate	5.4	3	4.4	4.2	3.3	3
Public-sector balance/GDP	2.3	2.3	4.5	1.6	−0.8	−1.1
National debt/GDP	55.1	49.6	38.8	36.5	34	34
Exports (% change)	21.4	15.7	17.8	8.4	6.9	6.7
Imports (% change)	25.8	11.9	16.6	7.7	7.7	7.9
Current account balance/GDP	0.9	0.4	−0.1	−0.3	−0.6	−1

e = estimated, f = forecast

PAYMENT AND COLLECTION PRACTICES

■ Payment

Bills of exchange are infrequently used for domestic commercial transactions and are only occasionally used for international trade.

The cheque, defined as 'a bill of exchange drawn on a banker and payable on demand', is more widely used for commercial transactions, but does not provide a complete guarantee insofar as issuing a bad cheque is not a criminal offence.

Bank transfers, in particular SWIFT transfers, are the most widespread means of payment as they can be quickly and effectively processed.

Payment orders issued via the website of the client's bank are a rapidly growing instrument.

■ Debt collection

As standard practice, the collection process begins with the delivery of a 'seven-days' letter by registered mail, whereby the debtor is requested to pay the principal along with any contractually agreed default interest. Where there is no specific interest clause, the European Central Bank's refinancing rate marked up by 7 basis points applies to commercial contracts concluded after 7 August 2002 (Regulations number 388, 2002).

For claims of 1270 euros (previously Irish Pound 1000) or more, creditors may threaten debtors with a statutory demand for the winding-up of their business. This entails issuing the debtor with a 21 day notice to pay. Where the debtor fails to pay within this deadline he is regarded as insolvent.

Irish law and the Irish legal system are mainly founded on British 'common law', although national legislation has subsequently been developed independently.

In ordinary proceedings, creditors who hold material evidence of their claim (contractual documents, acknowledgement of debt, unpaid bills of exchange) may petition the court to obtain a summary judgment where their claim is not contested, enabling them to rapidly obtain an enforcement order. Where a debtor fails to respond to a 'civil bill' or a 'summons' (depending on the appropriate jurisdiction), the creditor may obtain a judgment by default based on the submission of an 'affidavit of debt' without the need for a court hearing.

An affidavit of debt is a sworn statement attesting to the amounts outstanding as well as the cause of the debt. The supplier's signature on the affidavit must be notarized or certified by an Irish consular office.

Cases are heard by either a district court, a circuit court or the high court depending on the amount of the claim. Similarly, each court may hand down a summary judgment where justified by the circumstances of the petitioner's claim. Where defendants reply to a summons and refuse to settle their debt plenary proceedings may be instituted in which equal importance is given by the court to case documents submitted by the parties as to the barrister's arguments and oral evidence during the main hearing.

However, for claims under 6348.69 euros (previously Irish Pound 5000) brought before the district courts, the courts place greater importance on the plaintiff's evidence, whereas the written proceedings are greatly simplified.

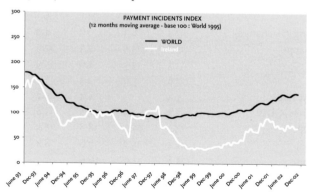

PAYMENT INCIDENTS INDEX
(12 months moving average - base 100 : World 1995)

— WORLD
Ireland

Italy

Coface analysis   Short-term: **A2**

STRENGTHS

- Increased productivity gains and cost savings as public administration reforms gather pace.
- Economic environment changed by continued privatizations and buoyed by liberalization of many sectors.
- Numerous regional networks of SMEs spur entrepreneurship and business in a wide variety of sectors, including textiles, footwear, mechanical engineering, ceramics, jewellery and luxury cars.

WEAKNESSES

- Underground economy forms a structural component of labour market, especially in the South, and continues to elude integration into mainstream economy, despite recently introduced incentives.
- Slow progress in reform of pension system, as measures so far adopted fail to address problem of low birth rate and rapidly ageing population.
- Persistent marked economic disparities between North and South.
- Public finances remain in the red, making it impossible to significantly reduce huge public debt.

RISK ASSESSMENT

Italy, initially protected by its fairly small market capitalization and low degree of specialization in high technologies, was finally hit by the world economic slowdown at the end of 2001. The downturn was greatly exacerbated, as shown by virtually stagnant growth in 2002. Exports were hit by the deteriorating economic situation in Europe, while consumer demand slumped under the impact of waning confidence, due to rising inflation not compensated by small wage increases. In contrast to private sector investment hit by the fall in demand, public sector investment remained strong within a budget in total disarray.

The situation should slowly turn around in 2003. Consumption could benefit from lower inflation and tax cuts for low and middle-income groups. Investment will not rise before the second half of 2003 due to the expiry of the second *Tremonti* law permitting companies to deduct, under certain conditions, 50 per cent of their investment expenses from taxable income. The government plans to cut the budget deficit by offsetting the tax breaks decided at three-way meetings between the government, trade unions and employers with reductions in expenditure and securitization of property assets. It also intends to grant tax amnesties to self-employed workers, enabling them to settle their position with the tax authorities by payment of a fixed sum.

Against this background the liquidity of Italian firms remained weak, with many experiencing payment difficulties or defaulting.

The default ratio has steadily deteriorated since the beginning of 2001, and at present seems to have stabilized some way above the European average. The debt collection ratio, though fairly satisfactory, has not offset the growing number of defaults. Apart from a tradition of late payment, the number of defaults rose as a result of corporate cashflow problems stemming from several years of disappointing growth. Firms operating in sectors such as textile fibres and yarn, furniture, process metallurgy, packaging and food remain particularly vulnerable

KEY ECONOMIC INDICATORS

%	1998	1999	2000	2001	2002 (e)	2003 (f)
Economic growth	1.8	1.6	2.9	1.8	0.4	1.7
Consumer spending (% change)	3.2	2.4	2.7	1.1	0	1.6
Investment (% change)	4	5.7	6.5	2.4	−2	2.5
Inflation	2.1	2.1	2.8	2.9	2.5	2.1
Unemployment	11.9	11.5	10.7	9.6	9.2	9
Short-term interest rate	5	3	4.4	4.2	3.3	3
Public-sector deficit/GDP	−3.1	−1.8	−0.6	−2.2	−2.3	−1.9
National debt/GDP	117.5	115.9	111.4	108.7	111	108
Exports (% change)	3.4	0.3	11.7	0.8	0	5
Imports (% change)	8.9	5.3	9.4	0.2	1.1	4.8
Current account balance/GDP	1.9	0.7	−0.5	0.3	−0.2	0

e = estimated, f = forecast

MAIN ECONOMIC SECTORS

Automobiles

In 2002 new passenger car registrations fell by some 10 per cent, reflecting the decline in consumer spending. Against a background of unfavourable trading conditions FIAT saw its market share shrink from 25 per cent to 22 per cent year on year. Sales in small and middle-size utility vehicles, on the other hand, rose sharply, largely due to the beneficial impact of the second Tremonti law.

In 2003 the market as a whole should decline slightly, with a slight improvement in passenger car sales and a fall in utility vehicle sales. Italian output should, more or less, follow market trends for the coming year.

Chemicals

In 2002 the Italian chemicals sector benefited from firmer domestic and foreign demand, resulting in a moderate increase in output and prices. The recovery in prices helped to offset the increase in oil prices. Nevertheless this upturn is relative as it is mainly based on the replacement of stocks that had fallen to dangerously low levels, rather than on a revival in real demand. In 2003 the upturn should be more marked on the back of stronger real demand

Cardboard

Sales rallied in 2002, largely due to export growth and, to a lesser extent, firmer domestic demand. Prices benefited from growth in demand. The upturn should continue in 2003.

Construction

High inventory levels slowed growth in 2002. The slowdown was accompanied by a fall in corporate profits in the sector. In 2003 business should pick up on the back of stronger performance by non-residential construction and civil engineering, offsetting the decline in the housing market. Industry profits should continue to grow.

Textiles and apparel

Italian textile sales continued to decline due to sagging domestic and external demand. The industry was particularly hard hit by the sharp rise in world sales of fabric from emerging Asian countries, in particular China. All of Italy's manufacturing regions, such as Prato and Biella, have been hit.

Garment sales did not suffer as much due to firmer external demand.

Trends at the end of 2002 point to an upturn in 2003. The projected increase in demand should enable textile groups to increase their prices as well as their profitability.

■ Electronics

After a grace period of some months compared with its foreign rivals the Italian electronics industry succumbed to the slump in demand in both telecommunications and information technology. While business is expected to pick up in 2003 profitability for the sector will continue to be depressed by fierce competition.

PAYMENT AND COLLECTION PRACTICES

■ Payment

Trade notes (cambiali) are available in the form of bills of exchange or promissory notes. *Cambiali* must be duly accepted by the issuer and stamped locally at 12/1000 of their value or at 6/1000 if stamped beforehand in France. In the event of default they constitute a *de facto* enforcement order as they are automatically admitted by the courts as a writ of execution (*ezecuzione forzata*) against the debtor.

Signed bills of exchange are a fairly secure means of payment but are rarely used on account of the high stamp duty, the rather lengthy cashing timeframes and the drawee's fear of damage to his reputation caused by the recording of protested unpaid bills at the Chamber of Commerce.

Cheques have also been widely used since the liberalization of legislation on cheque amounts in April 1990. Nonetheless, if they are to be cashed abroad, they must bear the wording *non trasferibile* and include the date and place of issue.

Bank vouchers (*ricevuta bancaria*) are not a means of payment but a mere notice of bank domicile drawn up by the creditor and submitted by him to his own bank for presentation to the debtor's bank for the purposes of payment (the vouchers are also available in electronic form, in which case they are known as *RI.BA elettronica*). Bank vouchers may be accepted by the courts as an admission of debt if they are signed by the buyer. However, they do not constitute a writ of execution.

Bank transfers are widely used (90 per cent of payments from Italy are made by bank transfer).

SWIFT transfers are also becoming more commonplace and are considerably faster than ordinary transfers. The bank transfer is an economical and secure means of payment once the contracting parties have established mutual trust.

■ Debt collection

As elsewhere, out-of-court settlements are always preferable to legal proceedings. Final notices and telephone dunning produce reasonable results, as do on-site visits by providing an opportunity to restore dialogue between supplier and customer, and so leading to a settlement.

Settlement negotiations focus on payment of the principal, plus any contractual default interest as may be provided for in writing and accepted by the buyer. In the absence of a benchmark rate of interest, the European Central Bank's refinancing rate marked up by 7 basis points applies to commercial contracts concluded after 8 August 2002 (Decree-law of 9 October 2002).

Where an agreement cannot be reached with the customer the form of legal proceedings varies with the type of document used to justify the claim. In the case of *cambiali notes* (bills of exchange, promissory notes) or cheques, creditors may obtain a writ of execution in the form of a demand for payment (*atto di precetto*) delivered by a bailiff. Such demands are a prelude to an attachment order if the trade notes remain unpaid.

Creditors may obtain an injuction to pay (*decreto ingiuntivo*) by way of a fast-track procedure if they can produce written proof of their claim. This helps avoid ordinary legal proceedings, still perceived as slow despite the reform of the civil procedure adopted in May 1995. Ordinary proceedings can take up to two years, although creditors may obtain, during the first instance, a provisional payment order that serves as a writ of execution.

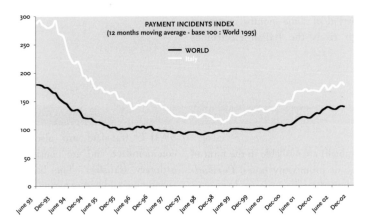

PAYMENT INCIDENTS INDEX
(12 months moving average - base 100 : World 1995)

— WORLD
— Italy

Kazakhstan

Short-term: **C**

Medium-term:
Quite high risk

Coface analysis

STRENGTHS

- Vast and diversified potential natural resources (oil and gas, minerals).
- Commissioning of oil pipeline to Black Sea in 2001 has boosted oil and gas exploitation.
- Country accounts for 75 per cent of all investment flows to Central Asia.
- Good relations with Russia, China and Western nations spur development and political stability.

WEAKNESSES

- Underdeveloped non-commodity sectors (agriculture and processing industries).
- External account structure carries risk as country exports commodities and imports virtually all of its capital and consumer goods.
- Export potential likely to be hampered by landlocked location.
- President Nazerbaev's government faces mounting political opposition.

RISK ASSESSMENT

Kazakhstan's economy has continued to perform well on the back of higher oil output spurred by direct foreign investment inflows and the opening of a new transit route via Russia in 2001. The country enjoys robust economic growth, sound finances and a healthy foreign trade position. The somewhat high financing need, driven by the input requirements of foreign-held firms, is amply covered by direct investment.

Relations between Western oil companies and the Kazakh government, however, became strained in 2002. While the prospects offered by Kazakh oil fields are far too lucrative to be ignored by large oil investors, any reduction in these investment inflows would have negative consequences for the Kazakh economy, in terms of both growth and financial equilibrium. Such a development can not be ruled out, although pragmatism should carry the day.

The exploitation of Kazakhstan oil potential is being hampered by the cost of offshore drilling. Modernization of the fragile banking system is continuing apace as part of a wider structural reform programme. Finally, President Nazerbaev's government is increasingly and openly at loggerheads with the country's elite.

KEY ECONOMIC INDICATORS

US$ million	1998	1999	2000	2001	2002 (e)	2003 (f)
Economic growth (%)	−1.9	2.7	9.8	13.2	9.5	7
Inflation (%)	7.3	8.4	13.4	6.4	6.5	6.4
Public-sector balance/GDP (%)	−7.8	−4.7	−1.8	−0.2	−0.3	−1.5
Exports	5871	6123	9795	9100	9900	11600
Imports	6672	5645	6849	8300	9600	10700
Trade balance	−801	478	2946	800	300	900
Current account balance	−1225	−37	700	−1400	−1100	−800
Current account balance/GDP (%)	−5.6	−1	3.7	−6.3	−4.6	−3.1
Foreign debt	9900	12100	12300	12100	12500	12400
Debt service/Exports (%)	14.4	19.3	17.4	13.4	15.4	12.3
Reserves (import months)	2.8	3.2	2.5	2	2.1	2.2

e = estimated, f = forecast

CONDITIONS OF ACCESS TO THE MARKET

■ Market overview

Almost 11 years after gaining independence on 16 December 1991 Kazakhstan has yet to complete its reform programme, despite its 'good pupil' image. A candidate for WTO accession, the country is plagued by corruption, bureaucracy, an inefficient tax system and widening social cleavages. However it has made excellent headway in public sector privatization, albeit in somewhat non-transparent conditions, and in the introduction of liberal trade legislation. Direct foreign investment between 1993 and the end of the first six months of 2002 amounted to US$18 billion. The country's current account surplus continues to grow on the back of strong oil, copper, steel and zinc exports.

■ Means of entry

Despite its designation as a market economy by the European Union in 2000 (and by the United States in 2002) and its fairly non-protectionist policies, landlocked Kazakhstan remains a difficult place in which to do business. Customs duties continue to be lowered, with the average rate of duty being cut to below 9 per cent. There is also 16 per cent non-refundable VAT. However, customs clearance is riddled with illegal practices and tariff hikes persist. A certain number of products are subject to certification. The fact that certificates from non-CIS countries are not valid in Kazakhstan significantly slows import formalities. Foreign businessmen should make allowance for corruption, even though it is not systematic.

■ Attitude towards foreign investors

At US$18 billion in mid-2002, Kazakhstan is the second largest recipient of direct foreign investment in the CIS, after Russia. Foreign investor interest is driven by the country's oil reserves and long-standing political stability. However, investors are worried by proposed investment legislation and have expressed reservations about a decree adopted (but not yet implemented) in the first half of 2002 requiring tenders to be submitted for all oil company procurements. In general the sustained improvement in the country's economic situation, which is extremely vulnerable to international trends, has set foreign investors at loggerheads with the government. Paradoxically, the government's awareness of the country's potential has been accompanied by a gradual deterioration in the business environment.

OPPORTUNITY SCOPE

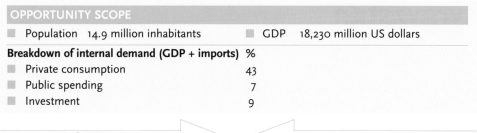

- Population 14.9 million inhabitants
- GDP 18,230 million US dollars

Breakdown of internal demand (GDP + imports) %
- Private consumption 43
- Public spending 7
- Investment 9

Exports: 59% of GDP   Imports: 47% of GDP

1

MAIN DESTINATIONS OF EXPORTS

Mn USD

Russia Germany China Sweden Italy

MAIN ORIGINS OF IMPORTS

Mn USD

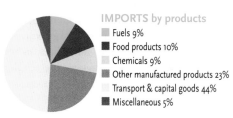

Russia Germany China Italy USA

EXPORTS by products
- Fuels 41%
- Ferrous metals 22%
- Food products 8%
- Chemicals 6%
- Other manufactured products 14%
- Transport & capital goods 5%
- Miscellaneous 4%

IMPORTS by products
- Fuels 9%
- Food products 10%
- Chemicals 9%
- Other manufactured products 23%
- Transport & capital goods 44%
- Miscellaneous 5%

STANDARD OF LIVING / PURCHASING POWER

Indicators	Kazakhstan	Regional average	DC average
GNP per capita (PPP dollars)	5940	7936	6548
GNP per capita	1260	3052	3565
Human development index	0.75	0.796	0.702
Wealthiest 10% share of national income	26	26	32
Urban population percentage	56	61	60
Percentage under 15 years old	27	20	32
Number of telephones per 1000 inhabitants	113	273	157
Number of computers per 1000 inhabitants	n/a	98	64

n/a – not available

Kyrgyzstan

Coface analysis

Short-term: **D**

Medium-term:
Very high risk

RISK ASSESSMENT

The recession observed in 2002 underlines the shortcomings of the Kyrgyz economy, especially its lack of diversification. The problems with gold mining are the main reason behind the drop in GDP, whereas gold was responsible for the country's strong growth over the last few years. Electricity and agriculture (40 per cent of GDP) are the other main sectors, but their low degree of modernization prevents them from acting as engines of growth.

The development of new gold mines in the future could revitalize an economy that remains dependent on sizeable inflows of multilateral finance. In this connection the country signed a debt rescheduling agreement with the Paris Club in March 2002. The political situation is somewhat less stable than before. President Akaev's government has toughened its line towards the increasingly hostile opposition, while benefiting from the deployment on Kyrgyz soil of international troops involved in the military campaign in Afghanistan, even though their continued presence remains uncertain

KEY ECONOMIC INDICATORS						
US$ million	1998	1999	2000	2001	2002 (e)	2003 (f)
Economic growth (%)	2.1	3.7	5.4	5.3	−3	1
Inflation (%)	16.8	39.9	9.6	3.70	5	5
Public-sector balance/GDP (%)	−10.8	−12.7	−9.7	−5.2	−4.8	−4.8
Exports	585	463	510.9	480.3	490	505.2
Imports	756	547	502.1	440.4	484.7	535.8
Trade balance	−171	−84	8.8	39.9	5.3	−30.7
Current account balance/GDP (%)	−22.9	−15.6	−7.5	−3.3	−3.8	−5.4
Foreign debt	1178	1359	1520	1655	1781	1800
Debt service/Exports (%)	19.2	21.7	22.5	28	26	20
Reserves (import months)	2.2	3.4	4.4	4.4	4.6	4.2

e = estimated, f = forecast

Latvia

Short-term: **A4**

Medium-term:
Coface analysis   **Quite high risk**

STRENGTHS
- Ongoing reforms driven by prospect of EU membership in 2004
- Cheap and skilled labour, attractive tax laws and secular trading tradition between East and West.
- External financial position strengthened by foreign direct investment.

WEAKNESSES
- High current account deficit.
- Dependent on Russia, especially for energy transit business.
- More effort must be put into improving administrative and legal environment.
- Lack of cohesion between political parties has led to a succession of coalition governments.

RISK ASSESSMENT

Growth slowed noticeably due to the sluggishness of the economic situation in the European Union, yet Latvia continues to post one of the highest growth rates in Central Europe. The economy should perform better in 2003 as consumer spending strengthens and foreign demand pick up slightly.

The main problem with this small, open economy remains the sizeable current account deficit. While exports to CIS and other Baltic countries held firm, partially offsetting the impact of poor economic conditions in the EU, imports, stimulated by the economy's modernization, have risen faster than sales. However, foreign direct investment should continue to cover the current account deficit without much difficulty.

Despite internal differences the centre-right coalition government, formed out of the parliamentary elections in October 2002, is expected to carry out reforms in taxation, public administration and the judicial system in view of the country's forthcoming membership of the European Union.

KEY ECONOMIC INDICATORS

US$ million	1998	1999	2000	2001	2002 (e)	2003 (f)
Economic growth (%)	3.9	1.1	6.8	7.6	4.5	5
Inflation (%)	4.5	2.4	2.7	2.5	1.7	2
Public sector balance/GDP (%)	−0.8	−3.9	−3.3	−1.9	−1.8	−1.5
Unemployment (%)	9.2	9.1	7.8	7.7	n/a	n/a
Exports	2011	1889	2058	2216	2341	2582
Imports	3141	2916	3116	3566	3863	4198
Trade balance	−1130	−1027	−1058	−1350	−1522	−1616
Current account balance	−650	−654	−494	−734	−743	−749
Current account balance/GDP (%)	−10.7	−9.8	−6.9	−9.7	−9.2	−8.5
Foreign debt	3098	3821	4489	5375	5704	6233
Debt service/Exports (%)	12	16.8	20.3	19.6	21	19.4
Reserves (import months)	2.1	2.6	2.5	3.1	3.2	3.1

e = estimated, f = forecast

CONDITIONS OF ACCESS TO THE MARKET

■ Market overview

The Latvian market is open and highly competitive, with no special protectionist measures.

Latvia is one of ten countries due to join the European Union. Accession talks, under way since March 2000, have stepped up harmonization of the country's legislation with the EU and implementation of the administrative machinery required for proper compliance with EU integration criteria. Latvia has completed accession talks and is due to join the EU in 2004–05 subject to a referendum in autumn 2003.

■ Means of entry

Following WTO membership in February 1999 Latvia has signed free trade agreements with 29 countries (15 from the EU; 4 from EFTA: Switzerland, Norway, Iceland, Liechtenstein; 7 of the 9 other candidate countries for EU accession in 2004, excluding Cyprus and Malta; and Turkey, Ukraine and Bulgaria). Talks are also under way on concluding similar agreements with Romania and the Faeroe Isles.

Except for agricultural products, still protected by customs duties at an average rate of 18.6 per cent and a top rate of 50 per cent, trade with the EU and the country's Baltic neighbours is not liable to customs duty. There is a ban on imports of beef, mutton and goat meat as well as on products containing these meats on account of BSE. Imports of pig meat from Lorraine are also prohibited.

The country's intellectual property laws are inadequate. Depending on relations with the customer, pre-payments are widespread, as are 30 to 45-day documentary credit and bank transfers.

Payments can be made in lats or in foreign currency. The euro has overtaken the dollar as the primary payment currency, with 45 per cent of trade denominated in euros, compared with 40 per cent in dollars, during the first half of 2002. There are no restrictions on capital transfers.

Business information can be obtained from the corporate information firm IGK BALT, a subsidiary of Coface based in the country.

■ Attitude towards foreign investors

The country is open to foreign investors, with direct foreign investment accounting for 5 per cent of GDP in the first half of 2002. Latvia will cut corporation tax from 22 per cent in 2002 to 19 per cent in 2003 and 15 per cent by 2004, making it one of the countries with the lowest corporation tax in Europe. The new Labour Code, adopted in 2002, is in line with European directives. Proposals to cut social security contributions (currently 35.09 per cent of wages, with 26.09 per cent borne by the employer and 9 per cent by the employee) have been indefinitely postponed.

A bilateral tax agreement has been in force since 1 May 2001.

■ Foreign exchange regulations

Pegged to special drawing rights since February 1994, the lat's value fluctuates in tandem with the fluctuations of the currencies comprising the SDRs. In the first half of 2002 this caused the lat to depreciate against the euro and appreciate against the dollar. At 31 October 2002 the exchange rate was 1.67 euros to the lat. There are no foreign exchange controls in the country.

OPPORTUNITY SCOPE

■ Population	2.4 million inhabitants	■ GDP	7150 million US dollars

Breakdown of internal demand (GDP + imports) %	
■ Private consumption	41
■ Public spending	12
■ Investment	17

Exports: 46% of GDP → ← Imports: 54% of GDP

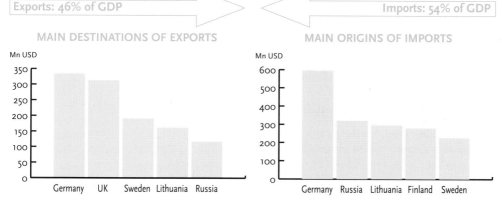

MAIN DESTINATIONS OF EXPORTS

Mn USD

Germany, UK, Sweden, Lithuania, Russia

MAIN ORIGINS OF IMPORTS

Mn USD

Germany, Russia, Lithuania, Finland, Sweden

EXPORTS by products
■ Food products 6%
■ Commodities 30%
■ Chemical products 6%
■ Other manufactured products 44%
■ Transport & capital goods 6%
■ Miscellaneous 8%

IMPORTS by products
■ Food products 12%
■ Fuels 11%
■ Chemical products 13%
■ Other manufactured products 31%
■ Transport & capital goods 30%
■ Miscellaneous 3%

STANDARD OF LIVING / PURCHASING POWER

Indicators	Latvia	Regional average	DC average
GNP per capita (PPP dollars)	7070	7689	6548
GNP per capita	2920	3229	3565
Human development index	0.8	0.796	0.702
Wealthiest 10% share of national income	26	26	32
Urban population percentage	69	61	60
Percentage under 15 years old	17	20	32
Number of telephones per 1000 inhabitants	303	273	157
Number of computers per 1000 inhabitants	140	98	64

Lithuania

Short-term: **A4**

Medium-term:
Quite high risk

STRENGTHS

- Prospect of EU membership in 2004 continues to drive reforms.
- Skilled manpower and low labour costs. Hub of East–West trade.
- Sound economic fundamentals and fiscal consolidation have ensured successful re-pegging of country's currency to euro in early 2002.
- Ethnic homogeneity promotes stability.

WEAKNESSES

- Large external account deficit due to economic modernisation.
- Exports highly dependent on transit trade.
- Low domestic savings.
- Transition to market economy could heighten social tensions against a background of high unemployment.

RISK ASSESSMENT

In 2002 the country posted strong economic growth on the back of buoyant domestic demand. However, the sluggish recovery in the European Union should affect growth in 2003, despite exports to CIS countries holding firm. Furthermore inadequate fiscal revenues and EU accession costs could prevent the government from meeting its fiscal objectives.

Soaring imports, buoyed by healthy domestic demand, are keeping the current account in the red,

the country's main weakness. Lithuania remains heavily dependent on international capital markets. But favourable terms of access to these markets, along with rising foreign direct investment, have helped cover the country's external financing requirement without difficulty.

The country needs to step up structural reforms in public (especially municipal) financial management, pensions, the business environment, labour legislation and energy and transport privatization.

KEY ECONOMIC INDICATORS

US$ million	1998	1999	2000	2001	2002 (e)	2003 (f)
Economic growth (%)	5.1	−3.9	3.8	5.9	5.7	4.5
Inflation (%)	5.1	0.8	1	1.3	0.4	1.5
Public-sector balance/GDP (%)	−5.9	−8.5	−2.8	−1.9	−1.5	−1.1
Unemployment	6.9	10	12.6	12.9	11.5	n/a
Exports	3962	3147	4050	4889	5490	6300
Imports	5480	4551	5154	5997	6960	8090
Trade balance	−1518	−1405	−1104	−1108	−1470	−1790
Current account balance	−1298	−1194	−675	−574	−860	−1051
Current account balance/GDP (%)	−12.1	−11.2	−6.0	−4.8	−6.2	−6.3
Foreign debt	3741	4528	4856	5259	5781	6465
Debt service/Exports (%)	21.1	18.7	19.3	28.8	21.9	19.9
Reserves (import months)	2.5	2.5	2.5	2.7	3.1	3.1

e = estimated, f = forecast

CONDITIONS OF ACCESS TO THE MARKET

■ Market overview

Purchasing power is growing steadily. The average wage at 1 July 2002 was 320 euros, up almost 5 per cent over the previous year.

The most buoyant sectors during the first half of 2002 were construction, transport, storage and industrial services. The electronics sector is also fast expanding.

Consumer spending, especially on household appliances, is picking up at a time of increasing competitiveness in the fast-growing mass food retailing sector.

■ Means of entry

Compliance with EU integration criteria is largely responsible for Lithuania's highly open market. The only duties that remain in force are excise duties for products such as alcohol, meat, sugar, cigarettes and oil. Certain products may be imported only by holders of an ad hoc licence. The conditions for obtaining such licences have been greatly relaxed, and the price of import licences for alcohol in particular slashed. The ban on imports of French beef is gradually being lifted.

The country's public tender legislation has been brought into line with EU criteria: open tenders, inclusion of utilities (water, energy, transport, tele-communications), the setting up of an independent commission to deal with disputes and monitoring of bids by a public tender committee. The national preference principle has been abolished. But the administrative machinery needs to be cranked up for the purposes of enforcement.

The Copyright Act of May 1999 and ratification of the Treaty of Rome have improved intellectual property protection. Intellectual property safe-guards, woefully inadequate until only recently, have been substantially enhanced in practice. Standards harmonization is making good progress and it is not difficult to obtain the relevant certificates as long as the products in question comply with a European standard.

Competition law is also broadly in line with EU criteria.

For payments, short-term credit is now widely available and has all but replaced pre-payment.

■ Attitude towards foreign investors

Foreign investors are treated on an equal footing with Lithuanian nationals, with no cases of discrimination reported. Lithuanian legislation offers foreign investors a number of incentives, including 15 per cent corporation tax. Foreign investors may freely repatriate profits, income and dividends derived from their activities upon meeting their tax obligations.

The workforce is highly skilled (technicians, engineers, scientists) and wage costs extremely low. Law and financial services firms offer the highest wages (about 600 euros a month).

Employer and employee social security contributions are 31 per cent and 3 per cent respectively of the gross wage. Contributions are paid to the country's social security agency, Sodra.

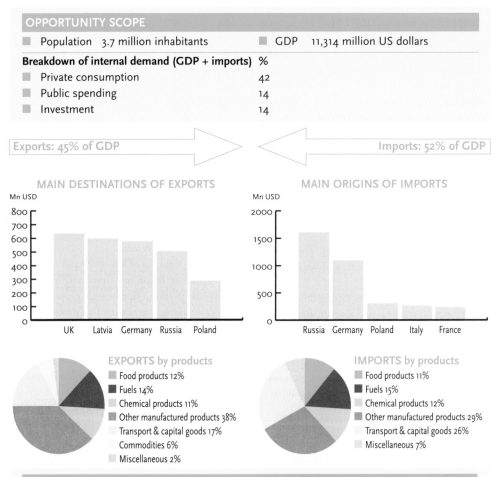

OPPORTUNITY SCOPE

- Population   3.7 million inhabitants
- GDP   11,314 million US dollars

Breakdown of internal demand (GDP + imports)   %
- Private consumption   42
- Public spending   14
- Investment   14

Exports: 45% of GDP   Imports: 52% of GDP

MAIN DESTINATIONS OF EXPORTS

Mn USD

UK   Latvia   Germany   Russia   Poland

MAIN ORIGINS OF IMPORTS

Mn USD

Russia   Germany   Poland   Italy   France

EXPORTS by products
- Food products 12%
- Fuels 14%
- Chemical products 11%
- Other manufactured products 38%
- Transport & capital goods 17%
- Commodities 6%
- Miscellaneous 2%

IMPORTS by products
- Food products 11%
- Fuels 15%
- Chemical products 12%
- Other manufactured products 29%
- Transport & capital goods 26%
- Miscellaneous 7%

STANDARD OF LIVING / PURCHASING POWER

Indicators	Lithuania	Regional average	DC average
GNP per capita (PPP dollars)	6980	7936	6548
GNP per capita	2930	3052	3565
Human development index	0.808	0.796	0.702
Wealthiest 10% share of national income	26	26	32
Urban population percentage	68	61	60
Percentage under 15 years old	20	20	32
Number of telephones per 1000 inhabitants	321	273	157
Number of computers per 1000 inhabitants	65	98	64

Macedonia

Coface analysis

Short-term: **D**

Medium-term:
Very high risk

RISK ASSESSMENT

The political situation in Macedonia remains precarious despite the formation after the elections in September 2002 of a new government coalition dominated by the centre-left party, the Social Democratic Alliance for Macedonia (SDSM), but also marked by the entry of the most powerful Albanian party, the Democratic Union for Integration, formed out of the National Liberation Army (UCK). The country's political stability is in fact heavily conditioned by the development of relations between the Slav majority and the strong Albanian minority against a background of still worrying social tensions (over 30 per cent unemployment).

The economy is nevertheless expected to grow in 2003, though this will depend on an increase in industrial and agricultural output as well as consumer spending. Moreover, the new government coalition will have to deal with the country's structural problems (public sector deficit, privatization, pensions, corruption) in order to win the support of foreign lenders, on whom the country relies so heavily. A stand-by agreement with the IMF is expected with this end in mind. The country's external position remains a cause for concern, as the burgeoning trade deficit weighs on the external account, while the level of foreign investment remains inadequate. However, some headway has been made, especially with supervision of the banking sector, which remains crippled by bad debt.

The prospect of WTO membership in March 2003 has helped bolster the reform programme, despite the persistence of many factors hampering the country's economic development.

KEY ECONOMIC INDICATORS						
US$ million	1998	1999	2000	2001	2002 (e)	2003 (f)
Economic growth (%)	3.4	4.3	4.6	−4.6	1	4
Inflation (%)	−0.1	−0.7	5.8	5.3	4	3
Public-sector balance/GDP (%)	−1.7	0	2.5	−6	−3.4	−3
Exports	1311	1191	1319	1155	1033	1186
Imports	1711	1584	1875	1581	1611	1795
Trade balance	−400	−393	−556	−426	−578	−609
Current account balance/GDP (%)	−9.6	−3.4	−3.1	−10.3	−13.8	−10.3
Foreign debt	1437	1490	1488	1372	1551	1863
Debt service/Exports (%)	8.3	10.8	9.6	16.4	11.3	9.2
Reserves (import months)	1.9	2.9	3.7	4.7	4.8	4.4

e = estimated, f = forecast

■ Payment

Bills of exchange are rarely used, as they do not correspond with local business practices. As in Germany, they are considered to reflect a supplier's lack of trust in buyers and thus to undermine the climate of confidence essential to lasting commercial relations.

Cheques are also infrequently used and are considered an unreliable mode of payment with cashing conditional on a cheque being covered by sufficient funds. Moreover, issuing bad cheques is not a criminal offence and those on the receiving end of a bad cheque incur high bank charges.

Under Dutch law–bills of exchange and cheques are especially useful in substantiating the existence of a debt.

In contrast, bank transfers ('Bankgiro') are by far the most common mode of payment. All large, main Dutch banks are connected to the SWIFT network, which facilitates timely, low-cost processing of international payments.

Concentration accounts, which permit centralized and simplified management of cashing of local payment and subsequent fund repatriation, are widely used.

■ Debt collection

The collection process begins with a formal notice inviting a debtor to pay the outstanding principal and past-due interest. If necessary, a bailiff or solicitor will then serve a summons. In the absence of prior contractual agreement, the applicable interest rate – since 1 December 2002 – is the European Central Bank's refinancing rate, increased by 7 basis points.

Where no payment is made or agreement reached creditors may engage a local lawyer to initiate legal proceedings. The Dutch legal system allows lawyers to act as both barristers and solicitors: they act as solicitors before courts in the jurisdiction where they are registered, whereas, as barristers, they may plead cases before any court in the country.

Before initiating legal proceedings effective pressure can be exerted on a debtor by filing a petition for winding up. This can be obtained without much difficulty if the creditor produces evidence of non-payment and the claim is not disputed. Such petitions are filed in civil courts (there are no commercial courts) and require the existence of another claim of any kind (commercial, alimony, tax debt, and so on).

Adversarial proceedings in the Netherlands are based mainly on written submissions. A simplified procedure heard before district courts (*kantongerecht*) is available for claims under 5000 euros (formerly 10000 guilders). Procedures for larger claims are heard by the court of first instance (*Rechtbank*) with adversaries arguing their case via written submissions. Unless the parties expressly request the right to make oral arguments, a right which is rarely invoked, the judge bases his ruling on the principal case documents submitted by the parties, but not before they appear in court (notably, to seek a possible amicable settlement).

For complex cases requiring special analysis the judge will follow a more formal procedure, examining respectively each adversary's briefs and counter-briefs.

In this respect the judge will carefully assess the parties' compliance with the general terms and conditions of sale appearing on invoices and purchase orders, which form the legal framework of the commercial contract.

Finally, recourse to arbitration is commonplace in the Netherlands. Most arbitration bodies work in specific fields and arbitrators are often selected from among specialized lawyers. Arbitral awards are usually more concerned with equity than with legal considerations.

PAYMENT INCIDENTS INDEX
(12 months moving average - base 100 : World 1995)

— WORLD
Netherlands

Norway

Coface analysis   Short-term: **A1**

RISK ASSESSMENT

In 2002 the economy continued to recover slowly on the back of consumer spending and steady oil revenues. Household consumption was spurred by the rise in consumer confidence stemming from higher wage increases and slower price increases. On the other hand investment remained weak due to sluggish external demand and high interest rates. Similarly, non-oil exports lost some of their competitiveness due partly to the strength of the krone and partly to the sharp increase in labour costs.

In 2003 consumer spending should continue to be buoyed by rising disposable incomes and additional public spending financed by a 4 per cent levy on 'petroleum funds'. However, the year should see a return to inflationary pressures, justifying the maintenance of a tight monetary policy. Against this background investment should continue to suffer. Only offshore investment is expected to climb. Finally, while oil and natural gas sales will continue to swell the nation's coffers, the competitiveness of traditional exports could be further eroded.

Continued low growth in 2002 was accompanied by an increase in the number of bankruptcies and defaults. The situation should stabilize in 2003.

KEY ECONOMIC INDICATORS

%	1998	1999	2000	2001	2002 (e)	2003 (f)
Economic growth	2.4	1.1	2.3	1.4	1.6	1.8
Consumer spending (% change)	3.4	2.2	3.5	2.5	2.8	2.9
Investment (% change)	10.6	−8.2	−1.1	−4.6	−1	2.5
Inflation	2.6	2	3.3	1.8	1.4	2.3
Unemployment	3.1	3.2	3.4	3.6	3.8	4
Short-term interest rate	5.8	6.5	6.7	7.2	7	7.1
Public-sector balance/GDP	3.5	5.9	14.8	15.2	14	11
National debt/GDP	26.6	27.6	30.9	26.8	25	25.8
Exports (% change)	0.3	2.8	2.7	4.2	2	1
Imports (% change)	9.3	−1.6	2.5	0.3	1	3
Current account balance/GDP	0	5.3	14.3	15.4	16	16

e = estimated, f = forecast

■ **Payment**

Bills of exchange and cheques are not frequently used in so far as strict formal requirements are placed on their validity and, as such, they are not to be recommended. In addition, creditors frequently refuse to accept cheques as a means of payment. Notwithstanding this, both bills of exchange and cheques are used above all to materialize the existence of a debt.

Promissory notes are much more commonly used in commercial transactions and offer superior guarantees where they are accepted in conjunction with an affidavit of debt by the buyer since, in the event of payment default, drawers may demand direct enforcement by the courts.

Bank transfers are by far the most widespread system of payment. All of the leading Norwegian banks are connected to the SWIFT network, offering a reliable, flexible and cost-effective means of issuing payments internationally.

Concentration accounts, which greatly simplify the settlement process by centralizing settlement procedures between locally based buyers and sellers, are also used from time to time.

Another rapidly growing payment method enables sellers to request orders for payment via the Internet site of their client's bank.

■ **Debt collection**

The recovery process commences with the issuance of a final notice inviting the debtor to make payment of the principal amount, plus any contractually agreed interest penalties, within 14 days. Where the parties have not made provision for interest penalties the applicable rate is that of the Late Interest Act, 1976.

Where no payment is received or agreement reached creditors may engage dispute remediation proceedings through the Conciliation Board (*Forliksrådet*), an administrative institution presided over by non-professional judges and enabling creditors to obtain a summary ruling by furnishing documents to authenticate their claim, which should be denominated in Norwegian krone.

Once the creditor has filed his petition the Conciliation Board summonses the debtor to acknowledge or dispute the claim before hearing the parties, either in person or in the form of their official representative (*Stevnevitne*). At this stage in the proceedings the presence of lawyers is not required.

Where no settlement is achieved the case is referred to the court of first instance for examination. However, where claims are deemed to be justified, the Conciliation Board has the power to deliver a ruling, which has the force of a court judgment.

Where a defendant fails to respond to the arbitrator's summons or fails to appear at the case hearing, a ruling in default is handed down and has the force of a court judgment.

For more complex or disputed claims cases are heard by the court of first instance (*Byret*). This notably involves plenary proceedings, which are based on both oral evidence and written submissions and are held to hear the parties' witnesses, arguments and legal proofs, before delivering a verdict.

Norway does not have a system of commercial courts, however the *Skifterett* (Probate Court) has jurisdiction to rule also on winding up proceedings.

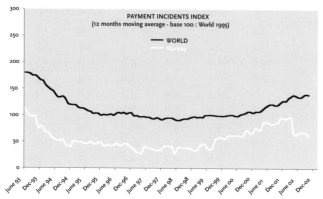

PAYMENT INCIDENTS INDEX
(12 months moving average - base 100 : World 1995)
— WORLD
— Norway

Poland

Coface analysis

Short-term: **A4**

Medium-term:
Quite low risk

STRENGTHS

- Foreign investment, though declining, continues to bolster country's economic modernisation.
- Political and economic stability strengthened by prospects of EU membership.
- Moderate foreign debt burden and comfortable foreign exchange reserves.

WEAKNESSES

- Worst performing economy of all the transition economies. Medium-term growth prospects marred by implementation of fairly tight monetary policies in the absence of credible measures to reduce the fiscal deficit.
- Increased vulnerability to capital outflows in the face of direct foreign investment's declining share of external financing needs cover. Sharp rise in private-sector debt over last few years.
- Rising unemployment makes it politically difficult to reduce social spending and pursue reforms.

RISK ASSESSMENT

The economy showed signs of recovery in late 2002 and growth is expected to rise in 2003 due to the zloty's depreciation, the easing of monetary policy and expectations of firmer external demand.

Weak growth and higher public spending sharply increased the fiscal deficit, which could become a source of concern in the medium term because of the swelling public debt.

The external accounts have improved, but the decline in external financing needs has been accompanied by a fall in foreign direct investment, thereby increasing the country's dependence on foreign borrowings. Consequently, Poland remains vulnerable to a crisis of confidence. Involving as it would a significant realignment of the exchange rate, loss of confidence would create fresh payment difficulties for companies with a high level of foreign currency debt. However, the country's ability to withstand capital withdrawals is strengthened by a free floating exchange rate system – which would limit the risk of an excessive exchange rate correction – and large foreign exchange reserves.

KEY ECONOMIC INDICATORS						
(US$ billion)	1998	1999	2000	2001	2002 (e)	2003 (f)
Economic growth (%)	4.8	4.1	4	1	1.3	2.5
Inflation (%)	11.8	7.3	10.2	5.5	2	1.7
Public-sector balance/GDP (%)	−3.2	−3.2	−2.7	−5.2	−6.7	−6.5
Unemployment (%)	10.4	13.1	15.1	17.4	19	n/a
Exports	32.5	30.1	35.9	41.7	44.7	51.9
Imports	45.3	45.1	48.2	49.3	51.6	−59.4
Trade balance	−12.8	−15.1	−12.3	−7.7	−6.9	−8.3
Current account balance	−6.9	−12.5	−10	−5.3	−5.2	−6.7
Current account balance/GDP (%)	−4.3	−8.1	−6.3	−3	−2.8	−4.3
Foreign debt	59.1	65.4	69.6	71	78.7	82.1
Debt service/Exports (%)	8.6	11.2	13.7	18.6	13.2	12.6
Reserves (import months)	5.9	5.8	5.2	4.9	5.3	4.8

e = estimated, f = forecast

CONDITIONS OF ACCESS TO THE MARKET

■ Market overview

Poland has suffered a sharp economic downturn since the second half of 2000. This has had serious consequences for fiscal revenues, business confidence and corporate balance sheets and investments.

At 1 January 2003 the minimum gross wage was 800 zlotys (200 euros). The average wage at end the end of 2002 was 2250 zlotys (560 euros).

■ Means of entry

Sweeping reforms in the laws and regulations governing the terms of access to the Polish market are bringing Poland closer into line with European Union standards. In matters of trade policy Poland continues to harmonize its trade arrangements with EU integration criteria and, through the WTO, co-ordinate its actions and policies with those of the European Union.

With the prospect of EU membership looming, considerable headway has been made in the most sensitive areas. Customs duties on cars have been cut to 0 per cent since 1 January 2002, whereas agriculture is covered by the 'double zero' agreement concluded with the EU in 2000. Some protective measures (non-tariff barriers) remain in place, especially under cover of agricultural or industrial restructuring, such as recent measures in respect of steel imports.

■ Attitude towards foreign investors

Drawing on the country's clear competitive advantage, the Polish government has already attracted US$61 billion in direct foreign investment, or 40 per cent of all DFI in the countries of Central and Eastern Europe. However, the pace of privatization has slowed since 2001, with many leading companies in the energy, banking, petrochemicals, heavy industry, defence and food sectors still waiting to be sold.

The new business law that took effect on 1 January 2001 places domestic and foreign companies on an equal footing. Almost all restrictions on foreign investment have been abolished and the number of activities requiring approval reduced.

Safeguards for foreign investors have also been enhanced. There are no restrictions on the repatriation of dividends. However, the administra-

PAYMENT INCIDENTS INDEX
(12 months moving average - base 100 : World 1995)
— WORLD

tive apparatus continues to be marred by lack of transparency, red tape and, in some cases, corruption. Administrative procedures for obtaining work permits, setting up companies or obtaining court rulings, for example, remain long and complex.

■ Foreign exchange regulations

The zloty's exchange rate is determined by the market, with a central peg set daily by the National Bank of Poland. Since 1 October 2002 the zloty has been fully convertible. However, some foreign exchange transactions, especially concerning securities trading, remain subject to restrictions.

PAYMENT AND COLLECTION PRACTICES

■ Payment

The bill of exchange and the cheque are not widely used as these instruments are subjected to a certain formality in order to be validly established.

For dishonoured and protested bills and cheques creditors may resort to a summary procedure for ordering payment.

Until now, cash payments were commonly used in Poland between individuals and firms alike, but the new Business Act that came into force on 1 January 2001 requires companies to carry out settlements via a bank account for transactions amounting to upwards of the equivalent of € 3000 in zlotys.

The original instrument is the *weksel in blanco*, an incomplete promissory note at the time of its establishment as only the word *weksel* and the issuer's signature appear on it. The signature constitutes an irrevocable promise to pay and this undertaking comes into force when the promissory note is completed (amount, place and date of payment), in accordance with a prior agreement between issuer and beneficiary. *Weksels in blanco* are commonly used as they also constitute a guarantee of payment in commercial agreements and payment rescheduling.

Bank transfers are by far the most widely used means of payment. Leading Polish banks – after an initial phase of privatization and a second phase of concentration – are now linked to the SWIFT system, which enables domestic and international payments to be processed more easily and quickly at a low cost.

■ Debt collection

It is advisable, as far as possible, not to initiate recovery proceedings locally due not only to the cumbersome formalities and the high cost of legal action but also to the country's lengthy court procedures: it takes almost two years to obtain a writ of enforcement due both to a lack of judges adequately trained in the rules of the market economy, and of insufficient equipment.

Following the submission of a demand for payment, accompanied by proof of debt, it is advisable to seek an amicable settlement based on a schedule of payment, preferably set up by a Public Notary, including an *enforcement formula* that allows creditors, in the event of default by the debtor, to go directly to the enforcement proceedings, after acknowledgement by the courts of the binding nature of this document.

Creditors may seek, through an order to pay (*nakaz zapłaty*), a fast-track and less expensive procedure if they produce positive proof of debt (bills of exchange, cheques or unpaid *weksels in blanco*, acknowledgements of debts, etc), it being understood that if the judge is not convinced of the substance of the claim – decisions being made under his own discretionary power – he can refer the case to full trial.

The plenary proceedings, for the written part, involve the filing of submissions by the parties and supporting case documents and, for the oral part, involve a hearing of the parties and their witnesses on the main hearing date. During such legal action the judge is required, wherever possible, to attempt conciliation between the parties.

Commercial disputes are generally heard by the commercial courts (*Sad Gospodarczy*), under the jurisdiction of district or regional courts (*Voivodies*) according to the amount involved.

Russia

Coface analysis

Short-term: **B**

Medium-term:
Quite high risk

STRENGTHS

- Abundant natural and human resources.
- Country's regional and nuclear power status reaffirmed since Vladimir Putin's election as president, especially after the support offered to the United States following the events of 11 September.
- Numerous changes in legislation introduced by the current government. Reform programme inspires confidence.
- Re-establishment of central control over regions, parliament and oligarchs creates political stability and starts to positively affect economic behaviour.

WEAKNESSES

- Output and investment well below pre-1990 levels.
- Ill-defined property and creditors' rights undermine foreign investor confidence.
- Commodity-based economy vulnerable to fluctuations in world prices. Domestic output hampered by rising real exchange rates.
- Risk of loose implementation of reforms voted by parliament as economic and regional actors not always keen on enforcing new laws.

RISK ASSESSMENT

Growth has been restrained owing to strong household spending and high oil prices. However, the slowdown in investment is a clear sign that the rising real exchange rate is hitting the competitiveness of companies operating in the domestic market and that corporate investment plans are being undermined by poor financial intermediation. Therefore the possibility of maintaining robust economic performance is increasingly dependent on the energy sector.

Russia's external position remains favourable, underpinned by oil exports boosted by growing production volumes and decreasing capital flight.

However, imports are growing more quickly than exports due to the real appreciation of the rouble.

Sovereign risk is not a cause for concern given the country's tight fiscal policy. Owing to a confidence crisis towards emerging markets in summer 2002 plans to return to the sovereign debt market have been shelved. A number of microeconomic problems remain: legislative progress on creditors' and property rights does not easily translate into behaviour on the ground. As for the banking system, it remains the Achilles heel of the Russian economy, however urgent the need for reform.

KEY ECONOMIC INDICATORS						
US$ billion	1998	1999	2000	2001	2002 (e)	2003 (f)
Economic growth (%)	−4.9	3.2	9	5	4	4.2
Inflation (%)	84.4	36.1	20.2	19	14.9	12.1
Public-sector deficit/GDP (%)	−8	−1.6	1.2	2.9	1.6	0.8
Exports	59	63.6	91.2	88.1	95.2	102.2
Imports	43.2	29.2	31.4	40.7	50.9	55.5
Trade balance	15.8	34.4	59.8	47.4	44.3	46.7
Current account balance	−2.3	22	44.2	31.7	23.7	23
Current account balance/GDP (%)	−0.9	11.5	17	10.1	8.6	8
Foreign debt	173	159	140.1	131.9	135.9	135.4
Debt service (DS)/Exports (%)	28.5	27.4	21.3	19.9	18.7	16.2
Reserves (import months)	1.3	2	5.1	5.7	6.1	7

e = estimated, f = forecast

CONDITIONS OF ACCESS TO THE MARKET

■ Market overview

The improvement in the country's macroeconomic indicators is borne out by the external account and budget surpluses, the steady increase in foreign exchange reserves and timely payments to the Paris Club. Russian companies have returned to the international financial markets, with the government announcing new issues for 2003. However the situation remains fragile, and calls for the intensification of structural reforms. The banking sector is in urgent need of wide-ranging reforms, significant investment is required to develop the country's infrastructure, especially in the field of energy, and greater transparency in the country's somewhat ineffectual business legislation is called for.

■ Means of entry

The implementation of root-and-branch reforms in such varied fields as customs procedures, taxation, land ownership and administrative formalities should help promote the buying and selling of goods and strengthen investor confidence. Continued pursuit and proper implementation of reforms, which should be spurred by the prospect of Russia's membership of the WTO, is the key to improving the business and investment climate in the country.

Since January 2001 Russia has carried out a series of customs reforms involving tariff reductions and unification. Only four rates of duty – from 5 per cent to 20 per cent - now remain. Despite these achievements customs procedures remain lengthy and costly due to chaotic customs reorganization and rigid customs clearance procedures. A new customs code, under review at the Douma, should be adopted over the next few months.

■ Attitude towards foreign investors

The introduction of a revised tax code, the most important piece of legislation in 2000–01, has permitted across-the-board tax cuts, including a sharp reduction in corporation tax from 35 per cent to a uniform 24 per cent (compared with more than 50 per cent for banks), a reduction in the outdated turnover tax from 4 per cent to 1 per cent, and a reduction in personal social security contributions and income tax to a uniform 13 per cent. Plans are also under way to abolish the remaining turnover tax as well as the sales tax.

The new land ownership code, which came into force on 30 October 2001, authorizes the sale of urban, industrial and commercial land, but not farmland. It gives foreign companies and individuals almost the same property rights as Russian nationals, permitting them to own land in all but a few cases.

A series of laws aimed at improving the business environment was adopted in early 2001. The measures involve simplifying licensing procedures, reducing the number of official inspections, streamlining investment registration procedures (setting up a one-stop shop for foreign investors) and amending product certification procedures. These reforms should help streamline investment regulations and curb certain bureaucratic practices.

■ Foreign exchange regulations
Exchange controls were eased slightly in 2001.

Under a law dating back to 1992 Russian-based exporters must convert 75 per cent of their income – generally generated in dollars – into roubles within 14 days of receiving payment. Since 1 January 2002 the conversion threshold has been lowered to 50 per cent.

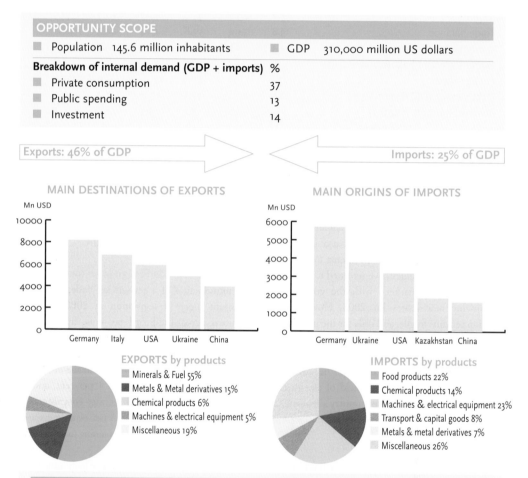

OPPORTUNITY SCOPE

■ Population   145.6 million inhabitants   ■ GDP   310,000 million US dollars

Breakdown of internal demand (GDP + imports)	%
■ Private consumption	37
■ Public spending	13
■ Investment	14

Exports: 46% of GDP   Imports: 25% of GDP

MAIN DESTINATIONS OF EXPORTS

Mn USD

(Germany, Italy, USA, Ukraine, China)

MAIN ORIGINS OF IMPORTS

Mn USD

(Germany, Ukraine, USA, Kazakhstan, China)

EXPORTS by products
- Minerals & Fuel 55%
- Metals & Metal derivatives 15%
- Chemical products 6%
- Machines & electrical equipment 5%
- Miscellaneous 19%

IMPORTS by products
- Food products 22%
- Chemical products 14%
- Machines & electrical equipment 23%
- Transport & capital goods 8%
- Metals & metal derivatives 7%
- Miscellaneous 26%

STANDARD OF LIVING / PURCHASING POWER

Indicators	Russia	Regional average	DC average
GNP per capita (PPP dollars)	8010	7936	6548
GNP per capita	1660	3052	3565
Human development index	0.781	0.796	0.702
Wealthiest 10% share of national income	39	26	32
Urban population percentage	73	61	60
Percentage under 15 years old	18	20	32
Number of telephones per 1000 inhabitants	218	273	157
Number of computers per 1000 inhabitants	43	98	64

Slovakia

Short-term: **A4**

Medium-term:
Quite low risk

Coface analysis

STRENGTHS

- The prospect of European Union membership in May 2004 enhances the country's economic and financial situation.
- Bank and industrial company privatizations have expanded the country's economic potential.
- Slovakia enjoys a privileged geographic position at the crossroads of Central Europe.

WEAKNESSES

- The economy has been registering substantial fiscal and external deficits.
- External financing needs are not negligible and the external debt is relatively high in percentage of GDP terms (about 50 per cent).
- Health system, civil service, and labour code reforms are lagging.
- Unemployment is high.

RISK ASSESSMENT

The government's expansionary fiscal policy contributed strongly to energizing the economy in 2002. With public spending expected to drop in 2003 to absorb the public sector deficit, investments and exports should pick up the slack. Meanwhile price deregulation will tend to spur inflation.

Concerning external accounts, the current deficit rose due notably to sustained capital goods imports growth linked to restructuring and foreign direct investment. Both privatization-linked and greenfield investments have been underpinning the local currency and contributing to the expansion of foreign exchange reserves.

Politically, renewal of a coalition favourable to reforms after the September 2002 legislative elections has bolstered investor confidence. Included in the EU wave of enlargement scheduled for May 2004, Slovakia is one of the first candidate countries to have closed all chapters of the *acquis communautaire* (the body of EU law).

KEY ECONOMIC INDICATORS

US$ million	1998	1999	2000	2001	2002 (e)	2003 (f)
Economic growth (%)	4.1	1.9	2.2	3.3	4	3.5
Inflation (%)	6.7	10.6	12	7.1	3.2	8.5
Public-sector balance/GDP(%)	−5.3	−3.6	−3.9	−4.8	−7	−5
Unemployment (%)	12.4	16.2	18.6	18.5	n/a	n/a
Exports	10667	10229	11835	12633	14100	15300
Imports	12959	11321	12709	14753	16400	17500
Trade balance	−2293	−1092	−874	−2120	−2300	−2200
Current account balance	−1994	−820	−676	−1756	−1900	−1800
Current account balance/GDP(%)	−9.4	−4.2	−3.4	−8.6	−7.9	−6.4
Foreign debt	11902	10518	10804	11269	11800	12400
Debt service/Exports(%)	13.8	15	17.5	14.3	11.4	15.4
Reserves (import months)	2.2	2.9	3.2	2.8	5.6	4.8

e = estimated, f = forecast

CONDITIONS OF ACCESS TO THE MARKET

■ Market overview

Slovakia's favourable macroeconomic environment is due to strong growth and plummeting inflation.

At 17.2 per cent in August 2002, unemployment is alarmingly high. In addition, the job market is affected by strong regional disparities. Despite substantial wage increases in 2002 the average monthly wage is a mere 310 euros.

Following completion of the banking sector restructuring programme and the partial privatization of gas and electricity supply companies, the ongoing privatizations of the Slovak electricity utility SE and the water supply company mark the last stage in Slovakia's economic liberalization programme.

While the expanding consumer goods market clearly offers many business opportunities, industrial joint ventures – sub contracting agreements, manufac-turing under licence and, above all, joint start-ups – have the highest growth potential.

■ Means of entry

Customs duty on industrial products has been lifted, but agricultural products are excluded from the exemptions and continue to be subject to duty. The last remaining barriers, in the form of certification and technical standards, are gradually being dismantled as Slovakia moves closer towards compliance with EU integration criteria.

Although the Slovak customs code implemented on 1 August 2001 is in line with European Union legislation, the entry of goods is subject to clearance by a sworn customs official.

The most widespread means of payment are SWIFT transfers, remittances and documentary credit. Disputes and litigation are relatively rare.

■ Attitude towards foreign investors

Slovak legislation is liberal, permitting investors to own a 100 per cent stake in local companies. A 34 per cent stake constitutes a blocking minority.

The law establishes equality of treatment between Slovak and foreign investors.

The Slovak investment and trade development Agency, SARIO, is more pro active than in the past in the promotion of Slovak manufacturing

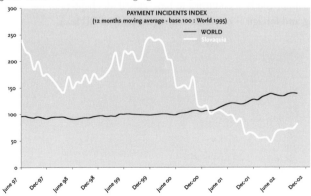

PAYMENT INCIDENTS INDEX
(12 months moving average - base 100 : World 1995)
— WORLD
— Slovaquia

businesses.

The new government's openly liberal policies, which include the lifting of restrictions on foreign interests in so-called strategic sectors (such as energy), will help strengthen direct foreign investment in the country.

The Franco–Czechoslovak dual taxation agreement concluded on 1 June 1973 is due to be revised shortly with a view to promoting investment.

■ Attitude towards foreign investors

The Slovak crown, which enjoys stable fixed parity with the euro, is freely convertible but rarely traded abroad. Since the abolition of exchange controls and the introduction of a new banking law the accent is on

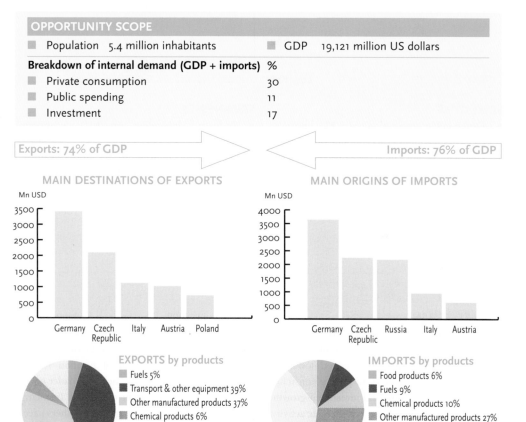

OPPORTUNITY SCOPE

■ Population 5.4 million inhabitants   ■ GDP 19,121 million US dollars

Breakdown of internal demand (GDP + imports) %
■ Private consumption   30
■ Public spending   11
■ Investment   17

Exports: 74% of GDP   Imports: 76% of GDP

MAIN DESTINATIONS OF EXPORTS

Mn USD

Germany | Czech Republic | Italy | Austria | Poland

MAIN ORIGINS OF IMPORTS

Mn USD

Germany | Czech Republic | Russia | Italy | Austria

EXPORTS by products
- Fuels 5%
- Transport & other equipment 39%
- Other manufactured products 37%
- Chemical products 6%
- Miscellaneous 13%

IMPORTS by products
- Food products 6%
- Fuels 9%
- Chemical products 10%
- Other manufactured products 27%
- Transport & capital goods 37%
- Miscellaneous 11%

STANDARD OF LIVING / PURCHASING POWER

Indicators	Slovakia	Regional average	DC average
GNP per capita (PPP dollars)	11040	7936	6548
GNP per capita	3700	3052	3565
Human development index	0.835	0.796	0.702
Wealthiest 10% share of national income	18	26	32
Urban population percentage	57	61	60
Percentage under 15 years old	20	20	32
Number of telephones per 1000 inhabitants	314	273	157
Number of computers per 1000 inhabitants	137	98	64

Slovenia

Coface analysis

Short-term: **A2**

Medium-term:
Low risk

STRENGTHS

- Forthcoming integration into EU improves country's medium-term economic prospects.
- One of the region's most developed economies, with a stable macroeconomic and political environment since the early 1990s.
- Ample foreign exchange reserves; foreign debt under control.
- Ethnically homogenous.

WEAKNESSES

- Industry dependent on EU's economic situation.
- Number of reforms to be undertaken or stepped up (reduction of state interference in economy, equal treatment for local and foreign investors, greater flexibility of labour market).
- High unemployment.

RISK ASSESSMENT

The country continued to enjoy moderate growth in 2002. Among the components of domestic demand, consumer spending trended lower. In 2003 the projected recovery in private consumption, together with export and investment growth, should lead to a slight pick up in economic activity. The prospect of EU membership should notably boost business confidence.

Thanks to growing sales to the rest of Central and Eastern Europe the country's external trade more or less weathered the slowdown in the eurozone in 2002. The current account deficit should however widen in 2003 because of the rise in imports driven by firmer domestic demand. But the country's external financial position should continue to improve on the back of broader cover by foreign direct investment of external financing needs as the privatization programme gathers pace.

Politically, the ruling centre-left coalition should remain stable following the victory of the outgoing prime minister at the presidential election in December 2002.

KEY ECONOMIC INDICATORS

US$ million	1998	1999	2000	2001	2002 (e)	2003 (f)
Economic growth (%)	3.8	5.2	4.6	3	3	3.7
Inflation (%)	7.9	6.2	8.9	8.4	7.4	4.1
Public-sector balance/GDP (%)	−0.9	−0.9	−1.4	−1.6	−2.9	−1.6
Unemployment (%)	14.5	13.6	12.2	11.6	11.9	n/a
Exports	9091	8623	8808	9342	10345	11277
Imports	9880	9868	9947	9964	11077	12382
Trade balance	−789	−1245	−1139	−622	−732	−1105
Current account balance	−147	−782	−612	−66	−57	−443
Current account balance/GDP (%)	−0.8	−3.9	−3.4	−0.4	−0.3	−1.9
Foreign debt	7474	7957	8774	9274	9554	9554
Debt service/Exports (%)	13.2	7.7	9.2	13.4	11.4	11.2
Reserves (import months)	3.7	3.2	3.2	4.3	4.9	4.9

e = estimated, f = forecast

CONDITIONS OF ACCESS TO THE MARKET

■ Means of entry

Average customs duty on goods imported from the EU is 1 per cent. This applies almost exclusively to consumer goods. These include milk (up to 10.9 per cent), meat (up to 30 per cent) and cosmetics and drugs, which are subject to high rates of duty and cumbersome customs procedures.

Public tenders are now officially open to EU firms. Until 2001 a national preference clause allowed local companies to win bids that were 10 per cent higher than those submitted by foreign bidders. Two new public tender laws establish equality between Slovenian and foreign tenderers, but as this legislation lacks teeth an amendment is due to be passed in 2003. There is a tendency towards arbitrary enforcement of certification rules and standards, as reflected in the heavy-handed food inspections and plant health tests carried out recently by Slovenian customs.

SWIFT transfers are a widespread means of payment. Many Slovenian companies settle their invoices through deferred payment arrangements thanks to their creditworthiness and good credit rating. Defaults are scarce and debt collection firms efficient. However, court procedures on the whole are slow.

The lack of competitively priced and timely sources of local finance is a major obstacle to the development of both Slovenian and foreign business.

■ Attitude towards foreign investors

Investment is unrestricted, except in armaments, compulsory pension funds and health insurance. However, there are no special incentives for foreign investment. Government approval is needed to acquire over 25 per cent of a Slovenian company with a capital of 800 million tolars or more (approximately 4 million euros). Foreign companies enjoy equal access to tax-free trade areas in Maribor, Celje and the fast-expanding port of Koper.

The market as a whole is open, although in a number of sectors (retail, locally manufactured consumer goods, financial services) Slovenian companies bitterly resist foreign competition. However, the situation is changing as compliance with EU integration criteria grows.

There is still a deplorable lack of transparency in the way public tenders are conducted, with public opinion and the government supporting cartels in public works and construction, telecommunication, etc.

There are growth opportunities for French companies in Slovenia – as exemplified by Suez, Renault, Lafarge, Sanofi-Synthélabo, E LeClerc – through tightly managed joint venture projects.

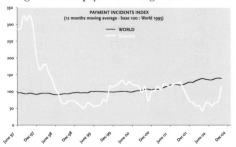

PAYMENT INCIDENTS INDEX
(12 months moving average - base 100 : World 1995)
— WORLD

■ Foreign exchange regulations

The tolar is a fully convertible, floating currency.

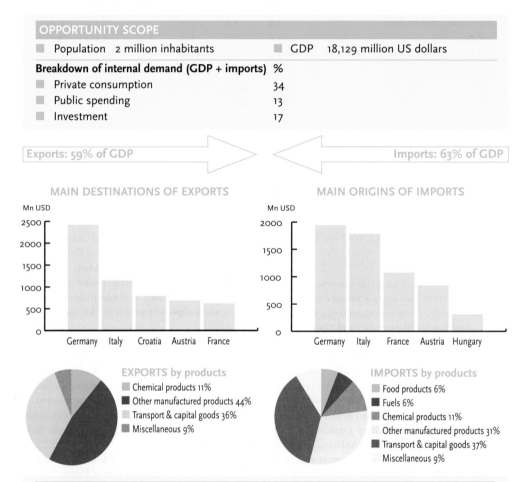

OPPORTUNITY SCOPE

■ Population   2 million inhabitants   ■ GDP   18,129 million US dollars

Breakdown of internal demand (GDP + imports) %
■ Private consumption   34
■ Public spending   13
■ Investment   17

Exports: 59% of GDP   Imports: 63% of GDP

MAIN DESTINATIONS OF EXPORTS

Mn USD

Germany Italy Croatia Austria France

MAIN ORIGINS OF IMPORTS

Mn USD

Germany Italy France Austria Hungary

EXPORTS by products
■ Chemical products 11%
■ Other manufactured products 44%
■ Transport & capital goods 36%
■ Miscellaneous 9%

IMPORTS by products
■ Food products 6%
■ Fuels 6%
■ Chemical products 11%
■ Other manufactured products 31%
■ Transport & capital goods 37%
■ Miscellaneous 9%

STANDARD OF LIVING / PURCHASING POWER

Indicators	Slovenia	Regional average	DC average
GNP per capita (PPP dollars)	17,310	7936	6548
GNP per capita	10,050	3052	3565
Human development index	0.879	0.796	0.702
Wealthiest 10% share of national income	23	26	32
Urban population percentage	50	61	60
Percentage under 15 years old	16	20	32
Number of telephones per 1000 inhabitants	386	273	157
Number of computers per 1000 inhabitants	276	98	64

Spain

Coface analysis   Short-term: **A1**

1

STRENGTHS

- Public finances should remain balanced amid a large primary balance surplus and a law forbidding central and regional governments from running up deficits.
- Decentralisation of power to regions has been proceeding successfully.
- Continued government infrastructure investment has been enabling the country to modernise its communications networks.
- Market liberalisation has been going forward even though privatisations and breaking up monopolies do not mean the end of dominant national companies or their influence.

WEAKNESSES

- Labour legislation remains rigid despite reforms as reflected in the still high level of structural unemployment.
- Low productivity and wage indexing spurs inflationary pressures.
- The housing boom continues to drive up prices, which could result in a speculative bubble.
- Inadequate research spending, low productivity, and rising production costs will spur relocations.

RISK ASSESSMENT

Growth slowed markedly in 2002 largely due to an export collapse. The European slowdown along with declining tourist revenues hit the economy hard. While investment in housing and public infrastructure construction remained strong, capital goods investment fell sharply. The recent household spending boom has sagged considerably amid weaker job growth and erosion of real wages caused by wage restraint and high inflation.

In 2003 economic activity should pick up moderately underpinned by growth in all demand categories. Consumption should benefit from improved employment trends and the income tax reductions that balanced public accounts make possible. European Union handouts will continue to bolster public infrastructure investment thereby cushioning the impact of a possible housing slump. However, the moderate economic recovery remains dependent on uncertain European and US growth trends as well as on management of inflationary risks and unemployment.

The economic slowdown has affected the profitability of companies accustomed to strong sales growth. Spanish banks, meanwhile, have been exercising greater vigilance in granting loans. Payment incidents thus increased in frequency and size throughout 2002. While textiles and clothing remain the most vulnerable sectors, chemicals, pharmaceuticals and perfumes, furniture and packaging, and electrical equipment could also generate occasional defaults.

KEY ECONOMIC INDICATORS

%	1998	1999	2000	2001	2002 (e)	2003 (f)
Economic growth	4.3	4.1	4.1	2.8	1.9	2.5
Consumer spending (% change)	4.5	4.7	4	2.7	1.9	2.4
Investment (% change)	9.7	8.8	5.7	2.5	1.6	3.2
Inflation	2.2	2.4	3.2	3.2	3.8	3.1
Unemployment	15.4	12.9	11.4	10.5	11	10.8
Short–term interest rate	4.2	3	4.4	4.2	3.2	3.5
National debt/GDP	−2.6	−1.2	−0.3	0	−0.2	0
Public–sector balance/GDP	81.3	75.4	72.1	69.1	69	66
Exports (% change)	8.2	7.6	9.6	3.4	0.3	5
Imports (% change)	13.3	12.8	9.8	3.7	0.1	4
Current account balance/GDP	−0.5	−2.3	−3.1	−2.6	−2.4	−2.6

e = estimated, f = forecast

MAIN ECONOMIC SECTORS

■ Steel

Stagnant output amid rising sales and profitability marked 2002. Starting from a low level steel prices began rising in the year and should continue trending up in 2003. Company performance will closely depend on the customers they serve. Those manufacturing flat products for construction and more specifically for public works will continue to prosper. Conversely, those producing sheet steel for cars and household appliances will suffer from the downward trend in those sectors.

■ Food retailing

After the acquisition frenzy gripping the sector in recent years a consolidation process developed in 2002. Spanish-owned groups have performed well. They have been focusing on internal growth through store openings. The position of other retailers – acquired by foreign players at high prices – is weaker amid sagging consumer spending.

■ Paper and Cardboard

After a poor start in 2002 conditions seemed to improve. However, the improvement has been more a reflection of a restocking process than a true demand recovery. Prices have thus tended to stagnate or even decline since the summer. The problems facing Spain's publishing and press sectors have weakened the position of coated paper for printing. While the sector's major players

should be able to cope with the gloomy conditions smaller firms, particularly in the graphic arts sector, could suffer.

■ Construction

The construction sector again enjoyed strong growth in 2002. This trend will continue in 2003, even though a slowdown is expected. The infrastructure segment will remain extremely buoyant. By contrast, housing construction should slow. Housing demand will nonetheless remain firm, with interest rates remaining low and large age groups still entering the market. However, this trend could turn down if economic growth sags.

■ Automobiles

The Spanish car industry suffered not only from a shrinking domestic market but also from sagging exports to the European market, which represents 80 per cent of the country's production. Recovery seems unlikely before the second half of 2003. Local car parts manufacturers have thus been under strong pressure from their customers. They could suffer even more if manufacturers decide to relocate some of their production.

■ Textiles

With the sector continuing to shrink in 2002 both production and investment declined. European sales barely grew amid sagging consumption and strong competition, not only from countries with low production costs but also from Italy, France and Germany. Catalan thread manufacturers suffered indirectly from increased fabric and garment imports from Asia and Morocco. Large garment manufacturers have been increasingly relocating their production facilities, particularly from Galicia. A slight upturn could develop in spring 2003.

PAYMENT AND COLLECTION PRACTICES

■ Payment

The bill of exchange is frequently used for commercial transactions in Spain. In the event of default, bills of exchange offer creditors certain safeguards, including access to the new exchange procedure (juicio cambiario) introduced by the recent civil proceedings law, under which courts may order debtors to make payment within 10 days and issue an attachment order against debtors' property on the basis of the documents submitted. Where a claim is contested a court hearing is held to examine both parties' arguments and a judgment is handed down within 10 days of said hearing.

Widely accepted, though somewhat difficult to obtain, bills of exchange endorsed by a bank limit the risk of payment default by granting creditors the right to claim as well against the endorser.

The cheque, which is less widely used than the bill of exchange, offers similar legal safeguards under "the exchange procedure" in the event of payment default.

The same is true of the promissory note, which, like the bill of exchange, is an instrument enforceable by law, but in the event of payment default is not recorded in the register of unpaid debts (Registro de Aceptationes Impagadas) that banks and other financial institutions regularly consult before extending credit to clients.

SWIFT bank transfers are widely used by Spanish banks and offer a quick, reliable and cost-effective means of payment, it being understood that payment depends on the customer's good faith. Where a customer fails to order a transfer the only legal remedy available to creditors is to institute ordinary proceedings for non-payment of invoices.

■ Debt collection

To speed up court procedures and modernize the obsolete civil procedure law dating back to February 1881, a new civil procedure law came into force on 8 January 2001. The purpose of this law is to drastically cut the time taken up by litigation and to give oral arguments priority over written submissions – the cornerstone of the previous system – even though the new law still requires the authentication of large numbers of documents.

Where sellers cannot reach an amicable settlement with buyers, they may obtain their right to payment through the new juicio declarativo procedure, divided into juicio ordinario for claims upwards of 3000 euros (previously 500,000 pesetas), and juicio verbal for claims under 3000 euros. The aim of the new procedure is to speed up delivery of enforcement orders by reducing and simplifying the stages of the old procedure.

In addition, for commercial claims below 30,000 euros (previously 5,000,000 pesetas) a more flexible procedure has been introduced (juicio monitorio), under which, once an application form has been filed before the court along with supporting documents, the judge may order the debtor to pay within 20 days.

This ambitious law, which brings Spanish judicial practice into line with the rest of Europe, is slowly gaining force and breaking the tradition of formalism acquired by the Spanish judiciary over several decades.

1

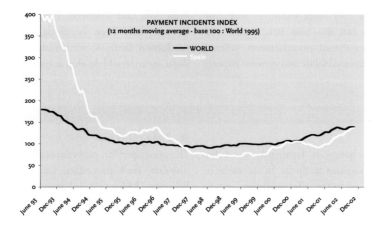

Sweden

Coface analysis   Short-term: **A1**

RISK ASSESSMENT

Despite a modest recovery in 2002 the economy remained fairly sluggish. Exports were depressed by slack external demand, especially in the telecommunications sector. The only positive aspect was a rally in consumer spending on the back of tax cuts and rising disposable incomes. However, consumer enthusiasm was dampened by the Central Bank raising interest rates in an attempt to check inflationary pressures. The decline in industrial output resulting from the slump in telecommunications exports, dearer credit and continuing uncertainties about the economy have, for the second year running, had a negative impact on investments.

In 2003 the economy should see a marked recovery, largely driven by more buoyant consumer spending, growth in disposable incomes outstripping inflation. Exports should rally as telecommunications equipment sales pick up. Against a background of firmer demand investment should see an upward trend despite the increase in interest rates.

The sharp growth in bankruptcies in 2001 slowed considerably in 2002. Despite the difficulties facing the telecommunications sector and the uncertainties affecting the paper industry, Swedish firms' overall payment behaviour remains satisfactory

KEY ECONOMIC INDICATORS						
%	1998	1999	2000	2001	2002 (e)	2003 (f)
Economic growth	3.6	4.5	3.6	1.3	1.8	2.5
Consumer spending (% change)	2.7	3.9	4.6	0.2	1.9	2.4
Investment (% change)	8.5	9.6	5	1.5	−2	3.8
Inflation	1	1	0.9	1.6	2.3	2.2
Unemployment	6.5	5.6	4.7	3.8	4	4
Short-term interest rate	4.2	3.1	4	4	4.2	4.5
Public-sector balance/GDP	2.1	1.3	3.7	4.8	1.8	1.6
Foreign debt/GDP	72.6	68.2	60.6	54	50	48
Exports (% change)	8.4	6.5	10.3	−1.1	2.1	5
Imports (% change)	11.2	4.4	11.5	−3.8	0.2	6
Current account balance/GDP	3.4	3.6	3.3	3.2	3.9	3.7

e = estimated, f = forecast

%	1998	1999	2000	2001	2002 (e)	2003 (f)
Economic growth	2.4	1.6	3	0.9	0.4	1.5
Consumer spending (% change)	2.3	2.2	2	1.8	1.2	1.4
Investment (% change)	4.5	3.7	5.8	−5.2	−5.8	3
Inflation	−0.2	0.4	0.9	1	0.6	0.7
Unemployment	3.9	2.7	2	1.9	2.7	3.1
Short-term interest rate	1.6	1.4	3.2	2.9	1	1.3
Public sector balance/GDP	−0.4	−0.2	2.4	−0.3	0.1	0.3
National debt/GDP	54.5	51.4	51.3	51.6	53	51
Exports (% change)	8.3	7.5	8.5	−0.1	−0.1	4.5
Imports (% change)	9.6	5.3	10.6	−0.3	−2	5
Current account balance/GDP	9.9	11	12.9	8.5	11	11

e = estimated, f = forecast

MAIN ECONOMIC SECTORS

Construction

The sector should remain sluggish in 2003, with slack conditions persisting in housing and commercial and industrial construction. Conversely, the old building renovation segment should remain buoyant. A strong economic driver until now, public works construction could sag with the completion of several large projects. Intense price competition has been widely affecting company profitability.

Tourism

Business continued to decline in 2002, particularly with fewer tourists coming from the United States and Germany. Even Swiss clientele has sagged. The Swiss franc's strength has also had a detrimental effect. All regions and all types of accommodation and food service are suffering. Little improvement appears likely in 2003. However, increased spending by Swiss customers shunning holidays abroad could partially offset the drop in foreign tourist business.

Watchmaking

This sector exports 70 per cent of its output, mainly to other countries in Europe and Asia. After weathering the drop in world tourism and air travel business began to sag from mid-2002 and should continue to decline in 2003. The decline is mainly attributable to a European sales slowdown. However, price increases permitted the sector to maintain profit levels.

Capital goods

With 66 per cent of its sales deriving from exports the sector continued to feel the effects of the investment slump worldwide, and particularly within Europe. Moreover, the Swiss franc's strength constitutes an additional impediment to export development. Domestic sales have also been severely depressed. Recovery seems very unlikely before mid-2003.

Retail

The sector has continued to grow but at a slower pace, which reflects sagging household consumption. A distinction should be made between sales of luxury goods, such as watches and jewellery, which have been falling; clothing and shoes, which have been stagnating; and foodstuffs, which have remained buoyant. This situation should remain stable in the coming months. Moreover, with major retail brands currently shielded from foreign competition, they can continue charging relatively high prices.

Food

Primarily driven by a mature but solid domestic

market the sector has continued to register moderate growth. Company earnings have been satisfactory. The opening of the European market to the sector is affording new opportunities to industrialists. These favourable conditions should persist in 2003.

■ Chemicals anad pharmaceuticals

The sector has continued to enjoy remarkable

growth. With 70 per cent of earnings coming from exports, it remains competitive because of the quality and specificity of its products. As such, the increased focus on biotechnologies augurs well for the future. Moreover, despite the pressure currently affecting prices, profit levels have remained satisfactory. The sector's performance should continue to improve in 2003.

1

PAYMENT AND COLLECTION PRACTICES

■ Payment

Bills of exchange and cheques are not commonly used owing to prohibitive banking and tax charges; the stamp duty on bills of exchange is 0.75 per cent of the principal amount, for domestic bills, and 1.5% for international bills. Similarly, commercial operators are particularly demanding as regards the formal validity of cheques and bills of exchange as payment instruments.

SWIFT bank transfers are the most commonly used payment system. Most Swiss banks are connected to the network, which facilitates rapid and effective payments.

■ Debt collection

The Swiss legal system presents technical specificities, as follows:

- The existence of an administrative authority (e.g. *Office des poursuites et des faillites or Betreibungs und Konkursamt*) in each canton that is responsible for executing court orders and whose functioning is regulated by federal law. Interested parties may consult or obtain extracts of the Office's records.
- Specific rules for legal procedure prevail in each canton (there are 26 different codes of civil procedure) which sometimes vary greatly depending on the legal doctrine that has inspired them. As such, before instigating actions, plaintiffs should ensure that their counsel is familiar with the law of the concerned jurisdiction as well as the language to be used before the court (French, German or Italian). These two key constraints hamper the

swift course of justice and a project to harmonize these various procedures is under review.

The debt collection process commences with the issuing of notice to pay by ordinary mail or registered letter (thus enabling interest penalties to be charged). This gives the debtor two weeks in which to pay the principal amount, plus – unless otherwise agreed by the parties – interest penalties equivalent to the bank rate applicable in the place of payment.

Where no payment is received after this 14-day period, the creditor may return a form to the *Office des poursuites et des faillites,* which then serves the debtor with a final order to pay within 20 days. This procedure, which is relatively simple to implement, nevertheless affords debtors the possibility of opposing the order without having to provide grounds. Where a claim is thus disputed the only alternative for creditors is to seek redress through the courts.

Conversely, where a seller holds an unconditional evidence of debt signed by the buyer (any original document in which the buyer recognizes his debt, bill of exchange, cheque, etc.), he may request the *temporary lifting* of the debtor's opposition without having to appear before the court. This is a summary procedure, quick and relatively easy to obtain, in which the court's decision is based upon the documents submitted by the seller.

Once this lifting order has been granted the debtor has 20 days in which to refer the case before the judge ruling on the merits of the matter, to obtain the debt's release and obtain, in turn an executory order. This entails instigating a formal procedure, with a written phase followed by a court hearing, lasting anything from between one to three years depending on the canton involved.

Legal costs also vary in each canton.

Once the court has handed down its definitive ruling, the *Office des poursuites et des faillites* delivers an execution order or, in the case of traders, a winding-up petition (*commination*). In all cases the law decides which measure – execution order or winding-up petition – is applied.

Procedures are either heard by a court of first instance or a district court. Commercial courts, presided over by a panel of professional and non-professional judges, exist in the cantons of Aargau, Berne and Zürich.

Once an appeal has been entered with the cantonal court (regarding the cantons that have a second instance court), cases in final step are heard by the Swiss Federal Court (the only federal court of justice) in Lausanne.

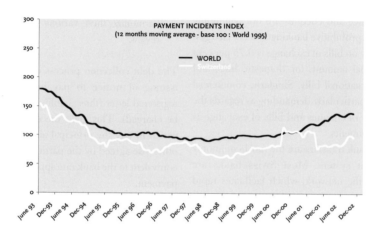

PAYMENT INCIDENTS INDEX
(12 months moving average - base 100 : World 1995)

Tajikistan

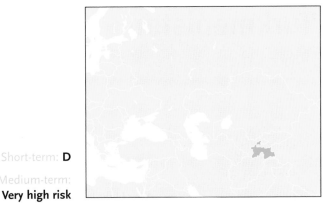

Coface analysis

Short-term: **D**

Medium-term:
Very high risk

1

RISK ASSESSMENT

The country's economic situation has improved thanks to the financial assistance it received as a result of government support for US military operations in Afghanistan. The country continues to receive vast amounts of Russian economic and military assistance, together with IMF financial help. After a record recession, underpinned by a long civil war in the 1990s, the economy has staged something of a recovery, with falling inflation and much sounder public finances.

The country's economic stability remains extremely vulnerable to climate (because of the dominant position of agriculture) and domestic political turmoil. Its solvency is undermined by the debt burden (the country is dependent on official funding). The fact that it enjoys the support of the major powers could help it to obtain better rescheduling terms. This would help sustain the current economic upturn.

KEY ECONOMIC INDICATORS

US$ million	1998	1999	2000	2001	2002 (e)	2003 (f)
Economic growth (%)	5.3	3.7	8.3	10.2	8	7.5
Inflation (%)	2.7	30.1	60.6	12.5	9.7	8.5
Public-sector balance/GDP (%)	−3.8	−3.1	−0.6	−0.1	1.1	−0.1
Exports	586	666	788	652	654	700
Imports	725	693	834	773	800	850
Trade balance	−139	−27	−46	−121	−146	−50
Current account balance	−120	−36	−62	−74	−64	−64
Current account balance/GDP (%)	−8.3	−3.4	−6.5	−7.1	−7	−7
Foreign debt	1179	1233	1226	1023	1021	1021
Debt service/Exports (%)	8.5	5.4	9.6	15.7	20.2	20
Reserves (import months)	1.5	1.7	2.1	1.9	2.3	3

e = estimated, f = forecast

Turkmenistan

Short-term: **D**

Medium-term:
Very high risk

Coface analysis

RISK ASSESSMENT

Although reliable data is hard to come by, the country's economic position has deteriorated. Oil and gas (80 per cent of exports) and agriculture still dominate the economy. In all likelihood recent economic performance has been hit by the poor cotton harvest. Many problems prevent the country's resources from being tapped.

First of all, a large proportion of gas supplies are paid for through barter. The country's land locked position means it has to depend on Russia for shipping its gas to Western markets. This does not always work in its favour. The geographical disadvantage affects its external financing needs, which have been covered by debt. The country could have difficulty meeting its debt repayments if its importers default.

Moreover, political risk has increased as a result of the dead-end policies adopted until now by President Niazov's government, which remains extremely reluctant to undertake any reforms or end the country's diplomatic isolation (brought about by its official policy of 'neutrality'). Under development hampers any moves to tap the country's potential. In the face of mounting opposition to its policies the government has toughened its line, as demonstrated by the all too frequent 'purges' as well as the recent assassination attempt on President Niazov.

KEY ECONOMIC INDICATORS

US$ million	1998	1999	2000	2001	2002 (e)	2003 (f)
Economic growth (%)	5	16	17.6	10	16	8
Inflation (%)	19.8	21.2	7.4	8	10	12
Public-sector balance/GDP (%)	−2.6	0	0.4	−1	−10	−10
Exports	614	1187	2506	2620	2700	2800
Imports	1137	1478	1785	2349	2400	2400
Trade balance	−523	−291	721	271	300	400
Current account balance	−934	−864	611	−149	−210	−250
Current account balance/GDP (%)	−32.21	−22.15	13.89	−2.48	−3.2	−3.9
Foreign debt	2259	2015	2300	2350	2500	2600
Debt service/Exports (%)	97	43.7	22.7	25.1	35	40
Reserves (import months)	10.3	9.4	8.9	6.2	6.1	6.1

e = estimated, f = forecast

Ukraine

Short-term: **D**

Medium-term:
Coface analysis   **Very high risk**

1

STRENGTHS

- Fairly diversified economy (agrifoods, heavy and light industries).
- Strategically located, soon with common borders with EU.
- Substantial earnings generated by transit fees for Russian gas exports to Western Europe.

WEAKNESSES

- Economic reforms hampered by recurrent political crises and influence of oligarchs.
- Key reason behind paucity of foreign investment.
- Metallurgy-dominated Ukrainian industry in need of greater restructuring.
- Dependent on political, economic and financial developments in Russia.

RISK ASSESSMENT

Despite a marked slowdown there is continued growth on the back of buoyant domestic demand and exports. External solvency has been boosted by the improvement in the current account and the increase in foreign exchange reserves. Moreover, Ukraine has hauled itself out of over-indebtedness.

However, lack of corporate restructuring and the downturn in world metal demand threaten the country's strong economic performance. In addition, the government has shown itself incapable of undertaking long-term reform. This has led international financial institutions to provide assistance in fits and starts and acts as a brake on direct foreign investment. The inability to reform is exacerbated by political uncertainty. Mounting opposition to President Koutchma from both the highly divided opposition and the United States (which provided massive aid in the 1990s) has increased short-term uncertainty in a country that continues to vacillate between Europe and Russia in its political affiliations.

KEY ECONOMIC INDICATORS

US$ billion	1998	1999	2000	2001	2002 (e)	2003 (f)
Economic growth (%)	−1.9	−0.2	5.9	9.1	4.3	4.5
Inflation (%)	20	19.2	25.8	6.1	−1	8
Public-sector balance/GDP (%)	−2.8	−2.4	0.6	−0.6	−1.8	−2
Exports	13.7	12.5	15.7	17.1	17.9	20.7
Imports	16.3	12.9	14.9	16.9	17.6	20.7
Trade balance	−2.6	−0.5	0.8	0.2	0.3	0
Current account balance	−1.3	0.8	1.5	1.3	1.9	1.2
Current account balance/GDP (%)	−3.1	2.6	4.7	3.7	4.5	2.8
Foreign debt	12.4	13.5	11.9	11.6	11.9	11.9
Debt service/Exports (%)	11.1	16.6	10	6.4	6.5	7.3
Reserves (import months)	0.5	0.8	0.9	1.7	2.2	2.2

e = estimated, f = forecast

CONDITIONS OF ACCESS TO THE MARKET

■ Market overview

The standard of living grew by another 8 per cent year on year. The official national average wage is US$65, which is supplemented with income from the grey economy (50–60 per cent of GDP). Expanding sectors include agriculture, agri-foodstuffs, timber, textiles, transport infrastructure and energy installations.

The stability of the national currency (the hryvnia) vis-à-vis the dollar is an asset. However, at over US$2 billion or two months of imports, current foreign exchange reserves fall below the three-month security threshold. The hryvnia may therefore be slightly devalued late this year or early next year to spur exports of low value-added heavy machinery, which declined during the last quarter of the year as a result of Russian import duties and anti-dumping measures in North America.

■ Means of entry

The market remains difficult to penetrate on account of many tariff and non-tariff barriers. Product certification remains an obstacle to entry, which only local specialist teams familiar with current procedures are able to surmount. In the service sector, the country's concept of intellectual property remains out of line with international standards and has led to the relocation of CD production units in neighbouring Belarus and Russia.

A new tax code is due to be voted on by parliament. A number of concrete measures could be in place by the end of the year if a certain degree of political stability is restored.

Measures to combat smuggling have proved ineffective, as has the country's anti-money laundering drive. As a result Ukraine has been blacklisted by the international Financial Action Task Force and is threatened with sanctions.

■ Attitude towards foreign investors

Officially, foreign investors are in great demand. In practice, however, Western investors seem to be treated very differently from their Russian counterparts, who enjoy preferential treatment in strategic sectors such as energy, petrochemicals and metal processing.

The government frequently equates foreign investment with the acquisition of companies earmarked for privatization. Start-ups remain scarce in Ukraine and it is advisable to set up new companies with a foreign majority stake. Due to high operating costs and the length of time it takes to see a return on investment (four to five years), large companies have a greater chance of success than small and medium-sized ones.

The country's special economic areas have not lived up to the expectations of the government, which alternately encourages and discourages their development. The resultant uncertainty deters investors at a time when they should be giving greater priority to satisfying domestic demand waiting to be unleashed.

OPPORTUNITY SCOPE

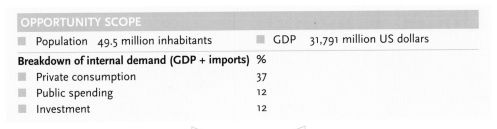

- Population   49.5 million inhabitants
- GDP   31,791 million US dollars

Breakdown of internal demand (GDP + imports) %
- Private consumption   37
- Public spending   12
- Investment   12

Exports: 61% of GDP   Imports: 57% of GDP

MAIN DESTINATIONS OF EXPORTS

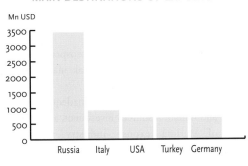

Mn USD — Russia, Italy, USA, Turkey, Germany

MAIN ORIGINS OF IMPORTS

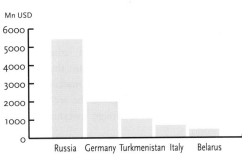

Mn USD — Russia, Germany, Turkmenistan, Italy, Belarus

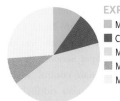

EXPORTS by products
- Minerals & combustibles 10%
- Chemical products 11%
- Metals & manufactured products 44%
- Machines & electrical equipment 9%
- Miscellaneous 26%

IMPORTS by products
- Minerals & combustibles 47%
- Metals & manufactured products 5%
- Chemical products 6%
- Plastic & rubber 5%
- Machines & electrical equipment 14%
- Miscellaneous 23%

STANDARD OF LIVING / PURCHASING POWER

Indicators	Ukraine	Regional average	DC average
GNP per capita (PPP dollars)	3700	7936	6548
GNP per capita	700	3052	3565
Human development index	0.748	0.796	0.702
Wealthiest 10% share of national income	23	26	32
Urban population percentage	68	61	60
Percentage under 15 years old	18	20	32
Number of telephones per 1000 inhabitants	199	273	157
Number of computers per 1000 inhabitants	18	98	64

United Kingdom

Coface analysis   Short-term: **A2**

STRENGTHS

- Fiscal restraint, simplified administrative procedures, integration into the English-speaking world and labour market flexibility make the United Kingdom the second largest recipient of direct foreign investment in the world.
- The City, the world's leading currency market and second largest venture capital market, and Edinburgh's financial centre are a powerful magnet for the services industry.
- Very low unemployment, with jobs growing in services and shrinking in manufacturing.

WEAKNESSES

- Persistent cleavage between prosperous service and housing sector and weak manufacturing sector.
- Low productivity, due to inadequate capital and human resources investment, and strength of sterling expose industry to foreign competition.
- Housing boom, while spurring spending, has forced households into heavy debt and caused house prices to soar in the South East.
- Privatization of public services has not produced better or cheaper services in every case. Sectors still under state control, such as health and education, are also riddled with problems.

RISK ASSESSMENT

Economic growth remained strong in 2002, although it is trending lower. Consumer spending, the economy's main driving force, has been buoyed by rising property values, wage increases, low unemployment and attractive interest rates. Government spending on health, education and transport has also boosted economic activity. Despite the recovery in high-tech sales exports have suffered because of the strong pound. Corporate investment has sharply declined because of low utilization of production capacity, uncertainties about the recovery and the fairly high cost of financing.

In 2003 the economy should gradually pick up thanks to higher foreign demand and the recovery in investment. Consumer spending should fall back slightly as house prices start to decline. However, spending could plummet if house prices slump. The government's economic policy will remain easy. Despite the reappearance of a slight deficit, the government should maintain a high level of public spending without raising taxes. The Bank of England is expected to leave interest rates unchanged until the end of the year.

The persistent difficulties plaguing the manufacturing sector led to a rise in the number of bankruptcies and defaults recorded by Coface. Sectors exposed to international competition, such as textiles, apparel and metal processing, were the hardest hit. The improvement in trading conditions for manufacturing, if sustained, should reduce the number of defaults.

KEY ECONOMIC INDICATORS

%	1998	1999	2000	2001	2002 (e)	2003 (f)
Economic growth	3	2.4	3	2	1.6	2.3
Consumer spending (% change)	3.8	4.5	5.1	4.1	3.5	2.5
Investment (% change)	13.2	0.9	3.9	0.3	−4.7	1.9
Inflation	2.7	1.5	0.7	2.4	1.6	1.3
Unemployment	6.3	6	5.5	5.1	5.1	5.2
Short-term interest rate	7.3	5.4	6.1	5	4	4.3
Public-sector balance/GDP	0.4	1.1	3.9	1	−1	−1.5
National debt/GDP	61.4	56.4	54	52.5	53	52
Exports (% change)	3	5.4	10.3	1.2	−0.9	4
Imports (% change)	9.6	8.9	10.9	2.8	1	5.5
Current account balance/GDP	−0.6	−2.1	−1.8	−2.1	−2	−2.2

e = estimated, f = forecast

MAIN ECONOMIC SECTORS

■ Textiles and clothing

Britain's embattled weavers and garment makers are caught on the horns of a dilemma: on the one hand, they are subject to increasing competition from South-East Asian rivals and, on the other, their exports are hamstrung by the strength of the pound. The UK market continues to provide growth opportunities, but consumer demand for the latest fashions is putting manufacturers under pressure. Traditional retailers are finding it difficult to weather competition from discount stores, department stores and new foreign stores.

■ Retail

Against a background of strong demand the retail sector on the whole continued to perform well in 2002. The expansion of out-of-town chain stores has slowed, while there are signs that food chains are turning to smaller premises located within town-centre shopping malls. Food chains are continuing to diversify into non-food retail segments, while the DIY market continues to expand significantly.

■ Meat trade

The meat industry has started to recover from the problems caused by the foot-and-mouth crisis in 2001. Vast sums have been committed to ensuring that meat supplies for export as well as supermarkets are properly sourced and tracked. Trading conditions for animal feeds and additives remain difficult

becasue it is taking a long time to rebuild livestock.

■ Telecommunications

Mobile telephony grew moderately, while it is early days still for the 3G equipment (UMTS standard) business. Many question marks hang over the impact, and adoption by the consumer, of this technology, which analysts expected would fuel the sector's growth. Cable TV and telephone operators continue to grapple with the debt contracted to build new networks.

■ Construction

Economic stability has continued to drive growth in residential and office construction in the major cities, in particular London. Sizeable orders have been placed to improve mainline railway tracks and the London Underground.

■ Iron and steel

The year 2002 was again a difficult one for the British iron and steel industry. Overcapacity persists in many segments despite the recent winding-up of ASW. Although the domestic market offers growth opportunities iron and steel producers, dealers and processing companies have felt the squeeze on margins caused by fierce foreign competition. Industrial customers, particuliarly in the automobile sector, are increasingly turning to foreign suppliers, mainly from the Far East. However, there was no dumping on the UK market as leading European steel producers forced, for better or worse, higher prices on the United Kingdom.

■ Payment

Cheques are a widely used means of payment, representing 60 per cent of transactions. However, they do not guarantee any genuine security since issuing bad cheques does not constitute a criminal offence. The drawer of a cheque may refuse payment at any time, via the RDPR (Refer to Drawer Please Represent) option. Cheques remain valid for six months.

Although payment by bill of exchange is uncommon in domestic commerce, it affords greater security than a cheque.

Bank transfers represent about 35 per cent of all transactions. Besides SWIFT transfers used for international payments, leading British companies use two highly automated inter-bank transfer systems–BACS (Bankers' Automated Clearing Services) and CHAPS (Clearing House Automated Payment Systems).

■ Debt collection

Debt collection agencies or solicitors handle the recovery of overdue payment. With regard to the Late Payment of Commercial Debts (Interest) Act 1998, small companies have – since 1 November 1998 – the right to demand interest penalties on overdue payments owed by large companies, whether public or private.

This law, which went into effect in successive stages with the last stage in force since 7 August 2002, now permits all commercial companies to bill interest once they encounter a late payment. Unless otherwise stipulated in the contract, the applicable rate will be the Bank of England's dealing rate increased by 8 basis points.

Recovery by legal means aims at obtaining a ruling after submission of a 'claim form' to the appropriate legal authority.

A summary judgment, which can be obtained rapidly for undisputed claims, is more difficult to obtain whenever the defendant files a defence.

However, the reform of procedural rules known as the Woolf reform, considered by lawyers to be a major breakthrough in dealing with disputed debts, went into effect on 26 April 1999.

Application of the new procedural rules has been progressively shortening litigation timeframes since the parties will have more incentive to find a negotiated settlement either directly or through mediation (ie ADR: Alternative Dispute Resolution).

Introduction of different 'tracks', depending on the amount outstanding and establishment of hearing timetables by the courts, are two of the approaches in use to speed up proceedings.

Judgments are enforced either through conventional methods (service by bailiff, attachment of debtor assets with subsequent auction) or directly by order of 'statutory demand', affording a debtor 21 days to settle his debt or face a winding-up petition. After expiration of a new 21-day period, and in the absence of serious payment proposals, filing such a petition results in a liquidation order by the court, as the debtor is regarded as insolvent.

Under specific conditions where claims are undisputed, that enforcement procedure may be applied directly without requiring a prior ruling.

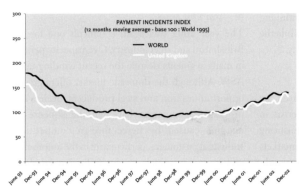

PAYMENT INCIDENTS INDEX
(12 months moving average - base 100 : World 1995)

— WORLD
— United Kingdom

Uzbekistan

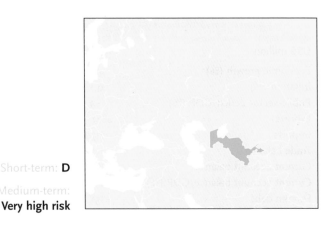

Coface analysis

Short-term: **D**

Medium-term:
Very high risk

STRENGTHS

- Rich in natural resources (mainly cotton and gold).
- Moves to diversify into other raw materials (oil and gas) and industries (cars).
- Market with good potential as most densely populated Central Asian country within the CIS (over 25 million inhabitants).
- Home to US military bases since military intervention in Afghanistan. Official financial assistance slowly renewed.

WEAKNESSES

- Country's main assets subject to exogenous pressures (world prices, climate).
- Government's tight control over economic policy and lack of reform constitute obstacles to continued assistance from multilateral organizations.
- Prospect of currency market liberalization could create high level of indebtedness.
- Islamic fundamentalism curbed, but underlying causes (social discontent) unaddressed.

RISK ASSESSMENT

Uzbekistan's macroeconomic performance reveals the problems with the 'Uzbek path' of transition: growth has weakened and inflation is high. Industry is obsolete and the country is increasingly dependent on cotton and gold, its main export earners.

The external deficit was covered by debt. Debt service is increasing the country's borrowing requirement. While moves are under way to liberalize the foreign currency market, the gradual harmonization of the official exchange rate with the market rate has revealed an unbearable level of debt burden.

IMF assistance will be much needed to avoid difficulties in servicing the foreign debt. But such assistance will be hard to materialize in the long term. The government, whose structural reform record is extremely poor, will not favour reforms regarded as too constraining. Nevertheless, the country's strategic importance to the West was highlighted by the setting up of US bases prior to the military offensive in Afghanistan and is demonstrated by growing Western financial assistance.

KEY ECONOMIC INDICATORS

US$ million	1998	1999	2000	2001	2002 (e)	2003 (f)
Economic growth (%)	4.4	4.1	4	4.5	3	3
Inflation (%)	26.1	25.2	28	26.6	27	27
Public-sector deficit/GDP (%)	−3	−2.8	−1	−1	−2.9	−3.1
Exports	2888	2671	2935	2940	2960	2750
Imports	2717	2594	2441	2490	2560	2650
Trade balance	171	77	494	450	400	100
Current account balance	−39	−203	72	−60	−230	−210
Current account balance/GDP (%)	−0.4	−2	−0.5	−0.5	−3	−3
Foreign debt	2751	4163	4300	4500	4900	5200
Debt service/Exports (%)	10.7	16.3	25.8	22.6	23	23
Reserves (import months)	1.8	2.6	2.1	2.4	2	1.6

e = estimated, f = forecast

CONDITIONS OF ACCESS TO THE MARKET

■ Market overview

Uzbekistan does not yet constitute a 'market' for foreign firms, especially small and medium-sized ones. There is no regular trade, and therefore no market development opportunities for consumer goods. Imports into the area are limited to basic foodstuffs (sugar, flour, oil, etc). Large companies can nonetheless find business opportunities if they come up with the necessary funding.

The country's debt servicing capacity is restricted by plummeting export revenues, which smeans that foreign business projects are closely vetted.

Foreign investment in the country is stagnant. The situation will improve only when trade is liberalized and structural reforms begin in earnest.

■ Means of entry

Other than foreign exchange controls there are no special restrictions on imports of consumer and capital goods. At present the number of licences and quarterly foreign exchange quota levels for imports into Uzbekistan are extremely low. These restrictions are presented as an essential launching pad for the soum's free convertibility.

The recommended means of payment is the irrevocable and confirmed letter of credit. Locals holding a licence and a conversion quota are permitted to make a maximum 15 per cent down-payment on import contracts. Imports are thus made mainly on consignment, with payment of the remaining 85 per cent being effected only on sale of the products and conversion of the local currency into foreign exchange.

■ Attitude towards foreign investors

A painstaking review of foreign investment legislation has been undertaken and is still in progress. In general, the fast-changing and volatile situation in the country makes it difficult to give accurate information. Current Uzbek legislation offers safeguards against discrimination, nationalization, expropriation and changes to legislation that would affect investments in the years ahead, while permitting unrestricted repatriation of profits. However, foreign exchange controls dilute the latter measure.

Substantial barriers remain in force. They include continued restrictions on the acquisition and use of foreign exchange against a background of multiple exchange rates and centralized decision making; a marginal private sector; profit repatriation that is allowed in principle but problematic in practice; cumbersome administrative procedures and controls; and highly changeable and unpredictable legislation.

■ Foreign exchange regulations

Nobody yet knows the date for the introduction of a freely convertible currency based on a single exchange rate. It seems that this is scheduled for spring 2003. Failure to implement such a scheme would result in the country's further isolation, from which it will be difficult to bounce back.

OPPORTUNITY SCOPE

■ Population   24.8 million inhabitants   ■ GDP   7,666 million US dollars

Breakdown of internal demand (GDP + imports)   %
■ Private consumption   46
■ Public spending   14
■ Investment   8

Exports: 44% of GDP ▷   ◁ Imports: 39% of GDP

1

MAIN DESTINATIONS OF EXPORTS

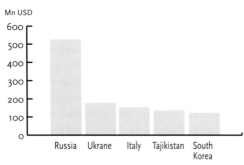

Russia Ukrane Italy Tajikistan South Korea

MAIN ORIGINS OF IMPORTS

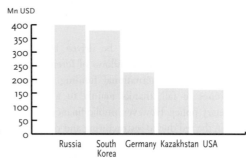

Russia South Korea Germany Kazakhstan USA

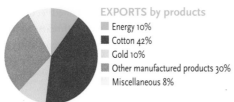

EXPORTS by products
■ Energy 10%
■ Cotton 42%
■ Gold 10%
■ Other manufactured products 30%
■ Miscellaneous 8%

IMPORTS by products
■ Equipment 50%
■ Food products 16%
■ Miscellaneous 34%

STANDARD OF LIVING / PURCHASING POWER

Indicators	Uzbekistan	Regional average	DC average
GNP per capita (PPP dollars)	2360	7936	6548
GNP per capita	360	3052	3565
Human development index	0.727	0.796	0.702
Wealthiest 10% share of national income	33	26	32
Urban population percentage	37	61	60
Percentage under 15 years old	36	20	32
Number of telephones per 1000 inhabitants	67	273	157
Number of computers per 1000 inhabitants	n/a	98	64

n/a – not available

Federal Republic of Yugoslavia

(Serbia-Montenegro)

Short-term: **D**

Medium-term:
Very high risk

Coface analysis

RISK ASSESSMENT

Economic growth should be driven by reconstruction and increasing inflows of foreign direct investment and international funding. Inflation continues to fall, thanks mainly to a sensible monetary policy. However, public finances remain well in the red due to restructuring and rising debt service.

The country's external position is even worse: high financing needs underpinned by a large current account deficit. As these needs are largely covered by international financial assistance there is little risk of a short-term crisis. The planned agreement with London Club private creditors on the partial restructuring of the country's foreign

debt is taking a long time to work out.

The political and social situation remains precarious. The invalidation of the presidential elections held in December 2002 in Serbia, on account of the low turn-out, has revived the struggle for power between the moderate nationalist Kostunica, winner of the election, and the reformist Prime Minister Djinjic. It has also exacerbated the constitutional crisis and could delay reforms designed to bring about a sustained economic recovery. There are also many threats to the country's territorial integrity, even though Montenegro's desire for independence seems for the time being to have abated.

KEY ECONOMIC INDICATORS						
US$ million	1998	1999	2000	2001	2002 (e)	2003 (f)
Economic growth (%)	2.5	−18	5	5.5	4	5
Inflation (%)	29.5	42.1	69.9	91.1	21.2	12.6
Public-sector balance/GDP (%)	n/a	n/a	−3	−1.3	−5.7	−5.3
Unemployment (%)	25.1	26.5	27.3	28.5	32	30
Exports	3033	1676	1923	2003	2250	2618
Imports	4849	3295	3711	4837	5567	6119
Trade balance	−1816	−1619	−1788	−2834	−3318	−3500
Current account balance	−660	−764	−610	−1187	−1646	−1722
Current account balance/GDP (%)	−4.8	−7.5	−7.6	−10.9	−12.8	−12.4
Foreign debt	10539	10744	11403	11948	8598	9397
Reserves (import months)	0.7	0.9	1.4	2.5	2.9	3.3

n/a – not available   e = estimated, f = forecast

The Americas

2

The US Economy and Foreign Policy in 2003

Experts from Oxford Analytica, London

The inflation-adjusted, trade-weighted value of the dollar begins 2003 higher than at the outset of the recession in the first quarter of 2001. It is 30 per cent higher in real-effective terms than it was in 1995. Assuming the world does not have an unlimited capacity to accumulate claims on the US economy, dollar adjustment is inevitable. How it occurs will have major ramifications for growth.

The US Economy

Flight-to-safety capital inflows and currency intervention by Asian central banks over the past two years have offset the falling US stock market and a growing interest rate differential with the rest of the developed world to sustain the value of the dollar. This in turn has supported low interest rates across the yield curve and facilitated an expansion of household debt and consumer expenditure. Hence, economic growth in the next two to three years depends upon a continuation of this dynamic, meaning that the dollar holds the fortunes of the economy. Yet in the final analysis, the world cannot provide unlimited funds to the US economy, making a weaker dollar inevitable.

Prior to the current business cycle, the last synchronous global downturn was in 1980-81. The ensuing five-year period saw the dollar climb 53 per cent in trade-weighted, inflation-adjusted ('real-effective') terms as US growth leapt ahead of that of trading partners. Real year-on-year GDP growth recovered from the 'double dip' of 1982 to above 3 per cent for most of the remainder of the decade. Yet in a crucial respect the two instances are wholly dissimilar: the current account was in surplus during 1981-82, leaving ample scope for trade deficits as US growth outpaced the rest of the world, without putting undue pressure on the dollar. (The current account fell into deficit from 1983, reached 3.3 per cent of GDP in 1987, and returned to balance in 1991.) Today's global downturn finds the US economy encumbered with a current account deficit of close to 5 per cent of GDP. Continued US growth in excess of European and Japanese growth will only add to this deficit, putting greater pressure on the dollar.

Real depreciation. The capacity of the US economy to attract global capital is formidable, suggesting a further period of dollar strength and US GDP 'outperformance'. However, at some point, dollar depreciation is inevitable. It need not be wholly nominal: the real-effective exchange rate can depreciate through bilateral exchange rates as well as the domestic price level. A constant nominal exchange rate accompanied by domestic deflation yields real depreciation. Using a global macro-economic model to simulate such an outcome is useful for understanding the implications for growth and other aspects of the economy. This exercise assumes that inflation slows to 0.6 per cent in 2003 (it is 1.0 per cent on the eve of 2003, as measured by the GDP deflator) and deflation manifests in 2004 at a 1.4 per cent annual rate and 2.7 per cent annual rate in 2005.

Because conventional economic dynamics are embedded in the model, the simulation results in a large monetary policy-induced boost to private sector spending. The Federal Reserve reacts promptly to the decline in consumer prices, reducing interest rates to zero in the first quarter of 2003. The federal funds rate remains at zero for two years. This massive monetary expansion raises the demand for stocks, providing a strong boost to equity prices, which reach a level 20 per cent higher than baseline projections by the end of 2005. These gains raise private sector wealth, triggering strong advances in private consumption: annual growth in household expenditure increases by several percentage points during the simulation period compared to the baseline trajectory. Lower interest rates and higher equity prices also reduce the cost of investment, sparking growth in business investment to rates seen in the mid- to late-1990s.

Liquidity trap. While this outcome is welcome news – and explains the bullish expectations of some forecasters – the responses which underlie it are unrealistic in the current environment. The economy faces something of a 'liquidity trap' in the aftermath of the (record-breaking) debt-financed binge of the 'new economy' era, as it did in the aftermath of the 1920s and as Japan did in the aftermath of the 1980s. Not only is debt at record high levels, but also the outlook for inflation is at record low levels, meaning that economic agents will increasingly understand the real burden of their debts – distinctly higher now than in earlier episodes of debt expansion, which were accompanied by higher levels of inflation, which erodes debt values. Although current conditions are exceptional, to ignore them – as most models and most consensus economists do – is naive.

More realistic results from the deflation/ nominal dollar rigidity scenario require imposing something of a liquidity trap on the model: the response of private consumption, housing investment and business investment to monetary expansion should be dampened to reflect high current indebtedness and the precaution of economic decisionmakers, which results in increased savings by households and deferred investment by firms. Altogether, the assumptions of a mild liquidity trap, rigid nominal exchange rate and domestic deflation produce results which contrast markedly with consensus forecasts for the US economy (which are proxied by the macro-economic model's baseline forecast):

- **Real GDP growth.** Growth under the baseline forecast is 2.5, 3.2 and 2.9 per cent in 2003-2005 respectively. Under the hypothetical scenario, it is 1.1, 1.4 and 1.9 per cent. Baseline private consumption growth is 1.4, 1.9 and 2.0 per cent , compared to -0.5, -0.6 and +0.4 per cent in the hypothetical scenario. Baseline private investment growth is 5.6, 7.6 and 6.5 per cent, compared to 1.9, 1.4 and 5.1 per cent.

- **External balance.** In the baseline scenario, exports grow 8.7 per cent in 2003, 10.1 per cent in 2004 and 8.7 per cent in 2005, outpacing import growth of 5.6, 7.9 and 6.7 per cent. In the hypothetical scenario, export growth is roughly the same but import growth collapses to 1.7 per cent in 2003, 1.5 per cent in 2004 and 1.4 per cent in 2005. Thus, as expected, the real depreciation – aided by slower GDP growth – results in a markedly smaller external imbalance. The current account deficit falls to 3.5 per cent of GDP in 2003, 2.6 per cent of GDP in 2004 and 1.8 per cent of GDP in 2005 – compared to baseline deficits of 4.0, 3.6 and 3.4 per cent.

- **Other indicators.** Unemployment rises to 6.1, 6.6 and 7.2 per cent in the hypothetical scenario.

In the baseline forecast, unemployment actually falls to 5.5, 5.0 and 4.9 per cent. The US government budget deficit in the hypothetical scenario is 3.1, 2.8 and 2.2 per cent of GDP; in the baseline forecast, it is 2.7, 2.1 and 1.6 per cent of GDP.

- **Global impact.** The painful US adjustment under the hypothetical scenario would produce a tougher global economic climate. Inflation in the developed world would fall to 0.6 in 2004 and zero in 2005. Growth would fall to 1.7, 2.0 and 2.3 per cent in 2003-05 respectively. Global growth would fall to 3.0, 3.1 and 3.2 per cent.

Counterfactual. If one does not impose the liquidity trap, but maintains the deflation assumption, households then continue to respond to easier borrowing conditions (short-term rates fall to zero under the deflation scenario), and the economy runs up staggering deficits. Real GDP growth rates exceed 6 per cent by 2004 and 2005. Import growth picks up even in the face of the real depreciation. As a consequence, the current-account deficit does not narrow, but hits 5.9 per cent of GDP at the end of 2005, compared to the baseline forecast of 3.4 per cent. Yet maintaining this dynamic requires a limitless ability of the US economy to issue dollar liabilities to the rest of the world. Despite the numerous advantages of the US economy, and the US dollar's central role in the global system of payments, such an outcome is impossible. It would mean not only infinite foreign appetite for US assets, but also a painful and politically intolerable dislocation of the US tradable-goods sector.

The opposite of this outcome – ie a shrinking current account deficit – requires a real depreciation of the dollar. Yet significant bilateral dollar adjustment is being consistently prevented by 'flight to safety' capital inflows and East Asian interventions to stem local currency appreciation. The latter are plainly visible during 2001-02 in correlations between the dollar trade-weighted exchange rate and East Asian purchases of dollar-denominated reserves. This suggests that the burden of real dollar adjustment will be shared by modest nominal depreciation and outright deflation. An economy producing below-potential GDP growth for 2003 and into the medium term would be consistent with deflation, thanks to the burden of an output gap (see OADB, October 28, 2002, II).

In conclusion, a year of continued consumer debt expansion and GDP 'outperformance' (vis-a-vis the rest of the developed world) is possible – given

2

the proclivity of external capital to seek shelter in US assets and Asian central banks to resist local currency appreciation. However, this will produce current-account deficits so large as to trigger adjustment in subsequent years. Such adjustment requires a depreciated real dollar, which looks increasingly likely to be accomplished through domestic deflation due to the rigidity of bilateral dollar exchange rates.

US Foreign Policy

US foreign policy in 2003 will be dominated by Iraq. While the 'war on terror' will continue, its public profile will probably be lower than during the past twelve months. President Bush's Iraq stratergy will remain a major factor in foreign policy considerations in the months ahead. Many other policy areas will be influenced by what happens to Saddam Hussein's regime and the stance that other states choose to take vis-a-vis the evolution of events in the Gulf.

Resolution 1441, adopted by the UN Security Council on November 8, represented a compromise within the US administration, as well as between the five permanent members of the Council. The Bush team was divided between those who favoured immediate unilateral action and others who were insistent that such a venture should not precede an attempt to build an international coalition. These divisions will continue to shape the internal debate within Washington in coming weeks.

Scenarios. Within the range of plausible scenarios, the starkest would be Iraq's absolute compliance with the UN inspectors or an early decision by Baghdad to stage a showdown with the UN and, by extension, the United States:

1. **Compliance.** On December 8, Saddam formally declared that Iraq had no biological, chemical or nuclear programme, but published a lengthy list of 'dual use' material, which Baghdad insists exists only for benign purposes. The aim is keep UN inspectors busy for months. In these circumstances, having started along the 'UN route', it could be very difficult for the United States to repudiate it. However, infighting inside the administration would intensify as those who favour toppling Saddam directed blame toward moderates, notably Secretary of State Colin Powell, for the failure to bring down Saddam.

2. **Defiance.** Saddam may yet be willing to engineer a showdown with the UN inspectors. This could occur for one of three main reasons:

- Saddam senses his own authority has been undermined at home by the inspectors' return;
- The stronger UN resolution combined with an advance in technological capacity means that the UN uncovers material that Iraq had been confident that it could keep concealed.
- Saddam calculates that the apparent unanimity at the UN is weak and that either Russia or France would not actually permit a resolution endorsing military force to prevail. This would be a serious miscalculation: an act of outright defiance by Saddam would probably prompt the White House speedily to initiate an air war.

Other outcomes. However, Washington is focused on two other options:

1. **Periodic minor infringement.** The 'hawk' faction fears that Saddam will regularly impede, but not directly obstruct, the efforts of inspectors. They assume that he will trigger a series of mini-crises, in a new version of the 'cheat and retreat' tactics he has employed in the past. None of these acts of intransigence would be on a scale large enough, despite the robust language of Resolution 1441, to prompt the UN to challenge Saddam. In such a scenario, Washington would be subject to a degree of humiliation that would become an issue in US domestic politics. In that case, the administration would revisit the entire unilateralist versus multilateralist debate, but with momentum sliding towards the unilateralists.

2. **Compliance then defiance.** In this scenario, Saddam would comply for the first four to six months of the new inspection arrangements. However, by late spring, Iraq would be less accommodating. The calculation in Baghdad would probably be that beyond March, the Pentagon would be reluctant to despatch a large army given the high temperatures in the Gulf region. The further assumption would be that Bush would be reluctant to risk conflict in late 2003 or during 2004 – the year of his re-election effort. If this is Saddam's thinking, it could be a substantial miscalculation as it cannot be assumed that a war would not be fought in the summer of 2003 or in 2004. Policy therefore remains in flux and is highly susceptible to the development of events as the inspectors renew their activities. The most plausible assumption remains that conflict is still more likely than not, although it is less likely now than before Bush took the UN route.

Other policy areas. Many other key areas of policy are likely to be affected by how the course of events proceed in Iraq:

1. **Middle East peace process.** It is widely ex-

pected in Washington that Likud will win the Israeli election. The uncertain element is whether the next government will be drawn exclusively from the Right or whether the coalition will include other elements. This will help shape whether or not the administration considers it worth pursuing a high-profile peace initiative in 2003 or settles for seeking what it perceives to be just enough to assist friendly Arab states whose citizens may be further embittered if Saddam is toppled. The balance of probability is that despite the efforts of Powell and UK Prime Minister Tony Blair, the more modest strategy will be followed.

2. Russian relations. After a period this autumn when Russia relations deteriorated due to disagreements over Iraq, it has now become a key priority for the White House to restore its relationship with Vladimir Putin and provide reassurances to Russia over its interests in Iraq. The administration is thus likely to indulge Moscow on several fronts, from economic policy to the conduct of the Chechen conflict. A war in Iraq need not trigger a major Bush-Putin split.

3. Europe. Relations between Washington and Western Europe are particularly volatile. Much will depend on whether military action against Iraq takes place and, if so, with what degree of UN authority. If the UN does not back a US campaign, most Europeans states will tacitly oppose the war.

4. China. Two factors suggest that the improvement in US-China relations secured in 2002 will endure into 2003: the desire of the Bush administration to retain Beijing's support in the 'war against terror'; and the determination of the new leadership in Beijing to avoid foreign policy crises, especially involving the United States. In this respect, the outlook is brighter than it has been for some time, with Beijing's recent concessions towards Taiwan (on the question of direct flights between the island and the mainland) helping (temporarily) to defuse a perennial source of friction in Sino-US ties.

5. North Korea. Pyongyang's recently disclosed covert nuclear programme challenges US interests in non-proliferation and security in North-east Asia. Washington's stated preference for a diplomatic solution reflects a qualitative distinction drawn between the threats posed by Iraq's and North Korea's weapons of mass destruction. Despite its renewed brinkmanship and bellicose rhetoric, Pyongyang is more interested in trading its weapons for guarantees of regime survival than aggression. However, the Bush administration has no desire to be seen to give in to blackmail, or to repeat the accommodation reached by Clinton administration during the 1994 North Korean nuclear crisis.

6. South Asia. In Afghanistan, renewed US pledges of aid and to expanding the international peace-keeping remit beyond Kabul should bolster the still-precarious authority of the interim administration. Although Washington's focus has moved elsewhere, the task of flushing out al-Qaida remnants in the border region with Pakistan is unfinished. Moreover, Afghanistan's prominence in the initial phase of the war against terrorism means that US policy there is seen as symbolic of its long-term commitment to stabilising weak states in the Islamic world.

As Washington currently enjoys close relations with India and Pakistan, its leverage will remain key to containing their posturing over Kashmir. If the rise of political Islam in Pakistan puts Islamabad under pressure to ration its support for US positions on Iraq and other issues, Washington's strengthening bond with India (a greater strategic long-term priority than its post-September 11 expedient compact with Pakistan) may assert itself in tacit support for Delhi's position on the territorial dispute.

War on terror. The Iraq factor is likely to crowd out the broader 'war on terror'. The anti-terrorism campaign has in any case largely moved on to a stage whereby there is now a person-by-person, cell-by-cell identification and arrest/elimination of al-Qaida operatives. Attention within the 'war of terror' is likely to edge away from the Afghan theatre towards Pakistan, Yemen and areas of South-east Asia where al-Qaida sympathisers exist and toward attempts to break the finances of terrorist organisations. However, US foreign policy priorities could change if Osama bin Laden were to re-emerge as a persistent, prominent and public figure. Unless that happens, or al-Qaida succeeded in conducting another truly spectacular act of terrorism, the war on terror will probably adopt a lower profile.

In conclusion, the prospect of war against Iraq will have a number of secondary consequences for US policy, including a desire to avoid friction with Russia. Policies towards the Middle East will nonetheless remain incremental and opportunistic. There remains little enthusiasm in the White House to invest real political capital in what is still viewed as a highly implausible peace initiative.

2

Country @rating scale for the Americas

Sylvia Greisman and Olivier Oechslin
Coface Country Risk and Economic Studies Department, Paris

The country @rating scale measures the average level of short-term non-payment risk presented by companies in a particular country. It reflects the extent to which a country's economic, financial and political outlook influences financial commitments of local companies. It is thus complementary to @rating Credit Opinions on companies.

Uncertainty surrounding the economic recovery in conjunction with the profusion of financial scandals has triggered a financial market collapse and prompted investors to be overly cautious. That heightened aversion to risk has exacerbated financing difficulties for companies in both North and South America. Macroeconomically, this climate of mistrust has impeded an investment recovery, notably in the United States, and caused sharp depreciations of emerging country currencies. A return to growth will thus largely depend on restoring confidence in financial markets amid a still uncertain geopolitical context that notably affects oil product prices and investment decisions.

In North America, US authorities reacted quickly in implementing expansionary monetary and fiscal policies, which have also benefited the Canadian and, to a lesser extent, Mexican economies. However, despite relative improvement in company profitability and the introduction of new accounting standards intended to restore investor confidence, the long-awaited investment recovery has not really developed. USA growth has thus remained largely driven by consumption, which has been showing signs of flagging.

In South America, recession, financial imbalances, and political instability have marked the continent. Brazil, very dependent on financial markets, has suffered the most from the crisis of confidence. Higher-risk premiums and the real's depreciation have undermined the country's public finances and companies carrying dollar debt. Argentina has remained in the grip of a severe economic, financial and political crisis. In Venezuela, the political crisis has plunged the country into deep depression. Only Chile can boast a macroeconomic environment and a geographic distribution of exports somewhat comparable to those found in North America.

Those difficulties have spurred aspirations for political change resulting in the election of political figures who question the validity of economic liberalization. However, they enjoy little room for manoeuvre, squeezed notably by financial equilibriums that could hamper implementation of ambitious programmes and disillusion a large proportion of the electorate.

This uncertain environment has severely undermined company solvency in both North and South America and prompted the downgrading of several countries. The ratings of Brazil, Paraguay and Uruguay have thus been downgraded to category C and that of Venezuela to category D. The United States continues to be rated A2. Conversely, a brighter growth outlook and improved payment behaviour have prompted the removal of two countries' ratings from the negative watchlist, Canada (A1) and Mexico (A4).

2

■ Countries rated A2

Default likelihood has remained low on average even though the country's economic and political environment or local company payment behaviour is slightly less good than in countries rated A1.

In the United States, household consumption has basically been carrying the economy. An investment recovery has remained slow in coming despite both monetary and tax incentives. Positive signs for companies, such as profitability improvement and stabilization of the number of bankruptcies, have accompanied a rebound of orders in some economic sectors, notably electronics. However, companies have been sticking to their wait-and-see attitude amid low production capacity utilization rates, stock market volatility, and the greater selectivity exercised by banks in the face notably of the downgrading of many companies by rating agencies.

The economic upturn led to a reduction in the number of bankruptcies in 2002 and resulted in a decline in payment incidents at the end of the year. However, both the number of bankruptcies and frequency of payment defaults have remained above their 2000 level. The most exposed companies belong to a variety of sectors such as new technologies, textiles, car industry subcontracting or metal and paper product wholesalers.

■ Countries rated A3

Company payment behaviour is generally less good than in the preceding categories and could be affected by a change in the country's economic and political environment, although the likelihood of that leading to large-scale payment defaults remains relatively low.

Chile has had to contend with the collapse of copper prices and the contraction of its export markets. The country has nonetheless remained sheltered from financial crisis since, unlike other regional economies, Chile does not suffer from macroeconomic imbalances. Sagging growth and the peso's decline have affected company payment behaviour while the foreign exchange debt carried by some companies has been increasing significantly. However, the growth upturn expected in 2003 should favour improvement.

■ Countries rated A4

These countries often present fairly mediocre payment behaviour that could be affected by an economic downturn, although the probability of that causing a large number of payment defaults remains moderate.

After a slight recession in 2001 the Mexican economy has been progressively finding its way back to growth. The crisis of confidence buffeting South America has only moderately affected Mexico. In the near term its economy will especially depend on the situation in the United States, as well as on the exchange rate trend. Although the peso's appreciation had been handicapping Mexican exports until spring 2002, its depreciation has now been helping to stimulate sales. However, that has also been increasing inflationary pressures, prompting tighter monetary policy and penalizing private investment.

The economic upturn and concomitant decline in payment defaults prompted the removal of Mexico's rating from the negative watchlist in 2002. Some companies carrying dollar debt nonetheless remain vulnerable, notably in the textile and computer sectors.

■ Countries rated B

A precarious economic environment could affect company payment behaviour, which is often mediocre.

Colombia has been contending with a resurgence of political violence. Meanwhile, the country's external debt has grown substantially in recent years and now constitutes a significant weakness. The debt burden has left the new president with little room for manoeuvre to increase security spending. In this context growth has remained moderate and the profit decline caused by the gloomy economic conditions of 2002 have undermined company solvency.

Since late 2001, Peru's growth has gained momentum, driven essentially by exploitation of the Antamina copper and zinc mine. Sustaining a high growth rate in 2003 will depend on this sector generating a possible knock-on effect that benefits the rest of the economy. Thus far no such effect is discernible.

■ Countries rated C

A very precarious economic and political environment could worsen payment behaviour that is already often poor.

Very dependent on market sentiment, Brazil has suffered from investor risk aversion and the Argentina crisis contagion amid a climate of uncertainty linked to the electoral campaign. That situation has resulted in a sharp depreciation of the real, higher risk premiums on international markets and higher interest rates. The new Brazilian president has very little room for manoeuvre in a very tight financial situation and difficult international environment. Growth should remain weak in 2003 and, despite a significant reduction of the current account deficit, the economy has remained vulnerable to a market confidence crisis due to its still substantial financing needs.

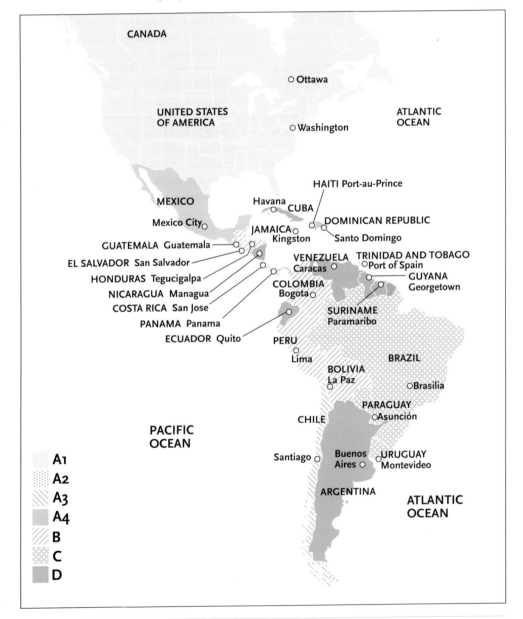

Although some companies have been able to exploit the competitive edge resulting from the real's decline, the depreciation has also weakened companies carrying heavy dollar debt or integrating imports to a substantial extent in their production. In a context of sluggish domestic demand companies are encountering difficulties in passing the increased costs on to customers, which affects company profitability. In that difficult environment

payment defaults by Brazilian companies have increased progressively. That deterioration, in conjunction with the country's difficult economic and financial situation, has prompted the downgrading of Brazil's rating to category C.

In Uruguay, economic activity fell sharply in 2002 with the country reeling from the Argentina crisis contagion, massive withdrawals by depositors in the banking sector, and the collapse of the

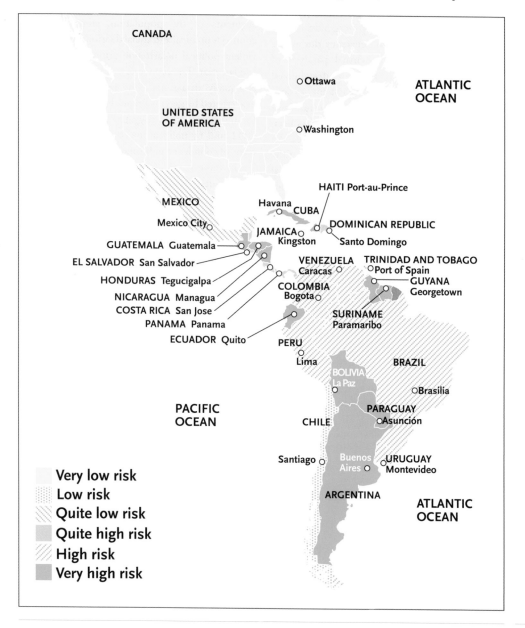

Very low risk
Low risk
Quite low risk
Quite high risk
High risk
Very high risk

currency. Growth should remain negative in 2003. Amid severe deterioration of company payment behaviour the country rating has been downgraded to category C.

■ Countries rated D

The economic and political environment presents a very high level of risk that exacerbates generally deplorable payment behaviour.

A severe economic, financial, and political crisis has continued to grip Argentina. The collapse of the economy and currency during the first half of 2002 and the virtual paralysis of financial channels have seriously destabilized companies and triggered a payment default explosion. Since summer economic indicators have steadied. Although domestic production has been benefiting from a new competitiveness the conditions for durable recovery (restoration of the State's credibility, renegotiation of the external debt, a viable banking sector rescue plan and so on) are still far from being met.

The November 2002 elections in Ecuador brought to power a candidate dissociated from the country's traditional political class. The new president's room for manoeuvre will nonetheless be very narrow, considering the very heavy debt burden. Moreover, the current account deficit has been increasing dangerously due to the loss of competitiveness resulting from the economy's dollarization.

Venezuela's political situation deteriorated sharply in 2002. After the failed coup in April President Chavez' return, backed by the poorest segments of the population, stigmatized the country's political and social divisions. A climate of violent political polarization gripped the country late last year. The economic and financial situation is equally disastrous. The recession has been exacerbated by sagging oil production, accentuated by the general strike triggered in early December 2002, and by political uncertainties linked to the crisis of confidence in business circles.

In these conditions the business climate has deteriorated sharply, causing significant late payments and bankruptcies. That situation has prompted Coface to downgrade the country's rating to category D.

Argentina

Coface analysis

Short-term: **D**

Medium-term:
Very high risk

2

STRENGTHS

- Numerous assets: vast natural resources, developed agri-foodstuffs sector and skilled labour.
- Fall of peso boosts exports and local manufacturing.
- Economy radically changed by structural reforms undertaken in 1990s.

WEAKNESSES

- Unsustainable foreign debt ratio – foreign debt accounts for nearly 400 per cent of export earnings and over one year of output – has led country to default on its debt repayments. Debt write-off inevitable.
- Financial system seriously undermined by crisis of depositor confidence and collapse of peso's fixed parity.
- Government has little room for fiscal manoeuvre and is unable to bring regional spending under control.
- Domestic savings insufficient to finance economy in the absence of foreign capital.
- Rampant unemployment, especially among middle class and poorest sections of society.
- Extreme political uncertainty.

RISK ASSESSMENT

Argentina is in the grip of a severe economic, financial and political crisis. The economy and currency collapsed in the first six months of 2002 with disastrous social consequences. The economic indicators have since stabilized. Local manufacturing may have regained sufficient competitiveness to boost exports and substitute imports, but conditions for a sustained recovery are nowhere near fulfilment.

The government must first and foremost renegotiate the foreign debt without discouraging foreign capital inflows, and restore the currency and banking system's credibility. But its insolvency means it does not have the resources to support the financial system, especially if it must first persuade the regions that they have no alternative but to curb spending.

The top priority, however, is to restore the government's credibility and, in so doing, rebuild the confidence of the people and the international financial community.

KEY ECONOMIC INDICATORS						
US$ billion	1998	1999	2000	2001	2002 (e)	2003 (f)
Economic growth (%)	3.9	−3.4	−0.8	−4.4	−11	2
Inflation (%)	0.7	−1.8	−0.7	−1.5	76	60
Public-sector balance/GDP (%)	−2.2	−4.2	−3.6	−5.4	−2.5	−2.5
Exports	26.4	23.3	26.4	26.7	25.5	27
Imports	29.5	24.1	23.9	19.1	8.9	13.3
Trade balance	−3.1	−0.8	2.6	7.5	16.6	13.7
Current account balance	−14.6	−12	−8.9	−4.4	5	2.7
Current account balance/GDP (%)	−4.9	−4.2	−3.1	−1.6	5.7	2.9
Foreign debt	140.7	145.4	146.5	140.5	142	145.3
Debt service/Exports (%)	56.4	75.2	76.8	99.3	60	69.7
Reserves (import months)	5.7	6.8	6.3	4.2	3.5	5

e = estimated, f = forecast

CONDITIONS OF ACCESS TO THE MARKET

■ Market overview

The peso's devaluation has made the Argentine economy extremely competitive, with business opportunities to be seized in the export sectors. The agri-foodstuffs sector, for example, offers foreign investors good growth prospects as the government and some agricultural trade organizations build and develop a niche strategy focusing on organic products, biotechnology, biofuel and plastics. There are also niche industries in chemicals, tyres (import substitution), aluminium and a number of steel products. Over the last few years growth in foreign investment has mainly been driven by privatization of the country's public services.

The Argentine government is currently engaged in talks with companies awarded public service concessions on adapting the concession contracts to the new economic environment. Upon their completion foreign investment in the privatization programme should pick up.

Network infrastructures (electricity, telecommunications, etc) should enjoy robust growth in the months ahead, as should environment-related industries and services, in particular water supply and waste treatment, transport and mining. Argentine labour is one of the cheapest in Latin America. The average monthly wage is US$450 (US$700 in Buenos Aires) and social security contributions have fallen from 33 per cent to 24 per cent since 1999. The revised labour laws passed in 2000 should make for greater flexibility, especially as the country's workforce is one of the most skilled in South America.

■ Means of entry

Goods from non-Mercosur countries are subject to the common external tariff (CET) which ranges from 0 per cent to 28 per cent (average 15 per cent). Within Mercosur member countries have maintained customs barriers for certain products, such as cars and automobile spare parts.

Imports are liable to 0.5 per cent statistical tax on the CIF value, 21 per cent VAT (CIF value, plus customs duties, plus statistical tax), 9 per cent additional VAT on goods intended for sale and 30 per cent tax on profits. Special procedures apply to imports of pharmaceuticals and agri-foodstuffs. The Argentine government has recently erected what appear to be trade barriers that could delay customs clearance and mark up imports of these products.

■ Attitude towards foreign investors

The legal system governing foreign investment in Argentina seems very liberal. Nevertheless the stability of the legal and tax system

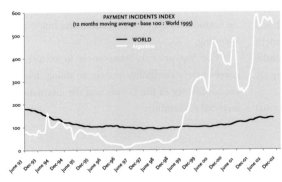

PAYMENT INCIDENTS INDEX
(12 months moving average - base 100 : World 1995)
— WORLD
— Argentina

applicable to foreign investment can not always be taken for granted, especially in the current state of economic and financial emergency, characterized by the adoption of unpredictable policies, unilateral measures (in particular the regional government laws affecting the financial viability of public service concessions) and national preference schemes such as the 'Buy Argentine' campaign.

■ Foreign exchange regulations

Under an economic and financial emergency law passed in 2002 the Argentine government has abolished the convertibility system and introduced a free currency market.

2

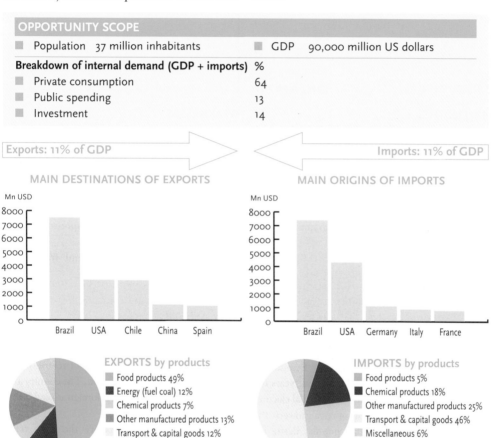

OPPORTUNITY SCOPE

■ Population   37 million inhabitants   ■ GDP   90,000 million US dollars

Breakdown of internal demand (GDP + imports)	%
■ Private consumption	64
■ Public spending	13
■ Investment	14

Exports: 11% of GDP   Imports: 11% of GDP

MAIN DESTINATIONS OF EXPORTS

Mn USD
(bar chart: Brazil, USA, Chile, China, Spain)

MAIN ORIGINS OF IMPORTS

Mn USD
(bar chart: Brazil, USA, Germany, Italy, France)

EXPORTS by products
■ Food products 49%
■ Energy (fuel coal) 12%
■ Chemical products 7%
■ Other manufactured products 13%
■ Transport & capital goods 12%
■ Miscellaneous 7%

IMPORTS by products
■ Food products 5%
■ Chemical products 18%
■ Other manufactured products 25%
■ Transport & capital goods 46%
■ Miscellaneous 6%

STANDARD OF LIVING / PURCHASING POWER

Indicators	Argentina	Regional average	DC average
GNP per capita (PPP dollars)	n/a	6339	6548
GNP per capita	2400	3369	3565
Human development index	0.844	0.761	0.702
Wealthiest 10% share of national income	n/a	40	32
Urban population percentage	89	73	60
Percentage under 15 years old	28	33	32
Number of telephones per 1000 inhabitants	213	129	157
Number of computers per 1000 inhabitants	51	41	64

n/a – not available   **129**

Bolivia

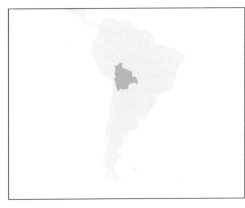

Short-term: **B**

Medium-term:

Coface analysis **Very high risk**

STRENGTHS

- Foreign investors attracted by abundant mineral resources, especially of natural gas.
- Wide-ranging structural reforms undertaken in recent years.
- Supported by international financial community. First Latin American country to benefit from HIPC debt reduction programme.

WEAKNESSES

- Landlocked; one of Latin America's poorest countries.
- Exports dominated by commodities (zinc, soya, natural gas, gold, silver).
- Over reliant on foreign funding because of low domestic savings.
- Heavy debt despite HIPC-sponsored debt relief.
- Widespread social unrest and fragmented political system.

RISK ASSESSMENT

With economic growth lagging way behind the demographic growth rate for the last four years the spectacular performance at the presidential election last summer of the champion of coca growers, the Indian Eva Morales, reflects a popular desire for change. The winner, Gonzalo Sanchez de Lozada, was only elected as a result of the cobbling together of a loose grouping of traditional parties. The fragility of the new ruling coalition is a severe handicap in the face of the many challenges to be overcome.

Oil and gas sales have not offset the downturn in other sectors, partially triggered by the drop in foreign remittances on account of the Argentine crisis. Falling tax revenues have led to a sharp rise in the public debt necessitating urgent reform of the public sector and pension system. The country also remains highly dependent on foreign capital for its development.

The only bright spots are the debt relief obtained under the renewed HIPC initiative and the favourable long-term prospects for natural gas exports should ease the external account deficit. However, disagreement over the gas pipeline's route could delay the project's implementation. Finally, greater economic diversification is called for if the problems posed by the current industrial strife and the radicalization of coca growers demands are to be addressed.

KEY ECONOMIC INDICATORS

US$ billion	1998	1999	2000	2001	2002 (e)	2003 (f)
Economic growth (%)	5.5	0.4	2.4	1.2	1.8	2.5
Inflation (%)	4.4	3.1	3.4	1.6	0.8	2.9
Public-sector balance/GDP (%)	-4.6	-3.4	-3.7	-6.0	-7.0	-7.0
Exports	1.1	1.1	1.2	1.3	1.3	1.5
Imports	1.8	1.5	1.6	1.5	1.6	1.7
Trade balance	-0.7	-0.5	-0.4	-0.2	-0.3	-0.2
Current account balance	-0.7	-0.5	-0.5	-0.4	-0.5	-0.4
Current account balance/GDP (%)	-8.0	-5.9	-5.6	-4.8	-6.6	-5.3
Foreign debt	6.5	6.2	5.8	5.6	5.9	6.1
Debt service/Exports (%)	25.7	27.1	27.4	31.5	26.2	25.3
Reserves (import months)	4.2	4.6	4.0	3.6	3.4	3.3

e = estimated, f = forecast

CONDITIONS OF ACCESS TO THE MARKET

Market overview

A small, landlocked state surrounded by powerful neighbours, Bolivia has steadfastly focused on opening its borders and moving towards closer trade integration with the other countries of the region. Since 1995 the five-tier Common External Tariff of the Andean Community of Nations (0 per cent, 5 per cent, 10 per cent, 15 per cent and 20 per cent) has been in force in the country. The other Community members have agreed to let Bolivia apply a de facto 10 per cent flat-rate ad valorem customs duty to all its imports from non-ACN countries, excluding capital goods, which are subject to a reduced rate of duty. In the aftermath of the development programmes linked to key privatizations foreign investment has dropped to around US$750–800 million year on year. Unfortunately the investment is concentrated in low job growth sectors such as oil and gas, energy and telecommunications.

Unskilled Bolivian labour is widely available and cheap. Wages can be fairly high for positions of responsibility. Employment of foreign staff is in principle limited to 15 per cent of a company's workforce.

Means of entry

Food, vegetable and animal products require health certificates complying with ACN standards. The national agency Senasag is responsible for enforcing all health standards relating to imported meat and meat products. Imports worth more than US$ 3000 are subject to inspection by one of two government-approved companies, Inspectorate and SGS. Under revised Bolivian customs legislation a customs valuation department is to be set up shortly and outsourcing discontinued.

Documentary credit is the most widespread means of payment for both cash and deferred settlements. Delivery against payment is also used, but much less frequently. Where business relations are well established payments are usually made by bank transfer. Corporate defaults have surged over the last two years. Against this background irrevocable and confirmed documentary credit is strongly recommended if there is any doubt about the buyer's creditworthiness.

Attitude towards foreign investors

There is no discrimination against foreign investors, who are subject to the same rules as Bolivian nationals. Foreign investors are only required to register their investments with the Vice-ministry of Foreign Trade and Investment and to submit various company incorporation documents. Despite political will and favourable legislation foreign investors can still face serious problems arising from lack of legal safeguards or exposure to local situations beyond the government's control.

Foreign exchange regulations

There are no foreign exchange controls and no restrictions on the buying and selling of currencies or capital transfers. Bolivia is a highly dollarized country, with more than 95 per cent of bank deposits denominated in dollars.

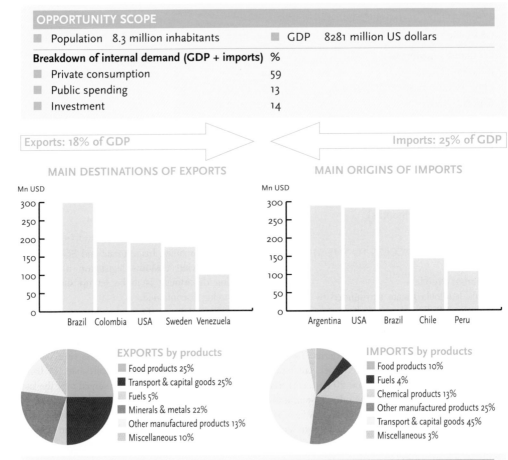

OPPORTUNITY SCOPE

- Population   8.3 million inhabitants
- GDP   8281 million US dollars

Breakdown of internal demand (GDP + imports)   %
- Private consumption   59
- Public spending   13
- Investment   14

Exports: 18% of GDP

Imports: 25% of GDP

MAIN DESTINATIONS OF EXPORTS

Mn USD

Brazil   Colombia   USA   Sweden   Venezuela

MAIN ORIGINS OF IMPORTS

Mn USD

Argentina   USA   Brazil   Chile   Peru

EXPORTS by products
- Food products 25%
- Transport & capital goods 25%
- Fuels 5%
- Minerals & metals 22%
- Other manufactured products 13%
- Miscellaneous 10%

IMPORTS by products
- Food products 10%
- Fuels 4%
- Chemical products 13%
- Other manufactured products 25%
- Transport & capital goods 45%
- Miscellaneous 3%

STANDARD OF LIVING / PURCHASING POWER

Indicators	Bolivia	Regional average	DC average
GNP per capita (PPP dollars)	2360	6339	6548
GNP per capita	990	3369	3565
Human development index	0.653	0.761	0.702
Wealthiest 10% share of national income	32	40	32
Urban population percentage	65	73	60
Percentage under 15 years old	40	33	32
Number of telephones per 1000 inhabitants	61	129	157
Number of computers per 1000 inhabitants	17	41	64

Brazil

Short-term: **C**

Medium-term:
Coface analysis
High risk

STRENGTHS

- Abundant natural resources and fairly diversified economy.
- Drop of real boosts competitiveness of Brazilian firms.
- Cautious and pragmatic fiscal and monetary policies.
- Growth potential of domestic market continues to attract foreign investors.
- Enjoys support of international financial community.

WEAKNESSES

- Heavy public debt due to excessively high interest rates and extremely short maturities.
- Unsustainable foreign debt in the long term.
- External financing needs too high compared with foreign currency earnings.
- New president has very little room for manoeuvre between electors' aspirations for change, the need for compromise with other coalition partners and economic constraints.

RISK ASSESSMENT

The new Brazilian President, Luiz Inacio Lula da Silva, who came to power on a wave of popular desire for change, has very little room for manoeuvre because of the country's precarious financial situation within a difficult international environment.

In the short term restoration of business confidence would facilitate a significant cut in interest rates, a major realignment of the exchange rate and an economic recovery. This is necessary to reduce the public debt. While a marked improvement in the trade balance that brought about the fall of the local currency has clearly reduced the borrowing requirement, a further depreciation of the real cannot be ruled out in

2003, despite IMF support, if financial inflows from lenders and private investors are not restored. Another slide of the currency will further weaken dollar-indebted companies, already battered by the currency's fall in 2002.

In the longer term the challenges remain daunting. The size of the country's foreign debt remains a major obstacle to growth. To generate the income for loan repayments and foreign dividend payments the country needs to boost its weak export sector, which is over dependent on agricultural products and commodities. But to deal with inadequate infrastructure, poor education and sharp inequalities a proactive approach is demanded of a government hamstrung by the size of the national debt.

US$ billion	1998	1999	2000	2001	2002 (e)	2003 (f)
Economic growth (%)	0.1	0.8	4.4	1.5	1.2	2
Inflation (%)	2.5	8.4	5.3	9.4	11	11
Public-sector balance/GDP (%)	−7.5	−9.2	−4.6	−5.2	−7.5	−5
Exports	51.1	48	55.1	58.2	59.5	63.9
Imports	57.7	49.3	55.8	55.6	47.3	49.3
Trade balance	−6.6	−1.3	−0.7	2.6	12.2	14.6
Current account balance	−33.4	−25.4	−24.7	−23.2	−8.9	−9.3
Current account balance/GDP (%)	−4.2	−4.8	−4.2	−4.6	−2	−2.2
Foreign debt	243.3	243	237.8	228.1	239.4	255.2
Debt service/Exports (%)	85.5	121	101.1	88.8	68.8	82.7
Reserves (import months)	5.2	4.8	4.1	4.5	5.4	6.8

e = estimated, f = forecast

CONDITIONS OF ACCESS TO THE MARKET

■ Market overview

Brazil's estimated working population is 136 million. The minimum monthly wage is 200 reis (about 74 euros). Employer social security and compulsory benefit contributions amount to about 50 per cent of gross wages.

■ Means of entry

The average rate of customs duty is approximately 14 per cent and the ceiling rate 35 per cent. Having negotiated far higher duties with the WTO than it actually applies Brazil is unlikely to call into question its multilateral commitments. Brazil is subject to Mercosur's Common External Tariff, which is under pressure as a result of the adoption of unilateral measures and large numbers of exceptions by member countries.

Brazil maintains a number of non-tariff barriers to imports, including import licences, customs valuation and prior registration.

The most widespread means of payment are down payments, pre payments, cash against documents, acceptance bills and irrevocable letters of credit confirmed by a Brazilian or foreign bank.

Brazil places restrictions on the employment of foreigners. There are two types of work permit – permanent and temporary – which are issued on a restricted basis.

■ Attitude towards foreign investors

Foreign investors may set up a wholly owned subsidiary without a local partner. There are still restrictions on foreign investment, especially in the nuclear energy and aeronautics sectors. Once a company is set up foreign investors are not subject to any regulatory restrictions. However, they must be represented by an attorney in Brazil.

Foreign fund transfers involving the repatriation of capital and/or reinvestment or the repatriation of profits and dividends are authorized once the capital is registered. Such transfers must be handled by financial institutions trading on the currency market but do not require central bank clearance. There is no tax on the transfer of profits and dividends.

■ Foreign exchange regulations

Since January 1999 the exchange rate has been set freely by the inter-bank market. The central bank still intervenes on the markets, occasionally and indirectly, to counter erratic exchange rate fluctuations. The new government formed after the elections in October 2002 has declared its commitment to maintaining a flexible exchange rate system.

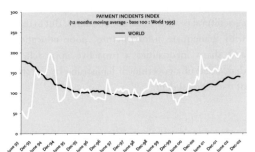

PAYMENT INCIDENTS INDEX
(12 months moving average - base 100 : World 1995)
— WORLD

OPPORTUNITY SCOPE

- Population   170.4 million inhabitants
- GDP   595,458 million US dollars

Breakdown of internal demand (GDP + imports) %
- Private consumption   56
- Public spending   16
- Investment   19

Exports: 11% of GDP   Imports: 12% of GDP

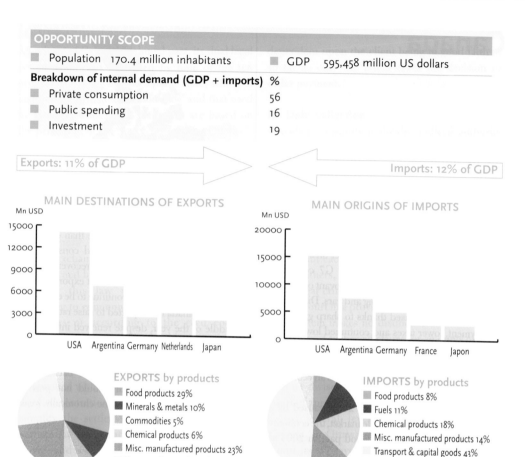

MAIN DESTINATIONS OF EXPORTS

Mn USD

USA   Argentina Germany Netherlands Japan

MAIN ORIGINS OF IMPORTS

Mn USD

USA   Argentina Germany France Japon

EXPORTS by products
- Food products 29%
- Minerals & metals 10%
- Commodities 5%
- Chemical products 6%
- Misc. manufactured products 23%
- Transport & capital goods 24%
- Miscellaneous 3%

IMPORTS by products
- Food products 8%
- Fuels 11%
- Chemical products 18%
- Misc. manufactured products 14%
- Transport & capital goods 43%
- Miscellaneous 6%

STANDARD OF LIVING / PURCHASING POWER

Indicators	Brazil	Regional average	DC average
GNP per capita (PPP dollars)	7300	6339	6548
GNP per capita	3580	3369	3565
Human development index	0.757	0.761	0.702
Wealthiest 10% share of national income	48	40	32
Urban population percentage	81	73	60
Percentage under 15 years old	29	33	32
Number of telephones per 1000 inhabitants	182	129	157
Number of computers per 1000 inhabitants	44	41	64

foundation of the plaintiff's claim, ordinary proceedings take place in three phases: the writ of summons under which the plaintiff presents his claim against the defendant; the 'examination for discovery', which outlines the petition made against the defendant along with the proofs to be submitted before the court by each party; and, finally, the trial proper, during which the judge hears the adverse parties and their respective witnesses, who are directly examined and cross-examined by the parties' legal counsels.

It should nonetheless be noted that, although the vocabulary used to describe the stages in proceedings is not standardized, the sequence of phases is generally applied throughout the country.

Chile

Coface analysis

Short-term: **A3**

Medium-term:
Low risk

STRENGTHS

- Significant mineral and fishery resources.
- Absence of major economic imbalances and sound finances should trigger sustained medium-term economic growth.
- Public and private sector enjoy lowest risk premium in region.
- Healthy financial sector.
- Stable political environment.

WEAKNESSES

- Extremely open economy heavily reliant on exports of commodities, especially copper.
- Significant outflows of foreign currency due to high levels of direct foreign investment.
- Vast foreign debt accumulated by private sector.
- Strong social inequalities.

2

RISK ASSESSMENT

Chile, a country with an extremely liberal trade policy, is being hit hard by plummeting copper prices and the slump in world demand.

Nevertheless the country has been spared a financial crisis because, unlike other Latin American countries, it does not suffer from macro-economic imbalances. Inflation is moderate, the external account deficit is under control, foreign exchange reserves are ample and, given the small public debt, the country's finances are sound. The financial sector is the strongest in the region and there is consensus across the political spectrum on maintaining balanced national accounts.

Chile's sound fundamentals should enable it to benefit from the world economic recovery. However, the economy suffers from two major long-term weaknesses. Private sector debt amortization, and above all dividend repatriation resulting from the high level of direct foreign investment, could widen the current account deficit. And the rigorous fiscal policy, often pursued at the expense of spending on education, health or infrastructure, inhibits the development of added-value sectors. If the country fails to diversify into such sectors its economic performance will remain over exposed to mining.

KEY ECONOMIC INDICATORS

US$ billion	1998	1999	2000	2001	2002 (e)	2003 (f)
Economic growth (%)	3.2	−1	4.4	2.8	2.2	4.5
Inflation (%)	4.7	2.3	4.5	2.6	2.5	3
Public-sector balance/GDP (%) (1)	0.4	−1.4	0.1	−0.3	−1.2	n/a
Exports	16.4	17.2	19.2	18.5	18.7	20.3
Imports	18.4	14.7	17.1	16.4	17.2	18.4
Trade balance	−2	2.5	2.2	2.1	1.5	1.8
Current account balance	−4	0.3	−1.1	−1.2	−1.1	−0.5
Current account balance/GDP (%)	−5.1	0.4	−1.4	−1.9	−1.7	−0.8
Foreign debt	35.7	36.3	36.8	37.8	38.9	39.6
Debt service/Exports (%)	16.9	16.6	18.2	23.4	22.2	27.3
Reserves (import months)	7.3	7.5	6.9	6.9	6.6	6.2

(1) central government

e = estimated, f = forecast

CONDITIONS OF ACCESS TO THE MARKET

■ Market overview

The Chilean market is secure and stable. The country's sound political and economic situation, satisfactory infrastructure and stable laws and regulations create an attractive business environment, especially for small and medium-sized companies.

Chile has sought little or no tariff protection for many years, adopting unilateral measures to cut import duties backed by bilateral and regional trade agreements. On 1 January 2003 flat-rate customs duty was cut from 7 per cent – the rate in force since 1 January 2002 – to 6 per cent. Moreover, under the free trade agreement with the EU, due to be ratified by parliament in early 2003, customs duties on most industrial goods will be slashed to 0 per cent.

■ Means of entry

There are few non-tariff barriers. However a number of measures with a similar effect are in place, including a surtax on luxury goods, variable levies on agri-foodstuffs and health and plant health regulations for food products (sampling procedures, etc).

The Intellectual Property Act 1991 provides inadequate protection for pharmaceuticals, especially with regard to formulae registered before 1991. The bill being reviewed by Congress will bring Chilean intellectual property legislation into line with WTO standards.

Chilean trademark and designation of origin laws are not yet fully WTO compliant.

All common means of payment are accepted in Chile.

■ Attitude towards foreign investors

There is equality of treatment between foreign and local investors. Foreigners are not required to tie up with a local partner. Foreign investment status within the meaning of Decree-Law 600 is applicable to deals in excess of US$1million. The central bank controls capital inflows of US$ 10000 or more, but some regulations have been relaxed. For instance, the one-year capital residence requirement has been scrapped, along with the mandatory zero-interest deposit scheme for foreign capital (encaje).

Corporation tax is 15 per cent, but there is an additional 20 per cent tax on profits repatriated abroad.

Labour legislation is not burdensome in terms of social security contributions. Despite the introduction of unemployment benefits from 2002 and the increase in severance pay stipulated by the recently revised labour code, employer social security contributions are extremely low and limited to industrial accident protection premiums.

PAYMENT INCIDENTS INDEX
(12 months moving average - base 100 : World 1995)
— WORLD

To counter the decline in foreign investment inflows in 2002 the government is looking to enhance prospects for foreign start-ups in the country.

■ Foreign exchange regulations

The central bank abandoned the peso's crawling peg at the end of September 1999. The exchange rate has since been determined solely by the market, with the monetary authorities intervening only on an exceptional basis.

2

OPPORTUNITY SCOPE

■ Population	15.2 million inhabitants	■ GDP	70,545 million US dollars

Breakdown of internal demand (GDP + imports) %
- ■ Private consumption — 48
- ■ Public spending — 9
- ■ Investment — 18

Exports: 32% of GDP ⟹ ⟸ Imports: 31% of GDP

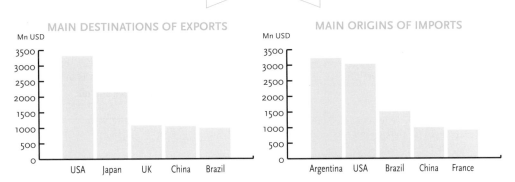

MAIN DESTINATIONS OF EXPORTS

Mn USD

USA, Japan, UK, China, Brazil

MAIN ORIGINS OF IMPORTS

Mn USD

Argentina, USA, Brazil, China, France

EXPORTS by products
- ■ Food products 27%
- ■ Commodities 10%
- ■ Minerals & metals 42%
- ■ Chemical products 5%
- ■ Misc. manufactured products 8%
- ■ Transport & capital goods 3%
- ■ Miscellaneous 5%

IMPORTS by products
- ■ Food products 9%
- ■ Fuels 13%
- ■ Chemical products 13%
- ■ Misc. manufactured products 25%
- ■ Transport & capital goods 37%
- ■ Miscellaneous 3%

STANDARD OF LIVING / PURCHASING POWER

Indicators	Chile	Regional average	DC average
GNP per capita (PPP dollars)	9100	6339	6548
GNP per capita	4590	3369	3565
Human development index	0.831	0.761	0.702
Wealthiest 10% share of national income	46	40	32
Urban population percentage	85	73	60
Percentage under 15 years old	29	33	32
Number of telephones per 1000 inhabitants	221	129	157
Number of computers per 1000 inhabitants	82	41	64

Colombia

Coface analysis

Short-term: **B**

Medium-term:
High risk

STRENGTHS

- Abundant natural resources (agriculture, oil and gas, mining).
- Development of niche industries reduces dependence on commodity price fluctuations.
- Highest business productivity in Andean Community of Nations. Plays key strategic role in the zone.

WEAKNESSES

- Heavy foreign debt.
- Inadequate reform of public finances.
- Growth hit by guerrilla attacks and waning foreign investor interest.
- Social tensions exacerbated by high unemployment and poverty.
- Weak banking sector.
- Exports over dependent on trends in prices of commodities such as coffee and oil.

RISK ASSESSMENT

Colombia has two main weaknesses: high debt and rampant political violence.

The last few years have seen a sharp increase in the country's foreign debt. Today this has become a major handicap. Colombia has been fairly well shielded from the Argentine crisis by its foreign exchange reserves that cover six months of imports of goods and services. The debt burden, however, has become unsustainable over the longer term and, above all, leaves the new president few opportunities to increase much-needed security spending.

The financing requirement may become more difficult to cover in future as the upsurge in violence could deter foreign investors. The country carries a high political risk as hopes of restoring calm fade yet again with the renewal of hostilities between government and the FARC (Colombian Revolutionary Armed Forces).

It should, however, be noted that until the 1998–99 crisis violence never hampered growth, which was usually higher than the regional average, especially in the 1980s. The country's growth today is driven by the development of an entrepreneurial private sector and non-traditional exports that reduce exposure to world commodity prices. The main uncertainty remains the impact of the deteriorating macroeconomic and political environment on the microeconomic environment.

KEY ECONOMIC INDICATORS

US$ billion	1998	1999	2000	2001	2002 (e)	2003 (f)
Economic growth (%)	0.6	−4.2	2.7	1.4	1.5	2
Inflation (%)	16.7	9.2	8.8	7.7	6.3	5.5
Public-sector balance/GDP (%)	−3.9	−6.2	−3.8	−3.8	−3.8	n/a
Exports	11.5	12	13.6	12.8	12.5	12.8
Imports	13.9	10.3	11.1	12.3	11.7	12.1
Trade balance	−2.5	1.8	2.5	0.5	0.8	0.7
Current account balance	−5.2	0.5	0.4	−1.5	−1.5	−1.9
Current account balance/GDP (%)	−5.3	0.6	0.5	−1.9	−1.9	−2.6
Foreign debt	36.9	37.5	36.9	39.9	39.6	39.4
Debt service/Exports (%)	53.8	38.9	43.9	43.6	49.5	48.1
Reserves (import months)	5.2	6.1	6	6.3	6.7	6.4

n/a – not available   e = estimated, f = forecast

2

CONDITIONS OF ACCESS TO THE MARKET

■ Market overview

While modest economic growth and the peso's devaluation prevent across-the-board increases in imports of consumer goods steadily changing patterns of consumption, largely spearheaded by French mass retailers, act as a stimulus to imports. There are also high-growth niche markets, especially in mid-range agri-foodstuffs. The year 2003 should be a promising one for capital goods in particular due to firm demand and the government's temporary tax incentives for sectors such as textiles and garments, leather goods, automobiles, pharmaceuticals and food processing. A number of ambitious public schemes are to be planned in 2003 and launched in 2004. French exports grew for the second consecutive year, up 20 per cent in 2002 on the previous year. French exports of semi-finished goods, such as light iron and steel products, could also climb.

■ Means of entry

The few barriers to trade that remain arise mainly from the complexity and cumbersomeness of the Colombian legal system, the proliferation of supervisory bodies and the lack of uniform criteria. The situation is expected to change for the better in 2003, with the adoption in late 2002 of amendments to the labour law and the pension system aimed, *inter alia*, at introducing greater flexibility in lay-offs and overtime pay.

Changes are also expected in environmental licencing (faster procedures) and in telecommunications legislation, with a new law under preparation.

Tax reforms carried out in late 2002, which initially provide for an increase in income tax and VAT, will facilitate access to the Colombian market by enabling importers to claim back VAT paid on imports of capital goods not manufactured in the country and even obtain VAT-free admission, on top of the exemption from customs duties granted in 2003, if more than 70 per cent of their turnover is generated from exports. It should be noted that the temporary 1.2 per cent tax on the FOB value of imports was finally repealed by the constitutional court in 2002.

■ Attitude towards foreign investors

All sectors of the economy are open to foreign investment except for defence

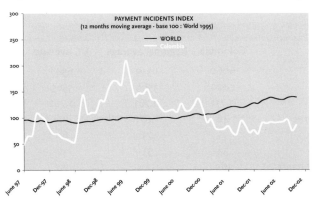

PAYMENT INCIDENTS INDEX
(12 months moving average - base 100 : World 1995)
— WORLD
— Colombia

143

and the processing of toxic, hazardous or radioactive waste not produced in the country. Investment in financial services, oil and gas and mining are subject to prior government approval

Foreign exchange regulations

Since September 1999 the peso has been floating freely against the dollar. In 2002 the currency finally underwent, albeit somewhat haphazardly, an average devaluation of 9 per cent against the dollar, or 3 per cent in real terms. This trend is likely to continue in 2003.

OPPORTUNITY SCOPE

- Population 42.3 million inhabitants
- GDP 81,283 million US dollars

Breakdown of internal demand (GDP + imports)	%
Private consumption	57
Public spending	16
Investment	10

Exports: 22% of GDP

Imports: 20% of GDP

MAIN DESTINATIONS OF EXPORTS

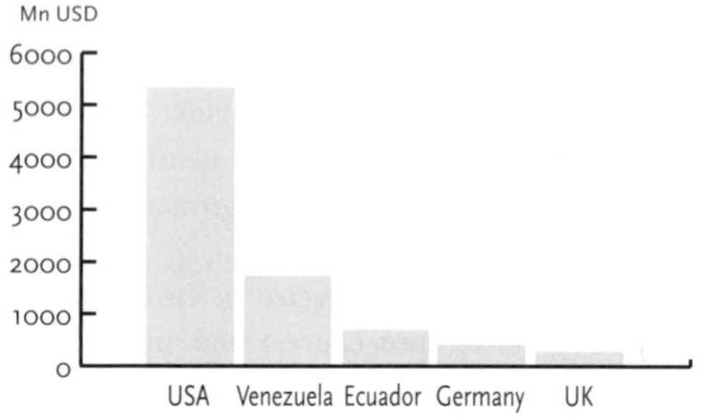

Mn USD
6000
5000
4000
3000
2000
1000
0
USA
Venezuela
Ecuador
Germany
UK

MAIN ORIGINS OF IMPORTS

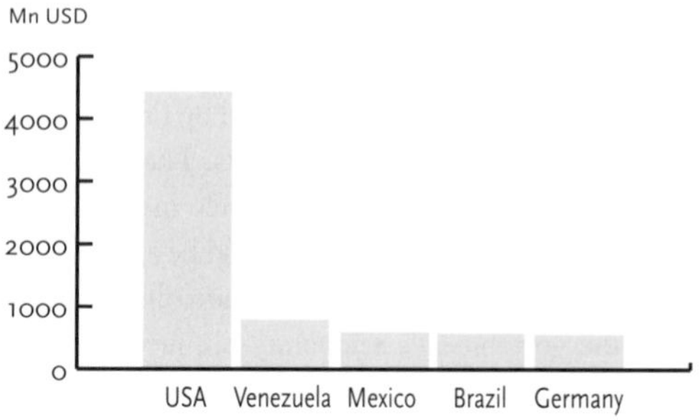

Mn USD
5000
4000
3000
2000
1000
0
USA
Venezuela
Mexico
Brazil
Germany

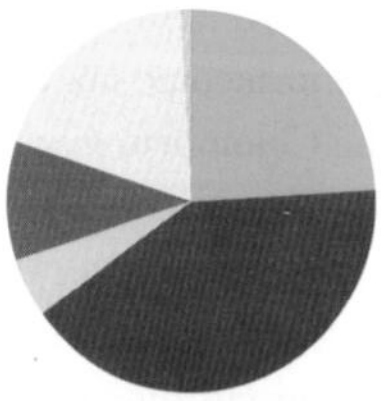

EXPORTS by products

- Food products 24%
- Fuels 41%
- Commodities 5%
- Chemical products 10%
- Misc. manufactured products 19%
- Miscellaneous 1%

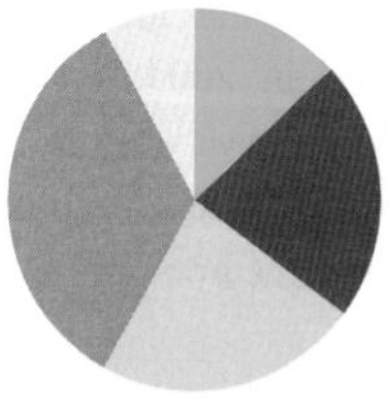

IMPORTS by products

- Food products 13%
- Chemical products 22%
- Misc. manufactured products 23%
- Transport & capital goods 34%
- Miscellaneous 8%

STANDARD OF LIVING / PURCHASING POWER

Indicators	Colombia	Regional average	DC average
GNP per capita (PPP dollars)	6060	6339	6548
GNP per capita	2020	3369	3565
Human development index	0.772	0.761	0.702
Wealthiest 10% share of national income	46	40	32
Urban population percentage	75	73	60
Percentage under 15 years old	33	33	32
Number of telephones per 1000 inhabitants	169	129	157
Number of computers per 1000 inhabitants	35	41	64

Costa Rica

Short-term: **B**

Medium-term:

Coface analysis **Quite high risk**

RISK ASSESSMENT

The sharp economic upturn between 1997 and 1999, spurred by the siting of the computer firm Intel in the country, has proven to be ephemeral after three years of mediocre growth. The positive spin-offs from the buoyant performance of the free zones and, above all, from the rapid expansion of tourism have been negated by high interest rates which, though necessary to contain double-digit inflation, have strangled economic activity.

The extremely heavy domestic public debt burden gives the government no scope to support demand. Moves to reduce the budget deficit, in urgent need of correction, and undertake vital reforms have been hampered by the failure to produce a clear majority at the last parliamentary elections.

The country nevertheless enjoys relative prosperity in the region. The social indicators are enviable, unemployment remains low and foreign debt moderate. While the prospect of mediocre growth cannot be ruled out a crisis is less likely in Costa Rica than in other Latin American countries.

2

KEY ECONOMIC INDICATORS						
US$ billion	1998	1999	2000	2001	2002 (e)	2003 (f)
Economic growth (%)	8.4	8.2	2.2	0.9	2.5	2.7
Inflation (%)	12.4	10.1	10.2	11	10.1	9.9
Public-sector balance/GDP (%)	−2.5	−2.2	−2.9	−2.7	−2.7	−2.7
Exports	5.5	6.6	5.8	4.9	5.1	5.5
Imports	5.9	6	6	5.7	6.2	6.6
Trade balance	−0.4	0.6	−0.2	−0.8	−1.1	−1.1
Current account balance/GDP (%)	−3.7	−4.3	−4.4	−4.6	−5.4	−5
Foreign debt	3.7	3.9	4	4.2	4.7	5
Debt service/Exports (%)	7.8	8.3	10	11.3	10.2	10.9
Reserves (import months)	1.7	1.9	1.8	2	2	2

e = estimated, f = forecast

Cuba

Coface analysis

Short-term: **D**

Medium-term:
Very high risk

STRENGTHS

- Vast natural (nickel, oil) and agricultural (sugar, tobacco) resources, fish stocks and tourism potential.
- Skilled manpower.
- Economic liberalization partially offsets shortcomings of centralized economy.

WEAKNESSES

- With the economy dependent on a limited number of commodities, foreign trade remains highly vulnerable to world commodity price movements.
- Economic development hampered by economic centralization.
- Access to less costly foreign funding (in particular long term) will remain restricted until payment of outstanding debt.
- Conflict with United States constitutes major stumbling block to Cuba's integration into world trading community.

RISK ASSESSMENT

Cuba's economy has been hit by the decline in tourism related to the events of 11 September 2001, but especially by low sugar prices. As the world's fourth largest sugar exporter Cuba must cut half its production capacity in this sector, the island's leading employer. Agricultural output also suffered from the havoc caused by the various hurricanes that struck the country. Finally, growth plunged on the back of the slump in foreign investment underpinned by the uncertain business climate.

Despite the drop in exports and tourist revenues the country's external account deficit has not widened thanks to the reduction in imports.

However, the borrowing requirement continues to be covered mainly by short-term loans due to Cuba's limited access to other types of foreign funding. The appalling shortage of foreign exchange has led the government to renew talks with the main creditor countries in an attempt to deal with the problem of medium and long-term outstanding debt.

Despite a visit by former President Carter in May 2002 and pressure from certain US companies a substantial improvement in relations with the United States is unlikely in the short term due to the international context and the new political configuration produced by the US mid-term elections held in November.

KEY ECONOMIC INDICATORS

US$ billion	1998	1999	2000	2001	2002 (e)	2003 (f)
Economic growth (%)	1.3	6.2	5.6	3	0	3.5
Inflation (%)	2.8	−0.5	−0.1	−4.1	3.9	2.2
Public-sector balance/GDP (%)	−2.3	−2.4	−2.7	−2.8	−3	−3
Exports	1.5	1.5	1.7	1.8	1.8	1.8
Imports	4.2	4.3	5	4.8	4.8	4.8
Trade balance	−2.7	−2.9	−3.3	−3.1	−3.1	−3
Current account balance	−0.4	−0.5	−0.6	−0.6	−0.8	−0.6
Current account balance/GDP (%)	−1.9	−2.1	−2.6	0	−3.2	−2.4
Foreign debt	12.1	12	11.9	11.9	12.5	13.1
Debt service/Exports (%)	21.8	20.6	18.8	19	19.9	20.7
Reserves (import months)	1	1	1.2	1.3	1.1	1.1

e = estimated, f = forecast

2

CONDITIONS OF ACCESS TO THE MARKET

■ Means of entry

Cuba is an active founding member of the WTO and maintains fairly good trade relations with countries around the world, except with the United States, which continues to maintain its embargo. The Helms-Burton and Torricelli Acts have made Cuban imports more expensive. However, a few agricultural and pharmaceutical goods are traded against cash between the United States and Cuban non-governmental entities. The market is only open to staples and goods matching government-defined requirements.

Price and funding are of the utmost importance, although quality, guarantees and after-sales service are gaining significance. Customs duties on the whole are more attractive than in most Latin American countries. However, Cuba is encountering serious payment difficulties and the risk of default is high. The country is forced to seek short-term financing (12 to 24 months) at Libor plus some 7 per cent. Payments usually take one year or more due to the shortage of foreign currency. The preferred means of payment for foreign trade is the irrevocable documentary credit confirmed by a leading bank, and for domestic trade credit cards issued by non-US banks and cash. Cheques are increasingly used for ordinary business transactions.

In theory, the euro has been the official trading currency since July 1999.

■ Attitude towards foreign investors

Cuba encourages foreign investment and has concluded bilateral investment promotion and protection agreements with 53 countries. The sectors covered by these agreements include tourism, basic industry, energy, telecommunications and banking. However education, military, health-care and construction are closed to foreigners. Foreign investment is governed by very cumbersome regulations, under which the government reserves the right to grant, renew or refuse import licences without explanation. The Helms-Burton Act also hampers foreign investment on the island, although Cuba has adopted 'remedial' legislation. The tax system offers a number of conditional incentives.

The free trade areas in Havana and Cienfuegos award companies exemptions from business and labour taxes, customs duties and corporation tax. Conversely, companies must export 75 per cent of their production within three years of start-up. Labour on the whole is skilled but expensive and not highly motivated. The employing entity, necessarily Cuban, can decide pay rises unilaterally and lay off essential employees. Severance pay-ments are compulsory and exorbitant.

■ Foreign exchange regulations

The exchange rate has steadied since the revalua-tion of the currency between 1994 and 1996 to 22 pesos to the dollar. The rate of exchange shown in the national accounts is 1 peso to the dollar.

OPPORTUNITY SCOPE

■ Population	11.2 million inhabitants	■ GDP	30,300 million US dollars

Breakdown of internal demand (GDP + imports) %

■ Private consumption	59
■ Public spending	19
■ Investment	8

Exports: 16% of GDP   Imports: 18% of GDP

MAIN DESTINATIONS OF EXPORTS

Mn USD

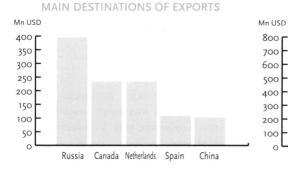

Russia   Canada   Netherlands   Spain   China

MAIN ORIGINS OF IMPORTS

Mn USD   n/a – not available

Spain   China   Italy   Canada   Mexico

EXPORTS by products
- ■ Sugar 26%
- ■ Nickel 33%
- ■ Tobacco 9%
- ■ Minerals 5%
- ■ Miscellaneous 27%

IMPORTS by products
- ■ Equipment 25%
- ■ Fuel 24%
- ■ Food Products 16%
- ■ Chemical products 9%
- ■ Miscellaneous 26%

STANDARD OF LIVING / PURCHASING POWER

Indicators	Cuba	Regional average	DC average
GNP per capita (PPP dollars)	n/a	6339	6548
GNP per capita	n/a	3369	3565
Human development index	0.795	0.761	0.702
Wealthiest 10% share of national income	n/a	40	32
Urban population percentage	75	73	60
Percentage under 15 years old	21	33	32
Number of telephones per 1000 inhabitants	44	129	157
Number of computers per 1000 inhabitants	11	41	74

n/a – not available

Dominican Republic

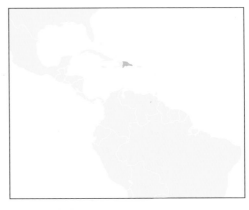

Short-term: **A4**

Medium-term:
Coface analysis **Quite high risk**

STRENGTHS

- Vast natural (nickel) and agricultural (sugar, coffee, cocoa) resources.
- Successful diversification into exports of manufactured goods from free zones and development of tourism.
- Close to North American market and signatory to various international and regional trade agreements.
- Moderate debt ratios.

WEAKNESSES

- Vulnerable to external crises mainly because of chronic shortage of foreign exchange.
- Loan repayments and dividend repatriations stemming from sizeable direct foreign investment in infrastructure schemes should have adverse long-term effect on balance of payments.
- Strong social tension against a background of enduring poverty (50 per cent of population), low average social indicators for the region and large-scale corruption.
- Prone to natural disasters

RISK ASSESSMENT

Since the second half of the 1990s when the Dominican Republic had the highest growth rate in Latin America due to substantial direct foreign investment inflows, the Dominican economy has been hit by the international economic downturn. Nevertheless the economic situation remains satisfactory largely due to the strong performance of construction, mostly financed by public borrowings and foreign investment.

On the other hand the external account has deteriorated due to the poor performance of tourism and free zone exports. Despite the relatively high level of direct foreign investment the country's growing borrowing requirement has depleted foreign exchange reserves to less than one month of imports and forced the country to seek debt financing.

The level of foreign debt nevertheless remains moderate. Increasing indebtedness, however, could undermine the country's solvency if, as the effectiveness of certain public investments is called into question by analysts, it is not brought under control.

KEY ECONOMIC INDICATORS						
US$ billion	1998	1999	2000	2001	2002 (e)	2003 (f)
Economic growth (%)	7.3	8.3	7.6	2.7	3.7	4.4
Inflation (%)	4.8	6.5	7.7	8.9	4.7	4.6
Public-sector balance/GDP (%)	−2.1	−3	−2	−2	−1.5	−1.5
Exports	5	5.1	5.7	5.3	5.2	5.6
Imports	7.6	8	9.5	8.8	8.9	9.4
Trade balance	−2.6	−2.9	−3.7	−3.5	−3.7	−3.7
Current account balance/GDP (%)	−2.1	−2.5	−5.2	−3.9	−5	−3.8
Foreign debt	4.5	4.8	4.6	5	5.3	5.4
Debt service/Exports (%)	3.8	3.6	5.2	5	5.8	5.5
Reserves (import months)	0.6	0.8	0.6	1.1	0.9	0.9

e = estimated, f = forecast

Ecuador

Coface analysis

Short-term: **D**

Medium-term:
Very high risk

STRENGTHS

- Well endowed with natural resources (oil, agriculture, fisheries).
- Dollarization has helped stabilize economy and position of banking sector.
- Rescheduling of bond-related debt and construction of new oil pipeline have improved medium-term growth prospects.

WEAKNESSES

- High degree of political instability hampers reform.
- Traditional antagonism between coastal and hilly regions undermines cohesion.
- External account and public finances vulnerable to oil fluctuations.
- High debt ratios despite restructuring.
- Weak banking sector.
- Falling standard of living in recent years

RISK ASSESSMENT

The victory in the November presidential elections of the progressive Colonel Lucio Gutierrez (who enjoys widespread support among the Indians and had contributed to the resignation of former President Jamil Mahuad in January 2000) is a reflection of Ecuadorians' disenchantment with the political establishment. However, just as the hopes for change are high, so the new president's room for manoeuvre is small.

The president must first come to terms with a hostile parliament in a country which has seen five presidents since 1996, two through resignations before their tenure had ended. The country's massive debt in a dollarized economy leaves practically no scope to develop economic policy.

The decision to replace the local currency with the dollar has clearly helped stabilize the economy after the violent crisis in 1999 that triggered a strong recession and caused the government to default on its debt. Inflation has fallen sharply and growth has picked up, largely due to investment connected with the construction of the new oil pipeline. However, the current account deficit has widened substantially because of the loss of competitiveness of Ecuadorian industry in the aftermath of dollarization. In line with the requirements of the IMF, whose support is essential, there is need for strict fiscal discipline, which the country has so far been incapable of observing.

KEY ECONOMIC INDICATORS						
US$ billion	1998	1999	2000	2001	2002 (e)	2003 (f)
Economic growth (%)	0.4	−7.3	2.3	5.6	2.9	3.5
Inflation (%)	43.4	60.7	91	22.4	11	6.7
Public-sector balance/GDP (%)	−6.1	−5.9	1.7	0.6	0.7	0.5
Exports	4.3	4.6	5.1	4.8	4.9	4.9
Imports	5.5	3	3.7	5.3	6	6.4
Trade balance	−1.1	1.6	1.4	−0.5	−1.1	−1.5
Current account balance	−2.1	0.9	0.9	−0.7	−1.3	−1.6
Current account balance/GDP (%)	−10.6	6.7	6.7	−4.2	−6.7	−7
Foreign debt	16.4	16.4	13.6	14.4	15.2	15.6
Debt service/Exports (%)	38.9	31.8	24.2	21.3	20.3	20.8
Reserves (import months)	2.4	3.5	1.8	1.2	1.2	1

e = estimated, f = forecast

2

CONDITIONS OF ACCESS TO THE MARKET

■ Market overview

Ecuador is a founding member of the Andean Community of Nations and complies, in principle, with the rules of the WTO, which it joined in 1996. While trade between Ecuador and its three 'main' ACN partners – Colombia, Bolivia and Venezuela – have been fully exempt from customs duties since 1994, a host of ad hoc tariff and non-tariff barriers hamper intra-ACN trade.

■ Means of entry

With regard to non-ACN tariff barriers, in April 2002 Ecuador brought out a rehashed version of the old customs tariff. In this schedule the rates of duty remain unchanged (0 per cent, 3 per cent, 5 per cent, 15 per cent, 20 per cent and 35 per cent), while tariff item numbers have been changed and a range of tariff sub-items introduced. It should be noted that a new ACN Common External Tariff will come into force no later than 31 December 2003, replacing the current one.

As well as the above-mentioned duties, there is 5.15 per cent to 77.25 per cent consumption tax (ICE) on a number of so-called 'luxury' products plus 12 per cent VAT. The 2–10 per cent surtax known as the 'safeguard clause' has been abolished. Despite the introduction of a single import declaration form (*Documento unico de importación*), and its recent replacement by the DAU, import procedures remain lengthy and constitute a major stumbling block to the free flow of trade. Ecuador runs a highly complex system of controls, prohibitions, authorizations and permits. Besides, frequent changes in legislation make people extremely wary of the legal system.

■ Attitude towards foreign investors

In theory, non-discrimination between domestic and foreign investors is the norm, except in so-called strategic sectors (such as the ban on property ownership along the borders). In practice, however, this liberalism is negated by the extreme complexity of the legal and judicial system, which breeds insecurity. The high concentration of political, economic and financial power can also distort law enforcement.

■ Foreign exchange regulations

The widespread use of the dollar provides a certain degree of monetary stability.

OPPORTUNITY SCOPE

- Population 12.6 million inhabitants
- GDP 13,607 million US dollars

Breakdown of internal demand (GDP + imports) %
- Private consumption 45
- Public spending 7
- Investment 12

Exports: 42% of GDP → ← Imports: 31% of GDP

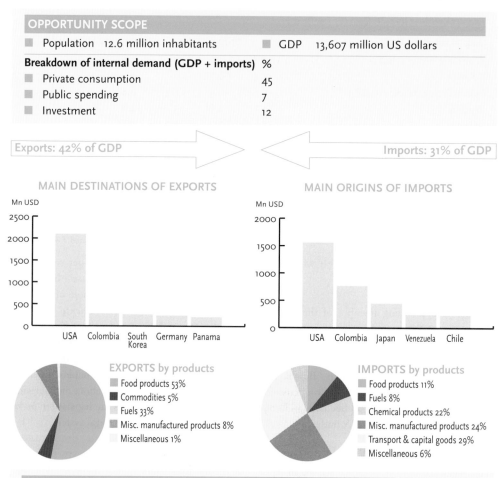

MAIN DESTINATIONS OF EXPORTS

Mn USD

USA Colombia South Korea Germany Panama

MAIN ORIGINS OF IMPORTS

Mn USD

USA Colombia Japan Venezuela Chile

EXPORTS by products
- Food products 53%
- Commodities 5%
- Fuels 33%
- Misc. manufactured products 8%
- Miscellaneous 1%

IMPORTS by products
- Food products 11%
- Fuels 8%
- Chemical products 22%
- Misc. manufactured products 24%
- Transport & capital goods 29%
- Miscellaneous 6%

STANDARD OF LIVING / PURCHASING POWER

Indicators	Ecuador	Regional average	DC average
GNP per capita (PPP dollars)	2910	6339	6548
GNP per capita	1210	3369	3565
Human development index	0.732	0.761	0.702
Wealthiest 10% share of national income	34	40	60
Urban population percentage	62	73	59
Percentage under 15 years old	34	33	32
Number of telephones per 1000 inhabitants	100	129	157
Number of computers per 1000 inhabitants	22	41	64

El Salvador

Short-term: **B**

Medium-term:
Coface analysis   **Quite high risk**

RISK ASSESSMENT

The economy has rebounded after two years of slowdown due to the earthquakes in 2001. Against the background of a sluggish US economy and falling prices for traditional exports (mainly coffee), growth has been driven by huge public spending, mainly on construction, and by moderate rates of interest due largely to the economy's dollarization.

However the deteriorating public finances and current account balance, financed until now by foreign capital inflows, has led to a marked increase in debt that will make it more difficult to attract

foreign capital in 2003, especially in a climate of mounting risk aversion towards Latin America.

The political conflict between the party in government, the Arena (Alianza Republicana Nacionalista), and the main opposition party, the FMLN (Frente Farabundo Marti para la Liberacion Nacional), could also contribute to a loss of market confidence. The political antagonisms are being played out against a background of spreading popular discontent and rising insecurity in the run-up to municipal and parliamentary elections in March 2003 and presidential elections in 2004.

2

KEY ECONOMIC INDICATORS

US$ billion	1998	1999	2000	2001	2002 (e)	2003 (f)
Economic growth (%)	3.7	3.4	2.2	1.8	2.9	3.9
Inflation (%)	4.2	−1	4.3	1.4	3	2.2
Public-sector balance/GDP (%)	−2.3	−2.8	−3.7	−4.9	−5.4	−4.8
Exports	2.5	2.5	3	2.9	3.1	3.4
Imports	3.8	3.9	4.7	4.8	5.3	5.7
Trade balance	−1.3	−1.4	−1.7	−2	−2.2	−2.3
Current account balance/GDP (%)	−1.1	−2.2	−3.5	−1.5	−4.5	−4.4
Foreign debt	4.4	5	5.5	6.3	7.2	7.9
Debt service/Exports (%)	11.1	11.3	9.6	14.6	14.8	14.6
Reserves (import months)	5.2	5.4	4.4	4	3.6	4

e = estimated, f = forecast

Guatemala

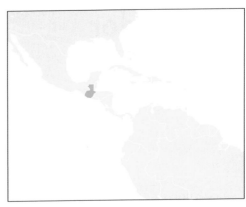

Coface analysis

Short-term: **B**

Medium-term:
Very high risk

STRENGTHS

- Receives international financial aid.
- Moderate public debt despite increased borrowings.
- Cautious fiscal and monetary policies.
- Conclusion of peace agreement with Belize has ended border disputes that hampered economic relations between the two countries.

WEAKNESSES

- Exports over concentrated on traditional and agricultural products, the prices of which are highly volatile.
- Weak savings and investment. Extremely low tax ratio and poor infrastructure.
- Weak banking sector.
- Highly inegalitarian country with declining per capita income due to rising population.
- Extremely unstable politically.

RISK ASSESSMENT

Growth has been stunted by the continued economic slowdown in the United States and neighbouring countries, the slump in commodity prices (especially coffee, the country's main export) and the mediocre performance of tourism. Moreover the aversion of international investors to the risks carried by Latin American countries has caused foreign investment to shrink. As this covers only a small proportion of the borrowing requirement the country is running deeper into debt.

However, thanks to an agreement concluded with the IMF, the still shaky financial sector should see gradual consolidation. The privatization programme should continue to make headway, although the inadequate tax ratio and the public sector deficit will limit the government's room for manoeuvre.

Political instability is the main source of uncertainty. Divisions within the government in the run-up to the elections due in late 2003 between supporters of President Portillo and those of the former dictator Rios Montt restrict government action. In addition corruption, drugs trafficking and the bitter antagonism between government and opposition (the scars left by 36 years of violent civil war have yet to heal) undermine the country's social cohesion and deter foreign investors and lenders.

KEY ECONOMIC INDICATORS						
US$ billion	1998	1999	2000	2001	2002 (e)	2003 (f)
Economic growth (%)	5	3.8	3.6	2.1	2.3	3
Inflation (%)	7.5	4.9	5.1	8.9	6	4.5
Public-sector balance/GDP (%)	−2.2	−3.3	−2.2	−2.8	−1.3	−1.3
Exports	2.8	2.8	3.1	2.9	2.9	3.1
Imports	4.6	4.6	5.2	5.6	6.1	5.7
Trade balance	−1.8	−1.8	−2.1	−2.8	−3.2	−2.6
Current account balance	−1	−1	−1.5	−1.2	−1.1	−1.4
Current account balance/GDP (%)	−5.4	−5.5	−5.4	−5.9	−4.8	−6.5
Foreign debt	2.9	3.3	3.2	3.6	3.2	1.9
Debt service/Exports (%)	15	18	16.7	16.9	16.9	16.9
Reserves (import months)	3	2.7	4	4.8	3.9	3.6

e = estimated, f = forecast

2

CONDITIONS OF ACCESS TO THE MARKET

■ Means of entry

Under the Common External Tariff of the Central American Common Market the rates of duty are 0 per cent for commodities and capital goods, 15 per cent for finished goods and between 5 per cent and 10 per cent for semi-finished goods. A certain degree of tariff protection remains in place for some agricultural products or locally manufactured goods, along with a system of temporary exceptions introduced under the state of emergency.

The average rate of duty in the customs tariff is 7.6 per cent, compared with the WTO's 40 per cent consolidated rate. Import licences are not required. Some tariff protection is provided for certain local industries (shoes) and certain basic agricultural products. The new health regulations on wine and alcohol labelling are restrictive, but applied in a non-discriminatory manner.

The two main audit companies (SGS and Bureau Veritas) operate on a non-compulsory contractual basis at the request of the importer or exporter. In spite of the shaky banking sector there are no difficulties with payments. Interest rates are very high. Letters of credit are the most widespread means of payment. Transfers are usually carried out in a timely manner.

■ Attitude towards foreign investors

Foreign investors benefit from non-discriminatory treatment and the most-favoured nation clause and are subject to more or less the same procedures as national investors. There are no restrictions on investment, other than in so-called strategic sectors, such as domestic air and land transport in which the minimum stake held by Guatemalans must be 60 per cent and 51 per cent respectively. This restriction will be gradually lifted for land transport firms by 2004. Post-establishment difficulties derive from the socio-cultural and political environment prevalent in Central America rather than from actual discrimination against foreign investors. At least 90 per cent of a firm's staff must be made up of Guatemalans, and wages paid to foreigners may not exceed 15 per cent of the total payroll. In principle the legal system offers identical safeguards to foreign and national investors, but corruption and opaque administrative procedures often place foreigners at a disadvantage.

■ Foreign exchange regulations

There are no restrictions on capital, dividend and currency transfers and no exchange controls either. The so-called 'Free Currency Trading' Act has legalized the circulation of the dollar within the economy and allows people to open dollar-denominated accounts and make all types of payment in that currency. There are no restrictions on investment of capital or reinvestment of earnings by foreign investors exercising their shareholder rights.

OPPORTUNITY SCOPE

- Population   11.4 million inhabitants
- GDP   18,988 million US dollars

Breakdown of internal demand (GDP + imports) %
- Private consumption   65
- Public spending   5
- Investment   13

Exports: 20% of GDP   Imports: 28% of GDP

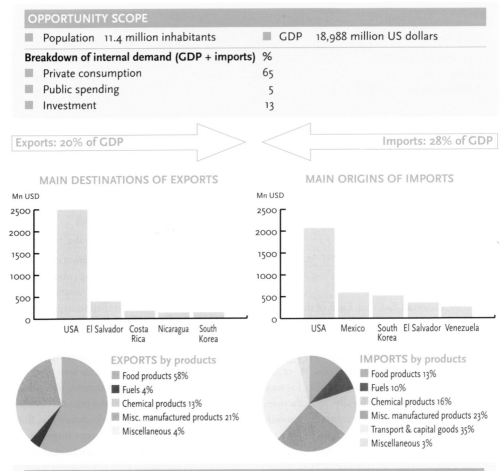

MAIN DESTINATIONS OF EXPORTS

Mn USD

USA   El Salvador   Costa Rica   Nicaragua   South Korea

MAIN ORIGINS OF IMPORTS

Mn USD

USA   Mexico   South Korea   El Salvador   Venezuela

EXPORTS by products
- Food products 58%
- Fuels 4%
- Chemical products 13%
- Misc. manufactured products 21%
- Miscellaneous 4%

IMPORTS by products
- Food products 13%
- Fuels 10%
- Chemical products 16%
- Misc. manufactured products 23%
- Transport & capital goods 35%
- Miscellaneous 3%

STANDARD OF LIVING / PURCHASING POWER

Indicators	Guatemala	Regional average	DC average
GNP per capita (PPP dollars)	3770	6339	6548
GNP per capita	1680	3369	3565
Human development index	0.631	0.761	0.702
Wealthiest 10% share of national income	46	40	32
Urban population percentage	40	73	60
Percentage under 15 years old	44	33	32
Number of telephones per 1000 inhabitants	57	129	157
Number of computers per 1000 inhabitants	11	41	64

Haiti

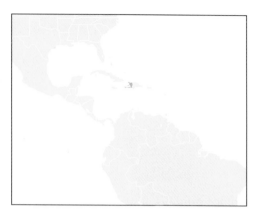

Short-term: **C**

Medium-term:
Very high risk

Coface analysis

RISK ASSESSMENT

The economic position of Haiti, the poorest country in Latin America, continues to be undermined by political instability. The legitimacy of President Aristide's election victory that returned him to office in 2001, and the worsening law and order situation, have been called into question by both the opposition and the international community. While grants to alleviate the country's poverty are gradually being restored political instability is preventing the return of foreign investors and contributing to the economic malaise.

Against this background growth was stagnant, increasing the impoverishment of the fast-growing population. Sporadic outbursts of discontent are also rising. The state of the country's finances, already extremely precarious because of meagre incomes, a huge budget deficit and extremely low foreign exchange reserves, leaves the government little room for manoeuvre and keeps the country dependent on expatriate remittances and international aid. The normalization of political life is therefore a precondition for restoring the minimum amount of confidence needed to kick-start the economy.

US$ million	1998	1999	2000	2001	2002 (e)	2003 (f)
Economic growth (%)	3.1	2.2	1.2	−1.1	0	0.8
Inflation (%)	8.3	9.9	15.3	12.3	11.7	12
Public-sector balance/GDP (%)	−3.3	−3.7	−5.2	−3.6	−3.4	−3
Exports	299	349	327	317.4	310	320
Imports	822	940	1014	981.6	968	1058
Trade balance	−523	−591	−687	−664	−658	−738
Current account balance	−205	−205	−252	−177	−229	−294.9
Current account balance/GDP (%)	−5.5	−5	−6.4	−4.8	−6	−8.9
Foreign debt	1090	1079	1096	1090	1097	1100
Debt service/Exports (%)	8	8.3	7.9	9.4	8.1	8.6
Reserves (import months)	2.3	2.2	1.6	1.8	2	2

KEY ECONOMIC INDICATORS

e = estimated, f = forecast

Jamaica

Short-term: **C**

Medium-term:
High risk

Coface analysis

RISK ASSESSMENT

The world economic downturn is making it difficult for Jamaica to shrug off the recession. Tourism's performance since the events of 11 September 2001 and rising violence have also hit the economy. The competitiveness of Jamaican companies continues to be undermined by an overvalued currency underpinned by the government's high interest rate policy.

Direct foreign investment does not enable Jamaica to cover its growing borrowing requirement. Rising foreign debt has caused the country's total debt burden to reach alarming proportions, although steps have been taken to reduce the budget deficit.

While the People's National Party (PNP) has managed to hang on to its parliamentary majority, violent clashes with the Jamaican Labour Party (JLP), its main rival, have undermined the implementation of measures to reduce poverty, unemployment and, above all, crime, the island's scourge. The army has been given policing powers in an attempt to eradicate crime, often drug related. The country's reputation for violence, which is the worst in the Caribbean, hampers the development of tourism, deters foreign investors and encourages large numbers of the country's young graduates to emigrate.

KEY ECONOMIC INDICATORS						
US$ billion	1998	1999	2000	2001 (e)	2002(e)	2003(f)
Economic growth (%)	−0.4	−0.1	1.1	1.1	2.5	2.5
Inflation (%)	6	8.4	6.4	8.1	8	7
Public-sector balance/GDP (%)	−10.9	−7.2	−5.6	−6.8	−6.6	−5
Exports	1.6	1.6	1.5	1.4	1.5	1.6
Imports	2.7	2.7	3	2.9	3.1	3.2
Trade balance	−1.1	−1.2	−1.5	−1.5	−1.6	−1.6
Current account balance/GDP (%)	−2.9	−4.2	−5.6	−7.6	−7.9	−8.1
Foreign debt	4	3.9	4.4	5.2	5.7	5.8
Debt service/Exports (%)	18.3	17.6	14.6	18.5	30.1	31.9
Reserves (import months)	2.8	3.1	4.9	7.1	5.4	5.5

e = estimated, f = forecast

Mexico

Coface analysis

Short-term: **A4**

Medium-term:
Quite low risk

STRENGTHS

- Vast natural resources, fast-expanding manufacturing sector and increased diversification of foreign trade.
- Membership of North American Free Trade Area provides foothold in North America.
- Sounder fundamentals than other large Latin American countries attracts international investors.
- Democratic political system.

WEAKNESSES

- Vulnerable to external crisis largely because of insufficient foreign exchange reserves in relation to short-term debt and portfolio investment.
- President encountering opposition to implementation of essential structural reforms.
- Public finances remain dependent on oil revenues.
- Strong social tensions exacerbated by continuing inequalities still evident.

RISK ASSESSMENT

Following a slight recession in 2001 the Mexican economy has gradually staged a recovery. In the short term, Mexico's economic performance is closely linked to the state of the US economy as well as exchange rate fluctuations. The depreciation of its currency has helped stimulate exports, but it has also built up inflationary pressures leading to a tightening of monetary policy, which in turn has hit private investment.

Mexico has seen sweeping structural changes over the last few years as a result of NAFTA membership that has opened up the country in a big way to international trade and capital flows. Spectacular export growth, coupled with a cautious economic policy, have sharply reduced the debt ratio to its current moderate level.

While the sizeable volume of volatile capital flows raises fears of a sudden change of attitude on the part of foreign investors, Mexico is only moderately affected by the crisis of confidence that has struck South America as its economy is closely tied to that of the United States. The growing rift between President Fox and the Congress, however, is creating a climate of uncertainty that could undermine investor confidence.

KEY ECONOMIC INDICATORS

US$ billion	1998	1999	2000	2001	2002(e)	2003(f)
Economic growth (%)	5	3.6	6.6	−0.3	1.4	3
Inflation (%)	15.9	16.6	9.5	6.4	4.9	4.7
Public-sector balance/GDP (%)	−1.2	−1.1	−1.1	−0.7	−0.8	−0.8
Exports	117.5	136.4	166.5	158.4	163.0	169
Imports	125.4	142	174.5	168.4	170.8	177.2
Trade balance	−7.9	−5.6	−8	−10	−7.8	−8.2
Current account balance	−16.1	−14	−18.1	−17.8	−18.6	−21.3
Current account balance/GDP (%)	−3.8	−2.9	−3.1	−2.9	−3	−3.4
Foreign debt	164.4	167.5	159.5	159	163.7	167.4
Debt service/Exports (%)	23.6	22.9	19.8	16.4	15.3	16.1
Reserves (import months)	2.4	2.2	2	2.6	2.7	2.6

e = estimated, f = forecast

CONDITIONS OF ACCESS TO THE MARKET

■ Means of access

Since joining the North American Free Trade Association Mexico has offered foreign companies incentives to gain a strategic foothold on the continent. These include the gradual elimination of tariff barriers, industrial property protection and free movement of capital. Mexico has also signed nine other free trade agreements with 30 countries across the world.

The free trade agreement concluded between the European Union and Mexico on 1 July 2000 has paved the way for European countries to win back market share and step up declining investment under the impact of NAFTA and competition from Asian products. By 1 July 2000 47 per cent of trade in industrial products had been liberalized and granted duty free access. A further 5 per cent has been liberalized from 1 January 2003. Customs duties for the remaining 48 per cent (mainly consumer goods) will be gradually lifted by 2007. It should be noted that from 1 January 2003, no European industrial product is liable to more than 5 per cent duty.

Government-licenced independent audit companies are responsible for checking compliance with Mexican Official Standards and issuing certificates of conformity. The services of these companies are widely used but fairly expensive.

The most frequently used invoicing currency is the US dollar. Payments are made within 30 – 45 days. This is fairly quick considering the high rates of interest and shortage of credit. Documentary credit is the safest means of payment for export firms but expensive for the buyer.

■ Attitude towards foreign investors

While the economy is gradually opening up to foreign investment a certain number of strategic sectors are reserved for Mexican companies and are strictly off limits to foreign companies. Foreigners may invest in these sectors only through the 'neutral investment' mechanism (without decision-making powers). For sectors open to foreign investment foreigners are required to obtain an authorization from the National Commission on Foreign Investment for investments above a certain threshold (currently US$8.5 million). For investments below US$8.5 million dollars foreign investors may acquire a 100 per cent stake in Mexican firms without the

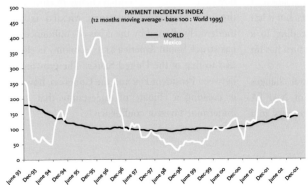

PAYMENT INCIDENTS INDEX
(12 months moving average - base 100 : World 1995)

— WORLD
Mexico

Commission's prior approval. Since 1999 foreigners have been allowed to invest in commercial and merchant banks without a capital ceiling. The Reciprocal Investment Promotion and Protection Agreement between France and Mexico has reinforced the legal framework for French investment.

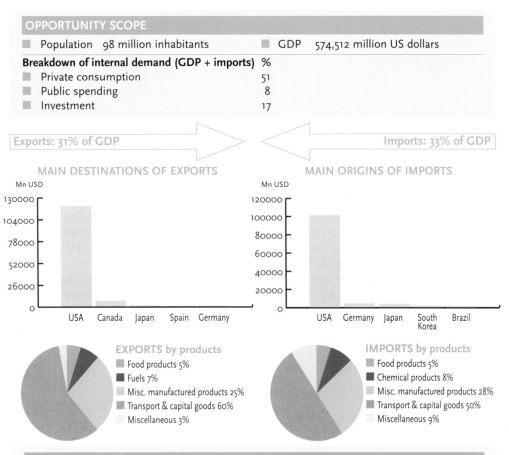

OPPORTUNITY SCOPE

- Population   98 million inhabitants
- GDP   574,512 million US dollars

Breakdown of internal demand (GDP + imports) %
- Private consumption   51
- Public spending   8
- Investment   17

Exports: 31% of GDP

Imports: 33% of GDP

2

MAIN DESTINATIONS OF EXPORTS
Mn USD

USA   Canada   Japan   Spain   Germany

MAIN ORIGINS OF IMPORTS
Mn USD

USA   Germany   Japan   South Korea   Brazil

EXPORTS by products
- Food products 5%
- Fuels 7%
- Misc. manufactured products 25%
- Transport & capital goods 60%
- Miscellaneous 3%

IMPORTS by products
- Food products 5%
- Chemical products 8%
- Misc. manufactured products 28%
- Transport & capital goods 50%
- Miscellaneous 9%

STANDARD OF LIVING / PURCHASING POWER

Indicators	Mexico	Regional average	DC average
GNP per capita (PPP dollars)	8790	6339	6548
GNP per capita	5070	3369	3565
Human development index	0.796	0.761	0.702
Wealthiest 10% share of national income	42	40	32
Urban population percentage	74	73	60
Percentage under 15 years old	33	33	32
Number of telephones per 1000 inhabitants	125	129	157
Number of computers per 1000 inhabitants	51	41	64

Nicaragua

Short-term: **D**

Medium-term:

Coface analysis **Very high risk**

RISK ASSESSMENT

Economic growth slumped as a result of the international economic situation, falling agricultural commodity prices and a tighter budget policy. The budget and external account remain sharply in the red, reflecting the country's heavy dependence on multilateral financial assistance to cover its deficits. Nicaragua should be eligible for foreign debt relief and assistance under a growth and poverty reduction agreement sponsored by the IMF.

However, to qualify for this aid, the government must adopt a tight fiscal policy. But the conflict between the president, Enrica Bolanos Geyer, and his predecessor, Arnaldo Aleman, is hampering the pursuit of economic reforms, especially in the field of taxation. Because of this fratricidal struggle within the ruling party the government has been forced to compromise with the Sandinista National Liberation Front (FSLN), which is ill-disposed towards budgetary austerity. While the anti-corruption drive ensures the support of the international community political uncertainty discourages direct foreign investment in what is one of the poorest countries of Central America.

KEY ECONOMIC INDICATORS

US$ billion	1998	1999	2000	2001	2002 (e)	2003 (f)
Economic growth (%)	4.1	7.4	4.1	3	0.8	2.6
Inflation (%)	18.5	7.2	9.9	7.4	3.9	5.6
Public-sector balance/GDP (%)	−5.2	−13.9	−14.4	−11.6	−7.7	−7.7
Exports	0.6	0.6	0.7	0.6	0.6	0.7
Imports	1.4	1.7	1.6	1.6	1.7	1.8
Trade balance	−0.8	−1.1	−1	−1	−1.1	−1.1
Public-sector balance/GDP (%)	−24.4	−31.5	−21.1	−21.5	−25.5	−24.6
Foreign debt	6.4	7	7	6	5.8	5.7
Debt service/Exports (%)	22.1	16.2	22.8	27.6	34.5	30.5
Reserves (import months)	2.2	2.7	2.6	2.7	2.7	2.6

e = estimated, f = forecast

Panama

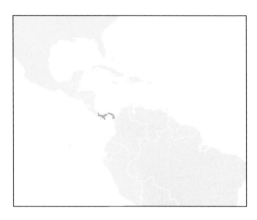

Short-term: **A4**

Coface analysis

Medium-term:
Quite high risk

RISK ASSESSMENT

Shrinking external demand in this open market economy has led to economic stagnation. Nevertheless the service sector has weathered the crisis despite being affected by the world economic slowdown. The growth in income from the Panama Canal, banking and tourism has helped offset the drop in earnings from the Colon Free Zone. The latter, mainly a transit point for products of Asian origin on their way to other Latin American countries, has been hit by the regional crisis. Several years of decline in sectors such as manufacturing, construction and agriculture have

led to an upsurge of social tensions in what is one of the world's most inegalitarian countries.

A series of corruption scandals as well as conflict with the opposition are partly responsible for the stagnation of the reform programme, the deterioration in the country's finances and the perpetuation of a climate inimical to foreign investment, which is in sharp decline. The medium-term prospects for recovery hinge on the construction of a third system of waterways, which would facilitate the passage of container ships, and on the creation of other activities across the country aimed at reducing the duality of the economy.

2

KEY ECONOMIC INDICATORS						
US$ billion	1998	1999	2000	2001	2002 (e)	2003 (f)
Economic growth (%)	4.4	3.2	2.5	0.3	0.5	2
Inflation (%)	1.4	1.5	0.7	0	0.1	0.3
Public-sector balance/GDP (%)	−2.9	−1.4	−0.8	−3.1	−3.1	−3.1
Exports*	0.7	0.7	0.8	0.9	0.8	0.9
Imports*	3.4	3.5	3.4	3	3	3.1
Trade balance	−2.7	−2.8	−2.6	−2.1	−2.2	−2.2
Current account balance/GDP (%)	−15.5	−17	−12.1	−6	−7.5	−7.8
Foreign debt	6.5	6.8	7.1	7.7	7.9	8.5
Debt service/Exports (%)	20	20.4	16.9	24.1	30.5	17.3
Reserves (import months)	2	1.7	1.6	2.6	2.3	2.4

*excluding Colon Free Zone

e = estimated, f = forecast

Paraguay

Coface analysis

Short-term: **C**

Medium-term:
Very high risk

STRENGTHS

- Abundant hydroelectric resources, with significant foreign currency earnings derived from agriculture.
- Fairly low foreign debt to export ratio.

WEAKNESSES

- Country's development hamstrung by abnormally large and inefficient public sector, delays in structural reforms and widespread corruption.
- Chronic political instability prevents implementation of reforms.
- Overdependent on primary sector, imports of consumer and capital goods and economic developments within Mercosur.
- Extremely weak banking sector.
- Unemployment, underemployment and poverty encourage smuggling, corruption and drugs trafficking.

RISK ASSESSMENT

The Argentine crisis and the economic slowdown in Paraguay's main trading partners have led to a slump in the country's exports, exacerbating the recession that has been around since 1998. As well as contributing to rising social tensions the return of emigrant workers has reduced foreign exchange earnings. The sharp depreciation of the Paraguayan currency, the guarani, has weakened corporate and bank balance sheets given the economy's high level of dollarization. The falling value of the currency has undermined the country's capacity to pay against a background of low foreign exchange reserves and restricted access to foreign funding.

To avoid defaulting on its public debt in the long term the country has sought IMF assistance. But because of the atmosphere of near rebellion prevailing in the country the government has been unable to undertake the reforms required by the IMF, especially the restructuring of the abnormally large public sector. The high degree of political instability remains the biggest obstacle in this poor, landlocked country.

KEY ECONOMIC INDICATORS

US$ billion	1998	1999	2000	2001	2002 (e)	2003 (f)
Economic growth (%)	−0.4	−0.8	−0.4	−0.1	−4.5	−1.0
Inflation (%)	14.6	5.4	8.6	7.3	11.5	12.3
Public-sector balance/GDP (%)	−1.0	−4.7	−5.7	−2.4	−2.7	−2.7
Exports	3.5	2.7	2.4	2.4	2.0	2.2
Imports	3.9	3.0	2.9	2.9	2.4	2.4
Trade balance	−0.4	−0.4	−0.5	−0.5	−0.3	−0.3
Current account balance	−0.2	−0.1	−0.1	−0.2	−0.1	−0.1
Current account balance/GDP (%)	−1.9	−1.2	−1.8	−3.3	−2.0	−1.4
Foreign debt	2.3	2.5	2.8	3.3	3.3	3.4
Debt service/Exports (%)	4.8	6.4	9.6	8.9	9.1	8.4
Reserves (import months)	2.2	3.1	2.6	2.3	2.7	2.7

e = estimated, f = forecast

2

CONDITIONS OF ACCESS TO THE MARKET

■ Market overview

In general Paraguay has a very open trade policy as its nascent industrial sector is unable to meet domestic demand. Membership of Mercosur has forced it to raise customs duties on most products in line with the Common External Tariff gradually phased in by the four member countries. Under Decree No. 13385, 10 per cent ad valorem duty has been applied to a list of 320 products (agri-foodstuffs, textiles, apparel, cast iron, etc) from 10 July 2001 to 31December 2002.

This Decree has had very little impact on French exports. The privatization of three public services – fixed telephones (Antelco), water/waste management (Corposana) and railways (FCPCAL) – launched in October 2000 and due to be completed in 2002, has been indefinitely postponed by Law No. 1932/02 of 5 June 2002.

The most widely used invoicing currency is the US dollar. Documentary credit is only used for little-known importers, occasional sales or relatively large amounts.

■ Means of access

The import of certain products is prohibited. The most awkward non-tariff barrier is that set up by Law No.194 because it unfairly protects the interests of Paraguayan agents, representatives and importers.

While mandatory inspections by an approved audit firm of goods exported to Paraguay were abolished in 1999, export documents must first be cleared with the Paraguayan consulate, in the country of origin of the goods or the nearest consulate, and the relevant stamp duty paid.

Copyright infringement and smuggling are rife in Paraguay. Despite repeated assurances from the government the country's new intellectual property legislation lacks teeth.

■ Attitude towards foreign investors

There is no discrimination between national and foreign investors, except in the case of contractual relationships (Law No.194). Foreign investment is not subject to approval or compulsory registration, except for investment covered by the Tax Incentives Act (No. 60/90) and the so-called 'Maquilla Act' (No. 1064 of 3 July 1997). Disputes between foreign investors and the government are brought before local courts.

A new 'Arbitration and Mediation Act' (No. 1879/02) was passed in April 2002 based on the model proposed by Unsitral, which handles both domestic and international arbitration. The Act replaces Book V of the Civil Proceedings Code on disputes, particularly in the business arena.

■ Foreign exchange regulations

There are no exchange controls. In the first 11 months of 2002 the guarani depreciated by more than 50 per cent against the US dollar.

KEY ECONOMIC INDICATORS

US$ billion	1998	1999	2000	2001	2002 (e)	2003 (f)
Economic growth (%)	−0.5	0.9	3.1	0.2	4.2	2.5
Inflation (%)	6	3.7	3.7	−0.1	1.5	2.8
Public-sector balance/GDP (%)	−0.8	−3.1	−3.2	−2.5	−2.5	−2.5
Exports	5.8	6.1	7	7.1	7.7	8.4
Imports	8.2	6.7	7.4	7.2	7.5	7.8
Trade balance	−2.5	−0.6	−0.3	−0.1	0.3	0.6
Current account balance	−3.6	−1.9	−1.7	−1.2	−0.9	−0.6
Current account balance/GDP (%)	−6.4	−3.7	−3.1	−2.2	−1.7	−1.1
Foreign debt	30.3	29.6	29.2	28.6	30.8	30.7
Debt service/Exports (%)	40.3	40.3	39.8	36.6	34.8	32.5
Reserves (import months)	8.9	9.3	8.4	9.1	9.9	9.6

e = estimated, f = forecast

CONDITIONS OF ACCESS TO THE MARKET

■ Market overview

Sectors include:

- The Camisea oil field. Investment in the oil field's current phase of development amounts to US$1.5 billion. In the medium term the oil field project should lead to the development of a large petrochemicals industry. In 2003 Camisea will account for 1 per cent of GDP.
- Mining. The year 2001 saw the commissioning of Antamina, the world's largest copper and zinc mine, which generates US$800 million in annual exports. The mining sector will continue to grow in 2003.
- Construction, which after two years of recession is picking up on the back of a vast housing programme.
- Textiles, which will benefit from the inclusion by the United States of apparel from four Andean countries in the generalized system of preferences (ATPDEA) over a four-year period (2002–06).

■ Means of entry

The market is open and import payments do not pose any problems. The average rate of customs duty is 11 per cent, following the introduction of a new 4 per cent rate of duty. Talks are under way between the five member countries of Andean Community of Nations on setting up a Common External Tariff.

■ Attitude towards foreign investors

Peru's legislation provides foreign investors with a wide range of incentives and safeguards, including equality of rights with domestic investors, the option to sign 10-year legal stability agreements, unrestricted transfer of profits, dividends and capital, freedom of entreprise, freedom to import and export, etc.

Foreign investment is not subject to prior approval. However, investment eligible for special legal treatment and incentives must be registered with *Proinversión*.

Foreign investors may conclude a tax stability agreement with the authorities.

Peru's current tax system consists of income tax, 18 per cent general sales tax (including 2 per cent municipal tax), 10 per cent-30 per cent selective consumer tax for a range of products (fuel, cars, cigarettes, wines and spirits, etc), various customs duties and administrative levies, and land tax.

The special 2 per cent solidarity tax levied on the employee's gross wage will remain in force in 2003.

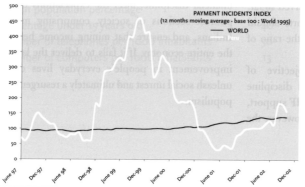

PAYMENT INCIDENTS INDEX
(12 months moving average - base 100 : World 1995)
— WORLD
Peru

On l January 2002 corporation tax was cut to 27 per cent of reinvested profits. Reinvested profits are liable to an additional 4.1 per cent tax. Since July 1995 companies have been able to lay off up to 5 per cent of their staff on grounds of 'operational necessity' without being required to justify such a decision. As this has sparked off a great deal of political controversy redundancy legislation may be amended in favour of employees in the not too distant future.

There are no difficulties obtaining work or residence permits in connection with an investment.

■ Foreign exchange regulations
Peru has a floating yet managed exchange rate.

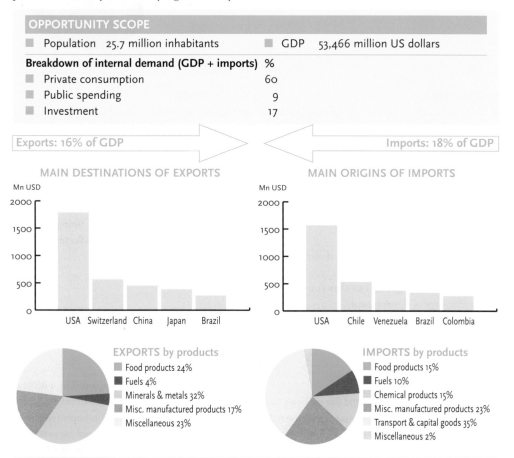

OPPORTUNITY SCOPE

■ Population 25.7 million inhabitants ■ GDP 53,466 million US dollars

Breakdown of internal demand (GDP + imports) %
■ Private consumption 60
■ Public spending 9
■ Investment 17

Exports: 16% of GDP   Imports: 18% of GDP

MAIN DESTINATIONS OF EXPORTS
USA Switzerland China Japan Brazil

MAIN ORIGINS OF IMPORTS
USA Chile Venezuela Brazil Colombia

EXPORTS by products
■ Food products 24%
■ Fuels 4%
■ Minerals & metals 32%
■ Misc. manufactured products 17%
■ Miscellaneous 23%

IMPORTS by products
■ Food products 15%
■ Fuels 10%
■ Chemical products 15%
■ Misc. manufactured products 23%
■ Transport & capital goods 35%
■ Miscellaneous 2%

STANDARD OF LIVING / PURCHASING POWER

Indicators	Peru	Regional average	DC average
GNP per capita (PPP dollars)	4660	6339	6548
GNP per capita	2080	3369	3565
Human development index	0.747	0.761	0.702
Wealthiest 10% share of national income	35	40	32
Urban population percentage	73	73	60
Percentage under 15 years old	33	33	32
Number of telephones per 1000 inhabitants	64	129	157
Number of computers per 1000 inhabitants	41	41	64

United States

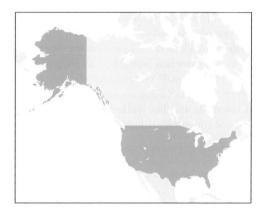

Coface analysis Short-term: **A2**

STRENGTHS

- Vast domestic market ensures significant outlets for firms.
- Swift reaction of economic players, underpinned by government fiscal and monetary policy, enables rapid adjustment to economic developments.
- Geographical mobility, immigration and flexible labour legislation enables labour supply and demand to be matched.
- Despite economic difficulties, dollar remains benchmark currency.
- Higher potential growth rate than countries at a similar stage of development.

WEAKNESSES

- Inadequate public investment. Often dilapidated rail and road infrastructure hampers balanced regional development.
- Shaky welfare, education (primary and secondary) and healthcare systems.
- Several industrial sectors, including steel and textiles, will require massive government aid to cope with much-needed restructuring.
- Inadequate domestic savings reflected in huge current account deficit.

RISK ASSESSMENT

Despite the slowdown in late 2002 the economy has picked up. The upturn has been spurred by the rally in consumer spending. On the other hand business investment has continued to fall as over capacity is nowhere near being absorbed and investors' risk aversion increases financing costs.

Growth should continue in 2003. The small drop in consumer spending triggered by the levelling off of car and house sales should be offset by the recovery in investment and exports, especially from the second half of the year. Interest rates should not rise before the summer, while there could be a fresh round of tax cuts. The outlook for stock markets and property prices remains uncertain.

The upturn has been accompanied by a decline in the number of bankruptcies and defaults. Nevertheless, caution is called for. The improvement in corporate profitability in 2002 should be viewed in the context of the declines of previous years. Many firms will moreover have to pump money into the pension funds of their employees and retired staff. Litigation related to asbestos and health risks could lead to heavy compensations being paid. Sporadic bankruptcies therefore cannot be ruled out. Apart from this, the most exposed sectors remain new technology start-ups, construction, textiles, automobile subcontracting and metal and paper wholesale.

KEY ECONOMIC INDICATORS

%	1998	1999	2000	2001	2002 (e)	2003 (f)
Economic growth	4.3	4.1	3.8	0.3	2.3	2.6
Consumer spending (% change)	4.8	5	4.3	2.5	3.1	2.6
Investment (% change)	10.3	7.9	6.7	−5.2	−5	3
Inflation	1.1	1.6	2.5	2.0	1.5	1.7
Unemployment	4.5	4.2	4	4.8	5.8	6
Short-term interest rate	5.5	5.4	6.5	3.7	1.8	2
Public-sector balance/GDP	0.3	0.8	1.4	−0.5	−2.9	−3
National debt/GDP	68.3	65.3	59.4	59.2	61.4	62.8
Exports (% change)	2.1	3.2	9.5	−5.4	−1.1	7
Imports (% change)	11.8	10.5	13.4	−2.9	3	6
Current account balance/GDP	−2.3	−3.2	−4.2	−3.9	−4.8	−4.7

e = estimated, f = forecast

2

MAIN ECONOMIC SECTORS

■ Automobiles

There were 16.6 million passenger car registrations in 2002, close to the record levels of 2000 and 2001. This excellent performance, however, masks the shaky position of US carmakers who continue to lose market share to the Japanese, Germans and Koreans. They would have fared even worse without the advertising campaigns offering 0 per cent loans and deferred instalment payments. The year 2003 should see a decline due to the gradual saturation of the world market.

■ Paper and cardboard

The upturn in the United States as well as the restructurings carried out since 2000 pushed up paper and cardboard prices at the end of 2002. Factory closures caused by bankruptcies and mergers should improve earnings of the surviving companies in 2003. Through better control of supply, facilitated by consolidation in the sector, companies have gained greater control over market prices.

■ Steel

The protectionist measures adopted by the Bush government have had repercussions since spring 2002, including shortages of some specialist products and longer delivery times. This lifted 'spot' prices, with the increases being passed on to multi-annual contracts in the autumn. As a result US steel makers, many of whom are placed under the protection of 'Chapter XI', saw an improvement in their trading accounts. This trend should continue into 2003. However, the upturn could serve as a pretext for not undertaking much-needed restructuring, especially as the government does not want to address the sensitive issue of pensions and social cover for steelworkers.

■ Telecommmunications

The stagnant fixed telephone market was subject to ever-fiercer competition as a result partly of the dismantling of borders between operators (regional and long-distance) and partly of the growth in mobile phones. Against this background several companies sought the protection of 'Chapter XI' in 2002.

Cell phones have enjoyed strong growth. Nevertheless the disparity in standards, falling subscriber income, saturation of transmission equipment and the huge investments required for third generation telephony, should trigger mergers between the six leading operators on the market. The sluggishness of the fixed telephones sector and the wait-and-see attitude of mobile operators is affecting equipment manufacturers in the telecommunications sector.

Textiles

As a result of the continued downturn in 2002 the textiles sector is still in the throes of restructuring. The competitiveness of Asian countries and fiercer competition between large distributors have further weakened an already shaky situation. Retail prices for garments have never been so low. This trend should intensify over the next few months in accordance with the aims of trade policy.

Retail

Consumer spending remained on an upward trend in 2002, focusing mainly on household products, apparel and electronic goods. However, given the uncertain economic context, consumers favoured outlets offering better prices, so much so that mass retailers outperformed all other retailers. Department stores and specialist outlets are the most at risk in this environment. In 2003 strong consumer demand should prolong this situation.

PAYMENT AND COLLECTION PRACTICES

Payment

Exporters must exercise particular caution as to the provisions of sales contracts that are payable on credit, and ensure that they obtain payment conditions which are appropriate for the context.

Cheques and bills of exchange are very basic payment devices that do not allow creditors to bring actions for recovery in respect of exchange law (droit cambiaire).

Cheques are widely used but do not presuppose, at their issue, notions of sufficient funds, which means that they offer relatively limited guarantees. Account holders may stop payment on a cheque by way of a simple written request made within 14 days of the cheque's issue. Moreover, in the event of default, a cheque's beneficiary must still provide proof of the existence of his claim.

More difficult to obtain, but providing greater security, banker's cheques that are drawn directly on the bank's account, offer a direct undertaking to pay by a bank.

Bills of exchange and promissory notes are less commonly used and offer no specific proof of a debt.

SWIFT transfers are frequently used and the majority of US banks are connected to the system. Such payments, which are relatively rapid and simple to use, are particularly suitable where trust exists between contracting parties, in so far as the seller depends on his client's good faith to order the transfer (a system known as *open account*).

Debt collection

Owing to the complexity and high cost of the US legal system, exporters are always better advised to negotiate with clients and, wherever possible, to settle out of court.

The judicial system comprises two basic types of court, those in the federal court system (district courts) and state courts (circuit or county courts).

The broad majority of actions are heard by state courts that uphold state and federal law in disputes occurring within their jurisdictions (ie actions concerning persons domiciled or resident in the state).

However, federal courts rule on disputes involving state governments, cases involving interpretations of the constitution or federal treaties, disputes between citizens of different states and foreign countries as well as, in certain cases, those concerning plaintiffs and defendants from foreign countries.

A key feature of the US judicial system is the 'pretrial discovery phase' which allows each party to demand evidence and testimonies concerning a dispute from his adversary before the case is heard by the court. During the trial itself judges also afford considerable leeway to plaintiffs to produce any pertinent document.

Another feature of the US procedure is that parties may request that cases be heard by a jury made up of ordinary citizens whose task is to deliver a verdict based, over all, on the facts presented in the case.

Lastly, in matters of special complexity or cases involving long periods of time or considerable costs, courts frequently authorize creditors, in winding up matters, to invoke the liability of professionals who have counselled the defaulting enterprise, in so far as it is demonstrated that such advisers have committed breaches in the exercise of their activity.

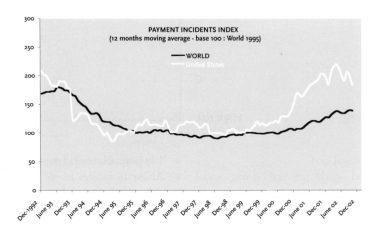

2

Uruguay

Short-term: **C**

Medium-term:

Coface analysis   **High risk**

STRENGTHS

- Rich agricultural land.
- Well-trained workforce and strong social indicators.
- Politically stable country backed by international financial community.

WEAKNESSES

- Unsustainable level of debt.
- Ability to redeem mostly dollar denominated debt closely linked to exchange rates movements.
- Collapse of banking sector could do lasting damage to country's finances and Montevideo's reputation as a financial centre.
- Extremely vulnerable to economic development of Argentina and Brazil.
- Poorly diversified exports consisting mainly of agricultural products.
- Rising unemployment driving emigration of many skilled workers.

RISK ASSESSMENT

After three years of recession Uruguay is now reeling from the effects of the Argentine crisis, massive fund withdrawals by depositors and the collapse of its currency. Economic activity plunged by over 10 per cent in 2002. Growth is expected to remain negative in 2003 due to lack of liquidity, restrictive fiscal and monetary policies and continued uncertainties in an unfavourable regional environment.

Unlike Argentina, rapid action by the government and international financial institutions helped ward off a systemic crisis in the banking sector. Nevertheless Montevideo's role as a financial centre seems to have suffered lasting damage.

The chances of economic modernization are low as financial restructuring will be a long and painful process, putting severe strain on the country's finances. The magnitude of the recession and the collapse of the currency have seriously undermined the solvency of both the public and private sectors as most of their debt is denominated in foreign currency. Debt ratios are now among the highest for emerging countries.

KEY ECONOMIC INDICATORS

US$ billion	1998	1999	2000	2001	2002 (e)	2003 (f)
Economic growth (%)	4.5	−2.8	−1.4	−3.1	−11.5	−4.3
Inflation (%)	8.6	4.2	5.1	3.6	39.2	49.1
Public-sector balance/GDP (%)	−1	−4.1	−4	−4.2	−3.6	−3
Exports	2.8	2.3	2.4	2.1	2.1	2.2
Imports	3.6	3.2	3.3	2.9	2.1	2.1
Trade balance	−0.8	−0.9	−0.9	−0.8	0	0.1
Current account balance	−0.5	−0.5	−0.5	−0.5	0.2	0.2
Current account balance/GDP (%)	−2.1	−2.4	−2.6	−2.5	1.5	1.5
Foreign debt	13.6	13.3	14.3	16	12.8	13.4
Debt service/Exports (%)	21.2	29.7	29.2	33.2	36.3	37
Reserves (import months)	4.7	6.4	6.6	8	2.2	3.4

e = estimated, f = forecast

2

CONDITIONS OF ACCESS TO THE MARKET

■ Market overview

Despite the split vote on the budget package, the Economic Stimulus Act authorizing the government to award a series of public service concessions (roads, ports, airport, etc) and the slight upturn in meat exports, Uruguay is having difficulty stabilizing its economy. The country's earning capacity is currently insufficient to service its debt, raising investors' fears that it might default on its payments. In 2001 per capita GDP was US$5585, down 3.1 per cent on 2000. Average monthly household income (excluding house values) is 472 euros. Labour is plentiful and in general fairly skilled. Basic wages are low in relation to qualifications, but social security contributions are fairly high.

The only growth sectors at present are agri-foodstuffs and services.

■ Means of entry

The Uruguayan market can be construed as very open, although complex customs clearance procedures delay the entry of goods. Goods may be freely imported into the country, with the exception of military equipment, some wines and spirits, second-hand vehicles and spare parts and live cattle from certain countries, including France.

A number of non-tariff barriers remain in place and should be gradually lifted within the framework of Mercosur. These include prior approval for wheat imports, benchmark pricing, import duty payment formalities, domestic tax and restrictive health tests and inspections for all foodstuffs.

Mercosur's customs union currently applies to 85 per cent of tariff items, excluding automobiles and spare parts and sugar.

Customs duties and levies are calculated on the Montevideo CIF value and vary between 0 per cent and 23 per cent. Additional levies include a port tax, the commission charged by the Bank of the Oriental Republic of Uruguay and VAT. The most widely recommended means of payment are the documentary credit and documentary collection.

■ Attitude towards foreign investors

Foreign investment is unrestricted and not subject to any notification requirement. Nearly all sectors are open to foreign investors, except oil refining, fixed telephones, railways, transport and electricity generation. The Foreign Investment Act 1998 offers significant financial incentives, including exemptions from tax and customs duties.

■ Foreign exchange regulations

There are no restrictions on currency inflows and outflows. The dollar is the de facto benchmark currency, with 85 per cent of loans and deposits denominated in dollars. The peso has been floating freely since July 2002. There are no exchange controls on import payments. However, under a recent measure any foreign exchange transaction worth US$10000 or more, or its equivalent value in another currency, is subject to the completion of a form. There are no restrictions on or authorizations required for the transfer of capital or profits.

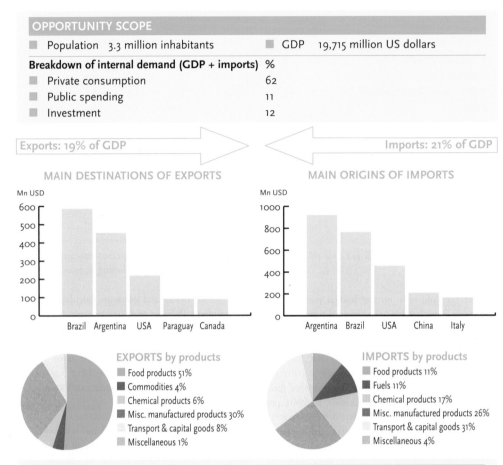

OPPORTUNITY SCOPE

- Population 3.3 million inhabitants
- GDP   19,715 million US dollars

Breakdown of internal demand (GDP + imports) %
- Private consumption   62
- Public spending   11
- Investment   12

Exports: 19% of GDP   Imports: 21% of GDP

MAIN DESTINATIONS OF EXPORTS

Mn USD

Brazil Argentina USA Paraguay Canada

MAIN ORIGINS OF IMPORTS

Mn USD

Argentina Brazil USA China Italy

EXPORTS by products
- Food products 51%
- Commodities 4%
- Chemical products 6%
- Misc. manufactured products 30%
- Transport & capital goods 8%
- Miscellaneous 1%

IMPORTS by products
- Food products 11%
- Fuels 11%
- Chemical products 17%
- Misc. manufactured products 26%
- Transport & capital goods 31%
- Miscellaneous 4%

STANDARD OF LIVING / PURCHASING POWER

Indicators	Uruguay	Regional average	DC average
GNP per capita (PPP dollars)	8880	6339	6548
GNP per capita	6000	3369	3565
Human development index	0.831	0.761	0.702
Wealthiest 10% share of national income	33	40	32
Urban population percentage	91	73	60
Percentage under 15 years old	25	33	32
Number of telephones per 1000 inhabitants	278	129	157
Number of computers per 1000 inhabitants	105	41	64

Venezuela

Coface analysis

Short-term: **D**

Medium-term:
High risk

2

STRENGTHS

- Substantial oil, gas and mineral resources. North America main market for oil exports.
- Progress in structural reforms (opening up of oil, gas, aluminium, electricity, banking and telecommunications sectors).
- Moderate level of foreign debt.

WEAKNESSES

- Economy heavily dependent on oil (over 80 per cent of exports and 50 per cent of fiscal revenues).
- Inefficient and mismanaged public sector.
- Lack of business confidence stemming from political uncertainties.
- Liquidity crunch caused by substantial capital outflows by residents.

RISK ASSESSMENT

Political uncertainty is the key risk factor. Absence of social progress, authoritarian methods and political and economic policies have engendered discontent, especially in business circles. After the failed coup attempt in April 2002 President Chavez's return to power with the support of the poorest sections of society has highlighted political divisions within the opposition and the army. The climate of political polarization could bring about a surge of violence and a state of emergency.

There are also concerns about the country's economic and financial situation. Oil output decline, amplified during the general strike launched on 2 December, and political uncertainty stemming from lack of business confidence have hit the economy. Despite the positive effect on fiscal revenues of firmer oil prices and the bolivar's devaluation, the country's growing inability to renew existing credit lines and raise capital could heighten inflationary pressures and intensify recession. It is unlikely that a recovery in world oil demand in 2003 will trigger a sustained economic recovery. The balance of payments deficit, caused by substantial capital outflows and weak foreign investment in an uncertain political environment, has forced the government to dip into the foreign exchange reserves and the Macroeconomic Stabilization Fund. Against this background the business climate has deteriorated significantly, leading to increased late payments and bankruptcies.

MAJOR ECONOMIC INDICATORS						
US$ billion	1998	1999	2000	2001	2002 (e)	2003 (f)
Economic growth (%)	0.2	−6.1	3.2	2.7	−8	0.8
Inflation (%)	29.9	20	13.4	12.3	32	31
Budget balance/GDP (%)	−3.2	−2	−2.5	−6.3	−4.5	−2.1
Exports	17.6	20.8	33	26.8	24	27.1
Imports	15.1	13.2	15.5	17.3	15.7	16.8
Trade balance	2.5	7.6	17.5	9.5	8.3	10.3
Current account balance	−3.3	3.8	13.1	4.1	3.3	5.7
Current account balance/GDP (%)	−3.4	3.6	10.8	3.3	3.8	6.8
Foreign debt	36.4	39.6	38.6	40.4	40.3	40.1
Debt service/Exports (%)	31.5	25.6	19.2	20.4	29.5	27.5
Reserves (import months)	5.8	7	6.5	4.1	3.8	3.7

e = estimated, f = forecast

CONDITIONS OF ACCESS TO THE MARKET

■ Market overview

While the liberalization programme adopted by the previous government has not been called into question by the new administration, protectionist measures have increased since 2000 against a background of economic recession. There are also signs of backtracking on intellectual property and trademark protection, especially in the pharmaceuticals sector. In an environment marked by the government's professed aim of food self-sufficiency, its wavering desire to promote domestic industry and the stark inefficiency of the local bureaucracy, it is difficult to pinpoint the everyday problems encountered by importers and investors. What is clear is that, despite government assurances to honour Venezuela's WTO commitments, there is a strong temptation for the country to withdraw into itself, as demonstrated by the measures adopted this year.

■ Means of entry

Certification and prior approval requirements were kept in place in 2002, slowing the sluggish bureaucracy even further. Customs clearance has become lengthier. The year saw an upsurge in tariff and non-tariff barriers designed to put a brake on imports. In the agri-foodstuffs sector these include a plethora of licensing procedures, discretionary award of licences (in particular for French cheese and milk powder), sweeping cuts in the number of licences awarded, blocking of containers at ports and stringent health restrictions on French apples and potatoes. Temporary protective measures have been introduced for certain products (steel, paper), together with a benchmark price band for a list of specific products (textiles, garments, etc), compulsory product labelling mentioning origin, and discrimination against imported products, including those originating in the ACN. The environment is conducive to corruption.

In the field of government procurement preferential measures have been adopted in favour of local companies that show a minimum of 20 per cent locally generated value added. This device is tantamount to knocking 20 per cent off the value of a local bid before comparing it with foreign bids.

■ Attitude towards foreign investors

The new constitution (Article 301) embodies the spirit of Decree 2096 of 13 February 1992, giving foreigners the same rights and

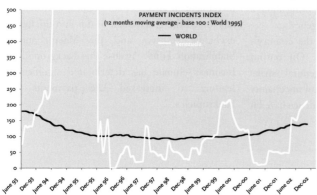

PAYMENT INCIDENTS INDEX
(12 months moving average - base 100 : World 1995)

— WORLD
Venezuela

duties as national investors. However, oil and gas and banking are the only sectors to have seen major investment in the past three years. The privatization of the state-owned steel company Sidor in 1998 and the takeover bid by the US company AES for the private company Electricidad de Caracas in 2000 are an exception.

The poor law and order situation, the U-turns by the new government on the privatization of public services and the political crisis currently engulfing the county combine to keep investors away, with the notable exception of the gas and alumina sectors.

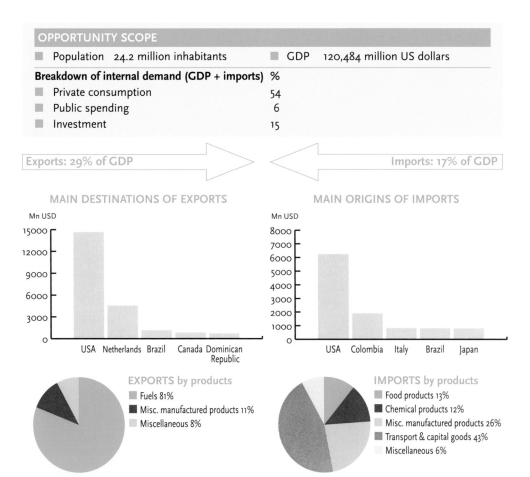

OPPORTUNITY SCOPE

- Population   24.2 million inhabitants
- GDP   120,484 million US dollars

Breakdown of internal demand (GDP + imports) %
- Private consumption   54
- Public spending   6
- Investment   15

Exports: 29% of GDP   Imports: 17% of GDP

MAIN DESTINATIONS OF EXPORTS
Mn USD

USA   Netherlands   Brazil   Canada   Dominican Republic

MAIN ORIGINS OF IMPORTS
Mn USD

USA   Colombia   Italy   Brazil   Japan

EXPORTS by products
- Fuels 81%
- Misc. manufactured products 11%
- Miscellaneous 8%

IMPORTS by products
- Food products 13%
- Chemical products 12%
- Misc. manufactured products 26%
- Transport & capital goods 43%
- Miscellaneous 6%

STANDARD OF LIVING / PURCHASING POWER

Indicators	Venezuela	Regional average	DC average
GNP per capita (PPP dollars)	5720	6339	6548
GNP per capita	4310	3369	3565
Human development index	0.77	0.761	0.702
Wealthiest 10% share of national income	37	40	32
Urban population percentage	87	73	60
Percentage under 15 years old	34	33	32
Number of telephones per 1000 inhabitants	108	129	157
Number of computers per 1000 inhabitants	46	41	64

Asia

3

The Outlook for South Asia and South-East Asia

Experts from Oxford Analytica, London

Tensions between India and Pakistan are now easing although political uncertainties prevent a fuller accommodation. In Pakistan the new coalition is struggling to consolidate, and in India the ruling government, though bolstered by its election victory in Gujarat, still faces a series of challenges.

The main economies in South-east Asia should experience relatively rapid growth in 2003, helped by China's growing role in regional trade and stronger domestic consumption. However, there are substantial risks to growth, including fallout from security tensions and limited private investment.

SOUTH ASIA

Tensions between Islamabad and Delhi have de-escalated since May – July when they came close to war. Both sides have pulled back their forces from the Line of Control in Kashmir where they had amassed over 1 million men. However, there are still grounds for concern:

■ Kashmir impasse

While the restoration of a limited form of democracy in Pakistan and regional elections in Indian-occupied Kashmir have paved the way for further stabilization, the Pakistan–India relationship is unlikely to move beyond the uneasy impasse of the last 50 years. One reason for this is the fact that Pakistan President Pervez Musharraf will not be able to forsake his country's claims to Indian-occupied territory, made in the name of the Kashmiri people. These claims justify both Pakistan's independent sovereignty and the military's dominant role, which form the basis of his power.

The Muttahida Majlis-i-Amal, an Islamist alliance with a strong anti-US orientation, came to prominence during the elections. If, as appears most probable, Musharraf maintains his security connection with the United States, it is unlikely that he would want to antagonize Islamist sentiment further by giving ground on Kashmir. Islamabad's decision to cancel a regional summit in January suggests that there is no imminent prospect of diplomatic progress on the dispute. Moreover, a recent spate of attacks in Kashmir suggests that Islamabad's 'informal' support of local militant groups will continue. In this context, Washington's hopes of India and Pakistan moving towards any fuller détente will remain limited, straining Islamabad's relationship with the United States.

■ Pakistan politics

Pakistan's new parliamentary government possesses a slender majority. A US-led war in Iraq could strengthen the hand of the Islamist opposition. The best hope of consolidation would be a tacit coalition arranged between Prime Minister Zafarullah Khan Jamali's party (which is loyal to Musharraf) and Benazir Bhutto's secular opposition Pakistan People's Party Parliamentarians (PPPP). The formation of such a coalition requires compromise and statesmanship on the part of both Bhutto and Musharraf and, if it fails, Jamali's government could struggle to survive.

■ Economic strains

Political strains may affect the economy, where the new government will continue the reform policies already instituted by Musharraf in concert with the IMF. While the reforms have stabilized the economy they have also moved it towards a low equilibrium trap. Strategies to escape this trap focus particularly on the development of gas pipelines from the Middle East and Central Asia. Such projects are only economic if inclusive of the much larger Indian market. Current forecasts of 4 – 5 per cent economic growth for Pakistan in the financial year 2003 are optimistic and the figure could be significantly smaller if the new government fails to consolidate its position.

■ Indian politics

The Indian government, led by the Hindu nationalist Bharatiya Janata Party (BJP) also faces tests on several fronts:

1 State polls

The BJP overcame one of them on 12 December, winning an enhanced majority in Gujarat, the first in a series of eight regional elections leading up to the general election due in 2004. A poor result for the BJP in Gujarat would have deepened fissures within the party and caused a collapse of the 24-party coalition government. Gujarat witnessed large-scale religious violence in March, in which chief minister and local BJP leader, Narendra Modi, was implicated. The violence brought to a head long-standing party tensions between Hindu nationalists and 'liberals', including Prime Minister Atal Behari Vajpayee. There is a significant risk that Modi's victory will send a signal to other BJP cadres that a strident rhetoric and orchestrated attacks on cultural and religious 'minorities' represents a recipe for electoral success. This is likely to increase the tensions surrounding subsequent regional elections.

With the pressures of the crises in Gujarat and Kashmir of 2002, Vajpayee's succession has already passed to the hard line Deputy Prime Minister LK Advani. These tensions may result in further splits. Many of the other parties who support the ruling coalition are uncomfortable with the BJP's brand of Hindu nationalism.

2 Opposition challenge

Developments within the main opposition Congress Party will be a key determinant of the BJP's political fortunes. Since 1998 the BJP national government has benefited from weakness and confusion within

the Congress. Italian-born party president Sonia Gandhi lacks widespread popularity. Recently there have been signs of change. Vajpayee's failure to prevent the BJP from becoming tainted with religious communalism in Gujarat has enabled Gandhi to advance a broad secularist platform. The Congress has performed well in several regional elections and slowly begun to orient itself towards coalition politics. For example, in Kashmir, the Congress accepted a second-rank berth behind the People's Democratic Party. Many of the small regional parties currently supporting the BJP are starting to sense that an alliance with the Congress could prove better. If so, the days of the BJP-led government could be numbered.

3 Reform resistance

Political uncertainty is bound to have an impact on economic policy. Vajpayee and the liberal wing of the BJP, together with certain coalition partners, are determined to press ahead with a second generation of liberal economic reforms. However, they have encountered resistance from protectionist elements within the BJP as well as from the populist demands of some of their coalition partners. The Congress, which initiated the programme in 1991, has become more critical of liberalization while in opposition. As the centre of gravity in economic policy has moved to the left it is unlikely that any radical measures will be passed in 2003.

However, the established momentum of reform should continue, particularly in the financial sector where the recent failure of several institutions has undermined trust in the public sector. However, there could be considerable hesitation about advancing the privatization of public sector industry and cutting public subsidies. If so, the budget, due in February, is unlikely to show much success in restraining the fiscal deficit – which remains a major structural problem. As long as this problem is unaddressed an economic growth rate of 5–6 per cent is the best that can be expected.

4 Foreign policy

Foreign policy is unlikely to be affected by the political uncertainties of the coming year since it is broadly agreed upon by all the major parties. India should continue its cautious rapprochement with the United States. However, in view of Washington's

3

ties with Islamabad, it will also seek to strengthen its relations with other powers, particularly Russia and Iran. Indeed, vacillation by the United States over Pakistan's support for 'terrorism' could see the revival of Delhi's once close relationship with Moscow. In comparison to the Congress, a BJP government might seek to make more domestic capital out a confrontation with 'Muslim' Pakistan. In basic policy and attitudes there is little to divide the two main contenders for national government.

In conclusion, a political need to pacify extremist opinion on both sides will constrain both governments' room for manoeuvre on Kashmir. Pakistan's economic rehabilitation will continue but the new government is weak and vulnerable to Islamist pressures. In India, policies will be dominated by political expediency, which could lead to delays in economic reform and an increase in religious conflicts.

SOUTH-EAST ASIA

Consensus Economics has forecast average real GDP growth in 2003 of 3.9 per cent for the 10 members of the Association of South-east Asian Nations (ASEAN), compared with an expected 3.6 per cent in 2002 and 2.3 per cent in 2001. Forecasts by the World Bank, Asian Development Bank and regional research groups range from 3.5–4.6 per cent, reflecting guarded optimism that the region will withstand the impact of weak growth in its two main export markets, the United States and Japan. There are grounds to believe that these forecasts are realistic but performance in the region remains hostage to external developments beyond its control, a number of which could have an adverse affect on growth.

On the positive side, recovery from the 1997–98 East Asian economic crisis is in some respects broadly based. It has survived the export slowdown of 2001 and the upheaval in equity markets that followed:

- **Domestic demand.** Domestic consumption rose strongly in the first three quarters of 2002 with the help of historically low interest rates, static inflation and higher prices for commodities. Household spending has benefited from increased bank lending in countries with lower levels of financial sector debt and

expansionary fiscal policies instituted during the 2001 exports slump.

- **External demand.** Export revenues have been eroded by weakening US and Japanese demand. However, this blow has to some extent been softened by closer economic integration within ASEAN, and growing trade with China. Intra-regional shipments accounted for an estimated 24 per cent of South-east Asian export sales during the first three quarters of 2002, and exports to China were up by at least 50 per cent over the same period in 2001.

- **Manufacturing output.** Manufacturing grew by an estimated 5 per cent year on year during January–September 2002, despite slow sales of electronic and technological goods, which contribute up to 40 per cent of total export revenues. It is expected to expand by 5–7 per cent in 2003, with Vietnam and Malaysia achieving the highest growth rates among the developing and industrialized countries, respectively.

- **Debt management.** Exchange-rate risks have markedly receded, with the five leading South-east Asian economies now maintaining sufficient international reserves to cover their short-term external debts. Ratios of offshore debt to GDP are lower than at the onset of 1997, while most outstanding loan repayment commitments have been converted into more stable long-term debt. Major currencies have appreciated by 15–20 per cent against the dollar during the past 12 months.

■ Growth threats

While South-east Asia has so far avoided contagion from the volatility in emerging South American markets, the region will be affected if the US recovery is delayed. Certain export-dependent ASEAN states showed signs of a slowdown in late 2002, with a third-quarter fall in demand for technology goods. Singapore and Indonesia recorded slower growth between July-September and output fell in Thailand and Singapore. Recurrent loan defaults have curbed bank lending in Thailand and Malaysia. While these setbacks do not suggest a sustained loss of impetus from the 2002 rebound their growth outlook will be largely determined by external conditions:

- **External trade.** The United States and Japan still account for about 40 per cent of combined exports of ASEAN countries and the EU a further 10–12 per cent. Intra-regional trade is therefore only a partial substitute for US demand. Most exports from the region are intermediate products that will undergo basic processing before being re shipped to markets in developed countries. In many cases, exports are the leading source of economic growth, providing 85 per cent of GDP in Malaysia, 40 per cent in Thailand, 35 per cent in the Philippines, 25 per cent in Indonesia and 20 per cent in Singapore.
- **Iraq war.** With its large Muslim population South-east Asia will be especially vulnerable if the United States leads a military offensive against Iraq. Tourism and foreign investment would suffer from retaliatory attacks in the region. Arrivals from the United States have fallen by almost 11 per cent since 2001 according to the Pacific Asia Travel Association. Higher oil prices would push up inflation and trim current account surpluses. The effect would be particularly severe in the Philippines and Thailand, which import 54 per cent and 46 per cent of their energy supplies respectively.
- **Capital flows.** Excess production capacity has so depressed investment levels that economic recovery will be difficult to sustain if security concerns deter foreign capital inflows. China will continue to draw foreign direct investment away from South-east Asia in 2003. Private fixed investment now accounts for only half its 1997 level in Malaysia, two-thirds in Thailand and the Philippines, and one-quarter in Indonesia. Only in Singapore does investment match consumption.

■ **Policy challenges**

Economic planners may have limited capacity to react to these external threats:

- **Domestic capital.** At least 50 per cent of Indonesian commercial bank loans are classed as non-performing. The figures are 43 per cent in Thailand and 18 per cent in the Philippines. Corporate debt remains a concern, despite an impressive recovery since 2000. The debt-to-equity ratio was 7.8:1.0 in Indonesia in 2001 and 4.3:1.0 in Thailand, but was almost at parity in Malaysia and the Philippines. Efforts to attract foreign capital are undermined by a nationalist upsurge leading to a partial roll-back in investment and business reforms of 1998-2000.
- **Structural changes.** Several processes are under way in the region. While structural reforms in manufacturing and finance have slowed as debt pressure has receded, the formal launch of the ASEAN Free Trade Area in January 2003 threatens uncompetitive industries, currently adjusting to lower export demand and rivalry from low-cost producers such as China. At the same time Indonesia, Malaysia and Thailand are struggling to make the transition to more sophisticated manufacturing processes to deflect the threat posed by China. In the long term China will be seen as an investment partner.

Policymakers will have to balance calls for further reforms with the need to shield major economic sectors against external pressures:

- **Monetary policy.** Average inflation is expected to grow by a manageable 2.5–3 per cent if oil prices remain relatively stable, but could reach 4 per cent in the event of a prolonged disruption of Middle East shipments. Another potential source of inflation is agricultural shortages due to unfavourable weather conditions caused by a return of the El Nino phenomenon in Indonesia, parts of Malaysia and the Philippines. In these circumstances, an increase in base interest rates may be unavoidable, though monetary chiefs might pressurize banks to absorb the initial shock without curtailing essential lending growth.

3

- Debt resurgence. Public debt is unsustainably high in Indonesia, Thailand, Malaysia and the Philippines, thus undermining the capacity of these countries to fall back on stimulus measures. At the end of 2001 Indonesia and the Philippines were carrying debt in excess of 90 per cent of GDP; 70 per cent in Malaysia; 60 per cent in Thailand, mainly as a result of post-crisis expansionary policies.

■ Sectoral outlook

Budgetary reforms will probably occur too late to release more public funding as a prop against lagging private investment. Countries with healthy levels of domestic consumption and an ability to compete for shrinking export markets will fare best:

- Developing economies. Vietnam, expected to record economic growth of 7 per cent in 2003 after a projected expansion of 6 per cent in 2002, is the most promising of the five developing ASEAN countries. Based on World Bank forecasts, Laos will match its 2002 expansion of 5 per cent, as will Cambodia, which grew by 4.5 per cent. These three countries have benefited from higher prices for farm produce. Tentative forecasts for Burma put growth at about 4 per cent due to a resumption of cross-border trade and increased activity in the lucrative resources sector.

- Mature economies. Healthy export figures in November suggest Singapore's GDP could grow by 4 per cent or above in 2003 if external conditions stabilize, although heavy reliance on electronic exports renders this forecast vulnerable. Malaysia should achieve 5 per cent growth, compared with 3.8 per cent in 2002, reflecting a strong rebound in manufacturing during the second half of 2002 and the growth of services. An expansion of 4.3 per cent is likely in the Philippines (4 per cent in 2002), following buoyant exports growth and robust consumer spending. Thailand will grow by 4 per cent (3.8 per cent in 2002), Indonesia by 3.2 per cent (3.2 per cent in 2002) and Brunei 3-3.5 per cent (3.5 per cent in 2002).

In conclusion, stable external conditions should allow growth to match 2002 levels, with private consumption providing a buffer against falling export demand. However, efforts to roll back bankruptcy and budgeting reforms could deter foreign investment. Moreover, regional security tensions could dampen business sentiment and force a rapid reappraisal of economic prospects.

Country @rating scale for Asia

Sylvia Greisman and Pierre Paganelli
Coface Country Risk and Economic Studies Department, Paris

The country @rating scale measures the average level of short-term non-payment risk presented by companies in a particular country. It reflects the extent to which a country's economic, financial and political outlook influences financial commitments of local companies. It is thus complementary to @rating Credit Opinions on companies.

At the start of 2003 Asia remains the continent enjoying the most buoyant growth. The robust economies of both China and South Korea have been driving this dynamism. Japan, meanwhile, still hampered by sluggish domestic demand and the slow process of consolidating the banking sector, has been progressively losing its role as a regional growth engine. That situation should persist this year.

Emerging Asian countries, whose dependence on financial markets remains relatively low, have registered satisfactory growth overall, despite doubts about the vigour of the US economic recovery and insecurity problems in some regional countries. Buoyant domestic demand and sustained regional trade have continued to buoy economic activity. In the more mature regional economies (Hong Kong, Singapore, Taiwan), traditionally more dependent on exports to industrialized countries, the recovery has been more moderate, due notably to sluggish North American and European demand for electronic equipment.

In a globally favourable regional context local company payment behaviour remains generally acceptable as evidenced by a payment incident index significantly below the world average. That situation, in conjunction with a still bright growth outlook, has permitted regional country ratings to remain remarkably stable.

PAYMENT INCIDENT INDICES
(12-month moving average; base 100: world in 1995)
— World
— Asia

■ Countries rated A2

Default likelihood has remained low on average even though the country's economic and political environment or local company payment behaviour is slightly less good than in countries rated A1.

In Japan, economic activity is unlikely to improve much. Despite buoyant sales to Asia exports could suffer from sagging household demand in the United States. Tax reductions will be unlikely to boost local consumption, depressed by declining wages, rising unemployment, and anxiety about pension financing. Moreover, monetary policy will have little impact, with real interest rates already negative. Public investment has continued to contract due to budgetary constraints, whereas company investment has continued to rise slowly.

In this context, the company financial situation remains shaky. Besides small and medium-size companies (often weakened by their dependence on large groups), leading companies in the distribution, finance and construction sectors have had to seek protection from creditors. Although

3

bankruptcies and payment incidents have been contained a resurgence of failures could develop as the process of consolidating the banking sector goes forward.

Admitted to the WTO in 2002, Taiwan should benefit from a slight external demand recovery. However, uncertainties about the vigour of the US recovery tend to undermine that outlook. The economy nonetheless rests on solid foundations although suffering from the banking sector situation (too many financial institutions and a high level of bad debts) and deterioration of public finances.

Taiwanese companies, thanks to repositioning in electronics and delocalization of their production to China, have stemmed the decline in turnover and begun to show profits again, which has contributed to their improved payment behaviour.

Hong Kong, still vulnerable to swings in the international situation due to its very open economy, has resumed modest growth. The outlook will depend, however, on redefinition of its positioning to permit it to avoid being marginalized due to China's increasing dynamism since joining the WTO.

Payment defaults are infrequent with companies that have succeeded in delocalizing their production to China. Conversely, companies operating exclusively in the domestic market have been weakened with a consequent increase in the frequency of bankruptcies of such companies, which suffer from high production costs resulting from high property prices and wages.

In Singapore, also exposed to swings in world trade, the recovery has remained moderate in the absence of a clear upturn in the predominant electronics sector. Faced with that extreme sectoral specialization, the city state has been attempting to diversify by focusing on services. Moreover, its fundamentals have remained very sound. While Singapore has been suffering from a loss of competitiveness due to high taxes and wages, it has been adapting its positioning, notably via closer ties to China and a multiplicity of economic agreements with several industrialized countries.

Payment incidents have risen only moderately, although electronics, construction and distribution have remained particularly vulnerable.

Economic expansion should continue in South Korea, driven by sustained domestic demand and increased sales to China, which has been partially offsetting poorer trade performance with industrialised countries. Furthermore, the external financial situation has remained solid and the banking sector has recovered relatively quickly since the 1997 crisis. Financial adjustment of certain conglomerates (chaebols) is still a major problem, with successful conclusion of their restructuring crucial to the modernization of the economy.

South Korean companies have nonetheless improved their profitability and globally reduced their debt, thereby permitting payment incident indices to remain at a low level.

In Malaysia, economic activity has picked up and that trend should gain momentum thanks to buoyant domestic demand and an export rebound that has been benefiting all sectors even though the electronics sector has remained predominant. Meanwhile, although the banking sector consolidation has been progressing satisfactorily, the company restructuring process has been lagging.

Although companies continue to carry substantial domestic debt there has been no apparent deterioration of their payment behaviour.

■ Countries rated A3

Company payment behaviour is generally less good than in the preceding categories and could be affected by a change in the country's economic and political environment, although the likelihood of that leading to payment default remains relatively low.

In China, recent political changes should not alter the regime's main economic orientations. The economic situation has remained favourable and WTO membership has permitted sustaining massive foreign investment inflows while affording China the opportunity to increase market share abroad. However, increasing competition has accentuated the need for deep reforms while industrial and banking sector restructuring, as well as essential spending on welfare, have been inflating public debt. Although the authorities have to effect reforms while preserving political and social stability, China still enjoys important advantages in its pursuit of modernization.

In this buoyant context the main risks for companies involve the difficulty of obtaining reliable financial information and the poor collection prospects in cases of non-payment.

In Thailand, a return to sustained growth will depend on acceleration of the process of consolidating the situation of companies and banks. The government, which has been lagging in implementing certain structural reforms, has nonetheless undertaken a bank-restructuring programme. It is subject to budgetary constraints, however, with public debt having increased markedly. The economy's competitiveness also poses a problem since it has failed to evolve sufficiently towards more value-added activities in response to competition from China. The country's

3

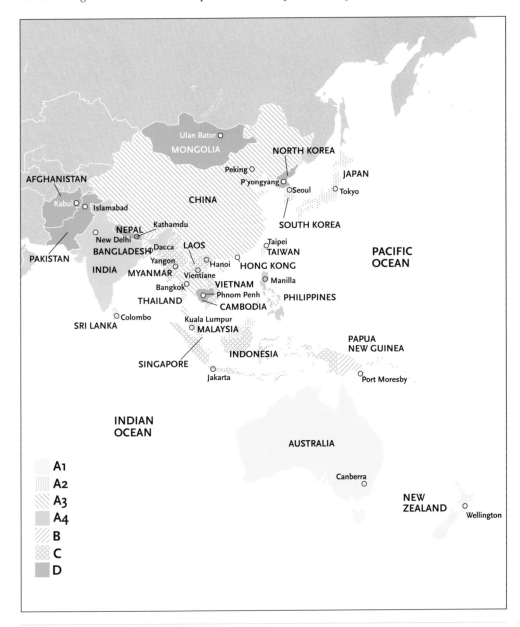

financial situation is nonetheless much sounder than in 1997, which substantially reduces risks of a balance of payments crisis.

The company situation has improved with a return to profitability and some debt reduction. Payment behaviour has been satisfactory.

■ Countries rated A4

These countries often present mediocre payment behaviour that could be affected by an economic downturn, although the probability of that causing a large number of payment defaults remains moderate.

In the Philippines, household demand's continued dynamism should permit sustaining moderate growth although structural problems will impede development of stronger growth. Deterioration of public finances has been generating substantial public debt, while insuffi-

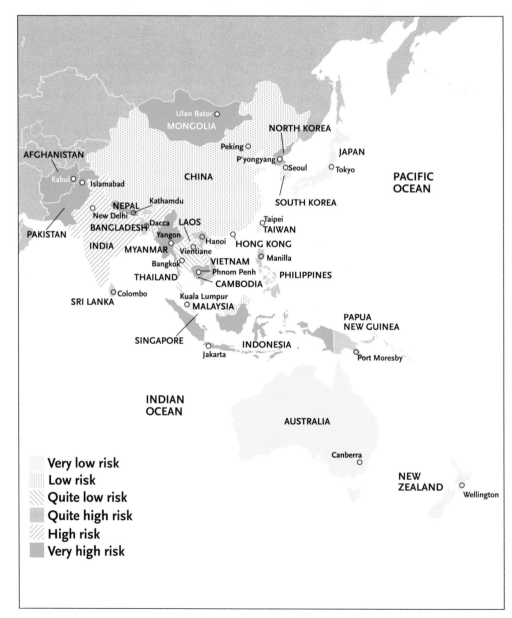

Very low risk
Low risk
Quite low risk
Quite high risk
High risk
Very high risk

cient domestic savings and foreign direct investment have made the country dependent on external capital and resulted in high external debt. Moreover, the banking sector situation has been deteriorating.

Although the payment behaviour of Philippine companies has not been deteriorating their situation remains vulnerable to an economic downturn.

The Indian economy, meanwhile, has been showing signs of weakness, with a growing fiscal deficit and public debt subject to an unsustainable medium-term dynamic. The concomitant economic and fiscal deterioration has nonetheless had no impact on foreign currency financing needs. Besides, the political situation has remained tense. Domestically, inter-religious conflicts have been particularly violent while, internationally, the risk of conflict with Pakistan remains high.

Regarding payments, difficulties in obtaining reliable information and the inadequacy of legal recourse for collection have continued to favour the occurrence of difficult to foresee payment incidents that offer poor prospects for collection. The payment default index has remained above the world average.

◼ Countries rated C

A very precarious economic and political environment could worsen payment behaviour that is already often poor.

The world's largest Muslim country, Indonesia's situation was again shaken by the Bali attack in October last year. Renewal of the IMF assistance programme and new external debt rescheduling agreements have nonetheless improved the country's growth prospects. However, slow implementation of structural reforms and terrorism's negative impact on tourism have been hindering development of a more robust economic recovery. Moreover, there are persistent doubts about the cohesiveness of that immense archipelago with many ethnic groups.

Finally, the Vietnamese economy's strong growth continues, underpinned by buoyant domestic demand, private company dynamism, and the initial positive effects of the trade agreement with the United States. Implementation since 2001 of an ambitious consolidation programme to overhaul the banking and industrial public sector instigated by the IMF reflects the authorities' firmer commitment to economic reforms. Acceleration of the process of opening the economy will nonetheless depend on a profound change in attitudes and substantial improvement of the business environment.

In this context vigilance is still in order, particularly since it is very difficult to obtain financial information on companies and obligations and bankruptcy law is virtually non-existent.

3

Australia

Coface analysis   Short-term: **A1**

RISK ASSESSMENT

In 2002 the economy grew sharply on the back of buoyant consumption and house purchases, underpinned by declining unemployment and inflation. Sounder public finances have also facilitated continued implementation of simpler and lower corporate taxation. The only blemish was the decline in agricultural exports caused by the drought, which was not offset by the rally in ore exports.

In 2003 the country should continue to post strong economic growth, largely due to the boom in commodity exports and corporate investment. The latter should partially offset the decline in spending on residential property.

Consumer spending should also fall slightly. Despite the improvement in the job market the enthusiasm of highly indebted consumers should be dampened by the central bank's decision to push up interest rates in order to prevent any risk of overheating.

Bankruptcies and defaults, which multiplied in the wake of the economic slowdown in 2001 (particularly in telecommunications and air transport), fell back to a satisfactory level in the second half of 2002. The upturn should endure in 2003. However, special attention should be paid to the housing market, which is expected to slow.

KEY ECONOMIC INDICATORS						
%	1998	1999	2000	2001	2002(e)	2003(f)
Economic growth	5.4	4.5	3.4	2.7	3.6	3.6
Consumer spending (% change)	4.7	5.1	2.7	3.4	4.2	3.5
Investment (% change)	7.4	6.6	0.3	−2.5	10	5.5
Inflation	1.3	0.8	3.2	3.5	2.9	2.7
Unemployment	7.7	6.9	6.3	6.7	6.3	6
Short-term interest rate	5	5	6.2	4.9	4.8	5.5
Public-sector balance/GDP	0.6	1.1	0.3	0	0.3	0.4
National debt/GDP	33.2	27.5	23.4	24.4	23	21
Exports (% change)	−0.2	4.6	10.6	1.1	2	6.5
Imports (% change)	6	9.2	7.1	−4.2	10	6.8
Current account balance/GDP	−4.5	−5.4	−3.5	−2.2	−3.5	−3.2

e = estimated, f = forecast

PAYMENT AND COLLECTION PRACTICES

As a former colony of the British Crown, Australia's legal system and legal precepts are broadly inspired by British 'Common law' and the British court system. Since 1901 the six states comprising Australia have formed an independent federated union within the Commonwealth.

■ Payment

Bills of exchange and promissory notes are not widely used in Australia and are considered, above all, to authenticate the existence of a claim.

Cheques, which are defined as a 'bill of exchange drawn on a bank and payable on presentation', are commonly used for domestic and international transactions.

SWIFT bank transfers are the most commonly used payment method for international transactions. The majority of Australian banks are connected to the network, offering a rapid, reliable and cost-effective means of payment.

Another fast growing payment method enables sellers to request orders for payment, via the Internet site of their client's bank.

■ Debt collection

The recovery process starts with the issuance of final notice, or 'a seven days letter', reminding the client of his obligations to pay together with any contractually agreed interest penalties or, where no penalty clause has been provided for, the legal rate of interest applicable in each state.

Where no payment is received and the creditor's claim is undisputed (or where a judgment has already been handed down), the creditor may issue a summons demanding payment within 21 days. Unless the debtor settles the claim within the required timeframe the creditor may lodge a petition for winding-up of the debtor's company, considered insolvent ('statutory demand under section 459E of the Corporations Law').

Under ordinary proceedings, once a statement of claim (summons) has been filed and where debtors have no grounds on which to dispute claims, creditors may solicit a fast-track procedure enabling them to obtain an executory order by issuing the debtor with an application for summary judgment. This petition must be accompanied by an affidavit (a sworn statement by the plaintiff attesting to the claim's existence) along with supporting documents authenticating the unpaid claim.

For more complex or disputed claims, creditors must instigate standard civil proceedings – an arduous, often lengthy process lasting up to two years given the fact that court systems vary from one state to the next.

During the preliminary phase the proceedings are written in so far as the court examines the case documents authenticating the parties' respective claims. During the subsequent 'discovery phase', the parties' lawyers may request their adversaries to submit any proof or witness testimony that is relevant to the matter and duly examine the case documents thus submitted. Before handing down its judgment the court examines the case and holds an adversarial hearing of the witnesses, who may be cross-examined by the parties' lawyers.

Aside from the local courts that hear minor claims not exceeding, on average, A$50,000, claims for amounts up to A$750,000 in New South Wales, A$250,000 in Queensland and Western Australia or A$200,000 in Victoria are heard either by a county or district court, depending on the state. Claims exceeding the aforementioned amounts are heard by the Supreme Court in each state.

As a general rule appeals lodged against Supreme Court decisions, where a prior ruling in appeal instance has been handed down by a panel of judges, are heard by the High Court of Australia, in Canberra, which may decide, only with 'leave' of the court itself, to examine cases of important legal subject.

The right of final recourse before the Privy Council, in London, was abolished in 1986.

Lastly, though the Australian legal system does not have commercial courts per se, in certain states, such as New South Wales, commercial sections of the district or supreme courts offer fast-track proceedings for commercial disputes.

Since 1 February 1977, federal courts have been created alongside the state courts and established in each state capital. The federal courts

3

have wide powers to hear civil and commercial cases (companies law, winding-up proceedings) in addition to matters concerning fiscal, maritime, intellectual property, consumer law.

In certain cases the jurisdictional boundaries between state and federal courts may be indistinct and this may lead to conflicts depending on the merits of each case.

Arbitration and mediation proceedings may also be used to resolve disputes and obtain out-of-court settlements, often at a lower cost than through the ordinary adversarial procedure.

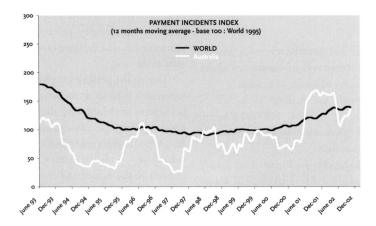

Bangladesh

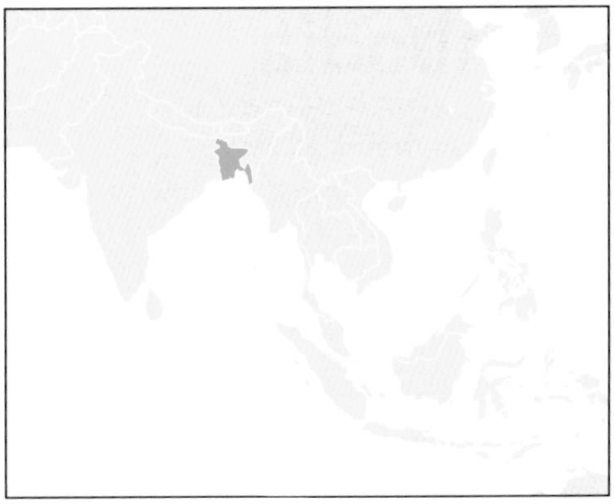

Coface analysis

Short-term: **B**

Medium-term:
High risk

RISK ASSESSMENT

Although Bangladesh remains one of the world's poorest countries it enjoys a fair degree of macro-economic stability. Growth is high, the modest current account deficit has shrunk and foreign exchange reserves have been rebuilt. However, the persistently large hole in public finances keeps the country financially dependent on foreign aid. Moreover the economy remains vulnerable to the domination of apparel (close to 70 per cent of exports) and agriculture (subject to the vagaries of climate). Finally, inadequate infrastructure and widespread corruption act as a brake on foreign investment.

The country remains politically unstable. Since the elections in October 2001 there has been no let-up in the rivalry between the main opposition party, the Awami League (AL), and the leading party in government, the Bangladesh Nationalist Party. The AL is engaged in discrediting the government over the presence in the coalition of two Islamic parties that could have links with terrorist organizations. The political feuding is hampering economic reforms, vital to the development of the country's growth potential.

3

KEY ECONOMIC INDICATORS						
US$ million	1998/99	1999/00	2000/01	2001/02 (e)	2002/03(f)	2003/04(f)
Economic growth (%)	4.9	5.9	5.2	3.8	4.5	4.4
Inflation (%)	8.9	3.5	1.5	3	4.5	5
Public-sector balance/GDP (%)	−5.1	−5.8	−5.1	−6.2	−6.1	−7
Exports	5324	5762	6477	5884	6375	6400
Imports	8342	8566	9524	8846	9470	9800
Trade balance	−3018	−2804	−3047	−2962	−3095	−3400
Current account balance/GDP (%)	−1.9	−0.9	−2.4	−1.4	−1.9	−2
Foreign debt	14840	16182	16591	17393	18000	18000
Debt service/Exports (%)	7.8	8.4	7.5	7.7	7.7	7.9
Reserves (import months)	2.19	2.24	1.64	2.15	1.71	1.71

e = estimated, f = forecast

Cambodia

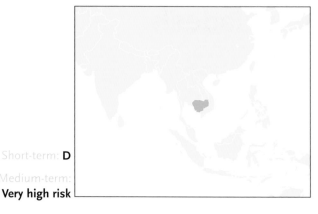

Short-term: **D**

Medium-term:

Coface analysis

Very high risk

RISK ASSESSMENT

Cambodia enjoys relative political stability. The party of the current Prime Minister Hun Sen improved its standing at the municipal elections in February 2002 and is, as a result, well placed (despite the possibility of rising tensions) to win the general election due at the end of July 2003. Moreover, since July 2002 the country has successfully capitalized on its first-ever annual rotating presidency of ASEAN, which it joined in 1999, to improve its diplomatic and economic image.

Against this background the boom in textiles and tourism, the latter providing the strongest growth potential, has helped kick-start the economy. With the dominant agricultural sector continuing to perform satisfactorily this bodes well for sustained growth, albeit inadequate for a country at such a backward stage of development.

Cambodia remains one of the world's poorest countries, highly dependent on international aid to finance its large, chronic budget and external account deficits. Besides, while it is engaged in WTO accession talks, the textile sector could be hit by restricted access to the North American market and competition from Vietnam.

Administrative, fiscal and banking reforms have been undertaken, with measures introduced to protect the environment and reallocate military spending. In spite of these efforts the poor law and order situation, endemic corruption and continued illegal deforestation and trafficking handicap the country and could affect the support of foreign donors.

KEY ECONOMIC INDICATORS						
US$ million	1998	1999	2000	2001	2002(e)	2003(f)
Economic growth (%)	2.1	6.9	7.7	6.3	4.5	5.5
Inflation (%)	14.8	4	−0.8	0.2	2	3.5
Public-sector balance/GDP (%)	−6	−4	−5.2	−6	−5.9	−5.6
Exports	863	1099	1383	1451	1529	1627
Imports	1091	1373	1742	1806	1918	2030
Trade balance	−228	−274	−359	−355	−389	−403
Current account balance/GDP (%)	−7.5	−8.4	−9.5	−9.4	−9.7	−9.5
Foreign debt/GDP (%)	73	68	67	65	42	43
Debt service/Exports (%)	13.4	10.6	8.8	3.6	1.2	2
Reserves (import months)	4.1	3.5	3.3	3.6	3.7	4

e = estimated, f = forecast

China

Coface analysis

Short-term: **A3**

Medium-term:
Low risk

STRENGTHS

- Clear determination on government's part to pursue structural reforms, as demonstrated by WTO entry.
- Extremely low foreign debt relative to foreign exchange reserves and very good debt structure, with low short-term debt.
- External account in black thanks to continued strength of exports.
- Significant foreign direct investment inflows boost foreign exchange reserves to world's second largest after Japan.
- Very high savings ratio.

WEAKNESSES

- Significant industrial overcapacities; many obstacles to public sector restructuring.
- Banking sector weakened by large number of bad debts run up by state-owned enterprises.
- Sizeable increase in budget revenues required to restructure banking and industrial public sectors and to alleviate social and environmental problems.
- Tensions generated by growing gap between rich coastal provinces and poor provinces.
- Strong social disparities and rising unemployment.
- Strained relations with Taiwan.

RISK ASSESSMENT

Changes in the leadership of the Communist Party and the country's governing bodies in late 2002 and early 2003 should not alter the focus of government economic policy on high growth, advancing reforms and smaller regional disparities.

The economic situation remains favourable largely on the back of strong domestic demand. WTO entry offers many opportunities, as illustrated by the massive foreign investment that continues to pour into China because of its huge market potential, and by the likelihood that the country will win new market share abroad. However, fiercer competition in the industrial, agricultural and banking sectors has heightened the need for wide-ranging reforms.

Public debt has soared under the impact of industrial sector reorganization, banking sector restructuring (with absorption of large volumes of bad debt), and essential spending on welfare, infrastructure development and the environment. However, the high level of domestic savings should cover the financing needs, while external debt looks likely to remain under control, particularly given the country's vast foreign exchange reserves.

The government is also having to pursue the conflicting objectives of undertaking essential reforms and preserving political and social stability (because of high social costs of the restructuring of agriculture and the least profitable public sector companies). But China possesses significant assets in its quest for modernization and, provided it overcomes these difficulties, should continue to enjoy robust growth.

3

KEY ECONOMIC INDICATORS

US$ billion	1998	1999	2000	2001	2002(e)	2003(f)
Economic growth (%)	7.8	7.1	8	7.3	7.5	7.6
Inflation (%)	−0.8	−1.4	0.2	0.7	−1	−0.7
Public-sector balance/GDP (%)	−2.1	−3	−2.8	−2.6	−3	−3.2
Exports	183.5	194.7	249.1	266.1	303	366
Imports	136.9	158.7	214.7	232.1	265	331
Trade balance	46.6	36	34.5	34	38	35
Current account balance	31.5	21.1	20.5	17.4	18	12
Current account balance/GDP (%)	3.3	2.1	1.9	1.5	1.4	0.9
Foreign debt/GDP (%)	18.8	17.6	16.1	14.7	13.8	12.5
Debt service/Exports (%)	8.3	8.5	6.2	5.5	5	4.4
Reserves (import months)	9.6	8.9	7.3	8.6	9.9	9.5

e = estimated, f = forecast

CONDITIONS FOR ACCESS TO THE MARKET

■ Means of entry

Access to the Chinese market is littered with obstacles that block, depress or mark up imports. However, China is required to lift certain barriers in line with its WTO membership obligations.

On 1 January 2002 the average customs tariff was cut from 15.3 per cent to approximately 12 per cent, which is still above the level applied by developed countries. It will be lowered to 10.9 per cent in due course as planned cuts in customs duties take effect. Imported goods are subject to restrictive and discriminatory industrial and technical standards. Despite the reform of goods inspection and safety certification procedures China has not made much progress towards lifting technical barriers to trade since joining the WTO.

Imported goods are reserved for Chinese companies authorized to trade internationally. This system must be totally dismantled by 2005. For the time being foreign companies are unable to set up local entities to distribute their products in China, even though a number of innovative measures could usefully be adopted in the free zones.

■ Attitude towards foreign investors

The opening of the Chinese market to direct foreign investment (DFI), handled with great maturity by the government, has gathered a great deal of pace since China's WTO entry.

The Chinese government has introduced four categories of DFI – encouraged, tolerated, restricted and prohibited – by sector. In March 2002 China revised its main legislation in the field, the foreign investment guidelines, to bring it into line with its WTO obligations. DFI is prohibited in postal services, air traffic control, publishing and the media, but sectors such as telecommunications, construction and urban gas, water and central heating supply have been opened up. In addition, various directives relating to the service sector will gradually be implemented in the years ahead according to a pre-established timetable. Foreign access to the retail sector, for example, will be practically unrestricted by 2005.

Each DFI scheme is subject to municipal, provincial or central government approval depending on the total amount of investment. The trend is to strengthen the powers of local authorities, which are more flexible in the enforcement of national legislation, with the central government retaining the right to oversee locally approved projects falling within its jurisdiction in the past.

DFI projects are generally carried out through foreign investment companies (FICs). Although such a practice is restrictive, it entitles FICs to tax incentives. Limited liability and share capital companies formed under the 1995 Companies Act have a promising future, as they enable foreigners to participate in the restructuring of Chinese firms (buy-ins, mergers and acquisitions), especially in the public sector.

Given the principle of public ownership of land, the use of which is only granted for a limited period (50 years for an industrial plant), foreign investors should examine carefully the status of land proposed by the local authority. The central government continues to strictly prohibit changes to the designated purpose of land, especially farmland.

In principle, foreign investment companies must give priority to hiring local labour and employ foreign workers only on an exceptional basis. The statutory working week is 40 hours and the duration of paid leave varies from 5 – 15 business days per year. China does not yet have a unified social welfare system.

■ Foreign exchange regulations

The yuan is freely convertible only for ordinary business transactions. It is more or less pegged to the US dollar (around 8.28 yuan to the dollar).

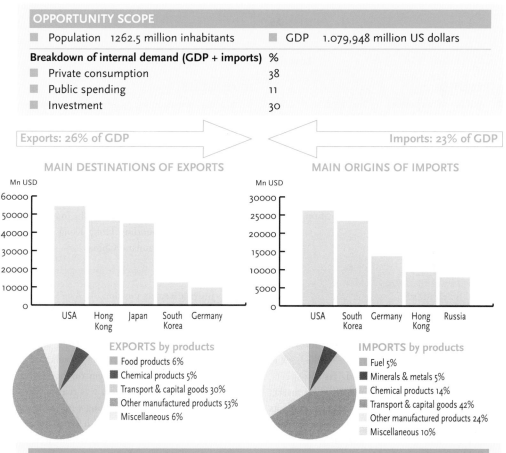

OPPORTUNITY SCOPE

■ Population   1262.5 million inhabitants   ■ GDP   1.079,948 million US dollars

Breakdown of internal demand (GDP + imports) %
- ■ Private consumption — 38
- ■ Public spending — 11
- ■ Investment — 30

Exports: 26% of GDP   Imports: 23% of GDP

MAIN DESTINATIONS OF EXPORTS

Mn USD

(Bar chart: USA, Hong Kong, Japan, South Korea, Germany)

MAIN ORIGINS OF IMPORTS

Mn USD

(Bar chart: USA, South Korea, Germany, Hong Kong, Russia)

EXPORTS by products
- ■ Food products 6%
- ■ Chemical products 5%
- ■ Transport & capital goods 30%
- ■ Other manufactured products 53%
- ■ Miscellaneous 6%

IMPORTS by products
- ■ Fuel 5%
- ■ Minerals & metals 5%
- ■ Chemical products 14%
- ■ Transport & capital goods 42%
- ■ Other manufactured products 24%
- ■ Miscellaneous 10%

STANDARD OF LIVING / PURCHASING POWER

Indicators	China	Regional average	DC average
GNP per capita (PPP dollars)	3920	8590	6548
GNP per capita	840	5794	3565
Human development index	0.726	0.725	0.702
Wealthiest 10% share of national income	30	32	32
Urban population percentage	32	51	60
Percentage under 15 years old	25	29	32
Number of telephones per 1000 inhabitants	112	192	157
Number of computers per 1000 inhabitants	16	105	64

Hong Kong

Short-term: **A2**

Medium-term:
Low risk

Coface analysis

STRENGTHS

- Advanced expertise in financial and other services and growing high-tech industry.
- Asia's leading financial centre after Japan, with well-capitalized banking sector.
- Gateway to vast Chinese market.
- Preservation of territory's special status in China's interest.
- Comfortable external financial position.

WEAKNESSES

- Market positioning and competitiveness difficulties relating, in particular, to Shanghai's increasing competition.
- Highly exposed to international economic changes because of economy's high degree of openness.
- Economic cost of the currency's fixed link with the US dollar leading to speculation over maintaining this exchange rate system in the long run.
- Uncertainty surrounding Hong Kong's future autonomy from mainland China.

RISK ASSESSMENT

Hong Kong's high degree of economic openness makes it extremely vulnerable to international economic changes. Nevertheless the territory seems to be returning to moderate growth on the back of slightly firmer external demand. Its prospects, however, depend on a redefinition of its market positioning with a view to preventing its marginalization in the face of China's growing economic stature following WTO entry.

Public finances, in the black for a long time, are now structurally in the red largely due to the extremely narrow tax base. However, vast fiscal reserves provide a safety cushion. As Asia's second largest financial centre Hong Kong boasts numerous assets, including a healthy current account surplus, low foreign debt, large foreign exchange reserves and well-capitalized banks.

The new 'accountability' system, on the basis of which the territory's government was reinstated in July 2002, could erode Hong Kong's institutional autonomy. In any event relations with China remain crucial, especially as the Chinese government, with an eye to reunification with Taiwan, is banking on the 'one country two systems' approach being a success.

KEY ECONOMIC INDICATORS						
US$ billion	1998	1999	2000	2001	2002(e)	2003(f)
Economic growth (%)	−5.3	3	10.4	0.2	1.5	3
Inflation (%)	2.9	−4	−3.7	−1.6	−2.8	−1.9
Public-sector balance/GDP (%)	−2.5	0.8	−0.6	−5	−5	−4
Exports	175.8	174.7	202.7	190.9	193	205
Imports	183.7	177.9	210.9	199.3	198	213
Trade balance	−7.8	−3.2	−8.2	−8.3	−5	−8
Current account balance	3.9	11.5	8.6	12.1	16	14
Current account balance/GDP (%)	2.4	7.3	5.3	7.5	9.9	8.6
Foreign debt/GDP (%)	29.7	24.2	26	23.4	21.3	19.3
Debt service/Exports (%)	1.2	1.2	1.6	2.2	1.9	1.6
Reserves (import months)	4.2	4.7	4.5	5	5.2	5

e = estimated, f = forecast

CONDITIONS FOR ACCESS TO THE MARKET

■ Means of entry

Hong Kong has built its reputation on effective and transparent free trade legislation and regulations. It is unquestionably the most open market in Asia and one of the most open in the world, even in the sensitive field of government procurement. Hong Kong's return to China on 1 July 1997 and its new status as a Special Administrative Region has not affected its openness to international trade. The territory has maintained its policy of unrestricted imports free from customs duties and direct taxes, with the exception of wines, spirits and fuel. There are no tariff barriers. Some foodstuffs, though, require a health certificate. For most imports the only requirement is an import notification. By special arrangement and under certain conditions it is possible to send in a monthly notification rather than one for each shipment. Hong Kong has adopted identical or similar standards to international ones, including the ISO 9000 series of quality standards. As the second largest Asian financial centre after Tokyo, Hong Kong has a highly internationalized banking sector.

Payments are usually made by a simple letter of credit, but given the poor economic climate it is advisable to insist on payment by irrevocable letter of credit when dealing with small and medium-sized businesses.

■ Attitude towards foreign investors

The territory's free trade traditions inherited from the British have been maintained by the government of the Special Administrative Region, without meddling by the mainland in the territory's legal, financial and economic affairs. In keeping with its free market philosophy Hong Kong places no restrictions on the activities of foreign investors. There are no prior notification or approval formalities, but the territory does not offer any tax incentive or subsidies to foreign investors. Local monopolies have succeeded in driving out foreign competitors. In the absence of a competition law the authorities only intervene when distortions damage consumer interests.

The legal system is simple and company incorporation formalities rapid. Tax laws too are simple and tax rates fairly low (15 per cent income tax and 16 per cent corporation tax). While regulations governing permanent employment in Hong Kong are vigorously enforced, the authorities now permit a small influx of professionals from China to plug gaps. Undeterred by declining commercial property values and small wage increases Hong Kong continues to impose high establishment costs on potential investors.

■ Foreign exchange regulations

There are no exchange controls. The Hong Kong dollar is 'pegged' to the US dollar at the rate of HK$ 7.8 to the dollar. This rate is guaranteed by a Currency Board System that automatically links Hong Kong's foreign currency reserves to the monetary base.

3

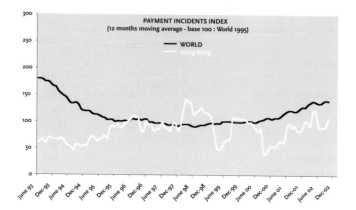

India

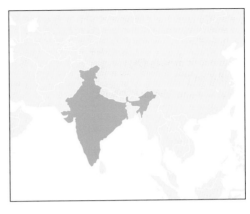

Short-term: **A4**

Medium-term:

Coface analysis   **Quite low risk**

STRENGTHS

- Vast potential market (1 billion inhabitants).
- Some progress in structural reforms (banking sector, trade liberalization, tax reforms).
- Development of information technology and communications sectors.
- Growth in currency reserves driven by service export incomes and private transfers.
- High but manageable foreign debt.

WEAKNESSES

- Alarming state of public finances and high domestic debt (public debt accounts for 87 per cent of GDP).
- Slowdown in economic activity for cyclical and structural reasons (underinvestment due to poor financial intermediation, weak infrastructure).
- Coalition government weakened by rise of regional parties ill-disposed to fiscal consolidation.
- Continued tensions between India and Pakistan, both nuclear powers.

3

RISK ASSESSMENT

Although the Indian economy has largely weathered the world economic slowdown it is showing signs of running out of steam. On the one hand growth has slowed down under the combined impact of poor weather conditions that have hit the agricultural sector and declining private sector investment. On the other hand the fiscal deficit has risen due to inefficient taxation and the burden of so-called incompressible spending. Consequently the public debt is unsustainable in the medium term. There is little political will to implement the reforms needed to bring public finances under control.

The deteriorating economy and public finances, however, do not impact on India's foreign currency borrowing requirement. If anything the country posts a slight current account surplus. The increase in foreign debt largely results from additional official financing.

The political situation, both at home and abroad, remains tense. Following a series of electoral setbacks the BJP government is increasingly dependent on regionalist factions within its ranks. In 2002 there were fresh eruptions of inter-religious violence. On the international front there remains a real danger of conflict with Pakistan, despite efforts at international mediation.

e = estimated, f = forecast

KEY ECONOMIC INDICATORS					
US$ billion	1999/00	2000/01	2001/02 (e)	2002/03(f)	2003/04(f)
Economic growth (%)	6.1	4	5.4	4	5
Inflation (%)	5.5	6.4	1.7	6.2	3.7
Public-sector deficit/GDP (%)	−9.7	−9.7	−9.9	−9.4	−9.4
Exports	37.5	44.9	44.9	48.6	54.6
Imports	49.8	53.3	51.9	55.4	59.1
Trade balance	−12.3	−8.4	−6.9	−6.8	−4.5
Current account balance	−4	−4.7	1.4	1.5	3.6
Current account balance/GDP (%)	−1.1	−0.6	0.3	0.3	0.6
Foreign debt	111.2	113.3	114.5	121.5	120.3
Debt service (Exports %)	19.2	15.8	14.7	15.3	17.4
Reserves (import months)	5.9	5.9	7.5	9	9.5

CONDITIONS FOR ACCESS TO THE MARKET

Means of entry

The landmark event is the lifting of non-tariff barriers on 750 or so products. Following a dispute between India and the United States, the Indian authorities have been forced to dismantle quantitative barriers. Consequently it is now theoretically possible to import anything into India.

To counterbalance what is seen as imposed tariff liberalization, New Delhi has erected a number of new tariff barriers on consumer goods, in particular wines and spirits, as well as a plethora of non-tariff barriers, such as new technical certification requirements and highly stringent health standards (systematic testing of imported foodstuffs and the introduction of a health permit).

Numerous products, especially in the agricultural sector, resist the trend towards lower customs duties. Oil, tea and coffee attract 70 per cent or more basic customs duty. The 75–150 per cent additional duty levied on wine and spirits on top of 100 per cent basic customs duty makes it practically impossible to import these goods into India. Second-hand cars are taxed at 105 per cent.

Conversely, certain products regarded as essential to the country's economic development benefit from reduced rates of duty (textile and computer equipment and semi-finished goods, certain uncut gems, film equipment).

Attitude towards foreign investors

A number of obstacles remain. These include: restrictions on the manufacture of over 800 goods that remain the preserve of small industry; the lack of a flexible redundancy policy; the protection of mass retailing from foreign investors; incomplete reform of industrial and intellectual property legislation (blocked by parliament); swingeing corporation tax (40 per cent for companies incorporated under foreign law compared with 35 per cent for Indian companies); and complex and obscure indirect taxation. But there have also been real improvements, including a gradual reduction in the number of industries required to obtain a manufacturing licence; planned changes to legislation aimed at lifting or reducing barriers to internal trade; reforms or draft reforms in company and competition law; more transparent procedures for approving direct foreign investment applications; etc.

There are no restrictions on the repatriation of profits,

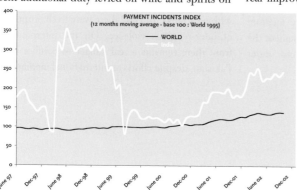

PAYMENT INCIDENTS INDEX
(12 months moving average - base 100 : World 1995)
— WORLD
— India

dividends or royalties derived from the sale of licences, patents, know-how, etc. To withdraw and repatriate equity from an Indian joint venture or subsidiary foreign companies require the permission of the Reserve Bank of India. Authorization is granted in almost all cases, although the authorities retain the right to oversee the price at which foreign companies sell their shares.

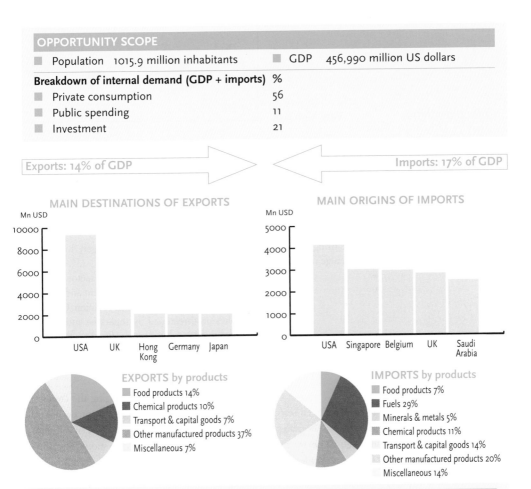

OPPORTUNITY SCOPE

Population 1015.9 million inhabitants

GDP 456,990 million US dollars

Breakdown of internal demand (GDP + imports) %

Private consumption 56
Public spending 11
Investment 21

Exports: 14% of GDP

Imports: 17% of GDP

MAIN DESTINATIONS OF EXPORTS
Mn USD

USA, UK, Hong Kong, Germany, Japan

MAIN ORIGINS OF IMPORTS
Mn USD

USA, Singapore, Belgium, UK, Saudi Arabia

EXPORTS by products
- Food products 14%
- Chemical products 10%
- Transport & capital goods 7%
- Other manufactured products 37%
- Miscellaneous 7%

IMPORTS by products
- Food products 7%
- Fuels 29%
- Minerals & metals 5%
- Chemical products 11%
- Transport & capital goods 14%
- Other manufactured products 20%
- Miscellaneous 14%

STANDARD OF LIVING / PURCHASING POWER

Indicators	India	Regional average	DC average
GNP per capita (PPP dollars)	2340	8590	6548
GNP per capita	450	5794	3565
Human development index	0.577	0.725	0.702
Wealthiest 10% share of national income	34	32	32
Urban population percentage	28	51	60
Percentage under 15 years old	34	29	32
Number of telephones per 1000 inhabitants	32	192	157
Number of computers per 1000 inhabitants	5	105	64

Indonesia

Short-term: **C**

Medium-term:
Very high risk

Coface analysis

STRENGTHS

- Vast natural resources (oil, gas, tin, copper, timber, rice and plantations) and huge population (210 million inhabitants).
- Diversified economy, with hydrocarbon's share of GDP and exports declining.
- Continued current account surpluses due, notably, to strong performance of manufacturing exports.
- Satisfactory level of foreign exchange reserves.

WEAKNESSES

- Foreign debt burden has led to its rescheduling and the country remains dependent on international financial assistance.
- Slow progress in structural reforms (privatizations, restructuring of legal system, anti-corruption drive).
- Very high public debt due largely to restructuring of fragile banking sector.
- Overindebtedness of corporate sector.
- Very high levels of unemployment and poverty.
- Tensions within government coalition. Country's cohesion threatened by separatist and terrorist movements and violent conflict in certain parts of archipelago.

RISK ASSESSMENT

The situation of the world's largest Muslim country has been further undermined by the Bali bombing in October 2002 after the damage done by the events of 11 September 2001. Moreover, Indonesia is still faced with a massive public and private sector debt, although help from the international financial community has been forthcoming. In 2002 the IMF restored its assistance programme and the Paris and London Clubs agreed new debt rescheduling terms. While such assistance has enhanced the country's growth prospects and political stability the economy is still reeling from the effects of the 1997 financial crisis. The slow pace of structural reforms and the negative impact of terrorism on tourism are preventing a more sustained economic recovery.

In addition the job of managing the country's deficit-ridden public finances has not been made any easier by the policy of regional decentralization. However the external accounts should remain in the black thanks largely to firm oil prices. But the country's financing needs remain huge, whereas the woefully inadequate level of foreign investment could fall further as investors are driven away by the climate of insecurity.

Besides, President Megawati is still struggling to establish her authority and implement an effective anti-corruption and anti-terrorism drive, against a background of strong nationalist opposition to the opening up of the economy to foreign investment and continued uncertainty over the cohesion of this vast archipelago with its multiplicity of ethnic groups.

KEY ECONOMIC INDICATORS

US$ billion	1998	1999	2000	2001	2002(e)	2003(f)
Economic growth (%)	−13.1	0.8	4.8	3.3	3.3	3.4
Inflation (%)	58.4	20.4	3.7	11.5	11.4	6.9
Public-sector balance/GDP (%)	−2.4	−1.6	−1.5	−3.6	−2.8	−2.6
Exports	50.4	51.2	65.4	57.4	57.3	59.6
Imports	31.9	30.6	40.4	34.7	34.5	37.1
Trade balance	18.4	20.6	25	22.7	22.8	22.5
Current account balance	4.2	5.8	8	6.9	5.8	4.7
Current account balance/GDP (%)	4.4	4.1	5.3	4.8	3.2	2.2
Foreign debt/GDP (%)	158.1	105	93.1	90.3	72.2	59
Debt service/Exports (%)	34.1	39.1	23	25.4	28.8	25.9
Reserves (import months)	5.1	5.2	5.1	5.5	6.1	5.9

e = estimated, f = forecast

CONDITIONS FOR ACCESS TO THE MARKET

■ Means of entry

A signatory to GATT since 1950 and a member of the WTO from the outset, Indonesia pursues a trade policy based on liberalisation and multilateralism. Since the Marrakech Agreement, customs duties have been significantly lowered. The unweighted average level of Most Favoured Nation (MFN) duty was cut from 20 per cent in 1994 to 8.9 per cent at the end of 1999 and 7.3 per cent in 2002. Cuts in MFN duties have been particularly sharp over the last two years, with the proportion of tariff items subject to 0 - 5 per cent duty rising from 60 per cent in early 1999 to 72 per cent today. While high levels of duty remain in force, particularly for imported manufactured goods, the liberalisation programme continues apace in keeping with the commitments made at Marrakech. Under Schedule XXI, maximum customs duty (ceiling rate) on imports of manufactured goods is due to be cut to 40 per cent over the 1995 – 2004 period (except for 500 tariff items). As well as reducing customs duties, Indonesia is gradually lifting non-tariff barriers. The number of tariff items subject to import licences was reduced from 261 to 160 between 1994 and 1999. In the agricultural sector, the import monopoly of the National Logistics Agency (Bulog) has been abolished for all items except rice. Indonesia is liberalising not only multilateral trade, but also regional trade with its ASEAN partners under the Asian Free Trade Agreement (AFTA).

■ Attitude towards foreign investors

The Indonesian government is extremely open to foreign investors. BKPM, the government investment agency, is responsible for promoting direct investment opportunities in Indonesia. Against a background of financial and economic turbulence, the government has adopted a policy of encouraging investments through 3-5 year tax incentives. With Indonesia relinquishing exchange controls, investors are free to repatriate, without prior permission, capital gains on shares after dividend distribution and payment of local taxes.

Despite free trade legislation, direct investment is subject to prior government approval. The BKPM is the gateway through which all foreign investment

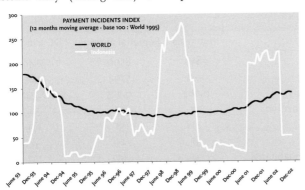

PAYMENT INCIDENTS INDEX
(12 months moving average - base 100 : World 1995)

— WORLD
— Indonesia

3

flows, regardless of sector. There are two exceptions to this rule: in banking, financial services and insurance, investment applications are subject to the approval of the Ministry of Finance, while for oil and gas exploration responsibility for investment lies with the Ministry of Energy. A *Negative List* sets out the sectors facing restrictions on direct investment. This list is due to be revised by the new investment bill, blocked by parliament since early 2002.

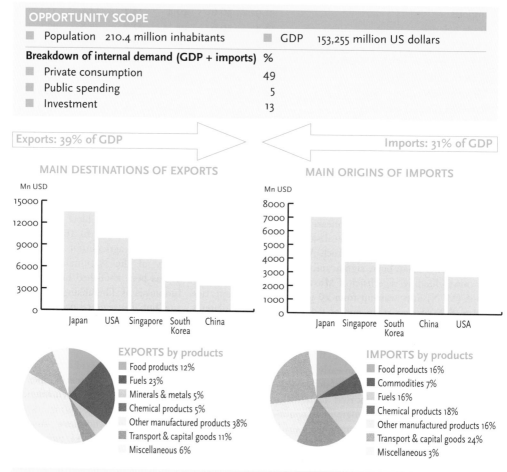

OPPORTUNITY SCOPE

Population	210.4 million inhabitants	GDP	153,255 million US dollars

Breakdown of internal demand (GDP + imports) %
- Private consumption — 49
- Public spending — 5
- Investment — 13

Exports: 39% of GDP   Imports: 31% of GDP

MAIN DESTINATIONS OF EXPORTS
Mn USD

Japan | USA | Singapore | South Korea | China

MAIN ORIGINS OF IMPORTS
Mn USD

Japan | Singapore | South Korea | China | USA

EXPORTS by products
- Food products 12%
- Fuels 23%
- Minerals & metals 5%
- Chemical products 5%
- Other manufactured products 38%
- Transport & capital goods 11%
- Miscellaneous 6%

IMPORTS by products
- Food products 16%
- Commodities 7%
- Fuels 16%
- Chemical products 18%
- Other manufactured products 16%
- Transport & capital goods 24%
- Miscellaneous 3%

STANDARD OF LIVING / PURCHASING POWER

Indicators	Indonesia	Regional average	DC average
GNP per capita (PPP dollars)	2830	8590	6548
GNP per capita	570	5794	3565
Human development index	0.684	0.725	0.702
Wealthiest 10% share of national income	27	32	32
Urban population percentage	41	51	60
Percentage under 15 years old	31	29	32
Number of telephones per 1000 inhabitants	31	192	157
Number of computers per 1000 inhabitants	10	105	64

Japan

Coface analysis   Short-term: **A2**

STRENGTHS

- Highly competitive industry in global environment.
- High standard of living and consumer spending despite mediocre growth.
- Strong social cohesion in the face of rising unemployment makes new government's reform package politically acceptable.
- Massive savings reserves available to government for stemming the deterioration in public finances and meeting additional economic restructuring costs.

WEAKNESSES

- Substantial overcapacity as pace of restructuring remains slow.
- Deflation fuelled by increasing use of foreign outsourcing.
- Sharp deterioration in banking asset positions as stock market investments fall in value and bad debt continues to rise.
- Increasingly impracticable and ineffective expansionary fiscal and monetary policies.

3

RISK ASSESSMENT

A boom in exports to the United States and Asia at the start of the year and slightly firmer consumer spending helped stabilize growth in 2002 and offset the continued decline in investment.

In 2003 growth should suffer as exports are hit by the US economic slowdown. While corporate investment should continue the slow recovery it has posted since end-2002 on the back of a number of tax incentives, public spending should remain on a downward trend due to strong fiscal constraints. Meagre planned tax cuts will do little to stimulate consumer spending, as will monetary policy with interest rates already at 0 per cent.

In this unfavourable environment the financial position of companies will continue to be adversely affected. SMEs, usually vulnerable because of their dependence on large groups and local government contracts, have been the first to feel the squeeze on bank lending. Many retailers and financial and construction firms have been forced into receivership. While bankruptcies and defaults have been few and far between until now the relaunch of the banking sector reform programme by Minister Takeneka could trigger a wave of insolvencies.

KEY ECONOMIC INDICATORS

%	1998	1999	2000	2001	2002(e)	2003(f)
Economic growth	−1.1	0.7	2.4	−0.3	−0.5	1
Consumer spending (% change)	0.1	1.2	0.6	1.4	0.8	0.6
Investment (% change)	−4	−0.8	3.2	0	−6.5	2
Inflation	−0.1	−0.5	−1.1	−1.5	−1.3	−1
Unemployment	4.1	4.7	4.7	5	5.4	5.6
Short-term interest rate	0.7	0.2	0.2	0.1	0.1	0
Public-sector balance/GDP	−5.5	−7.1	−7.4	−7	−7.5	−7.7
National debt/GDP	103	115.8	123.5	132.8	141	144
Exports (% change)	−2.3	1.4	12.4	−6.7	5	6
Imports (% change)	−6.8	3	9.6	−0.7	−1	3.5
Current account balance/GDP	3.1	2.4	2.4	2.3	3	3.1

e = estimated, f = forecast

MAIN ECONOMIC SECTORS

Automobiles

Despite unfavourable trading conditions on the domestic market in 2002 Japanese carmakers posted higher sales and profits on the back on increased sales to the North American and Asian markets. In 2003 they should post a similar performance due to stabilization of the world market.

Steel

In 2002 Japanese steel manufacturers increased output and profit, due to buoyant demand in Asia. In 2003 they should post higher profits as they consolidate the price increases achieved in the second half of 2002 and Asian demand gets firmer.

Construction

The construction market shrank further in 2002, due largely to the poor state of public finances and the decline in infrastructure spending as local authorities diverted funds to other sectors of the economy. Competition depressed prices, forcing many companies to the wall. The number of bankruptcies in the sector will continue to rise in 2003.

Electronics

The market for electronic components remained sluggish in 2002, with the majority of manufacturers suffering losses due to strong competition from Taiwan and South Korea. The sector will continue to see consolidation in 2003. In a saturated domestic market PCs were only able to stage a moderate recovery, in sharp contrast to the heady growth of previous years. Manufacturers will have to relocate abroad in order to remain competitive in world markets. Leisure electronics (especially video game consoles, digital photo equipment and DVD players and recorders) continued to perform satisfactorily despite the absence of truly new products and stronger competition from China in the bottom and mid-range products. Performance in 2003 will be largely influenced by the economic situation in North America.

Retail

Retail profits sagged due to the prolonged slump in consumption and strong price competition in a deflationary environment. Supermarkets and discount stores will have to face up to the new alliance between Seiyu and Wal Mart. Ito-Yokado and Aon Corporation are expected to lead the industry's reorganization. Department stores lost their competitiveness and dominant market share to discount stores, with many going bankrupt. The industry should reorganize under the aegis of Isetan, Takashimaya and Mitsukoshi. No upturn is expected in 2003.

■ Mechanical engineering

Heavy equipment manufacturers, hit by the slump in domestic electricity generation and shipbuilding, sought to build alliances and diversify. They increased business in neighbouring countries, posting sharp growth in energy demand. In precision tools Ricoh, Canon, Olympus and Hoya turned in strong performances, capitalizing on their clear technological edge in digital equipment. Trading conditions should remain favourable in 2003, despite Chinese penetration of certain segments.

PAYMENT AND COLLECTION PRACTICES

■ Payment

Japan ratified the International Conventions of June 1930 on Bills of Exchange and Promissory Notes and of March 1931 on Cheques, meaning that the same conditions for the validity of these instruments exist as in Europe.

The bill of exchange and the promissory note (the latter being in widespread use) allow recourse, if they remain unpaid and under certain conditions, to a summary procedure through the courts. Although the cheque allows for this same type of quick procedure it is far less common.

Clearing houses play an important role in the collective processing of the money supply arising from these instruments. Moreover, in the event of non-payment, the sanctions act as a deterrent effect: a debtor who, twice in six months, fails to honor the payment of a bill of exchange, a promissory note or a cheque, for clearing in Japan, is barred for a period of two years from undertaking banking transactions with financial establishments, that are members of the clearing house. All of this will result in the debtor's de facto insolvency.

This double rejection normally results default of bank loans granted to the debtor.

Transfers have become much more prominent in all fields of economic trade over the last few decades, thanks to the electronic medium widely used by the banking sector.

■ Debt collection

In theory, debt collection can only be carried out by lawyer offices. A recent law however instituted the 'servicer' profession; these are companies that can undertake debt collection, but only for certain types of debt (bank credits, loans from official groups, leasing agreements, credit cards, etc).

Collection by non-litigious means is always preferable and often involves having the debtor sign a notarial deed including a clause of acknowledgement of execution, which can thus be applied, in the event of payment default, without requiring a court judgment.

In general, the creditor will send to the debtor a registered reminder with return receipt requested (Naïyo Shomeï), the content of which, in Japanese letters, is certified by the post office. The effect of this letter is to set back the statute of limitations by six months (five years for commercial debts). During this period, if there is no response from the debtor, the creditor must bring court proceedings in order to conserve the benefit of the interruption of the limitation period.

The summary procedure (Shiharaï Meireï) applies to undisputed debts and allows a court order within a period of approximately three months. Procedural fees, which must be settled in the form of duty stamps payable by the applicant, vary according to the amount of debt. In the event of dispute the proceedings are converted to the standard procedure.

The standard procedure is brought before the 'summary court' for debts less than 900,000 yen and before the 'district court' for debts over this amount. Proceedings may last from one to three years and generate significant legal costs. With respect to procedural fees the amount of the stamp duty also varies depending on the amount of the debt.

Finally, the importance accorded to reconciliation must be underlined as being the main characteristic of the Japanese legal system. As part of legal reconciliation (conducted under review of the court), arbitration committees, usually made up

3

of a judge and two assessors, try to resolve civil and commercial disputes in an amicable way. In this situation, any arbitration award ratified by the court, becomes enforceable.

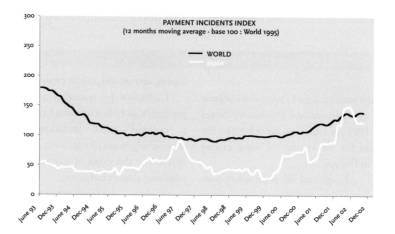

Malaysia

Short-term: **A2**

Medium-term:
Low risk

Coface analysis

STRENGTHS

- Diversified economy with special emphasis on training.
- High level of savings.
- Sound external finances (reasonable level of debt and low short-term debt).
- Proactive financial sector restructuring policy.
- Melting pot of Malay, Chinese, Indian and Western cultures.

WEAKNESSES

- Dependent on exports, in particular electrical and electronic equipment.
- High domestic public debt.
- Banking sector weakened by excessive indebtedness of large corporations.
- Upsurge of Islamic fundamentalism in Malay community, with risk of renewed ethnic tensions.

3

RISK ASSESSMENT

The Malaysian economy picked up in 2002 and should continue to strengthen in 2003 on the back of buoyant domestic demand and industry-wide export growth, despite the preponderance of electronic products.

The swelling budget deficit has created a massive public debt, but the borrowing requirement is covered by the high level of domestic savings. The country continues to post a healthy external account surplus, despite a slight drop, and the foreign debt is moderate especially in relation to exports. Moreover, the low level of short-term debt against foreign exchange reserves and the ringgit's continued peg to the US dollar shields the country somewhat from a crisis of confidence on

the markets. Banking sector restructuring is making good headway, although corporate reorganization is behind schedule.

The political uncertainties surrounding the succession of Prime Minister Dr Mahathir have been reduced with the appointment of Deputy Prime Minister Abdullah Badawi as his successor after October 2003. Mr Badawi is expected to maintain existing policies. However, the upsurge of Islamic fundamentalism has cast a shadow over peaceful co-habitation between the various ethnic groups as the government steers a middle course in an attempt to keep a lid on the risk of intercommunity tensions.

KEY ECONOMIC INDICATORS

US$ billion	1998	1999	2000	2001	2002(e)	2003(f)
Economic growth (%)	−7.4	6.1	8.3	0.4	4	5
Inflation (%)	5.3	2.7	1.5	1.4	2.3	2.1
Public-sector balance/GDP (%)	0.7	−1.4	−4.6	−4	−4.8	−3.9
Exports	71.9	84.1	98.4	88	95.5	105
Imports	54.4	61.5	77.6	69.6	80	90
Trade balance	17.5	22.6	20.9	18.4	15.5	15
Current account balance	9.5	12.6	8.4	7.3	6.4	6.1
Current account balance/GDP (%)	13.2	15.9	9.4	8.3	6.8	6
Foreign debt/GDP (%)	60	53.9	46.3	50.7	51.2	49.6
Debt service/Exports (%)	9.7	8.3	7.2	7.1	6	6.2
Reserves (import months)	4.1	4.3	3.3	3.8	4	4

e = estimated, f = forecast

CONDITIONS FOR ACCESS TO THE MARKET

■ Means of entry

Malaysia has a long-standing free trade tradition. In 2001 it was ranked the world's 18th largest importer and exporter. Most goods can be imported without restriction under the 'open general licence' arrangement. Trade liberalization within the framework of WTO and AFTA has resulted in a sharp reduction in tariff barriers over the last few years. The average rate of customs duty for all products is below 7.8 per cent, and there are few non-tariff barriers.

Imports that required export credit cover during the Asian crisis are being settled in cash again, even by large public sector groups (Tenegra, TeleKom, Petronas). The documentary letter of credit, rather than documents of payment, is the most widespread means of payment used by companies.

■ Attitude towards foreign investors

In general, the Malaysian government welcomes foreign investment, especially if it generates export income and does not compete with Malaysian companies. This attitude of openness has become more marked since the sharp decline in foreign investment in the country, as foreign companies develop a stronger bargaining counter vis-à-vis the government. The government aims to encourage the involvement of Malaysians, especially Bumiputras (the ethnic group comprising mainly Malays and natives) in the country's economic growth, by offering them a minimum 30 per cent stake in companies operating in a certain number of sectors. However, in the aftermath of the Asian crisis, in July 1998 it decided to temporarily liberalize its policy on equity ownership in the industrial sector. Under this policy foreign investors in the manufacturing sector may, with a few exceptions, hold a 100 per cent interest in companies without being required to export.

The Foreign Investment Committee approves the establishment of foreign businesses, but delegates its powers to the Malaysian Industrial Development Authority for industrial schemes.

The Malaysian government has introduced a number of tax incentives aimed at encouraging the establishment of foreign businesses (Pioneer Status, Investment Tax Allowance, International Procurement Centre Status, Operational Headquarters Status). There is an offshore site in Labuan for financial activities and 14 free zones where companies are exempt from taxes and customs duties.

The Malaysian employment environment offers a number of advantages (young, easy-to-train, usually English-speaking and relatively cheap workforce).

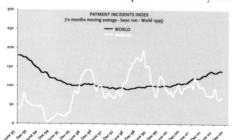

■ Foreign exchange regulations
In September 1998 the ringgit was pegged at 3.8 to the US dollar. In September 1999 the government introduced a more flexible exchange and capital control policy. Transfers are subject to the approval of the central bank, but this does not in any way hamper business transactions and direct foreign investment.

OPPORTUNITY SCOPE

■ Population 23.3 million inhabitants   ■ GDP 89,659 million US dollars

Breakdown of internal demand (GDP + imports)	%
■ Private consumption	21
■ Public spending	5
■ Investment	13

Exports: 125% of GDP   Imports: 104% of GDP

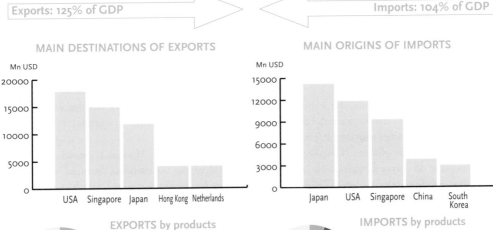

MAIN DESTINATIONS OF EXPORTS: USA, Singapore, Japan, Hong Kong, Netherlands

MAIN ORIGINS OF IMPORTS: Japan, USA, Singapore, China, South Korea

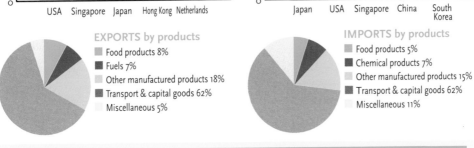

EXPORTS by products
■ Food products 8%
■ Fuels 7%
■ Other manufactured products 18%
■ Transport & capital goods 62%
■ Miscellaneous 5%

IMPORTS by products
■ Food products 5%
■ Chemical products 7%
■ Other manufactured products 15%
■ Transport & capital goods 62%
■ Miscellaneous 11%

STANDARD OF LIVING / PURCHASING POWER

Indicators	Malaysia	Regional average	DC average
GNP per capita (PPP dollars)	8330	8590	6548
GNP per capita	3380	5794	3565
Human development index	0.782	0.725	0.702
Wealthiest 10% share of national income	38	32	32
Urban population percentage	57	51	60
Percentage under 15 years old	34	29	32
Number of telephones per 1000 inhabitants	199	192	157
Number of computers per 1000 inhabitants	103	105	64

Mongolia

Coface analysis

Short-term: **D**

Medium-term:
Very high risk

RISK ASSESSMENT

The country is enjoying political stability since the landslide victory of the Revolutionary People's Party in the 2000 and 2001 elections, but the government continues to face simmering popular discontent and enormous difficulties.

For the last three years the economy has suffered extremely harsh winters that have decimated vast quantities of livestock. The problem could recur in the future. Despite a slight improvement in manufacturing the country's economic performance is closely influenced by world commodity prices. This is affecting its exports of copper, gold and cashmere, leaving its external account in the red.

The government's room for manoeuvre is limited in the face of a swelling budget deficit, which must be reduced, growing foreign debt that is almost as large as GDP and outstanding debt to Russia contracted prior to 1991. While it must continue to reform the banking sector and state-owned enterprises, there is a risk this will initially hamper already slow progress in poverty alleviation.

Consequently, Mongolia remains highly dependent on international financial assistance. Except for the mining sector, which continues to show good growth potential, its ability to attract foreign investment is marred by a narrow domestic market, the country's landlocked position and a structurally weak public sector.

KEY ECONOMIC INDICATORS

US$ million	1998	1999	2000	2001	2002(e)	2003(f)
Economic growth (%)	3.5	3.2	0.5	1.1	3	4
Inflation (%)	9.4	7.6	11.6	8	5	5
Public-sector balance/GDP (%)	−14.3	−12.2	−6.8	−7.3	−7.1	−6.6
Exports	462	454	536	523	630	648
Imports	582	567	676	693	798	771
Trade balance	−120	−113	−140	−170	−168	−124
Current account balance/GDP (%)	−13.3	−14	−15.8	−15.9	−15.8	−13.4
Foreign debt/GDP (%)	83.5	90.9	86.3	82.9	87	90.5
Debt service/Exports (%)	6.8	15	12.3	14.2	11.5	12.1
Reserves (import months)	1.3	1.8	2.1	2.3	2.5	3

e = estimated, f = forecast

Myanmar

Coface analysis

Short-term: **C**

Medium-term:
Very high risk

STRENGTHS

- Vast mineral (oil, gas, gems), forestry and agricultural (rice, sea foods, etc) resources and hydropower potential.
- Good geographical situation: located inside an economically vibrant area and close to China and India.
- Rich cultural heritage.
- Member of ASEAN since 1997.

WEAKNESSES

- Internationally isolated since 1989 following suspension of Western aid on grounds of serious human rights violations.
- Chronic instability stemming from conflict between government and country's various ethnic groups.
- Backward infrastructure and embryonic manufacturing sector hamper economic development of one of the world's poorest countries.
- Lack of wide-ranging structural reforms.
- Persistently large budget deficits and inadequate foreign exchange reserves.
- Problems with foreign debt service.

RISK ASSESSMENT

In May 2002 the State Peace and Development Council (the name of the ruling military junta) revoked the order placing Aung San Suu Kyi, leader of the democratic opposition, under house arrest in the hope, undoubtedly, of reducing the country's international isolation and attracting foreign investors. However the unwillingness of the divided junta to enter into meaningful discussions with the National League for Democracy is preventing the lifting of Western economic sanctions and continues to deny Myanmar the support of international financial institutions, despite ASEAN's policy of 'constructive engagement' towards the country.

Although reliable statistics are hard to come by Myanmar appears to be enjoying relatively strong growth largely on the back of rising gas exports. Nevertheless the country remains one of the poorest in the world. It suffers from a chronic budget deficit and its external financial position continues to be plagued mainly by a shortage of foreign currency. Inflation is soaring and the local currency continues to depreciate.

Lack of real structural reforms and political isolation prevent the country from staging a proper economic recovery and capitalizing on its assets, which include abundant forestry and mineral resources, valuable arable land, good tourism potential and a favourable geographical situation.

KEY ECONOMIC INDICATORS						
US$ million	1998	1999	2000	2001	2002(e)	2003(f)
Economic growth (%)	5	5.5	5	5.4	4.6	4.7
Inflation (%)	33.9	49.1	11.4	21.1	51.3	42.2
Public-sector balance/GDP (%)	−5.7	−4.6	−5	−6	−6	−5
Exports	1065	1281	1619	2225	2767	3067
Imports	2451	2160	2135	2625	2978	3234
Trade balance	−1386	−879	−516	−400	−211	−167
Current account balance/GDP (%)	−7.1	−3	−3.1	−2.8	−3.1	−3.4
Foreign debt/GDP (%)	85	69.6	60.7	57.2	54.3	51.9
Debt service/Exports (%)	13.4	14.7	12.9	11.2	10	8.2
Reserves (import months)	1.3	1.3	1	1.4	1.1	1.1

e = estimated, f = forecast

CONDITIONS FOR ACCESS TO THE MARKET

■ Means of entry

The problem with the country's trade is not really one of tariff barriers, as customs duties on imports vary between 1 per cent and 40 per cent. The main obstacles blocking access to the market are non-tariff barriers, lack of transparency of the local business environment and obsolete, unsuitable, changeable and unpredictable regulations, often applied retroactively in the absence of an official publication.

As with other impoverished countries, Burma's non-tariff barriers to trade include a restrictive system of import licences under which goods are listed as essential, non-essential or prohibited. Since 1998 imports of wine and spirits and canned food have been banned. These restrictions, never strictly enforced in the first place, are circumvented by means of a thriving border trade, mainly with Thailand and China. The ready availability of contraband goods in most Rangoon shops is a case in point.

Since 1998 importers have been required to generate, or 'purchase' from an export firm, hard currency for the payment of imported goods. But from March 2002 only Burmese export companies are allowed to import. The value of their imports is prorated to their export income. Foreign companies are denied import – export licences.

■ Attitude towards foreign investors

Legislation on the establishment of foreign companies is restrictive as potential investors have to be approved by the Myanmar Investment Commission where they are not de facto required to form a joint venture with a government entity, usually selected from army-owned or pro-army business groups (UMEH, MEC, USDA).

A dozen or so sectors are closed to foreign investors. With notable exceptions, such as Total and airline companies, the Myanmar Investment Commission has barred foreign companies from 12 sectors of the country's economy. Burmese legislation in this field is woefully inadequate. The present legal system is a legacy of the colonial past (the Burma Copyright Act, 1914 for copyright protection and the Indian Patent Act, 1911 for trademark and patent protection) and offers foreign investors few safeguards or remedies.

As a result of the US embargo and European sanctions Myanmar has received no international aid for the past 12 years. Its hand-to-mouth existence forces it to adopt expedients that push it further towards China – the country's main trading partner with which it carries out probably more than 50 per cent of its 'real' trade – which undoubtedly sees it as a cheap source of raw materials for its own fast-growing economy. Alternative outlets for Burmese manufactured goods usually require financing.

OPPORTUNITY SCOPE

- Population   47.7 million inhabitants
- GDP   11,178 million US dollars

Breakdown of internal demand (GDP + imports) %
- Private consumption   67
- Public spending   n/a
- Investment   10

n/a – not available

Exports: 27% of GDP   Imports: 30% of GDP

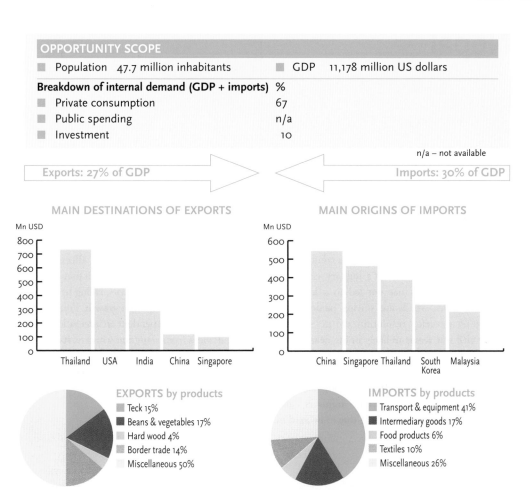

MAIN DESTINATIONS OF EXPORTS

Mn USD

Thailand   USA   India   China   Singapore

MAIN ORIGINS OF IMPORTS

Mn USD

China   Singapore   Thailand   South Korea   Malaysia

EXPORTS by products
- Teck 15%
- Beans & vegetables 17%
- Hard wood 4%
- Border trade 14%
- Miscellaneous 50%

IMPORTS by products
- Transport & equipment 41%
- Intermediary goods 17%
- Food products 6%
- Textiles 10%
- Miscellaneous 26%

3

STANDARD OF LIVING / PURCHASING POWER

Indicators	Myanmar	Regional average	DC average
GNP per capita (PPP dollars)	n/a	8590	6548
GNP per capita	n/a	5794	3565
Human development index	0.552	0.725	0.702
Wealthiest 10% share of national income	n/a	32	32
Urban population percentage	28	51	60
Percentage under 15 years old	33	29	32
Number of telephones per 1000 inhabitants	6	192	157
Number of computers per 1000 inhabitants	1	105	64

n/a – not available

Nepal

Short-term: **D**

Medium-term:
Very high risk

Coface analysis

RISK ASSESSMENT

The country's economic situation has continued to deteriorate. The government's military campaign against Maoist rebels has not led to a let-up in guerrilla attacks, which are sowing panic in the country. A peaceful resolution of the six-year bloody civil war seems unlikely in the near future. The conflict has been compounded by a constitutional crisis, thus adding to the political confusion, with King Gyanendra seizing executive power, dismissing the prime minister and indefinitely postponing elections due to be held in November 2002.

This situation has markedly affected the country's economic performance, with tourism, the country's main economic activity, falling by 34 per cent and putting a damper on growth. Financially, the country remains dependent on international aid and remittances from emi-grant workers. Its strong hydropower potential is under exploited and agriculture, which accounts for 40 per cent GDP, is in great need of modernization.

KEY ECONOMIC INDICATORS

US$ million	1998/99	1999/00	2000/01	2001/02(e)	2002/03(f)	2003/04(f)
Economic growth (%)	4.5	6.2	4.8	0.8	1	1
Inflation (%)	9	0.6	3.4	3.5	4.3	4
Public-sector balance/GDP (%)	−5.2	−5	−6.2	−6	−6	−5.6
Exports	763	971	942	762	782	836
Imports	1390	1713	1774	1605	1707	1826
Trade balance	−627	−742	−832	−843	−925	−990
Current account balance/GDP (%)	0.5	0.5	1.1	1.0	0.2	0
Foreign debt	2578	2890	2903	2732.4	3250	2999
Debt service/Exports (%)	5	4.7	6	5.2	5.6	5.6
Reserves (import months)	4.9	5.6	6.7	6.5	4.8	4.6

e = estimated, f = forecast

New Zealand

Coface analysis

RISK ASSESSMENT

The economy grew sharply in 2002 on the back of buoyant private consumption and soaring investment, especially in housing. The surge in domestic demand, accompanied by a narrow labour market and good utilization of production capacity, triggered inflationary pressures that the central bank was forced to control by maintaining a tight monetary policy. Exports benefited from strong demand for agricultural and forest products, while imports soared on the back of high domestic demand and a strong New Zealand dollar.

In 2003 the economy should slow down slightly on account of sluggish consumption and exports. However, the housing market will continue to grow. The economic slowdown, together with tighter monetary policies, will ease inflationary pressures somewhat. Fiscal policy is expected to remain cautious, generating a renewed budget surplus.

The persistence of favourable trading conditions is reflected in fewer bankruptcies and defaults. With regard to the economic outlook, this trend should continue in 2003.

3

KEY ECONOMIC INDICATORS						
%	1998	1999	2000	2001	2002(e)	2003(f)
Economic growth	−0.7	4.7	3.8	1.4	3.7	2.9
Consumer spending (% change)	1.7	4.2	2.3	2	3.3	2.3
Investment (% change)	−4.8	3.1	7.3	−1.7	4.6	4.8
Inflation	2.2	0.3	2.2	2	2.4	2.2
Unemployment	7.5	6.8	6	5.3	5.2	5.4
Short-term interest rate	7.3	4.8	6.5	5.7	5.7	6
Public-sector balance/GDP	−0.4	0.2	0.9	1.7	1.6	1.3
National debt/GDP	50.4	48.3	45.5	43	42	41
Exports (% change)	1.2	7.1	7.6	2.1	9	6.5
Imports (% change)	1.4	11.7	1.1	1.4	7	5
Current account balance/GDP	−4	−6.6	−5.4	−2.8	−2.8	−3.7

e = estimated, f = forecast

PAYMENT AND COLLECTION PRACTICES

As a former British colony in the 19th century and a Commonwealth member since 1907, New Zealand's legal code and precepts are largely inspired by British 'common law' and the British court system.

■ Payment

Bills of exchange or promissory notes are not frequently used for commercial transactions in New Zealand and are considered, above all, to authenticate the existence of a claim. Conversely, cheques are relatively widely used for domestic transactions.

Wire transfers or SWIFT bank transfers are the most commonly used payment method for international transactions. Most of the country's banks are connected to the network, which offers a rapid, cost-efficient means of effecting payments.

■ Debt collection

The recovery process starts with the issuance of final notice, or a 'seven days letter', by registered mail, in which the creditor notifies the debtor of his payment obligations.

Where no payment is received and where claims are undisputed (or once a judgment has been obtained) the creditor may summons the debtor to settle his debt within 15 days or to face a winding-up petition (Statutory demand under section 289 of the 1993 Companies Act). If no response is received within the required timeframe the debtor's company is considered insolvent.

Under ordinary proceedings, once a statement of claim (summons) has been filed and where debtors have no grounds on which to dispute claims, creditors may solicit a fast-track procedure enabling them to obtain an executory order by issuing the debtor with an application for summary judgment. This petition must be accompanied by an affidavit (a sworn statement by the plaintiff attesting to the claim's existence) along with supporting documents authenticating the unpaid claim.

For more complex or disputed claims, creditors must instigate standard civil proceedings, an arduous, often lengthy process lasting up to two years. Proceedings are heard by the District Courts or by the High Court, for claims exceeding NZ$ 200,000.

Under New Zealand's constitution the Privy Council, in London, has jurisdiction to hear appeals filed against decisions made by the NZ Court of Appeal, in Wellington, concerning claims for NZ$ 5000 or more. In addition the High Court may hold summary proceedings for commercial disputes that concern the fields of insurance, banking, finance, intellectual property, goods transport, and which are enumerated in its 'commercial list'.

During the preliminary phase proceedings are written in so far as the Court examines the case documents authenticating the parties' respective claims. During the subsequent 'discovery phase', the parties' lawyers may request their adversaries to submit any proof or witness testimony that is relevant to the case and duly examine the case documents thus submitted.

Before handing down its judgment the Court examines the case and holds an adversarial hearing of the witnesses, who may be cross-examined by the parties' lawyers.

Arbitration and mediation proceedings may also be used to resolve disputes and obtain out-of-court settlements, often at a lower cost than through the ordinary adversarial procedure.

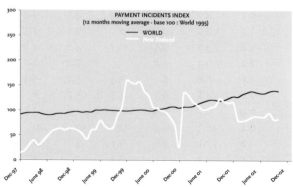

PAYMENT INCIDENTS INDEX
(12 months moving average - base 100 : World 1995)
— WORLD
— New Zealand

Pakistan

Coface analysis

Short-term: **D**

Medium-term:
Very high risk

STRENGTHS

- Financial position consolidated by international aid received in response to support for anti-terrorist alliance.
- Focus of US strategic considerations due to nuclear power status and risk of slipping into anti-Western camp.
- IMF-sponsored structural reforms and banking sector restructuring continue apace.
- Foreign exchange reserves bolstered by remittances from emigrant workers.

WEAKNESSES

- Economy heavily dependent on agriculture and, consequently, on vagaries of climate.
- Political risk hampers investment.
- Country's financial position shored up by creditor-backed debt relief and financial aid inflows.
- Continuing tensions with India carry strong risk of regional destabilisation.
- Lack of popular consensus on country's foreign policy.

3

RISK ASSESSMENT

Pakistan's policy of siding with the international coalition has earned it massive international financial assistance that acts as an economic spur. An agreement with the Paris Club and IMF financial aid have combined to improve the state's solvency, external financing needs and foreign currency liquidity. Moreover, growth and inflation are at satisfactory levels.

However, the country's economy continues to be plagued by structural difficulties. Growth prospects have been dampened, especially by the lack of foreign investment in the private sector. Moreover, with textiles making up 60 per cent of

exports and agriculture 26 per cent of GDP, the country remains exposed to the vagaries of climate.

The level of political risk remains high. On the domestic front, the parliamentary elections of 10 October 2002 demonstrated the power of Islamic parties opposed to President Musharraf's pro-US policy. On the external front, even though tensions have eased somewhat, Indo–Pakistan relations remain highly strained. Moreover, acute social tensions are making it difficult to step up the pace of structural reform essential to economic recovery.

KEY ECONOMIC INDICATORS

US$ billion	1998/99	1999/00	2000/01	2001/02(e)	2002/03(f)	2003/04(f)
Economic growth (%)	3.7	4.3	2.7	4.4	4.9	4.5
Inflation (%)	3.7	5.1	4.4	2.7	4	4
Public-sector balance/GDP (%)	−6	−6.6	−5.3	−5.1	−4.7	−4
Exports	7.5	8.2	8.9	9.1	9.9	10.6
Imports	9.6	9.6	10.2	9.5	10.5	11.2
Trade balance	−2.1	−1.4	−1.3	−0.4	−0.6	−0.6
Current account balance	−2.4	−1.1	−2	0	−0.8	−0.9
Current account balance/GDP (%)	−4.6	−3.4	−3.3	0.1	−1.1	−1.3
Foreign debt	34.1	34.1	36.2	36	35.7	34.9
Debt service/Exports (%)	50	54.9	32.5	41	39.6	35.8
Reserves (import months)	1.5	1.2	1.4	3.8	4.2	4.3

e = estimated, f = forecast

CONDITIONS FOR ACCESS TO THE MARKET

■ Means of entry

The country's economy is gradually being liberalized. Customs duties in the industrial sector are trending lower in line with the requirements of international bodies. The maximum rate of ad valorem customs duty (CIF value) is 25 per cent, except for certain products that are subject to a different system of taxation. The maximum rate of duty for the service sector is 10 per cent.

As a rule, Pakistani customs use the World Customs Organization's harmonized international nomenclature. However many businesses complain about the tendency of customs officials to unduly reclassify imported goods into a higher duty category. This leads to many disputes. The 6 per cent withholding tax that the government planned to abolish remains in force. Excise duties could be replaced by a 15 per cent general sales tax – a sort of VAT – at an unspecified date.

Foreign exchange regulations for business transactions and services tend to be liberal. Capital transfers can be made without major difficulty, testifying to the country's financial health according to certain bankers. The Pakistani rupee is fully convertible and transferable.

■ Attitude towards foreign investors

The government, formed out of a coup d'état in 1999, has created a liberal economic climate designed to attract foreign investors. Foreigners may hold a controlling interest in a local company.

It is regrettable that the administrative apparatus, notorious for its slowness and corruption, poses an obstacle to foreign investment.

Direct foreign investment, which amounted to only US$484.7 million in the financial year gone by, has not lived up to expectations for a country of Pakistan's stature. It should climb sharply this year if the privatization of Habib Bank, Pakistan State Oil and Pakistan Telecommunications Co Ltd bears fruit.

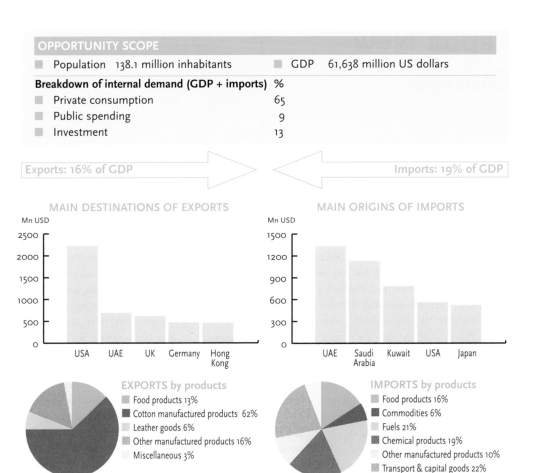

OPPORTUNITY SCOPE

■ Population   138.1 million inhabitants   ■ GDP   61,638 million US dollars

Breakdown of internal demand (GDP + imports) %
■ Private consumption   65
■ Public spending   9
■ Investment   13

Exports: 16% of GDP → ← Imports: 19% of GDP

MAIN DESTINATIONS OF EXPORTS

Mn USD

USA   UAE   UK   Germany   Hong Kong

MAIN ORIGINS OF IMPORTS

Mn USD

UAE   Saudi Arabia   Kuwait   USA   Japan

EXPORTS by products
■ Food products 13%
■ Cotton manufactured products 62%
■ Leather goods 6%
■ Other manufactured products 16%
■ Miscellaneous 3%

IMPORTS by products
■ Food products 16%
■ Commodities 6%
■ Fuels 21%
■ Chemical products 19%
■ Other manufactured products 10%
■ Transport & capital goods 22%
■ Miscellaneous 6%

STANDARD OF LIVING / PURCHASING POWER

Indicators	Pakistan	Regional average	DC average
GNP per capita (PPP dollars)	1860	8590	6548
GNP per capita	440	5794	3565
Human development index	0.499	0.725	0.702
Wealthiest 10% share of national income	28	32	32
Urban population percentage	37	51	60
Percentage under 15 years old	42	29	32
Number of telephones per 1000 inhabitants	22	192	157
Number of computers per 1000 inhabitants	4	105	64

3

Papua New Guinea

Short-term: **B**

Medium-term:
Quite high risk

Coface analysis

RISK ASSESSMENT

Since the general elections of June 2002 tensions in the country have decreased and the new prime minister, Sir M Somare, has unveiled a five-year export-led 'economic recovery and development plan'. While the 10-party coalition government may have difficulty implementing the plan, it will need to restore the main macro-economic balances, including the stabilization of public finances, and undertake structural reforms if the country is to shrug off three years of recession (2000–02) largely caused by political uncertainties, the shelving of mining schemes, the depletion of oil fields, unfavourable climatic conditions and plummeting coffee prices. Positive action along these lines will enable the country to retain the much-needed support of foreign lenders and international financial institutions.

To achieve sustainable growth Papua New Guinea must diversify its basically dual economy in which large-scale mining and farming generate 80 per cent of foreign currency earnings, and reduce its exposure to world commodity price movements. The country is also handicapped by backward infrastructure and geographical, ethnic and linguistic fragmentation. However, the completion of two major projects – a nickel and cobalt mine at Ramu and a gas pipeline to Queensland in Australia – could promote the country's development in the long term and trigger a moderate recovery in the short term (2003).

KEY ECONOMIC INDICATORS						
US$ million	1998	1999	2000	2001	2002(e)	2003(f)
Economic growth (%)	-3.8	5.4	-0.8	-2.6	-2.5	1.1
Inflation (%)	21.8	13.2	10	10.3	9.8	8.5
Public-sector balance/GDP (%)	-1.7	-2.5	-1.6	-3.9	-5.9	-5.1
Exports	1849	2019	2214	2033	2080	2060
Imports	1425	1525	1502	1643	1725	1740
Trade balance	424	494	712	390	355	320
Current account balance/GDP (%)	-5.0	-3.7	2.7	-2.9	-6.4	-5.1
Foreign debt/GDP (%)	71.2	78.6	76.4	91.3	91.0	87.0
Debt service/Exports (%)	25.6	29.9	17.4	22.2	22.1	20.7
Reserves (import months)	0.8	1.1	1.7	2.3	2.4	2.0

e = estimated, f = forecast

Philippines

Short-term: **A4**

Medium-term:
Coface analysis　**Quite high risk**

STRENGTHS

- Well-trained and highly productive workforce, which is attracting multinationals.
- Vibrant exports of electronic goods and products manufactured by special economic zones.
- External account surpluses.
- Fairly favourable regional environment.

WEAKNESSES

- Excessive domestic public debt and strong political will required to correct huge budget deficit.
- Deteriorating banking sector in need of reform.
- Growth insufficient to alleviate mounting poverty and social tensions.
- Exports dependent on electronics sector.
- Insecurity problems, created notably by Islamic separatist movements operating in south of archipelago, are deterring foreign investors.

3

RISK ASSESSMENT

Relatively firm consumer demand, buoyed by large expatriate remittances, should allow the country to post moderate economic growth despite the somewhat modest rally in external demand, particularly for electronic products, whose sales account for over 50 per cent of exports.

Continued structural problems are preventing the country from achieving higher growth. The alarming deterioration in the country's finances is generating a huge public debt, underlining the lack of credibility of the government's budget strategy. Unlike other Asian countries, inadequate levels of local savings and direct foreign investment force the country to rely partially on foreign capital to finance its requirements. At the moment this is not proving

too difficult, but it means that the country has to run up a large foreign debt to finance its needs. Banking supervision is inadequate to deal with the deteriorating position of the sector and the rising number of bad debts. The risk of a currency crisis is nevertheless limited due to the low level of short-term funding and the current account surplus.

President Gloria Arroyo is attempting to strengthen her political position, but is having difficulties making structural adjustments to the economy. The government's problems are compounded by the climate of insecurity created, in particular, by Islamic secessionist movements in the south of the country that are having a deterrent effect on foreign investors, as well as by social tensions stemming from worsening poverty.

KEY ECONOMIC INDICATORS

US$ billion	1998	1999	2000	2001	2002(e)	2003(f)
Economic growth (%)	-0.6	3.4	4.4	3.2	3.9	4.1
Inflation (%)	9.7	6.7	4.3	6.1	3.3	4
Public-sectorbalance/GDP (%)	-3	-3.3	-4.5	-4.3	-5.6	-4.7
Exports	29.5	34.2	37.3	31.2	32.6	34.8
Imports	29.5	29.3	30.4	28.5	30.4	32.9
Trade balance	0	5	6.9	2.7	2.2	1.9
Current account balance	1.5	7.9	8.5	4.5	4.8	4
Current account balance/GDP (%)	2.4	10.4	11.3	6.3	6.3	5
Foreign debt/GDP (%)	81.7	76.2	76.7	80.9	81.1	75.1
Debt service/Exports (%)	12.7	15.5	17.8	19	19.2	19.4
Reserves (import months)	2.6	4	3.8	4.3	4.3	4.1

e = estimated, f = forecast

CONDITIONS FOR ACCESS TO THE MARKET

■ Market overview

On the whole the market is very open and whatever import restrictions there are consist mainly of non-tariff barriers. It is difficult for foreigners to enter certain sectors (utilities), as they are protected by the Constitution. Imports of certain products are subject to regulatory restrictions involving the issue of documents by an inefficient administrative service.

The government has already met its tariff reduction targets for 2003, agreed with the WTO, in respect of 85 per cent of tariff items. Accordingly, duty on finished products has been cut to 10 per cent and on commodities to 3 per cent. By 2004 a single rate of 5 per cent should apply, although some exceptional protective tariffs will remain in force. At present there are six rates of duty: 0 per cent, 3 per cent, 5 per cent, 10 per cent 15 per cent and 20 per cent. Products, in particular agricultural goods, subject to preferential tariff quotas are taxable outside the quota system at rates as high as 45 per cent, 50 per cent or even 60 per cent.

Payment by irrevocable documentary letter of credit is strongly recommended.

PAYMENT INCIDENTS INDEX
(12 months moving average - base 100 : World 1995)
— WORLD

■ Attitude towards foreign investors

A 'one-stop action centre' disseminates practical information and facilitates registration formalities. Foreign companies are advised to make use of the services of a local lawyer. The 'Security and Exchange Commission' is the government agency responsible for the registration, regulation and monitoring of all companies and partnerships established in the Philippines. Registration with the SEC takes anything from one to four weeks. A 'fast-track' system has been set up to enable registration formalities to be completed within three days on condition that applications are made in English and invoices paid in cash.

By easing foreign investment regulations the Foreign Investments Act of 1991, amended in 1996 and again in 1998, has sharply boosted investment over the last 10 years. Foreign investors interested in infrastructure development can avail themselves of certain provisions of the Build-Operate-Transfer Act (1990). Another law allows foreign investors to lease land for the purposes of establishing a manufacturing facility. The Philippine Constitution also allows foreign businesses to repatriate their investment, together with any profits earned, in the original currency, and to raise loans on the local financial market. Foreign firms are protected against expropriation and confiscation of their investment. Various types of incentive are also available, with large zones having been set up for that purpose.

The Philippines is one of the most open countries in the region, even though some sectors of activity are reserved for local investors. The system of protection is based on a 'negative' list that sets out the sectors in which foreign interests are restricted or prohibited. Moreover, for overseas-funded projects, preference is given to local consultancy firms.

■ Foreign exchange regulations

There are no exchange controls, but for all imports in excess of US$1000 importers are required to make a foreign exchange application. The national currency has a floating exchange rate.

3

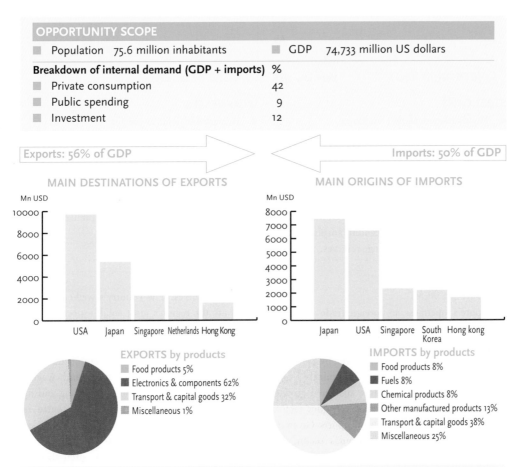

OPPORTUNITY SCOPE

■ Population 75.6 million inhabitants   ■ GDP 74,733 million US dollars

Breakdown of internal demand (GDP + imports) %
■ Private consumption   42
■ Public spending   9
■ Investment   12

Exports: 56% of GDP   Imports: 50% of GDP

MAIN DESTINATIONS OF EXPORTS

Mn USD

USA Japan Singapore Netherlands Hong Kong

MAIN ORIGINS OF IMPORTS

Mn USD

Japan USA Singapore South Korea Hong kong

EXPORTS by products
■ Food products 5%
■ Electronics & components 62%
■ Transport & capital goods 32%
■ Miscellaneous 1%

IMPORTS by products
■ Food products 8%
■ Fuels 8%
■ Chemical products 8%
■ Other manufactured products 13%
■ Transport & capital goods 38%
■ Miscellaneous 25%

STANDARD OF LIVING / PURCHASING POWER

Indicators	Philippines	Regional average	DC average
GNP per capita (PPP dollars)	4220	8590	6548
GNP per capita	1040	5794	3565
Human development index	0.754	0.725	0.702
Wealthiest 10% share of national income	37	32	32
Urban population percentage	59	51	60
Percentage under 15 years old	38	29	32
Number of telephones per 1000 inhabitants	40	192	157
Number of computers per 1000 inhabitants	19	105	64

Singapore

Short-term: **A2**

Medium-term:
Very low risk

Coface analysis

STRENGTHS

- Highly trained, skilled workforce.
- Significant role as regional hub underpinned by excellent infrastructure, growing financial centre status and robust banking sector.
- Economic success founded on policy of openness to foreign capital and on exports.
- Financial strength based on accumulation of budget and current account surpluses and significant foreign exchange reserves.

WEAKNESSES

- Remarkable political stability.
- Economy highly vulnerable to world economic developments. Exposure exacerbated by dependence on electronics sector.
- Competitiveness problems necessitating adjustment to changing regional environment.
- Inadequate innovation and entrepreneurial spirit linked to tight state control.
- Ageing population.

RISK ASSESSMENT

Singapore's openness to foreign trade makes it extremely vulnerable to changes in international market conditions. Economic recovery has been moderate, as it has been largely driven by growth in international demand for chemicals and pharmaceutical products. More sustained growth would require a pick-up in the electronics sector, which accounts for two-thirds of exports. Given its over-specialization in the electronics sector, the city–state has attempted to diversify into services.

The country's fundamentals, however, remain excellent. The accumulation of fiscal surpluses leaves the government plenty of room for manoeuvre, as do the huge external account surpluses, puny foreign debt and vast foreign exchange reserves. The country's well-capitalized banks are the region's most solid, especially after shedding most of their bad debt portfolios.

Singapore is nevertheless suffering from a loss of competitiveness vis-à-vis other countries in the region because of high taxation and wages. Moreover its re-export business is waning and its development as a regional financial centre is hampered by continuing regional political risks. But the seaport has held on to its many assets as it seeks to reposition itself, mainly by strengthening ties with China and promoting economic agreements with various industrialized countries.

KEY ECONOMIC INDICATORS

US$ billion	1998	1999	2000	2001	2002(e)	2003(f)
Economic growth (%)	0.4	5.4	9.9	−2	2.5	3.5
Inflation (%)	−0.3	0.4	1.4	1	−0.5	1
Public-sector balance/GDP (%)	1.6	5.5	4.6	−1.5	1	1.8
Exports	110.6	115.6	138.9	123.8	126.9	135.4
Imports	95.8	104.4	127.5	109.8	112.8	122.7
Trade balance	14.8	11.2	11.4	14	14.1	12.7
Current account balance/GDP (%)	24.9	25.2	23.6	23.3	20.1	17.8
Foreign debt/GDP (%)	13.5	12.6	10.5	9.1	8.7	8.4
Debt service/Exports (%)	0.9	0.9	0.6	0.7	0.7	0.6
Reserves (import months)	7.2	6.7	6	7.7	8.5	7.9

e = estimated, f = forecast

CONDITIONS FOR ACCESS TO THE MARKET

■ Market overview

A fervent advocate of multilateral trade through international institutions such as the WTO, of which it has been a member since 1995, and regional bodies such as ASEAN and Asia Pacific Economic Co-operation (APEC), Singapore has been engaged for some years in talks on concluding bilateral free trade agreements. The country has already signed agreements with New Zealand, Japan and EFTA and is in the process of negotiating others with the United States, Australia, Mexico, Canada, Taiwan and India.

■ Means of entry

The city–state's extreme openness to the outside world has been the key to its economic success. Foreign trade accounted for 277 per cent of GDP in 2001. Despite the sharp recession caused by the international economic downturn in 2001 Singapore continues to pursue liberal trade and investment policies, without the slightest inclination towards protectionism. Singapore's free trade policy is characterized by almost no tariff or non-tariff barriers. With a few exceptions, customs duties are zero.

■ Attitude towards foreign investors

Singapore has always keenly welcomed foreign investment and offers an economic and political environment that is both very open and highly planned. The government uses foreign investment to develop priority sectors known as clusters (electronics, chemicals, engineering and biotechnology). The aim is to encourage the growth of high value-added activities and turn the island into a trade, administrative and financial centre for foreign investors seeking to do business in the region. The Economic and Development Board has key responsibilities for developing and promoting investment inflows into, and outflows from, Singapore. The city–state also encourages foreign investment in industrial infrastructure.

However, Singapore's service sector (media, legal and financial services, transport, energy genera-tion and supply, water supply) is only partially open to foreign investment. The government has announced plans for the gradual liberalization and opening up of some of these areas.

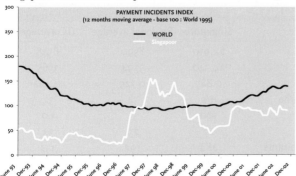

PAYMENT INCIDENTS INDEX
(12 months moving average - base 100 : World 1995)
— WORLD
— Singapoor

■ **Foreign exchange regulations**

Since the early 1980s the exchange rate has been the key instrument of government monetary policy. The main feature of this policy is a flexible exchange rate within an adjustable floating band. From now on, the declared aim of the 'Monetary Authority of Singapore' is to stabilize the Singapore dollar's nominal effective exchange rate against a basket of currencies of its main trading partners, the main component of which is the US dollar.

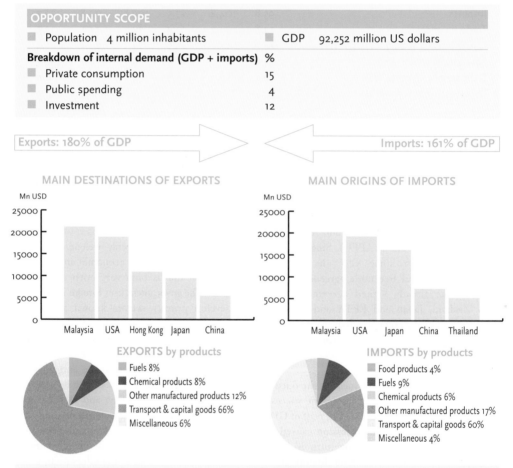

OPPORTUNITY SCOPE

■ Population   4 million inhabitants   ■ GDP   92,252 million US dollars

Breakdown of internal demand (GDP + imports) %
■ Private consumption   15
■ Public spending   4
■ Investment   12

Exports: 180% of GDP   Imports: 161% of GDP

MAIN DESTINATIONS OF EXPORTS
Mn USD

Malaysia USA Hong Kong Japan China

MAIN ORIGINS OF IMPORTS
Mn USD

Malaysia USA Japan China Thailand

EXPORTS by products
■ Fuels 8%
■ Chemical products 8%
■ Other manufactured products 12%
■ Transport & capital goods 66%
■ Miscellaneous 6%

IMPORTS by products
■ Food products 4%
■ Fuels 9%
■ Chemical products 6%
■ Other manufactured products 17%
■ Transport & capital goods 60%
■ Miscellaneous 4%

STANDARD OF LIVING / PURCHASING POWER

Indicators	Singapore	Regional average	DC average
GNP per capita (PPP dollars)	24,910	8590	6548
GNP per capita	24,740	5794	3565
Human development index	0.885	0.725	0.702
Wealthiest 10% share of national income	n/a	32	32
Urban population percentage	100	51	60
Percentage under 15 years old	22	29	32
Number of telephones per 1000 inhabitants	484	192	157
Number of computers per 1000 inhabitants	483	105	64

n/a – not available

South Korea

Short-term: **A2**

Medium-term:
Low risk

Coface analysis

STRENGTHS

- Highly diversified and sophisticated manu-facturing industry.
- Highly educated workforce.
- Decisive government action on financial restructuring, although industrial reorganiza-tion is proving more difficult.
- Vast savings ratio.
- Strong external financial position.

WEAKNESSES

- Export-led economy still vulnerable to external crisis.
- Financial restructuring of certain conglomerates (chaebols) vital to modernization of economy.
- Room for improvement in banking sector reorganization as privatization programme is not yet completed.
- Uncertainty about North Korea's future, with Korean reunificaion inevitable in the long run.

3

RISK ASSESSMENT

The victory at the presidential elections in December 2002 of the reformist Roh Moo-Hyun, of the ruling Millennium Democratic Party, should ensure continuity with the policies of his predecessor Kim Dae-Jung. The new government is expected to pursue dialogue with North Korea, under the 'sunshine policy', and the restructuring of the country's large industrial groups.

The economy should continue to grow, albeit at a somewhat slower pace on account of the uncertain international environment. Growth should continue to be driven by fairly firm domestic demand, boosted by the increase in consumer credit and, to a lesser extent, exports, with sales to China partially offsetting the downturn in exports to industrialized countries.

South Korea should continue to post an external account and budget surplus, underpinned by a solid external financial position, moderate foreign debt, ample foreign exchange reserves and a firmer won.

While banking sector restructuring has made fairly rapid headway since 1997 there is still room for improvement. The privatization programme has not been completed and the diversification of bank lending in favour of individuals carries certain risks. The financial restructuring of certain conglomerates (chaebols) continues to pose problems. Continued progress in their reorganization is vital to South Korea's economic modernization.

KEY ECONOMIC INDICATORS						
US$ billion	1998	1999	2000	2001	2002(e)	2003(f)
Economic growth (%)	−6.7	10.9	9.3	3	6	5.5
Inflation (%)	7.5	0.8	2.3	4.1	2.7	2.9
Public-sector balance/GDP (%)	−4.3	−3.3	1.3	1.3	1	0.5
Exports	132.1	145.2	175.9	151.4	163	173
Imports	90.5	116.8	159.1	138	150	162
Trade balance	41.6	28.4	16.9	13.4	13	11
Current account balance	40.4	24.5	12.2	8.6	5	2
Current account balance/GDP (%)	12.7	6	2.7	2.1	1.1	0.4
Foreign debt/GDP (%)	47.6	32.9	28.7	28.3	28.4	26.9
Debt service/Exports (%)	25.7	24.4	11.2	14	8.2	7.6
Reserves (import months)	5.1	5.8	5.7	6.9	7.6	7.5

e = estimated, f = forecast

CONDITIONS FOR ACCESS TO THE MARKET

■ Means of entry

South Korea has a very open trade policy. The vast majority of imports have been liberalized in recent years, particularly since OECD membership in 1996. The average rate of customs duty is 8 per cent, although high rates of duty remain in force, especially in the agricultural sector.

The trade barriers in the way of foreign companies are essentially of the non-tariff kind, such as technical standards and de facto discriminatory tax regulations, usually applicable to high value-added products.

Intellectual property remains poorly protected and abuses are frequent despite reforms aimed at harmonizing legislation with international standards. While the legal system appears to be satisfactory, its overall operation leaves much to be desired.

Despite the strong rebound of the Korean economy many companies continue to be affected by the 1997–98 crisis. Extreme caution is therefore called for when dealing with large industrial customers. Foreigners are advised to opt for secure means of payment. Exporters are strongly advised to secure payment by irrevocable documentary credit due to the guarantees it provides.

■ Attitude towards foreign investors

Since 1998, Korea has been one of the countries most open to direct foreign investment. In fact the Korean government actively encourages the establishment of foreign companies in the country. The few restrictions that remain in place are usually also found in the legislation of other OECD countries (utilities, defence, agriculture). Between 1995 and 2000 direct foreign investment inflows increased eightfold to US$15.7 billion. Even the 24 per cent contraction of DFI to US$11.9 billion in 2001 is fairly satisfactory considering the poor economic situation worldwide. The

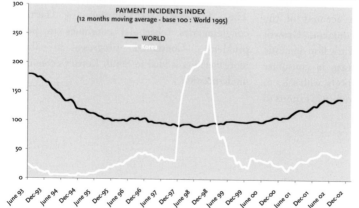

PAYMENT INCIDENTS INDEX
(12 months moving average - base 100 : World 1995)

— WORLD
— Korea

recent increase in investment inflows makes South Korea the third largest recipient of DFI in Asia after China and Hong Kong, but ahead of Japan. Most of the deals take the form of mergers and acquisitions. EU firms are the leading investors in South Korea, ahead of the US and Japanese companies.

Foreign exchange regulations

The parity of the won is determined by the currency market and since January 2001 the currency has been fully convertible and freely transferable. The only restriction concerns Korean residents, who are required to notify the authorities when exporting capital.

3

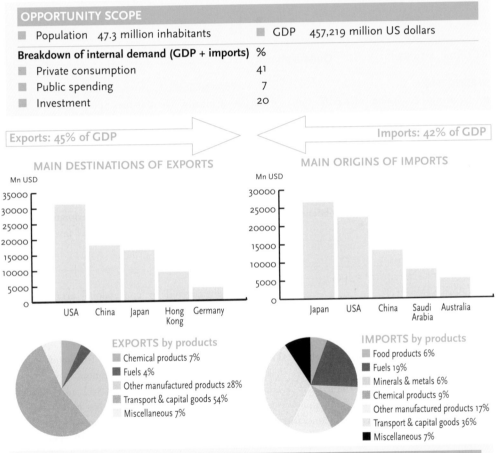

OPPORTUNITY SCOPE

Population	47.3 million inhabitants	
GDP	457,219 million US dollars	

Breakdown of internal demand (GDP + imports) %

Private consumption	41
Public spending	7
Investment	20

Exports: 45% of GDP
Imports: 42% of GDP

MAIN DESTINATIONS OF EXPORTS

Mn USD (USA, China, Japan, Hong Kong, Germany)

MAIN ORIGINS OF IMPORTS

Mn USD (Japan, USA, China, Saudi Arabia, Australia)

EXPORTS by products
- Chemical products 7%
- Fuels 4%
- Other manufactured products 28%
- Transport & capital goods 54%
- Miscellaneous 7%

IMPORTS by products
- Food products 6%
- Fuels 19%
- Minerals & metals 6%
- Chemical products 9%
- Other manufactured products 17%
- Transport & capital goods 36%
- Miscellaneous 7%

STANDARD OF LIVING / PURCHASING POWER

Indicators	South Korea	Regional average	DC average
GNP per capita (PPP dollars)	17,300	8590	6548
GNP per capita	8910	5794	3565
Human development index	0.882	0.725	0.702
Wealthiest 10% share of national income	24	32	32
Urban population percentage	82	51	60
Percentage under 15 years old	21	29	32
Number of telephones per 1000 inhabitants	464	192	157
Number of computers per 1000 inhabitants	238	105	64

Sri Lanka

Coface analysis

Short-term: **B**

Medium-term:
Quite high risk

STRENGTHS

- Growing economic diversification, with manufacturing and services making increasing contribution to growth.
- High potential for tourism.
- Moderate debt service, largely based on concessional terms.
- Peace talks between the government and Tamil separatists create climate of confidence.

WEAKNESSES

- Climatic factors play preponderant role: agriculture accounts for 19 per cent of GDP and hydropower meets 70 per cent of energy requirements.
- Textile industry, country's dominant export earner, exposed to strong competition from China and India.
- National debt swollen by deteriorating public finances. The weight of market financing is a factor of vulnerability.

RISK ASSESSMENT

The opening of peace talks between the government and the Tamil rebels has improved the political climate, after 19 years of bloody and costly conflict. Compromises have been made by both sides. However, the embryonic peace process is shaky, with the government undermined by rivalry between the president and the prime minister and the population divided over what concessions to make to the Tamil separatists.

The new climate of confidence has had a favourable impact on economic prospects. Growth is rising and moves are under way to diversify and restructure the economy. The current account deficit is under control and foreign debt, almost

entirely covered by concessional arrangements, gives no cause for concern. However, the borrowing requirement could slowly rise as the low-growth textiles and apparel export sectors come up against increasing competition within the framework of increasing world trade liberalization.

The fiscal deficit still mars Sri Lanka's financial situation. The deficit, which has been rising for several years, has created an excessive burden of public debt (100 per cent of GDP). The market component of this debt has risen sharply under pressure of domestic financial reforms and constitutes a risk factor.

KEY ECONOMIC INDICATORS						
US$ billion	1998	1999	2000	2001	2002(f)	2003(f)
Economic growth (%)	4.7	4.3	6	−1.4	3.7	2.5
Inflation (%)	9.4	4.7	6.2	14.2	9	9
Public-sector deficit/GDP (%)	−9.2	−7.5	−9.9	−10.9	−8.5	−11
Exports	4.8	4.6	5.5	4.8	5.1	5.3
Imports	5.9	6	7.3	6	6.3	6.7
Trade balance	−1.1	−1.4	−1.8	−1.2	−1.2	−1.4
Current account balance/GDP (%)	−1.8	−3.8	−6.4	−2.5	−3.3	−3.3
Foreign debt	8.80	9.97	10.09	9.68	10.3	10.68
Debt service/Exports (%)	10.9	15.2	14.7	13.3	12.5	12.5
Reserves (import months)	3.2	2.2	1.3	1.9	2	1.2

e = estimated, f = forecast

CONDITIONS FOR ACCESS TO THE MARKET

■ Means of entry

The new government, elected in December 2001, has been quick to deliver on its two main election pledges: peace and sound management of the economy. In matters of economic policy the government is committed to bringing spending under control, reducing the budget deficit and launching a restructuring and privatization programme.

Sri Lanka remains the most open country in South-east Asia, with 70 per cent of imports not subject to any restrictions. Its incentives for direct foreign investment, simplified customs duty arrangements and US- and UK-inspired trade policies make the island a relatively free and attractive market.

VAT was introduced from 1 August 2002, replacing the former 12.5 per cent goods and services tax (GST) and 6.5 per cent defence levy. Three rates of duty are applicable: 0 per cent, 10 per cent (commodities) and 20 per cent. The list of VAT-exempt items is shorter than that of GST-free products (300 in all). The surcharge on imports has been temporarily maintained, although it has been cut from 40 per cent to 20 per cent. Since 1 May 2002 stamp duty on imports has been abolished and replaced by a 1 per cent duty on the CIF value of imported products.

■ Attitude towards foreign investors

The Board of Investment is responsible for promoting and monitoring investments. Sri Lanka has adopted a number of measures to encourage foreign investment. These should bear fruit as the peace process makes headway. A bill to liberalize the labour market is currently under review.

The country's policy is one of non-discrimination between foreigners and nationals. However, some discrimination exists over the size of investment. In theory, foreign companies investing over US$5.5 million receive flagship status plus tax exemptions. In practice, however, the commitment to protect foreign investment is not always translated into reality.

The 2002 budget has abolished restrictions on foreign investment in the transport, construction, roads building, energy, water supply, banking and financial services sectors. The 100 per cent tax on land acquisitions by foreigners was also abolished.

3

OPPORTUNITY SCOPE

■ Population   19.4 million inhabitants   ■ GDP   16,305 million US dollars

Breakdown of internal demand (GDP + imports) %
■ Private consumption   48
■ Public spending   7
■ Investment   19

Exports: 40% of GDP   Imports: 51% of GDP

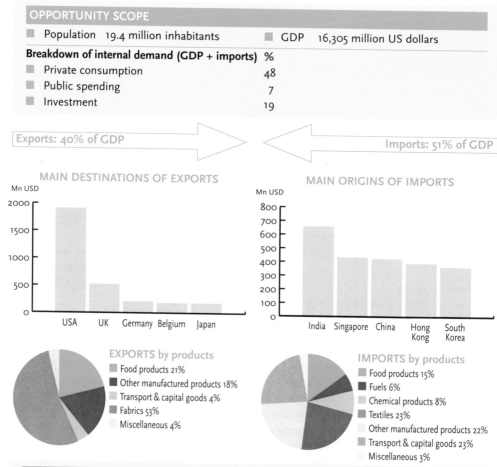

MAIN DESTINATIONS OF EXPORTS

Mn USD

USA · UK · Germany · Belgium · Japan

MAIN ORIGINS OF IMPORTS

Mn USD

India · Singapore · China · Hong Kong · South Korea

EXPORTS by products
■ Food products 21%
■ Other manufactured products 18%
■ Transport & capital goods 4%
■ Fabrics 53%
■ Miscellaneous 4%

IMPORTS by products
■ Food products 15%
■ Fuels 6%
■ Chemical products 8%
■ Textiles 23%
■ Other manufactured products 22%
■ Transport & capital goods 23%
■ Miscellaneous 3%

STANDARD OF LIVING / PURCHASING POWER

Indicators	Sri Lanka	Regional average	DC average
GNP per capita (PPP dollars)	3460	8590	6548
GNP per capita	850	5794	3565
Human development index	0.741	0.725	0.702
Wealthiest 10% share of national income	28	32	32
Urban population percentage	24	51	60
Percentage under 15 years old	26	29	32
Number of telephones per 1000 inhabitants	41	192	157
Number of computers per 1000 inhabitants	7	105	64

Taiwan

Coface analysis

Short-term: **A2**

Medium-term:
Low risk

STRENGTHS

- Firm economic foundations underpinned by highly skilled workforce and dynamic firms well positioned in growth sectors such as high-tech.
- Adaptable and fairly diversified industry.
- High savings and productive investment rates.
- Low foreign debt, especially in relation to huge foreign exchange reserves.
- Consolidation of democracy.

WEAKNESSES

- Political tensions with mainland China could dent foreign investor confidence.
- Slow adoption and implementation of structural reforms.
- Sharp deterioration in public finances necessitating tax reforms.
- Fragile banking sector.
- Increasing economic dependence on mainland China, despite diversity of trading partners.

3

RISK ASSESSMENT

With growth traditionally led more by exports than by domestic demand Taiwan, which became a WTO member in 2002, could benefit from a slight pick-up in external demand. Nevertheless prospects – in particular for the electronics industry – are weakened by the risk of another downturn in the United States and a worsening international political environment. The island is however protected from turbulence on the financial markets by its large foreign exchange reserves, which easily surpass its low foreign debt.

Taiwan's two main weaknesses are a highly fragmented banking sector hamstrung by a large number of non-performing loans and deteriorating public finances in need of tax reform. Nevertheless the country has solid economic foundations, underpinned by a highly educated workforce as well as dynamic and well-positioned firms.

Relations with mainland China remain the main source of uncertainty surrounding Taiwan's future. However, growing economic ties between Taiwan and China, as well as US support, reduce the risk of conflict. Besides, changes in China's leadership should not upset the status quo.

KEY ECONOMIC INDICATORS

US$ billion	1998	1999	2000	2001	2002(e)	2003(f)
Economic growth (%)	4.6	5.4	5.9	−1.9	3	4
Inflation (%)	1.7	0.2	1.2	0	0.2	1.3
Public-sector balance/GDP (%)	−3.4	−5.9	−4.7	−6.4	−6.5	−5.6
Exports	110.2	121.1	147.6	122.1	131.9	138.7
Imports	99.9	106.1	133.6	101.9	112.1	121.9
Trade balance	10.3	15	14	20.2	19.8	16.9
Current account balance	3.4	8.4	9	18.9	16.7	14.7
Current account balance/GDP (%)	1.3	2.9	2.9	6.7	5.9	4.7
Foreign debt/GDP (%)	11.2	9.4	7	6.6	7.2	7.9
Debt service/Exports (%)	2.3	2	2	2.5	1.8	2.2
Reserves (import months)	8.6	9.5	7.8	11.2	11.1	10.6

e = estimated, f = forecast

CONDITIONS FOR ACCESS TO THE MARKET

■ Market overview

There are no major restrictions on imports of goods and services into Taiwan. For the last 10 years the Taiwanese government has focused on opening the country's market and harmonizing its regulations with international standards in order to pave the way for WTO accession. Membership of the organization on 1 January 2002 provides foreign companies with an additional incentive to invest in the country. Under the terms of membership customs duties, low by comparison with those in other countries of the region, will be further slashed, together with tariff barriers. Tariff reductions for almost 4,500 imported products will be spread over a 10-year period from 2002 to 2011. Since 1 January 2002 the average nominal tariff has been cut from 8.25 per cent to 7.2 per cent. By 2005 it will be lowered to 5.5 per cent. The biggest cuts concern agricultural products, the average tariff for which has been cut from 20.02 per cent to 14.01 per cent in the first year of WTO membership, before being slashed to 12.9 per cent in three years' time.

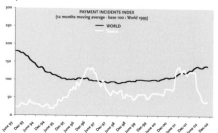

PAYMENT INCIDENTS INDEX
(12 months moving average - base 100 : World 1995)
— WORLD

The letter of credit, generally valid for 180 days, is the most widespread means of payment in Taiwan. To a lesser degree open accounts are also used for settlements between companies. However, other means of payment than the letter of credit should be used with caution owing to the difficulties of enforcing court judgments against defaulters.

Taiwan is not a member of large international organizations or a signatory to international treaties and so applies the principle of bilateral reciprocity, especially in matters of enforcement. This can pose problems for foreign companies involved in a dispute with Taiwanese firms. Many of the impediments to foreign business operations result from the general business environment rather than from specific regulations.

■ Attitude towards foreign investors

Foreign companies encounter few administrative obstacles to establishment. Most are engaged in sales and look to open a local office or branch in the country. Those with larger facilities, such as a manufacturing unit, are at times required to set up subsidiaries in the form of capital companies, with their own legal status and commercial capacity. The country's common system of company law contains discriminatory measures against the subsidiaries of foreign companies, but these can be waived by obtaining foreign investment approval. While such approval is not required to set up a business in the country it is strongly recommended as it allows foreign companies to obtain terms similar to those enjoyed by Taiwanese companies.

■ Foreign exchange regulations

In theory, the Taiwanese currency (new Taiwanese dollar or NTD) has a floating exchange rate. In practice, however, the central bank intervenes very actively on the currency market to control the currency's value. Investors should note that Taiwan's foreign exchange regulations are fairly strict.

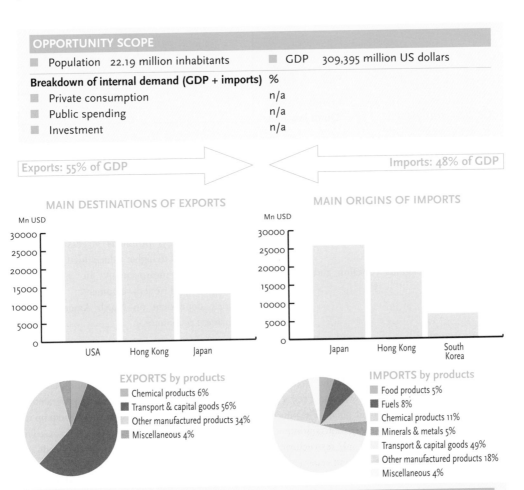

OPPORTUNITY SCOPE

■ Population   22.19 million inhabitants   ■ GDP   309,395 million US dollars

Breakdown of internal demand (GDP + imports)	%
■ Private consumption	n/a
■ Public spending	n/a
■ Investment	n/a

Exports: 55% of GDP   Imports: 48% of GDP

MAIN DESTINATIONS OF EXPORTS

Mn USD

USA   Hong Kong   Japan

MAIN ORIGINS OF IMPORTS

Mn USD

Japan   Hong Kong   South Korea

EXPORTS by products
■ Chemical products 6%
■ Transport & capital goods 56%
■ Other manufactured products 34%
■ Miscellaneous 4%

IMPORTS by products
■ Food products 5%
■ Fuels 8%
■ Chemical products 11%
■ Minerals & metals 5%
■ Transport & capital goods 49%
■ Other manufactured products 18%
■ Miscellaneous 4%

STANDARD OF LIVING / PURCHASING POWER

Indicators	Taiwan	Regional average	DC average
GNP per capita (PPP dollars)	n/a	8590	6548
GNP per capita	n/a	5794	4565
Human development index	n/a	0.725	0.702
Wealthiest 10% share of national income	n/a	32	32
Urban population percentage	75	51	60
Percentage under 15 years old	21	29	32
Number of telephones per 1000 inhabitants	545	192	157
Number of computers per 1000 inhabitants	197	105	64

n/a – not available

3

Thailand

Short-term: **A3**

Medium-term:
Quite low risk

Coface analysis

STRENGTHS

- Fairly well-diversified economy underpinned by strong agriculture (mainly rice and fish farming), tourism and some manufacturing sectors (automobiles, electronics).
- Attractive to foreign investors as regional hub.
- High savings ratio and external account surpluses.
- Ethnic and religious cohesion and political stability.

WEAKNESSES

- Incomplete industrial and financial sector restructuring puts heavy burden on public finances and widens public debt.
- Resistance to structural reforms and opening up of economy to foreign capital.
- Competitiveness problems, necessitating an industrial shift to higher value-added activities.
- Room for improvement in education, healthcare and rural development.
- Fairly dependent on North American and Japanese economies.

RISK ASSESSMENT

The economy is picking up gradually. Domestic demand should stabilize as the government starts to tighten its expansionary economic policy. The return to more sustained growth is, in any event, conditional upon quicker corporate and bank restructuring. There is also the problem of competitiveness of the economy which, in the face of Chinese competition, has not sufficiently developed higher value-added activities, largely due to inadequate vocational training.

Since the financial crisis in 1997 the disarray in the financial sector and overcapacity in the manufacturing and real estate sectors have put a brake on lending. Although T Shiwanatra's government is delaying the implementation of certain structural reforms it has undertaken a proactive banking sector restructuring programme. But it faces fiscal constraints as it tries to step up its populist programme. The public debt has soared in the last few years, although the financing needs are amply covered by abundant local savings.

The country, which has preserved external account surpluses, is in a much better financial position than in 1997, thanks to the external debt reduction, the sharp fall in short-term debt and the rebuilding of ample foreign exchange reserves. This substantially alleviates the risk of a balance of payments crisis.

KEY ECONOMIC INDICATORS

US$ billion	1998	1999	2000	2001	2002(e)	2003(f)
Economic growth (%)	−10.5	4.4	4.6	1.8	3.9	4.2
Inflation (%)	8.1	0.3	1.6	1.7	0.4	1.1
Public-sector balance/GDP (%)	−6.3	−6	−4.5	−3.5	−4.2	−2.8
Exports	52.8	56.8	67.9	63.2	65.1	67.2
Imports	36.5	42.8	56.2	54.6	57.3	60.4
Trade balance	16.2	14	11.8	8.6	7.8	6.8
Current account balance	14.2	12.4	9.3	6.2	5.3	4.5
Current account balance/GDP (%)	12.7	10.1	7.6	5.4	4.3	3.5
Foreign debt/GDP (%)	93.9	77.8	65.3	58.8	51	42.5
Debt service/Exports (%)	24.1	19.6	12.9	18.3	14.9	11.4
Reserves (import months)	6.2	6.5	5	5.2	5.7	5.2

e = estimated, f = forecast

CONDITIONS FOR ACCESS TO THE MARKET

■ Market overview

Thailand was hit by the downturn in electronics and stagnant international demand in 2001. The country's industrial output remains below pre-crisis levels. However, the economy rebounded in 2002 on the back of strong domestic demand, underpinned by a proactive government economic policy, growth in private investment and a rally in exports since April. Nevertheless questions remain about the recovery's sustainability in the face of the financial sector's persistent problems and substantial though declining industrial overcapacity, which keeps a curb on corporate lending.

■ Means of entry

Under WTO rules Thailand is engaged in the gradual reduction of import quotas and their steady replacement with customs duties and tariff quotas which, for consumer goods, are fairly high. However, the government plans to cut customs duties on many semi-finished and capital goods.

■ Attitude towards foreign investors

The government's legal reform programme continues apace. The purpose of the programme is to make Thailand more attractive to foreign investors (reform of banking and bankruptcy laws, tax incentives for siting regional headquarters in Thailand) and to facilitate the establishment of foreign-held businesses in the country (Foreign Business Act land, building and commercial property acquisition laws). While the Foreign Business Act does not lift all restrictions, it does create a more liberal environment by opening up new sectors to foreign investment.

■ Foreign exchange regulations

From the onset of the Asian crisis on 2 July 1997 the baht has been floating against the dollar. The Central Bank does not see the baht's relative weakness against the greenback as a major problem given the climate of uncertainty surrounding all the currencies of the region. It only intervenes on an ad hoc basis to cushion large fluctuations and counter speculation against the currency by restricting access to the baht market.

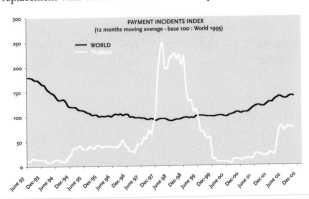

PAYMENT INCIDENTS INDEX
(12 months moving average - base 100 : World 1995)

— WORLD
Thailand

3

243

OPPORTUNITY SCOPE

- Population 60.7 million inhabitants
- GDP 122,166 million US dollars

Breakdown of internal demand (GDP + imports)	%
Private consumption	38
Public spending	8
Investment	14

Exports: 67% of GDP

Imports: 59% of GDP

MAIN DESTINATIONS OF EXPORTS

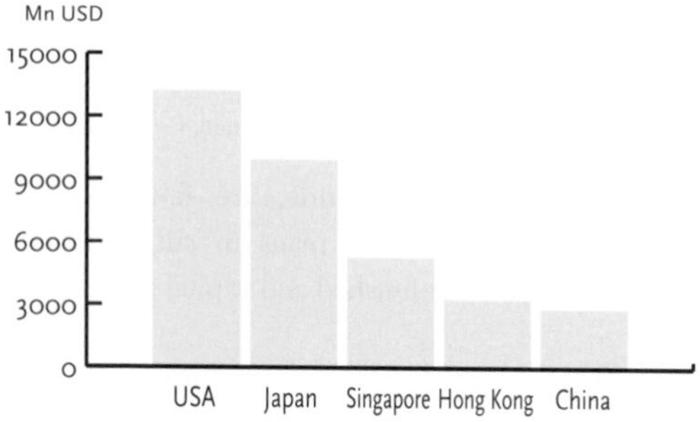

Mn USD
15000
12000
9000
6000
3000
0
USA
Japan
Singapore
Hong Kong
China

MAIN ORIGINS OF IMPORTS

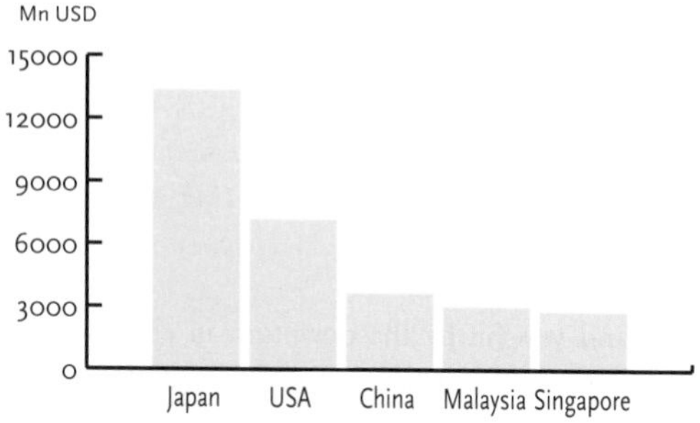

Mn USD
15000
12000
9000
6000
3000
0
Japan
USA
China
Malaysia
Singapore

EXPORTS by products

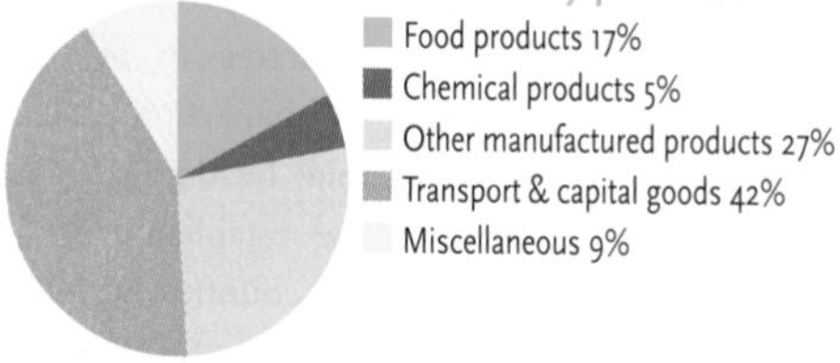

Food products 17%
Chemical products 5%
Other manufactured products 27%
Transport & capital goods 42%
Miscellaneous 9%

IMPORTS by products

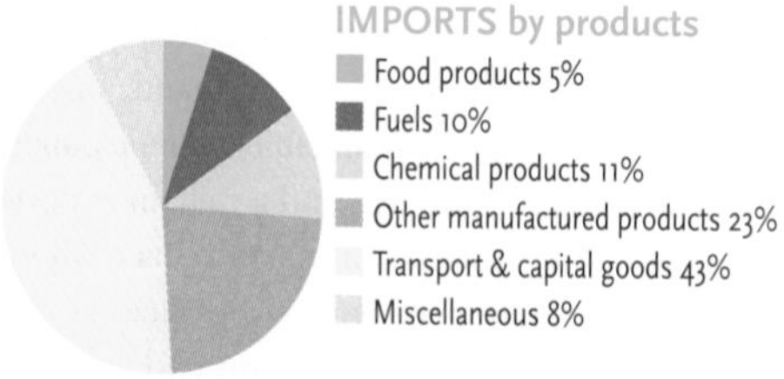

Food products 5%
Fuels 10%
Chemical products 11%
Other manufactured products 23%
Transport & capital goods 43%
Miscellaneous 8%

STANDARD OF LIVING / PURCHASING POWER

Indicators	Thailand	Regional average	DC average
GNP per capita (PPP dollars)	6320	8590	6548
GNP per capita	2000	5794	3565
Human development index	0.762	0.725	0.702
Wealthiest 10% share of national income	32	32	32
Urban population percentage	22	51	60
Percentage under 15 years old	27	29	32
Number of telephones per 1000 inhabitants	92	192	157
Number of computers per 1000 inhabitants	24	105	64

Vietnam

Short-term: **C**

Medium-term:

Coface analysis
Quite high risk

STRENGTHS

- Greater willingness to reform the economy since the change in leadership of the Communist Party in April 2001.
- As a member of ASEAN since 1995 the country benefits from integration into an economically vibrant area.
- Normalization of relations with United States since lifting of embargo in 1994 and conclusion of trade agreement implemented with United States at end-2001.
- Cheap, skilled workforce attracts multinationals.
- Dynamic and expanding private sector.

WEAKNESSES

- Alarming condition of state-owned enterprises and banks, whose reform is encountering resistance.
- Growing government debt because of public sector restructuring.
- Insufficient level of foreign exchange reserves.
- Legal and administrative environment unsuited to needs of foreign investors, despite improved legislation.
- Growing social inequalities, especially between urban and rural areas.
- One of Asia's poorest countries.

3

RISK ASSESSMENT

Vietnam's economy continues to post strong growth on the back of rising domestic demand, underpinned by an expansionary budget policy, and thanks also to a vibrant private sector, increased direct foreign investment and initial positive spin-offs from the trade agreement with the United States.

Continued reforms are essential for developing new businesses, attracting foreign investment and achieving sustained growth.

Since April 2001 changes in the leadership of the Communist Party and provision of IMF financial and technical assistance in exchange for an ambitious industrial and banking public sector restructuring programme have redoubled the country's commitment to economic reform. However, the high cost of reforms has led to an increase in public debt. While economic modernization is contributing to an increase in the imports of durables as well as a slight deterioration in the external account, it does not run into any funding difficulties as such. Nevertheless, the country's foreign exchange reserves are insufficient to eliminate the risk of foreign exchange shortage.

To pave the way for the opening of the country's economy it will be necessary to radically change attitudes at all levels and substantially alter the business environment. Progress in this area seems to be irreversible, especially with the prospect of WTO membership.

KEY ECONOMIC INDICATORS

US$ billion	1998	1999	2000	2001	2002(e)	2003(f)
Economic growth (%)	5.8	4.8	6.8	6.8	6.4	6.8
Inflation (%)	7.9	4.1	−1.7	−0.4	2	3.8
Public-sector balance/GDP (%)	−2.3	−2.6	−5.1	−4.6	−6.5	−7
Exports	9.4	11.5	14.4	15	15.6	17.5
Imports	10.3	10.5	14.1	14.4	15.8	18.2
Trade balance	−1	1.1	0.4	0.6	−0.2	−0.7
Current account balance	−1.1	1.3	0.6	0.7	−0.6	−1.1
Current account balance/GDP (%)	−3.9	4.5	2	2.1	−1.8	−3.3
Foreign debt/GDP (%)	38.8	37.3	40.8	41.6	44	43.9
Debt service/Exports (%)	12	11.7	9.6	9.6	8.1	6
Reserves (import months)	1.7	2.8	2	2.1	2.1	2.1

CONDITIONS FOR ACCESS TO THE MARKET

■ Means of entry

There is no doubt that Vietnam has spent many years liberalizing its trade. The first step consisted of membership of AFTA in 1995 as part of the country's regional commitments to ASEAN. In November 2001 it committed itself to pursuing and widening this policy under a bilateral trade agreement with the United States. These two agreements, along with a co-operation agreement with the European Union, set the stage for Vietnam's WTO accession, scheduled for 2004.

Vietnam's AFTA undertakings appear to serve as the guideline on tariff cuts. By 2005, most imports will be subject to less than 5 per cent customs duty. A programme of tariff cuts to be implemented by 2003 has been drawn up, under which the maximum rate of customs duty is set at 20 per cent. In the same vein Vietnam is gradually eliminating non-tariff barriers based mainly on a system of licences managed by the Ministry of Trade. However, the 'minimum price scheme' remains in place as an import control measure, even though it is totally unworkable. The country still needs to take substantial steps to ensure that its import arrangements attain the level of transparency expected of a country applying for WTO membership.

■ Attitude towards foreign investors

Vietnam's foreign investment regulations, though liberal in appearance, are not sufficiently transparent. The legal system is in a constant state of flux. The country's basic law enshrines principles that are extremely favourable to foreign investment. The Constitution, amended in 1992, encourages private investment and recognizes free enterprise as private ownership of the means of production, with the exception of land and mineral resources. Moreover, the country's foreign investment law, amended on several occasions, most importantly in 2000, is one of the most liberal in the region.

The government, however, exercises de facto control over investment via the prior approval requirement for all foreign investment projects. While the legal framework is attractive and relatively liberal it is incomplete, unstable and ambiguous. There are no safeguards for foreign investors, especially in matters of foreign currency availability. Investments in joint ventures are often difficult to manage if the Vietnamese partner proves uncooperative.

In matters of litigation and jurisdiction trial procedures and lack of proper enforcement of court decisions remain a problem. National arbitration is rare and little use is made of international arbitration. Moreover, licensed foreign investment during the first nine months of 2002 fell by 66 per cent to US$874.6 million, compared to the first nine months of 2001 (347 direct foreign investment projects totalling US$2 billion).

■ Foreign exchange regulations

The National Bank of Vietnam is responsible for the country's foreign exchange policy. The shortage of foreign currency has driven the government to control foreign currency outflows and to impose the local currency for domestic commercial transactions. However, the policy of asking foreign companies to balance income and expenditure in foreign currency has now been abolished.

OPPORTUNITY SCOPE

- Population   78.5 million inhabitants
- GDP   31,344 million US dollars

Breakdown of internal demand (GDP + imports) %
- Private consumption   44
- Public spending   4
- Investment   17

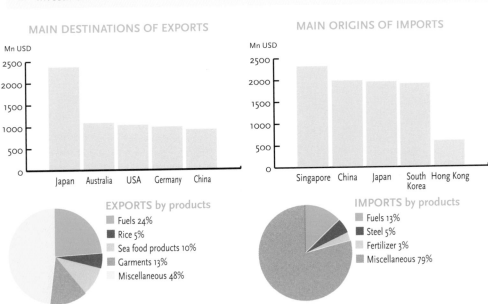

MAIN DESTINATIONS OF EXPORTS

Mn USD

Japan   Australia   USA   Germany   China

MAIN ORIGINS OF IMPORTS

Mn USD

Singapore   China   Japan   South Korea   Hong Kong

3

EXPORTS by products
- Fuels 24%
- Rice 5%
- Sea food products 10%
- Garments 13%
- Miscellaneous 48%

IMPORTS by products
- Fuels 13%
- Steel 5%
- Fertilizer 3%
- Miscellaneous 79%

STANDARD OF LIVING / PURCHASING POWER

Indicators	Vietnam	Regional average	DC average
GNP per capita (PPP dollars)	2000	8590	6548
GNP per capita	390	5794	3565
Human development index	0.688	0.725	0.702
Wealthiest 10% share of national income	30	32	32
Urban population percentage	24	51	60
Percentage under 15 years old	33	29	32
Number of telephones per 1000 inhabitants	32	192	157
Number of computers per 1000 inhabitants	9	105	64

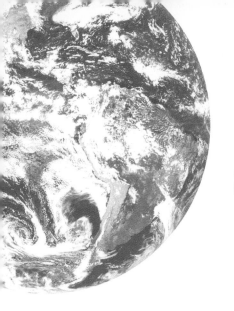

North Africa and the Middle East

4

The Outlook for the 'War Against Terror' and the Prospects for Iraq

Experts from Oxford Analytica, London

The attacks in Mombasa in November and in Bali in October raise questions about the efficacy of the war on terrorism. Specifically, they call into question the extent to which al-Qaida has been neutralized; whether more attacks can be expected; and whether military and law enforcement measures alone can bring peace.

The Outlook For The 'War Against Terror'

Since 11 September 2001 the United States has led a war against terrorism in which military forces and law enforcement agencies have pursued al-Qaida and associated groups of terrorists into and across many countries of the world. Recent significant terrorist attacks, notably November's attacks on Israeli tourists in Kenya and the bombing of a nightclub in Bali, Indonesia in October (in which 185 people died), inevitably raise the question of how successful the US campaign has been.

■ Long haul

The US administration has always said that the war against terrorism would be a 'long haul'. In this respect it is similar to the war against drugs; and, as with the war against drugs, there is a danger of perpetuating the struggle through a failure to overcome the sources that constantly regenerate the enemy. In the drugs field that source is the demand of the consumer. In the fight against Muslim fundamentalist terrorism – which is the kernel of President George Bush's war – the spring is the tacit sympathy of many, particularly young, people, throughout the Islamic world.

Since the end of the Afghan phase of the war al-Qaida has been elusive. There have been attacks that fit in roughly with al-Qaida's style: the murder of US journalist Daniel Pearl in Pakistan in January/February; the attack on a historic synagogue on the Tunisian island of Djerba in April; the killing of 11 French engineers in a suicide bomb attack in Karachi, Pakistan in May; the attack on the French oil tanker Limburg off the Yemeni port of al-Shihr in October; and the devastating bomb that killed so many young Western holidaymakers in Bali the same month. November's attacks on Israeli tourists in Mombasa, Kenya bore the hallmarks of al-Qaida.

True to form, al-Qaida did not claim responsibility for any of these attacks. However, the recent alleged tape-recording of Osama Bin Laden, which US experts seem to think is genuine, refers to them with approval; and the attacks have taken place against a background of what UK Prime Minister Tony Blair has described as a growing drum beat of rumours and imprecise information predicting further attacks across the Western world.

■ Remaining network

There can be no doubt that the successful US campaign in Afghanistan, and the concerted efforts of intelligence and law-enforcement services round the globe, will have caused major damage and disruption to al-Qaida as it existed in the days of the Taliban. However, it is equally certain that some, perhaps many, terrorists who had been trained by al-Qaida in Afghanistan were not in the country when the United States launched its attack. Some of these 'sleepers' will be known to or suspected by the Western agencies, but some will not. In addition, a significant number of trained terrorists escaped from Afghanistan. Putting these two groups together, there could be several hundred terrorists at large.

Terrorists need a sympathetic community in which to hide. They also need somewhere where they can in relative safety recuperate, plan, train and relax. In the 1980s such havens were provided by actively co-operating states, such as Iran, Syria, Iraq and Libya. When, in the 1990s, active co-operation by most states became too dangerous, Afghanistan became the principal home base. With Afghanistan now too dangerous, escaping terrorists will have looked for areas where the population is sympathetic and where the reach both of the local government and of the United States is attenuated, such as the tribal areas of Pakistan, Iran, Somalia and Yemen. However, such safe havens do not need to be in geographically remote areas, as evidence that substantial numbers of al-Qaida members are based in Karachi suggests. They can also live within Islamic communities in the West. Some may have decided to retire or to do the absolute minimum of active work, but others will plan new terrorist attacks and recruit new blood from among the young people in their community.

■ Franchise operation

It is far from clear that al-Qaida actively controls these cells. Centralized organizations are vulnerable, and al-Qaida may therefore have chosen to become a franchise, an umbrella loosely covering near-autonomous cells – a movement rather than an organization. If this is the case cells will presumably have to develop their own sources of funds. The continuing rallying cries to jihad, whether really made by bin Laden and other leaders or not, have also inspired unaffiliated 'copycat' would-be terrorists. These two factors are probably reflected in the varying size and sophistication of the attacks mounted or attempted by different groups over the past year.

It is possible to derive from these operations some tentative conclusions about the patterns of the network's current activities. They seem to confirm that the loss of a central and secure operating base in Afghanistan, coupled with the disruption of the leadership and of the broader network, and the increase in security around many 'hard' targets, have led to a reduced capacity to mount co-ordinated, 'spectacular' operations. Instead, smaller-scale, more varied attacks on 'softer' targets in easier operating environments have been the norm, generally using low-tech and 'traditional' methods rather than innovative or non-conventional weapons. (The Mombasa attacks also add to the evidence that al-Qaida is seeking to associate itself with the Palestinian issue.) However, none of this rules out the possibility that elements of the leadership still retain some capacity to plan and/or implement more ambitious operations.

■ Outlook

Some previous terrorist groups and movements have been defeated, although always after long and painful effort. Some of these were small, such as Baader-Meinhof in Germany, the Red Brigades in Italy and more recently the Greek November 17 group. The British and their ethnic-Malay-led allies defeated ethnic-Chinese communist insurgents in Malaysia, but these had no strong base in the Chinese population and were eventually isolated in the jungle. After the Second World War there was terrorist-type resistance to the Soviet Union in parts of Eastern Europe. These fighters operated from a largely sympathetic base in the community, but they and their communities were crushed by massive repression. However, in most cases where terrorist groups have had the continuing support of large populations, they have ultimately succeeded in gaining a seat at the negotiating table: examples include Cyprus, Kenya, Zimbabwe, Algeria, Ireland, Sri Lanka and even Palestine.

However, al-Qaida not only enjoys popular support and is thus difficult to eradicate, but also presents two additional challenges:

- Its political demands are essentially non-negotiable. By contrast even the Basque separatist ETA and the Colombian FARC are making demands that could, in theory at least, form the subject of negotiations. Furthermore it is not constrained, as other groups are, in the level of the violence it perpetrates by the negative impact of such actions on attainment of its political goals.
- The fact that it is a widely dispersed and franchised operation, perhaps without an active solid core, makes identifying potential negotiating partners particularly difficult.

■ Strategy lessons

One of the lessons from previous terrorism campaigns is that communities which have supported terrorists can become disenchanted by continuous strife and the loss of innocent lives. It is very much in the interests of the law enforcers to encourage this by means of 'hearts and minds' strategies. Al-Qaida is still at the stage of murdering innocent people indiscriminately and making demands that are impossible to meet. At present this uncompromising stance is still attractive to its sympathizers. However, in due course these attributes could in the right circumstances lose it support. In order to encourage this process of disenchantment the best strategy is usually to seek to engage more moderate elements and separate them from the hardliners.

Washington has embarked on a multi-pronged media campaign in order to address the 'hearts and minds' issue. However, current US policies in the Middle East make it hard to mount an effective counter-terrorist campaign without reinforcing those perceptions within Islamic society that enable the terrorists constantly to regenerate their forces.

There are indications that al-Qaida is becoming a loose mantle over near-autonomous cells. Based on sleeper terrorists who were clear of Afghanistan before the US attack, these cells are well placed to mount operations and to recruit new blood from among young members of the Islamic communities in which they live. Terrorists who have the sympathy of large communities are difficult to defeat. An effective 'hearts and minds' campaign will be needed to prevent al-Qaida from constantly regenerating its forces.

Prospects For Iraq

The Iraqi regime is struggling for survival under intense political pressure from the United States. Washington is applying that pressure under UN auspices through the issue of weapons of mass destruction (WMD). If Baghdad falls seriously short of its undertaking to co-operate with the UN arms inspectors, then the United States must return to the Security Council for consultations. It is likely that such consultations would amount to little more than a formality, prefacing the onset of US-led hostilities.

Given that such a conflict will mostly be fought by the US military, the regime would face a devastating onslaught. Even if President Saddam Hussein were to survive such a battle, his position would be much diminished. His best chance of survival is therefore to 'co-operate' with the weapons inspectors and hope that the climatic window of opportunity for a war is lost. He will calculate that it will be possible to remain in power indefinitely, in spite of the intrusive nature of the inspections and the heightened level of international interest, as was basically the case in the early 1990s.

◼ Playing for time

With this prospect in mind the Iraqi regime has decided to 'co-operate' with the weapons inspectors.

It is most likely to continue to do so in an effort to deny the United States its casus belli. This strategy of playing for time is predicated on one of two hopes:

- **Closed window.** Saddam will hope that co-operation will draw out the inspection process, thereby taking the United States beyond the climatic window of opportunity for a land war, somewhere around April 2003. At this point Baghdad could choose to reduce its level of cooperation with the inspectors. It is not clear that Washington has a fallback position, either in the event of Iraq choosing to renege on its commitments at this point, or should the weapons inspections process drag on indefinitely.
- **US distractions.** Saddam will also be hoping that something turns up by way of an international development or outrage that drags the attention of the US government away from the Iraqi issue. With its presumed access to considerable levels of foreign exchange generated through oil and products smuggling over the last six years, it is to be assumed that Iraq has significant resources to spend on expediting the emergence of such distractions. There has, for example, been speculation that an Iraqi hand was behind North Korea's recent revelations of the resumption of its own nuclear programme.

◼ Diversionary tactics

One may also expect to see Saddam, who enjoys a reputation for being a skilled tactician, especially when his back is to the wall, indulging in some diversionary strategies, aimed at winning over opinion in the region and further afield. Baghdad's somewhat chaotic release of all political prisoners in late October may be seen as such a gesture, as was the decision at the end of November by a supposed Iraqi opposition group to accept the regime's invitation to visit Baghdad for consultations.

Moreover, speculation is heightening that Saddam may make a major overture in the direction of the liberalization of the political system, to include the adoption of a new constitution, with the European Union rumoured to be the likely recipient of such an approach. However, it is unlikely that such measures would be any more than an exercise in window dressing, and would have little impact on regime power, at least over the short-to-medium term. Such gestures towards a formal opening of the system could include:

- the dissolution of the highest executive organization in the country, the Revolutionary Command Council, which Saddam chairs;
- the creation of a 'national unity government';
- Saddam relinquishing the premiership, as he did when in trouble domestically in 1991, perhaps with a Shia figure to be appointed in his stead; and
- the diminution of the profile of the Ba'ath Party.

War pattern

However, if war does indeed take place in Iraq at some stage during the first four months of 2003, it is likely, at least initially, to follow a predictable pattern:

- **Priority US targets.** The United States will focus on priority targets for initial military action. These will include: the Western desert, to reduce the likelihood that Iraq will be able to fire Scud missiles with non-conventional warheads at Israel; the oil fields of the south of the country, to ensure that the Iraqi regime does not set them ablaze, as it did in its scorched earth policy in Kuwait in early 1991; and sites that it feels may be significant in terms of the production of WMD, especially biological and chemical weapons.
- **Political victories.** The United States will post some easy political victories, both through defections from the regular Iraqi army and the rapid takeover of territory from Saddam's regime, either directly through its own forces, or indirectly through its local allies or through the medium of such local defectors.
- **Last stand.** Washington will then face the question of what to do about Baghdad. This is most likely to be the focus of a last stand by the regime – rather than Saddam's home town, the provincial centre of Tikrit, where regime insiders would be isolated and hence vulnerable – because of its significance as the capital and hence the seat of political power. It is possible, though not inevitable, that Saddam will be overthrown by a pre-emptive coup from within. If not, the US military will soon come face to face with his hard-core supporters. Saddam can only hope to count on such organs as the Special Republican Guard (between 15,000 and 26,000 men) and the Special Security organization (5000) as the bedrock of his regime, amounting in total to not much more than 30,000 armed supporters. It is thus unlikely that he will be able to defend the whole city. It is therefore more likely that the hard-core supporters of the regime will fall back on the affluent quarters in central Baghdad, such as Mansour, where they have their property and families.

Such a development would pose a test for the US administration and its ability to manage the denouement to the conflict. Its ability to win such a final contest is not in theory in doubt, though it might balk at the possible cost, either in terms of its own troop losses in street fighting or Iraqi casualties in a final, Dresden-style bombardment. Rather it might seek to manage the problem, perhaps by establishing the transitional seat of power in another part of the country.

4

This year will be decisive for the Iraqi regime. Either it will miscalculate and provide a casus belli for a US-led onslaught that it will be lucky to survive; or it will continue to co-operate with the UN weapons inspectors, and thwart the United States, but at the cost of a continuing intrusive investigation into its WMD programme. However the latter, while a constraint on national sovereignty, is unlikely to erode Saddam's domestic power base seriously during the course of 2003.

Country @rating scale for North Africa and the Middle East

Sylvia Greisman and Catherine Monteil
Coface Country Risk and Economic Studies Department, Paris

The country @rating scale measures the average level of short-term non-payment risk presented by companies in a particular country. It reflects the extent to which a country's economic, financial and political outlook influences financial commitments of local companies. It is thus complementary to @rating Credit Opinions on companies.

Political uncertainty constitutes the main risk factor in a region already marked by 11 September 2001 aftershocks and aggravation of the Israeli–Palestinian conflict, with the risk of war in Iraq compounding the climate of uncertainty.

If there is no armed conflict in the region, the growth of regional economies should accelerate, fuelled by improved external demand, while an easing of regional tensions should favour increased tourism and investment.

Forecasts for 2003 are difficult, however, supposing military intervention in Iraq. Such intervention could indeed compromise a growth upturn in non-oil countries whereas surging crude prices would benefit oil-exporting countries. Saudi Arabia could be the main beneficiary, being one of the rare countries capable of offsetting an Iraqi production shutdown.

Macro economically, last year's slowdown caused a slight deterioration of the payment incident index for regional companies, which remains nonetheless below the world average, as shown in the chart.

Partially offset by the steadiness of oil prices, uncertainties surrounding economic and political trends have only prompted a limited number of country rating changes. Israel's rating has thus been downgraded from A3 to A4 while Tunisia, rated A4, has been negatively watchlisted. Conversely Turkey, which had been downgraded to category C in 2001, has been positively watchlisted due to a growth rebound accompanied by improved company payment behaviour.

■ Countries rated A2

Default likelihood has remained low on average even though the country's economic and political environment or local company payment behaviour is slightly less good than in countries rated A1.

Qatar's financial situation has remained good. Considering the country's high debt ratios, however, it is nonetheless still vulnerable to a sudden reversal of the oil situation or aggravation of regional tensions. The country's development prospects are bright. The government has initiated a cautious process of economic liberalization and political opening, which is going forward despite resistance from conservative quarters.

■ Countries rated A4

These countries often present fairly mediocre payment behaviour that could be affected by an economic downturn, although the probability of

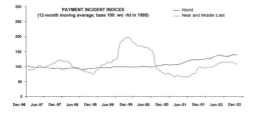

PAYMENT INCIDENT INDICES
(12-month moving average; base 100: world in 1995)
— World
— Near and Middle East

that causing a large number of payment defaults remains moderate.

The Saudi economy is structurally dependent on oil market trends. After two years of slowdown, economic activity should improve in 2003. However, the vigour of a recovery is uncertain and it will depend on durability of the growth rebound in the United States. Meanwhile, Implementation of the natural gas initiative, upon which the Saudi economy's redeployment will depend, has been lagging. Regional instability could also affect investments. The steadiness of oil prices last year permitted controlling the fiscal deficit. Whereas the government's payment speed has traditionally

affected the entire economy, company payment defaults increased only moderately in 2002 with the payment incident index remaining below average.

In Israel, economic activity has been declining. Since the new *intifada* began in September 2000, insecurity has affected most economic sectors, notably tourism, transportation, construction and farming. The high-technology sector, which had spurred a strong acceleration of economic growth in 2000, has since been suffering greatly from the economic downturn in the United States. It could suffer further from weakness of the recovery across the Atlantic. The downturn has affected fiscal revenues while spending on

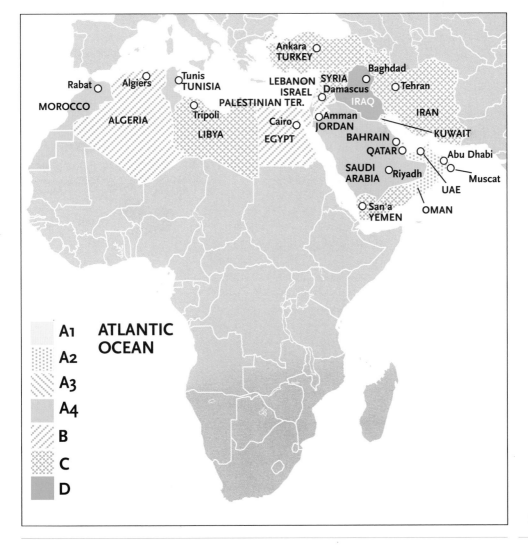

4

security has been increasing. The austerity budget that the authorities may continue to follow would constitute a further obstacle to economic recovery. Development of the political crisis, with no near-term solution in sight, has been weighing heavily on the country's economic and financial situation, which affects company solvency. Payment defaults and bankruptcies have thus been increasing. In this context, Israel's rating was downgraded from A3 to A4 during the year.

In Tunisia, after the deterioration registered last year with the drought, tourism decline and weak European demand, the 2003 outlook has remained positive although dependent on weather conditions and the evolving world geopolitical environment. Deficits should nonetheless remain under control while the increase in the external debt prompts no fear of any payment default by the country. Moreover, political stability and the expected continuation of privatizations and structural reforms should attract additional external financing. The payment behaviour deterioration, which had affected all economic sectors, but particularly farming and tourism, persisted last year. However, late payments by Tunisian companies – traditionally frequent – often result in collection.

In Morocco, the pace of economic activity should remain high this year. The economy has nonetheless remained vulnerable to exogenous factors affecting farm production output and tourism revenues. Meanwhile the government must continue the structural reforms intended to diversify and consolidate the industrial fabric. Export sectors (textiles–clothing, leather, fruit and vegetables) have particularly suffered from the European slowdown in 2002. They are also exposed to competition from Central European and Asian products. Payment defaults registered on Moroccan companies have often represented late payments that result in collection.

■ Countries rated B

A precarious economic environment could affect company payment behaviour, which is often poor.

In Egypt, while the climate of regional tensions has been discouraging investment that could drive long-term growth, political and economic fallout from 11 September 2001 has affected tourism, oil revenues, Suez Canal revenues, and emigrant worker remittances. Persistently difficult access to foreign exchange and the economic slowdown have continued to affect company payment capacity. Payment difficulties have increased sharply for companies in this country.

Conversely, Algeria's financial situation has never been better. The steadiness of oil prices has permitted restoring fundamental macroeconomic equilibriums while the external debt has continued to decline. Growth has nonetheless remained weak and grossly insufficient to raise the general standard of living. In the near term, the financial situation affords the authorities the means to pursue expansionary fiscal policy to stimulate the economy and meet some infrastructure needs. However, the private sector's development has led to the appearance of recently created companies that are often undercapitalized. Weaker than more established companies, the newcomers present a higher level of payment default risk. Meanwhile the great disparity between the oil sector and the rest of the economy underscores the need for reforms, which remain difficult to undertake considering the political and social context.

■ Countries rated C

A very precarious economic and political environment could worsen payment behaviour that is already often poor.

In Turkey, the economy has recovered faster than expected and inflation is in a better state than anticipated by the government. The Turkish financial situation remains nonetheless very exposed to a crisis of confidence in financial markets. Meanwhile, many uncertainties surround both the internal and domestic political situations. Nonetheless, IMF aid will doubtless permit the country to avoid a new financial crisis this year.

Turkish companies have been progressively recovering from the crisis. Although their payment behaviour has been improving it remains weakened by difficult access to foreign exchange. A major challenge facing the new government will be to pursue reforms (privatization, public sector streamlining, banking sector consolidation) essential to sustaining a climate of confidence.

In Iran, finally, it has remained difficult to obtain information on companies, which makes risk taking a haphazard enterprise. The country enjoys a favourable economic and financial situation, with its external debt representing a moderate constraint. The economy has nonetheless remained very dependent on the oil sector with the public sector continuing to predominate. Although pursuing the structural reform programme is necessary to consolidate the foundations of growth and limit unemployment, it is a slow process in a complex political context.

4

Algeria

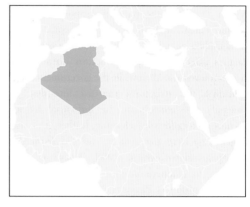

Short-term: **B**

Medium-term:

Coface analysis **Quite high risk**

STRENGTHS

- Vast natural resources (oil, gas).
- Support of Western countries guaranteed by foreign interests in the hydrocarbon sector and Europe's energy dependence on Algerian oil and gas.
- Engaged in economic liberalization and diversification.

WEAKNESSES

- Economy dependent on oil, gas and agriculture, itself vulnerable to climatic factors.
- Declining yet substantial foreign debt.
- Fiscal balance, burdened by rigid spending on wages and debt, heavily reliant on oil revenues. Limited access to capital markets hampers country's ability to finance public deficit when trading conditions in oil market are unfavourable.
- Barely noticeable improvement in living standards. Social tensions exacerbated by high unemployment.

RISK ASSESSMENT

Algeria's financial position has never been better thanks to firm oil prices, which have enabled the country to restore the key macroeconomic balances against a background of declining foreign debt. However, growth has been too weak to improve the living standards of a population whose increasingly strident demands across all areas of the economy (water, housing, education, healthcare, employment) remain unsatisfied, therefore creating social tensions.

In the short term the country's financial position allows the government to pursue an expansionary fiscal policy aimed at boosting economic activity and meeting a number of infrastructure requirements.

In the longer term the Algerian economy will remain shaky due to its exposure to a volatile oil market, the vulnerability of its agriculture to climatic factors, the inefficiency of public sector enterprises and the weakness of the banking sector. The government's structural reform programme is making painfully slow progress given the political and social context.

KEY ECONOMIC INDICATORS

US$ billion	1998	1999	2000	2001	2002(e)	2003(f)
Economic growth (%)	5.1	3.2	2.4	1.7	2.1	3.9
Inflation (%)	5.6	2.7	0.3	4.2	4.8	4.5
Public-sector balance/GDP (%)	−3.9	−2	9.8	3.4	1.7	n/a
Exports	10.1	2.3	21.7	19.1	18.4	18.8
Imports	8.6	9	9.3	9.8	10.4	11.4
Trade balance	1.5	3.4	12.4	9.29	7.96	7.43
Current account balance/GDP (%)	−1.9	0	16.6	12.3	10.2	8.5
Foreign debt/GDP (%)	64.3	59.5	47.5	42.1	40.2	34.6
Debt service/Exports (%)	45.5	37.4	19.2	21.2	18.9	18.7
Reserves (import months)	6.2	3.9	9.7	14.5	17	18.9

n/a – not available

e = estimated, f = forecast

CONDITIONS OF ACCESS TO THE MARKET

■ Market overview

Within the last two years Algeria has made sweeping changes to its customs tariff system. Customs duties have been streamlined and slashed – there are now three rates of duty: 30 per cent, 15 per cent and 5 per cent - and the administered prices system abolished. The new tariffs, which came into force in January 2002, lowers the average weighted rate of duty to below the 9 per cent mark. Duties are levied on the transaction value in line with the most favoured nation principle, pending enforcement of the Association Agreement with the European Union concluded in April 2002. In 2003 certain branches of the country's manufacturing industry will continue to be protected by 36 per cent provisional additional duty. This duty is transparent and will be gradually abolished by 2006. There are no further special import restrictions, licences or quotas, except for pharmaceuticals, where imports are subject to a subsequent investment in plant.

■ Attitude towards foreign investors

Algeria does not discriminate between local and foreign investment in manufacturing and services (development, extension of capacity, privatization-related buy-ins or buy-outs) or investments made in connection with the award of concessions and/or licences (Decree No. 01-03 of 20 August 2001). Tariff preferences and tax concessions designed to encourage investment are similar for both locals and foreigners. Foreign-held subsidiaries are permitted to operate in most sectors open to private investment, including financial services. The law guarantees repatriation of all capital invested and all income derived therefrom. A certain number of sectors (telecommunications, sea and air transport, electricity and gas supply, mining) have been opened to private investment in the last two years.

As a rule investment in plant is welcome. Conversely, trading and retail businesses are not treated as investments. Similarly, fee transfers relating to services and intangible investments (royalties, etc) pose problems.

■ Foreign exchange regulations

The dinar is fully convertible for imports of goods and equipment and, with foreign exchange reserves at an estimated US$22.5 billion in late 2002 the risk of default is limited. However, given the low capitalization of many recently established Algerian companies and the lack of transparency of balance sheets, which hampers the operations of the few audit firms in the marketplace, the most widely recommended means of payment is the bill of exchange and, in its absence, the documentary bill. The country's cumbersome banking procedures continue to pose problems.

The free convertibility of the dinar remains subject to exchange controls under which foreign currency applications for settlement of service contracts must first be cleared by the Central Bank.

4

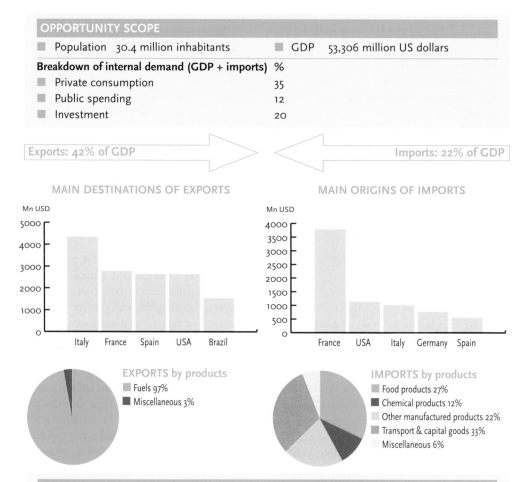

OPPORTUNITY SCOPE

- Population   30.4 million inhabitants
- GDP   53,306 million US dollars

Breakdown of internal demand (GDP + imports) %
- Private consumption   35
- Public spending   12
- Investment   20

Exports: 42% of GDP   Imports: 22% of GDP

MAIN DESTINATIONS OF EXPORTS

Mn USD

Italy   France   Spain   USA   Brazil

MAIN ORIGINS OF IMPORTS

Mn USD

France   USA   Italy   Germany   Spain

EXPORTS by products
- Fuels 97%
- Miscellaneous 3%

IMPORTS by products
- Food products 27%
- Chemical products 12%
- Other manufactured products 22%
- Transport & capital goods 33%
- Miscellaneous 6%

STANDARD OF LIVING / PURCHASING POWER

Indicators	Algeria	Regional average	DC average
GNP per capita (PPP dollars)	5040	7168	6548
GNP per capita	1580	4625	3565
Human development index	0.697	0.734	0.702
Wealthiest 10% share of national income	27	29	32
Urban population percentage	60	71	60
Percentage under 15 years old	35	36	32
Number of telephones per 1000 inhabitants	57	161	157
Number of computers per 1000 inhabitants	7	59	64

Bahrain

Coface analysis

Short-term: **A2**

Medium-term:
Quite low risk

STRENGTHS

- Economy diversified between industry (oil/gas, aluminium) and services (banks and tourism).
- Region's leading business hub due to geographical situation and offshore banking.
- Receives financial support from neighbouring states, mainly to contain Shiite opposition.
- Low foreign debt.
- Committed to democratization, becoming a constitutional monarchy on 14 February 2002.

WEAKNESSES

- Tiny oil reserves compared with neighbouring countries.
- Despite diversification economy highly dependent on oil sector.
- Rigid budgetary expenditure strains public finances.
- Social unrest among the Shiite majority in the Kingdom ruled over by the Sunni minority.
- Social tensions exacerbated by growing unemployment among Bahraini nationals.
- Slow progress in economic reforms.

4

RISK ASSESSMENT

The economy has strong growth potential. In the short term, however, growth could be dampened, as regional political uncertainties may slow investment in large-scale industrial projects. The increase in infrastructure spending, designed to create jobs and contain unrest within the Shiite population, should widen the fiscal deficit. Despite falling back slightly, firm oil prices should generate a current account surplus again this year.

Because of fairly low indebtedness the country's financial position is not worrying.

However, the country remains vulnerable to external crises. It has yet to adopt needed structural reforms and clear economic policies in order to attract foreign investment. While the reform process is already slowing in an attempt to contain social discontent, escalating regional tensions since 11 September 2001 are adding to difficulties.

Iraq

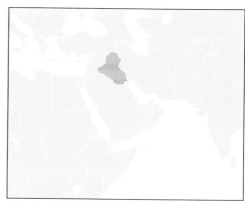

Short-term: **D**

Medium-term:

Coface analysis   **Very high risk**

RISK ASSESSMENT

Although the country has been placed under an embargo since the end of the Gulf war in 1991, the 'oil for food' programme introduced in 1996 has stemmed the slide in GDP and increased foreign exchange earnings, the use of which is under the tight control of the United Nations. The slump in growth over the last two years is due to the decline in crude oil output following the suspension of deliveries in 2001 and imposition of retroactive tariffs by the United Nations in early 2002.

Iraq's economic development is obviously conditioned by its relations with the international community and in particular the United States.

While Iraq possesses the world's second largest oil reserves after Saudi Arabia, the country's oil production, after more than 10 years of embargo, is well below capacity. If UN sanctions were lifted investment would be required to rehabilitate existing installations and increase long-term production capacity. The government would also have to give priority to tackling the country's debt. It will probably take a long time to return to normal.

KEY ECONOMIC INDICATORS					
US$ billion	1998	1999	2000	2001 (e)	2002(f)
Economic growth (%)	35	18	4	−6	−3
Inflation (%)	90	80	70	60	70
Exports	7.4	12.8	20.6	15.9	13
Imports	4	6.9	11.1	11	7.8
Trade balance	3.4	5.9	9.5	4.9	5.2
Current account balance/GDP (%)	6.4	8.5	10.3	3.7	8.7
Foreign debt	56	58	60	62	63.4

e = estimated, f = forecast

Israel

Coface analysis

Short-term: **A4**

Medium-term:
Quite low risk

STRENGTHS

- Diversified and open economy, equivalent in size to that of certain European countries, with 70 per cent of trade carried out with North America and Europe.
- Development of high-tech industries factor of growth, however heavily dependent on US markets.
- Political and financial support of United States and Jewish diaspora.

WEAKNESSES

- Regional integration negated by deteriorating relations with Palestinian Authority and most Arab countries.
- Economy hit by security situation.
- Public finances strained by social and military spending.
- Government stability undermined by political fragmentation along ethnic and religious lines

4

RISK ASSESSMENT

Economic activity declined as the breakdown in security caused by the launch of the new Intifada in September 2000 hit most sectors of the economy, in particular tourism. In addition the high-tech sector, the driving force behind the economy's rapid growth in 2000, has since been severely hit by the US economic slowdown. It could continue to suffer as a result of weak US recovery. The downturn has hit tax revenues, while spending on security has soared. The likelihood of the government sticking to its austerity budget will further hamper economic recovery.

Political developments, which do not point to a way out of the crisis in the short term, are placing a heavy economic and financial burden upon the country. Against this background defaults and bankruptcies are likely to rise.

KEY ECONOMIC INDICATORS						
US$ billion	1998	1999	2000	2001	2002(e)	2003(f)
Economic growth (%)	2.7	2.6	6.4	-0.6	-1.3	-1
Inflation (%)	5.4	5.2	1.1	1.1	6	3
Public-sector balance/GDP (%)	-2	-2.2	-0.6	-4.6	-4.8	n/a
Exports	23	25.6	30.8	27.4	27.1	29.6
Imports	26.3	30.1	34.2	30.9	31	32.9
Trade balance	-3.3	-4.5	-3.4	-3.5	-3.9	-3.3
Current account balance/GDP (%)	-1.4	-3	-1.3	-1.6	-2.5	-2
Foreign debt/GDP (%)	57	60.6	57.6	60.2	68	67.1
Debt service/Exports (%)	17.4	16.7	14	17.2	17.5	16.9
Reserves (import months)	7.9	5.6	4.9	5.6	5.7	5.5

n/a – not available

e = estimated, f = forecast

CONDITIONS OF ACCESS TO THE MARKET

■ Market overview

The Israeli government intends to pursue its policy of economic liberalization (privatization of banks, telecommunications and transport), tax reform and BOT infrastructure development.

■ Means of entry

Israel is one of only two countries in the world (the other is Mexico) to have a free trade agreement with the European Union and the United States. Similar agreements have been signed with EFTA countries: Turkey, Canada, the Czech Republic, Poland, Hungary, Slovenia and Mexico.

Except for some agricultural products, the products covered by the main free trade agreements are admitted into Israel free of customs duties.

They are, however, subject to 18 per cent VAT. A variable sales tax is levied on some consumer goods.

Under the Public Tender Act foreign bidders are subject to a set-off scheme based on a minimum 30 per cent of the tender's total value.

■ Attitude towards foreign investors

Investment is unrestricted (although an application must be made beforehand to obtain any benefits) except in protected sectors such as defence and some utilities. Israeli legislation contains various measures designed to encourage investment, whether of local or foreign origin.

Commercial payments between Israel and foreign countries are totally unrestricted. The transfer or repatriation of profits, dividends and financial receivables is unrestricted, after payment of Israeli taxes. Special tax benefits are granted to foreign investors, provided initial transactions are carried out through an approved agent.

The regulations governing foreign workers have become more restrictive.

The cost of living in Israel is high and is comparable to and, in some cases (consumer goods), higher than the European average.

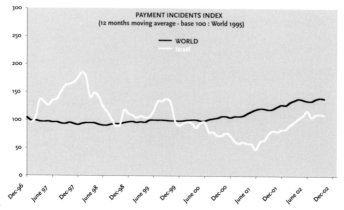

PAYMENT INCIDENTS INDEX
(12 months moving average - base 100 : World 1995)

— WORLD
— Israel

OPPORTUNITY SCOPE

- Population   6.2 million inhabitants
- GDP   110,386 million US dollars

Breakdown of internal demand (GDP + imports) %
- Private consumption   42
- Public spending   20
- Investment   13

Exports: 40% of GDP   Imports: 47% of GDP

MAIN DESTINATIONS OF EXPORTS

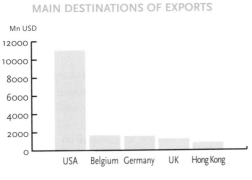

Mn USD

USA   Belgium   Germany   UK   Hong Kong

MAIN ORIGINS OF IMPORTS

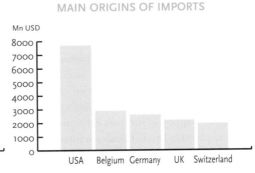

Mn USD

USA   Belgium   Germany   UK   Switzerland

EXPORTS by products
- Chemical products 14%
- Other manufactured products 48%
- Transport & capital goods 33%
- Miscellaneous 6%

IMPORTS by products
- Fuels 7%
- Food products 6%
- Chemical products 9%
- Other manufactured products 39%
- Transport & capital goods 35%
- Miscellaneous 4%

4

STANDARD OF LIVING / PURCHASING POWER

Indicators	Israel	Regional average	DC average
GNP per capita (PPP dollars)	19,330	7168	6548
GNP per capita	16,710	4625	3565
Human development index	0.896	0.734	0.702
Wealthiest 10% share of national income	28	29	32
Urban population percentage	91	71	60
Percentage under 15 years old	28	36	32
Number of telephones per 1000 inhabitants	482	161	157
Number of computers per 1000 inhabitants	254	59	64

Jordan

Short-term: **B**

Medium-term:
High risk

STRENGTHS	WEAKNESSES

STRENGTHS

- IMF-sponsored structural adjustment programme has improved economic fundamentals.
- Despite high debt, debt service reduced to sustainable levels under Paris Club agreements.
- Enjoys support of international community for role played in Israeli–Palestinian relations.
- Tourism and transport major areas of development.
- WTO membership, development of QIZs (Qualifying Industrial Zones) and free trade agreement with United States encourage investment and export.

WEAKNESSES

- High debt.
- Despite mineral resources (phosphate and potassium), limited foreign exchange earnings and dependent on international aid and expatriate remittances.
- Economy affected by embargo on Iraq, main trading partner in the past.
- Economy and society vulnerable to regional instability.
- Public sector deficit (excluding grants) affected by rigid spending (wages, pensions, interest on debt).
- High unemployment slowing reforms.

RISK ASSESSMENT

Despite the impact of regional tensions, on tourism in particular, the economy performed well. The country has reaped the benefits of reform to encourage investment and liberalize trade. Growth is driven by exports, underpinned by the free trade agreement with the United States and the Association Agreement with the European Union. However, the economy could be badly hit by a conflict in Iraq in light of the trade links between the two countries.

The country's financial position is not alarming. The borrowing requirement is under control and foreign debt service is sustainable thanks to IMF support, assistance from the international community and debt relief obtained under successive Paris Club agreements.

The public sector deficit, excluding grants, remains large. In the longer term continued reforms and debt reduction with the proceeds of privatization should enable sounder public finances.

A social and economic restructuring plan, partly financed through grants, has been adopted to alleviate poverty and reduce unemployment. It should allow the government to build on its structural adjustment programme without further inflaming social tensions in a population dominated by Palestinians and Iraqis.

KEY ECONOMIC INDICATORS

US$ billion	1998	1999	2000	2001	2002(e)	2003(f)
Economic growth (%)	2.9	3.1	4	4.2	4.5	5
Inflation (%)	0.6	0.6	0.7	1.8	3.2	2.1
Public-sector balance/GDP (%)	-9.7	-7	-8.9	-8	-10.1	n/a
Exports	1.8	1.8	1.9	2.3	2.7	3.1
Imports	3.8	3.7	4.6	4.8	4.8	5.3
Trade balance	-2	-1.9	-2.7	-2.5	-2.1	-2.1
Current account balance/GDP (%)	-4.4	0.2	-4.1	-5.3	-1.3	-2.2
Foreign debt/GDP (%)	132.8	138.8	127.5	119.6	113	104.9
Debt service/Exports (%)	24.5	21.5	23.3	15.7	18.1	17.4
Reserves (import months)	3.5	6.2	7.2	6.3	6.9	6.4

n/a – not available

e = estimated, f = forecast

CONDITIONS OF ACCESS TO THE MARKET

■ Means of entry

Business risk must be carefully assessed at all times.

While the banking system as a whole is solid and there are many first-rate financial institutions that continued to improve profitability in 2001, with 22 banks it remains oversized. However, there are moves towards concentration in the industry. The new Banking Act introduced in 2000 aims to strengthen prudential measures and give more powers to the Central Bank to prevent the collapse of banks that have seen their bad debt portfolio swell dangerously in recent years. The current slump in tourism should, from this year onwards, severely affect the finances of numerous banks heavily involved in this sector.

In the retail sector, a recipient of huge investments in the past, the situation has improved thanks to the conclusion of consolidation agreements with banks.

Caution is called for when dealing with private Jordanian customers. While there are few defaults, cases of overdue payment exist. Also, information on local firms is scarce and not very reliable. To avoid taking unreasonable risks exporters should check the credit history of potential customers and keep their ears open in the marketplace for any information about them.

■ Attitude towards foreign investors

Privatization has facilitated the influx of new foreign businesses, which already have a stabilizing influence and play a market-leading role. Foreign and local investors receive equal treatment. Moreover, Jordan's membership of the WTO and the structural reforms undertaken to modernize the economy (Amman Stock Exchange, introduction of VAT, intellectual property protection) are bringing the country into line with Western standards.

The deteriorating regional political situation has led Jordan to redouble efforts to attract foreign investors via tax benefits and preferential access to the US (free trade agreement) and European (Association Agreement) markets.

4

OPPORTUNITY SCOPE

- Population 4.9 million inhabitants
- GDP 8340 million US dollars

Breakdown of internal demand (GDP + imports) %
- Private consumption 48
- Public spending 15
- Investment 12

Exports: 42% of GDP

Imports: 69% of GDP

MAIN DESTINATIONS OF EXPORTS

Mn USD

India, Saudi Arabia, Israel, Japan, Pakistan

MAIN ORIGINS OF IMPORTS

Mn USD

Germany, USA, Italy, France, UK

EXPORTS by products
- Food products 16%
- Minerals & metals 27%
- Chemical products 32%
- Other manufactured products 18%
- Transport & capital goods 5%
- Miscellaneous 2%

IMPORTS by products
- Food products 23%
- Fuels 9%
- Chemical products 13%
- Other manufactured products 21%
- Transport & capital goods 29%
- Miscellaneous 5%

STANDARD OF LIVING / PURCHASING POWER

Indicators	Jordan	Regional average	DC average
GNP per capita (PPP dollars)	3950	7168	6548
GNP per capita	1710	4625	3565
Human development index	0.717	0.734	0.702
Wealthiest 10% share of national income	30	29	32
Urban population percentage	74	71	60
Percentage under 15 years old	40	36	32
Number of telephones per 1000 inhabitants	93	161	157
Number of computers per 1000 inhabitants	23	59	64

Kuwait

Short-term: **A2**

Medium-term:
Low risk

Coface analysis

STRENGTHS

- Vast oil reserves (10 per cent) of world's reserves). Production costs among the lowest in the world.
- Production capacity damaged by Iraq's occupation in 1990 has been restored.
- Solid financial position. Extensive overseas assets provide buffer against external crises.
- Moderate foreign debt.

WEAKNESSES

- Little diversified economy highly dependent on oil sector.
- Oil rentier system that does not benefit the entire economy and contributes to social inequality.
- Private sector highly dependent on foreign workers, who fill 98 per cent of jobs and repatriate the bulk of their incomes.
- Political divisions hamper reforms.

4

RISK ASSESSMENT

Cuts in OPEC production quotas and a series of accidents in refineries have contributed to Kuwait's economic downturn in the last two years. The restoration of normal conditions for oil output and higher quotas, as a result of firmer global oil demand, should facilitate an upturn in 2003.

Firm crude oil prices, although falling back from previous years' levels, should enable the country to post comfortable domestic and external account surpluses. The modest level of indebtedness does not affect the financial situation while the government pursues its accumulation of foreign assets for future generations.

The economy nevertheless remains vulnerable to a sharp reversal in the oil market. The government's structural reforms programme continues to be blocked by parliament, which is keen to preserve the system of oil rentier benefiting Kuwaiti nationals. In the circumstances it is likely that reforms will be painfully slow, unless the parliamentary elections due to be held in May 2003 bring about meaningful change.

The fact that political divisions may intensify when the question of the Emir's succession eventually arises is a source of instability. Finally, the country is highly exposed to a rise in regional tensions due to its geographical position.

KEY ECONOMIC INDICATORS

US$ billion	1998	1999	2000	2001	2002(e)	2003(f)
Economic growth (%)	3.2	−1.6	3.9	−1	−3.2	3.4
Inflation (%)	0.10	3	1.8	1.7	2.2	2
Public-sector balance/GDP (%)	0.3	30.7	39.3	19.7	15.5	n/a
Exports	9.6	12.3	19.5	16.2	15.7	16.2
Imports	7.7	6.7	6.5	6.9	7.3	7.7
Trade balance	1.9	5.6	13	9.2	8.3	8.5
Current account balance/GDP (%)	8.8	17.3	41	26.1	18.4	20.6
Foreign debt/GDP (%)	37.4	36	25.9	31.1	31.3	30.1
Debt service/Exports (%)	7.2	6.7	4.6	4.6	4	4.2
Reserves (import months)	2.9	3.9	6.1	8	8.2	7.8

n/a – not available

e = estimated, f = forecast

CONDITIONS OF ACCESS TO THE MARKET

■ Means of entry

Kuwait is an open market with one of the highest import to consumption ratios in the world (90 per cent). Customs duties are a symbolic 4 per cent and foodstuffs are not subject to any duty. Per capita income is high and demand for capital and consumer goods disproportionately large for a country of its size. But Kuwait is a highly coveted market demanding specific knowledge and perseverance.

Companies exporting to Kuwait are not required to have a sole local partner and may sell directly to several Kuwaiti importers. Similarly, they may run a customs warehouse from an office located in the free zone.

When relations with Iraq are ultimately restored there will be many opportunities as Kuwait has traditionally played the role of buffer between its two powerful neighbours, Iraq and Iran.

■ Attitude towards foreign investors

The Foreign Investment Law passed in March 2001 allows foreign companies to own a 100 per cent stake in a local company. It grants tax exemptions for 10 years upon recommendation of the Investment Commission and dispenses with the local sponsor or agent requirement for foreign investors. Only some sectors such as oil and gas exploration and production are closed to foreigners. Priority sectors include petroleum-related industries (petrochemicals), infrastructure (water, electricity, telecommunications), high-tech, banking, investment funds, insurance and tourism. The government has also announced its intention of cutting corporation tax for foreign companies from 55 per cent to 25 per cent.

It is likely that sensitive reforms will be undertaken after the parliamentary elections due to be held in spring 2003. The new regulations will offer investors attractive opportunities in this solvent and growing market

OPPORTUNITY SCOPE

- Population   2 million inhabitants
- GDP   35,800 million US dollars

Breakdown of internal demand (GDP + imports) %
- Private consumption   31
- Public spending   17
- Investment   8

Exports: 57% of GDP

Imports: 31% of GDP

MAIN DESTINATIONS OF EXPORTS

Mn USD

Japan | South Korea | USA | Singapore | Netherlands

MAIN ORIGINS OF IMPORTS

Mn USD

USA | Germany | Japan | UK | Italy

EXPORTS by products
- Fuels 91%
- Manufactured products 8%
- Miscellaneous 1%

IMPORTS by products
- Food products 17%
- Chemical products 8%
- Other manufactured products 30%
- Transport & capital goods 40%
- Miscellaneous 5%

4

STANDARD OF LIVING / PURCHASING POWER

Indicators	Kuwait	Regional average	DC average
GNP per capita (PPP dollars)	18,690	7168	6548
GNP per capita	18,030	4625	3565
Human development index	0.813	0.734	0.702
Wealthiest 10% share of national income	n/a	29	32
Urban population percentage	98	71	60
Percentage under 15 years old	31	36	32
Number of telephones per 1000 inhabitants	244	161	157
Number of computers per 1000 inhabitants	131	59	64

n/a – not available

Lebanon

Coface analysis

Short-term: **C**

Medium-term:
Very High risk

STRENGTHS

- Government committed to structural reforms.
- Financial support from the diaspora and the international community helps the country to surmount economic difficulties.
- Tourism and financial services continue to play an important economic role.

WEAKNESSES

- Unsustainable level of public debt.
- Banking sector extremely vulnerable to sovereign risk.
- Overvalued pound further erodes competitiveness of Lebanese exports. Structurally unfavourable trade balance.
- Regional political uncertainties undermine business climate.

RISK ASSESSMENT

The reconstruction programme of the 1990s has left a legacy of huge indebtedness. Economic growth has slumped and the country's financial position is under severe strain. Public spending restrictions, high interest rates, declining investment and the overvalued pound have put a brake on economic activity. The government is faced with a mounting public debt burden, while risk aversion has depleted the traditional sources of government finance. The external account remains deeply in the red. Foreign exchange reserves continue to dwindle as external financial inflows dry up.

Against this background, long-term preferential loans granted in November 2002 at the international conference of donor countries (Paris II) give the government some breathing space. However, sustained improvement in the country's financial position hinges on the government's ability to undertake much-needed privatization in order to reduce the debt stock. For the time being regional political uncertainties and the overvalued pound could discourage investors.

KEY ECONOMIC INDICATORS

US$ billion	1998	1999	2000	2001	2002(e)	2003(f)
Economic growth (%)	2.5	1	0	1.9	1.8	1.3
Inflation (%)	4.5	0.2	-0.4	-0.5	3.3	1.2
Public-sector balance/GDP (%)	-14.1	-14.5	-23.7	-16.8	-15.9	-13.4
Public debt/GDP (%)	109.3	131	148.2	168.5	174	185
Exports	0.7	0.7	0.7	0.9	1	1.1
Imports	6.6	5.8	5.8	6.8	6.2	6.4
Trade balance	-5.9	-5.1	-5.1	-5.9	-5.2	-5.2
Current account balance/GDP (%)	-38	-32.3	-30.5	-35.8	-29	-29.1
Foreign debt/GDP (%)	37.3	45.2	49.4	55.7	56.8	72.2
Debt service/Exports (%)	63.5	69.8	64.5	69.8	71.9	67.4
Reserves (import months)	9.9	12.8	9.6	7.4	7.3	5.8

e = estimated, f = forecast

CONDITIONS OF ACCESS TO THE MARKET

■ Means of entry

In late 2000 the rates of customs duty were drastically cut from 6 per cent and 105 per cent to 0 per cent and 70 per cent.

A new customs code was adopted in April 2001 in line with WTO requirements (relating to customs valuations) and World Customs Organization standards.

Although non-tariff barriers to import exist they are not insurmountable. Health regulations, the legal principles of which are not always defined with the greatest precision, are fairly liberal and usually comply with the recommendations of leading international organizations. Specific standards apply to the industrial sector. These can hamper exports to Lebanon.

All means of payment are accepted, although irrevocable and confirmed letters of credit and, to a lesser extent, documentary bills and bank transfers are strongly recommended.

Due to the unpredictability of the legal system and the lack of transparency of court procedures companies usually avoid litigation. The problem of bad debt is often sorted out amicably. For large contracts, international arbitration is the best way to resolve disputes as it is now recognized by the country's Civil Proceedings Code.

■ Attitude towards foreign investors

Paradoxically, while the legal machinery has been strengthened and improved to enable Lebanon to comply in due course with WTO business standards, the investment environment continues to deteriorate. The lack and repeated postponement of administrative reforms, arbitrary enforcement of laws, regulatory unpredictability and lack of transparency of procedures are examples of this general deterioration which, if it persists, could seriously damage the image of liberalism and openness to foreign investment that the country wishes to project.

Lebanon has not adopted any foreign investment legislation. In the absence of such legislation foreign joint ventures are automatically subject to common law in matters of taxation, employment rights, etc. Such companies are eligible for benefits under the country's Investment Promotion Act, adopted in August 2001. Under this Act responsibility for handling and facilitating investor formalities in certain sectors or in specially designated under privileged regions lies with the government one-stop shop, Investment Development Authority.

Lebanon's changing investment legislation, which should gather pace in the months ahead as WTO accession draws nearer, contains few insurmountable obstacles to the establishment of foreign businesses in the country.

4

OPPORTUNITY SCOPE

■ Population   4.3 million inhabitants   ■ GDP   16,488 million US dollars

Breakdown of internal demand (GDP + imports) %
■ Private consumption   64
■ Public spending   14
■ Investment   13

Exports: 13% of GDP ⟹ ⟸ Imports: 38% of GDP

MAIN DESTINATIONS OF EXPORTS

Mn USD

France USA Saudi Arabia UAE Switzerland

MAIN ORIGINS OF IMPORTS

Mn USD

Italy France Switzerland USA Syria

EXPORTS by products
■ Food products 19%
■ Textiles 6%
■ Chemical & pharmaceutical products 12%
■ Paper 7%
■ Metals 13%
■ Machines 13%
■ Jewellery 18%
■ Miscellaneous 12%

IMPORTS by products
■ Food products 18%
■ Textiles 6%
■ Chemical & pharmaceutical products 8%
■ Jewellery 7%
■ Metals 24%
■ Machines 23%
■ Miscellaneous 14%

STANDARD OF LIVING / PURCHASING POWER

Indicators	Lebanon	Regional average	DC average
GNP per capita (PPP dollars)	4550	7168	6548
GNP per capita	4010	4625	3565
Human development index	0.755	0.734	0.702
Wealthiest 10% share of national income	n/a	29	32
Urban population percentage	90	71	60
Percentage under 15 years old	31	36	32
Number of telephones per 1000 inhabitants	195	161	157
Number of computers per 1000 inhabitants	50	59	64

n/a – not available

Libya

Short-term: **C**

Medium-term:
High risk

Coface analysis

STRENGTHS

- Significant oil and gas resources.
- Lifting of UN embargo offers good growth prospects, despite US (ILSA) sanctions still in force.
- Political will to reform and restructure public sector underpinned by need to attract foreign capital.
- Large foreign currency reserves.
- Moderate debt.

WEAKNESSES

- Economy dependent on oil revenues.
- Economy weakened by state controls and seven years of embargo.
- Investors discouraged by unpredictable economic policies and lack of appropriate legal and financial framework.
- Deteriorating public services leading to social tensions.
- Erratic payment behaviour.

4

RISK ASSESSMENT

Firm oil prices strengthen the country's financial position, preventing a shortage of foreign exchange. Oil exports, which account for 96 per cent of total exports, help maintain a current account surplus. Foreign debt remains contained, with debt service using up only a small percentage of foreign exchange earnings.

The country's public account benefits from the dinar's devaluation, subsequent to the unification of exchange rates, and from high oil prices as well.

The country's economic performance, however, continues to be affected by OPEC oil production quotas. Similarly, the development of unprofitable projects in the non-oil sector is a drain on the economy.

The government is engaged in a programme of structural reforms to liberalize the economy and attract investors with a view to rehabilitating existing infrastructure and increasing oil output. But the programme's social implications are slowing its implementation. Moreover, regional political uncertainties are not conducive to investment. Despite attempts at normalization since the lifting of the UN embargo relations with the international community remain strained. The system's opaqueness and unpredictability are key risk factors.

KEY ECONOMIC INDICATORS						
(US$ billion)	1998	1999	2000	2001	2002(e)	2003(f)
Economic growth (%)	2.9	0.7	4.4	0.6	−0.4	0.5
Inflation (%)	3.7	2.6	−3	−8.5	6	6
Public-sector balance/GDP (%)	−4.2	12.4	10.6	6.4	4.8	n/a
Exports	6.3	6.8	12.2	9.8	9.4	9.3
Imports	5.9	4.4	4.5	5	6	6.3
Trade balance	0.5	2.4	7.7	4.8	3.4	3
Current account balance/GDP (%)	−2.9	5.2	20.2	14	13.5	10.7
Foreign debt/GDP (%)	12.5	18.9	15.1	19	30.2	29.2
Debt service/Exports (%)	6	3.2	7.1	8.4	6.1	9.2
Reserves (import months)	11.4	15.1	25.8	27.3	24.7	24

n/a – not available   e = estimated, f = forecast

CONDITIONS OF ACCESS TO THE MARKET

■ Market overview

Despite several years of sanctions, which were only lifted in April 1999, Libya's oil output remained stable throughout this period at 1.4 million barrels a day. Reserves amount to 60 years of current output.

The lifting of sanctions and firm oil prices continue to act as an economic spur despite the country's state-controlled economy, characterized by cumbersome, slow and inconsistent practices. These problems should be ironed out in the long term as reforms gather pace. The reform programme includes a number of planned privatizations, ongoing restructurings (National Oil Co) and those earmarked for the future, the transfer of economic powers to the regions since 1 January 2002 and the introduction of a uniform exchange rate.

Libya's policy of liberalisation and vast oil revenues offer investors a host of new business opportunities. Priority sectors include transport infrastructure and equipment (air, land, rail), telecommunications, electricity, oil and gas production and exploration (award of new licences) large-scale river development (water supply), desalination, environment, radio and television, food supply, etc.

■ Means of entry

Licences are no longer required to import goods into the country. All shipments must be accompanied by a certificate of origin.

Customs tariffs have been streamlined since January 1998 as part of a harmonised nomenclature. There is an import ban on so-called 'luxury' and locally manufactured products, a list of which is available. Sales contracts are settled exclusively by irrevocable letter of credit, which can take six months or more to open.

The law governing contracts with Libyan government agencies requires foreign suppliers to pay 2 per cent stamp duty on the total value of the contract, or 1 per cent in the case of sub contractors. Companies should factor in the cost of this duty when preparing bids.

The Libyan market should only be approached by financially solid companies used to long and arduous negotiations. SMEs can usefully engage in ordinary business where risks are controllable to a greater extent.

■ Foreign exchange regulations

The country's stringent foreign exchange regulations are overseen by the Exchange Control Department, an arm of the Central Bank. Since 1 January 2002, there has been a sharp convergence of exchange rates on the back of the dinar's 51 per cent devaluation against the official exchange rate. Exchange rates are published daily.

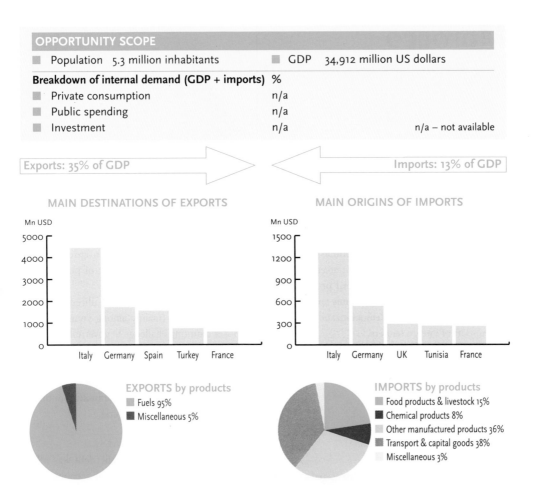

OPPORTUNITY SCOPE

■ Population 5.3 million inhabitants	■ GDP 34,912 million US dollars

Breakdown of internal demand (GDP + imports) %
- ■ Private consumption   n/a
- ■ Public spending   n/a
- ■ Investment   n/a   n/a – not available

Exports: 35% of GDP   Imports: 13% of GDP

MAIN DESTINATIONS OF EXPORTS
Mn USD

Italy   Germany   Spain   Turkey   France

MAIN ORIGINS OF IMPORTS
Mn USD

Italy   Germany   UK   Tunisia   France

EXPORTS by products
- ■ Fuels 95%
- ■ Miscellaneous 5%

IMPORTS by products
- ■ Food products & livestock 15%
- ■ Chemical products 8%
- ■ Other manufactured products 36%
- ■ Transport & capital goods 38%
- ■ Miscellaneous 3%

4

STANDARD OF LIVING / PURCHASING POWER

Indicators	Libya	Regional average	DC average
GNP per capita (PPP dollars)	n/a	7168	6458
GNP per capita	n/a	4625	3565
Human development index	0.773	0.734	0.702
Wealthiest 10% share of national income	n/a	29	32
Urban population percentage	88	71	60
Percentage under 15 years old	34	36	32
Number of telephones per 1000 inhabitants	108	161	157
Number of computers per 1000 inhabitants	n/a	59	64

n/a – not available

Morocco

Coface analysis

Short-term: **A4**

Medium-term:
Quite high risk

STRENGTHS

- Country's potential riches (natural resources, tourism, and population) attract investors.
- Political, economic and financial proximity to European Union acts as economic spur.
- Political stability and democratization ensures support of foreign lenders.
- Foreign debt burden reduced by active debt management policy.

WEAKNESSES

- Economy still too dependent on agriculture (16 per cent of GDP, 46 per cent of population), and therefore on climate.
- Alleviation of poverty, illiteracy and unemployment (mainly among young people) poses daunting challenge to government.
- Reform of these areas hampered by stretched public finances.
- Growing burden of domestic debt on economy.
- Deadlock over Western Sahara issue continues to cloud relations with Algeria.

RISK ASSESSMENT

Although the Moroccan economy has staged a strong recovery it remains far too dependent on the performance of the agricultural sector. To achieve the sustained growth needed to reduce unemployment and poverty structural reforms and investment must be stepped up. While the country's political stability appears to have been bolstered by the elections in September 2002, which returned the outgoing majority, the state of the public finances and the global economic environment make the prospects for growth uncertain.

The swelling domestic public debt was offset by an improvement in the external account and a reduction in the external financing requirement. In 2003 the financing requirement should remain moderate and should be easily covered, despite the potential impact on tourism of international uncertainty. Moreover, the country can count on the support of the international community, despite the tensions generated by the unresolved Western Sahara issue and deteriorating relations with Spain.

KEY ECONOMIC INDICATORS

US$ million	1998	1999	2000	2001	2002(e)	2003(f)
Economic growth (%)	6.8	−0.7	1	6.5	4.5	5
Inflation	2.8	0.7	4.1	5	6	7
Public-sector balance/GDP (%)	−3.4	−4.2	−6.5	−9	−6	−6
Exports	7.1	7.5	7.4	7.1	7.8	8.2
Imports	9.5	10	10.7	10.1	10.6	11
Trade balance	−2.3	−2.4	−3.2	−3	−2.8	−2.9
Current account balance/GDP (%)	−0.5	−0.5	−1.7	4.8	1.5	1.1
Foreign debt	21	19.6	17.9	15.8	15.4	14.4
Debt service/Exports (%)	24.2	23	19.9	18.9	20.3	17.5
Reserves (import months)	4.2	5.2	4.2	7.6	7.7	7.8

e = estimated, f = forecast

CONDITIONS OF ACCESS TO THE MARKET

Market overview

Customs duties range from 2.5 per cent to 50 per cent. Higher rates of duty continue to apply to basic agricultural commodities and agri-foodstuffs. The Association Agreement with the European Union, which came into force on 1 March 2000, was marked in the second year by cuts in the weighted average rate of duty. The agreement forms the basis for the establishment of a free trade area by 2012.

The last few years have seen wide-ranging reforms aimed at stabilizing the business environment. A new Business Code was adopted in 1996; a Private Limited Liability Company, Partnership and Joint Venture Law came into force in 1997; commercial courts were also set up in 1997. New government procurement legislation was adopted in 1998 along French lines. In 2000 a number of new laws were passed, including a new Customs Code (an outcome of the modernization process begun earlier), a Competition and Price Act, an Intellectual and Industrial Property Protection Act (pending implementation decrees), and a Literary and Artistic Property Act (which came into force on 1 January 2001).

The Public Limited Companies Act, adopted in 1996, finally came into force in January 2001. An Insurance Code Bill abolishing all caps on foreign investment in the sector has been enacted by parliament after years of review. The year 2002, which was marked by elections, was one of consolidation.

Attitude towards foreign investment

The past year has seen one significant development: the announcement by King Mohammed VI, in a letter to the Prime Minister dated 9 January 2002, of the setting up of 16 regional investment centres. Overseen by walis (prefects), the centres will have two main functions: to assist start-ups and provide help for investors. The local business community and foreign investors have waited a long time for such a measure. The relevant ministries and civil service departments have conducted an in-depth study to ensure that the recommendations are adopted within set deadlines. CRIs in Rabat, Casablanca, Marrakesh and Agadir are already in operation. Once implemented, the centres will greatly ease cumbersome administrative procedures and spur investment in Morocco.

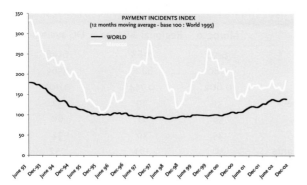

PAYMENT INCIDENTS INDEX
(12 months moving average - base 100 : World 1995)
— WORLD

4

■ Foreign exchange regulations

A supervised foreign exchange market remains in place. The exchange rate is set by the central bank, Bank Al Maghrib, on the basis of a confidential basket of currencies. The revision of this basket on 25 April 2001, which involved a re adjustment of the euro's weighting against the dollar, automatically resulted in a 5 per cent devaluation of the Moroccan currency.

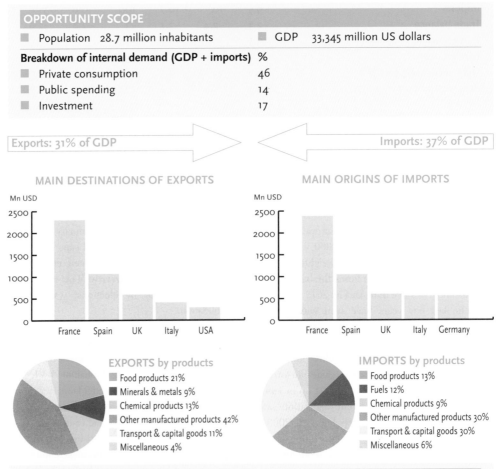

OPPORTUNITY SCOPE

■ Population 28.7 million inhabitants   ■ GDP 33,345 million US dollars

Breakdown of internal demand (GDP + imports)	%
■ Private consumption	46
■ Public spending	14
■ Investment	17

Exports: 31% of GDP → ← Imports: 37% of GDP

MAIN DESTINATIONS OF EXPORTS

Mn USD

(Bar chart: France, Spain, UK, Italy, USA)

MAIN ORIGINS OF IMPORTS

Mn USD

(Bar chart: France, Spain, UK, Italy, Germany)

EXPORTS by products
- ■ Food products 21%
- ■ Minerals & metals 9%
- ■ Chemical products 13%
- ■ Other manufactured products 42%
- ■ Transport & capital goods 11%
- ■ Miscellaneous 4%

IMPORTS by products
- ■ Food products 13%
- ■ Fuels 12%
- ■ Chemical products 9%
- ■ Other manufactured products 30%
- ■ Transport & capital goods 30%
- ■ Miscellaneous 6%

STANDARD OF LIVING / PURCHASING POWER

Indicators	Morocco	Regional average	DC average
GNP per capita (PPP dollars)	3450	7168	6548
GNP per capita	1180	6425	3565
Human development index	0.602	0.734	0.702
Wealthiest 10% share of national income	31	29	32
Urban population percentage	56	71	60
Percentage under 15 years old	35	36	32
Number of telephones per 1000 inhabitants	50	161	157
Number of computers per 1000 inhabitants	12	59	64

Oman

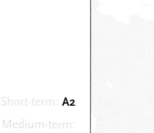

Coface analysis

Short-term: **A2**

Medium-term:
Quite low risk

STRENGTHS

- Significant natural resources (gas and oil).
- Government committed to opening up economy and developing private sector.
- Foreign investment encouraged by WTO accession.
- Focus of development on tourism

WEAKNESSES

- Economy dependent on oil revenues and vulnerable to price fluctuations.
- Public finances burdened by capital expenditure, public sector wage bill and military spending.
- Invisible trade balance weakened by outward workers' remittances.

RISK ASSESSMENT

After slowing down in 2002, mainly because of the drop in world oil demand, the economy should post faster growth in 2003 on the back of higher oil and gas output. Unless oil prices were to slide, firm crude prices should enable the government to maintain the major balances on a sound footing. The external financial position is not worrying, thanks to the fairly modest level of the debt service.

Despite growing economic diversification, due largely to the development of the gas industry, the economy remains dependent on developments in the oil market. The country's growth prospects are nevertheless promising. The liberalization and diversification programme has continued apace within the framework of the five-year plan (2001–05). WTO accession has been accompanied by measures to stimulate investment. This should attract foreign investors and facilitate privatization. Both are economically vital, as they will reduce budgetary costs and boost the private sector. Yet progress in these areas may be slowed by regional political uncertainties and deteriorating market conditions in certain sectors.

4

KEY ECONOMIC INDICATORS						
US$ billion	1998	1999	2000	2001	2002(e)	2003(f)
Economic growth (%)	2.7	−0.2	5.1	7.3	3.3	3.8
Inflation (%)	−0.5	0.5	−1.2	−1.1	−0.3	1.5
Public-sector balance/GDP (%)	−7.6	−0.3	9.6	4	3.2	2.4
Exports	5.5	7.2	11.3	11.1	11.2	11.5
Imports	5.2	4.3	4.6	5.3	5.8	6.6
Trade balance	0.3	2.9	6.7	5.8	5.4	4.9
Current account balance/GDP (%)	−21.1	−2.1	17.3	11.5	9.3	6
Foreign debt/GDP (%)	44.8	43.4	33.4	29.2	27.8	29.3
Debt service/Exports (%)	12.7	8.8	10.3	10.4	7.1	7
Reserves (import months)	2.5	4.1	3.3	3	3.4	3.4

e = estimated, f = forecast

CONDITIONS OF ACCESS TO THE MARKET

■ Market overview

Oman remains highly dependent on the oil sector. The decline in output and the downturn in prices during the first six months of 2002 have not deflected the government from pursuing the main objectives of its five-year plan, or its aim of diversifying the economy via industrial development. This consists in the development of natural gas, through large-scale industrial schemes, as a source of energy or as a commodity, and the promotion of the private sector's role in the economy (boosted by the privatization of companies and public services). The third plank of government policy concerns the Omanisation of jobs.

■ Means of entry

For private contracts, exporters of consumer goods not requiring any after-sales service do not need to be represented by a local agent. For public tenders open to foreign companies, the foreign supplier must have a local office or be represented by an Omani company.

General customs duty for the majority of products is 5 per cent on the CIF value. However, a prior licence is mandatory for some products on grounds of health, religion or protection of local manufacture.

There are no exchange controls and foreign currency may be sold freely. Transfers of corporate profits are unrestricted and there are no barriers to the free movement of capital.

■ Attitude towards foreign investors

With a few exceptions, Omani legislation tends to encourage foreign investment in manufacturing and infrastructure projects, especially as part of the country's privatization programme. Foreigners can now acquire a stake in manufacturing, trading and service companies, whereas in the past they were rarely allowed to own shares in the latter two.

On 27 February 2000 the government granted yet another concession, allowing foreign companies with more than 10 years of operation and at least three foreign subsidiaries to open a local sales office without a local sponsor.

Tax incentive schemes have been introduced to reduce discrimination against foreign companies and encourage local companies to open their capital to foreigners.

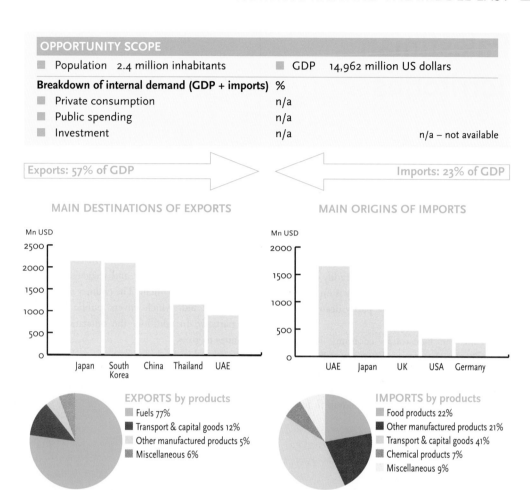

OPPORTUNITY SCOPE

- Population   2.4 million inhabitants
- GDP   14,962 million US dollars

Breakdown of internal demand (GDP + imports) %
- Private consumption   n/a
- Public spending   n/a
- Investment   n/a   n/a – not available

Exports: 57% of GDP   Imports: 23% of GDP

MAIN DESTINATIONS OF EXPORTS

Mn USD

Japan, South Korea, China, Thailand, UAE

MAIN ORIGINS OF IMPORTS

Mn USD

UAE, Japan, UK, USA, Germany

EXPORTS by products
- Fuels 77%
- Transport & capital goods 12%
- Other manufactured products 5%
- Miscellaneous 6%

IMPORTS by products
- Food products 22%
- Other manufactured products 21%
- Transport & capital goods 41%
- Chemical products 7%
- Miscellaneous 9%

STANDARD OF LIVING / PURCHASING POWER

Indicators	Oman	Regional average	DC average
GNP per capita (PPP dollars)	n/a	7168	6458
GNP per capita	n/a	4625	3565
Human development index	0.751	0.734	0.702
Wealthiest 10% share of national income	n/a	29	32
Urban population percentage	84	71	60
Percentage under 15 years old	44	36	32
Number of telephones per 1000 inhabitants	89	161	157
Number of computers per 1000 inhabitants	32	59	64

n/a – not available

Palestinian Territories

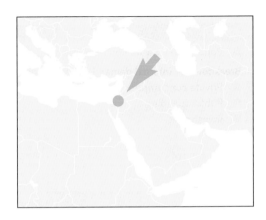

Coface analysis

RISK ASSESSMENT

Since the launch of the Intifada in late September 2000 the conflict with Israel has steadily escalated. As a result the Territories' economy is on the brink of collapse, its infrastructure partly destroyed and its institutions tottering.

While the Palestinian economy is heavily dependent on Israel (employer, tax collector and leading trade partner, with 80 per cent of the Territories' trade), the Territories' closure, the confiscation of taxes (VAT), the slump in tourism and investment and the suspension of ongoing contracts due to the climate of insecurity have crippled economic activity and triggered a sharp increase in unemployment. The country is living off international aid, which covers public spending only partially. In addition, the outstanding debt continues to grow.

Against this background it is unlikely that reforms – a precondition for resuming peace talks with Israel – will be forthcoming and elections held as planned.

MAJOR ECONOMIC INDICATORS					
US$ billion	1997	1998	1999	2000	2001 (e)
Economic growth (%)	3.3	7.9	7.4	−6	−10
Inflation (%)	7.6	5.6	5.5	2.8	2.2
Public-sector balance/GDP (%)	−1.2	−2.7	−1.2	−4.6	−14.8
Unemployment (%)	20.3	16	14	12.7	50
Imports	2.2	2.4	2.6	n/a	n/a
Exports	0.48	0.4	0.37	n/a	n/a
Trade balance	−1.7	−2	−2.2	n/a	n/a
Current account balance/GDP (%)	−19	−18.5	−31	n/a	n/a
Foreign debt	0.18	0.14	n/a	n/a	n/a

n/a – not available

Qatar

Short-term: **A2**

Medium-term:

Coface analysis

Quite low risk

STRENGTHS

- Bright development and growth prospects, underpinned by huge gas reserves (world's third largest).
- Growth of energy-intensive activities (iron and steel, petrochemicals) will boost external financial situation.
- Supported by United States.
- Al-Jazeera television serves as showcase for country's openness and efficiency.

WEAKNESSES

- Gas and industrial projects have required extensive investment that has led to high foreign debt.
- Weight of short-term debt relative to foreign exchange reserves factor of fragility.
- Fiscal revenues dependent on oil market developments.
- Non-transparent economic and financial data.

RISK ASSESSMENT

Economic activity was hit in 2002 by the drop in oil output, against a background of falling world oil demand, while the gas output reached a plateau. In 2003, although gas and non-oil activities should continue to grow at the current rate of around 5 per cent, OPEC oil product-ion quotas could put a damper on economic recovery.

Despite increased infrastructure spending the country should post a fiscal surplus this year as well, on the back of strong crude prices. A large current account surplus should continue to cover the country's still heavy debt service. Qatar's financial position remains strong, but is vulnerable to a sharp reversal in the oil market on account of the high debt ratio.

Qatar enjoys bright growth prospects, although it could be affected by rising regional tensions. The government's cautious policy of economic liberalization and political openness continues to make headway, despite opposition from the more conservative elements within the political establishment.

4

KEY ECONOMIC INDICATORS

US$ billion	1998	1999	2000	2001	2002(e)	2003(f)
Economic growth (%)	6.2	5.3	11.6	7.2	3.2	4
Inflation (%)	2.6	2.2	−1	1.4	1.9	2.4
Public-sector balance/GDP (%)	−10.4	−4.3	8.4	0.1	1.4	n/a
Exports	4.8	7.7	11.1	10.9	10.8	12.1
Imports	3.1	2.3	2.9	3.4	3.6	4
Trade balance	1.7	5.4	8.2	7.5	7.2	8.1
Current account balance/GDP (%)	−6.9	21.8	29.3	26.6	23.5	27.1
Foreign debt/GDP (%)	95.1	95.8	86.3	91.4	95.7	95.3
Debt service/Exports (%)	22	16.4	15.2	20.3	22.4	21.5
Reserves (import months)	2	2.8	2	2.4	2.4	2.4

e = estimated, f = forecast

CONDITIONS OF ACCESS TO THE MARKET

■ Market overview

The Qatari market is free and open to trade. Imports are nevertheless subject to rules of origin that vary from country to country. Trademark and intellectual property protection legislation is relatively recent. Qatar has been a signatory to the Geneva Convention (industrial property) and the Bern Convention (intellectual property) only since 5 July 2000. Consequently the country still lacks the means to enforce and implement this legislation on a systematic basis.

■ Means of entry

From 1 January 2003 all goods are subject to 5 per cent duty, except for products directly competing with local manufacture (steel: 20 per cent), products taxed on grounds of health (cigarettes: 100 per cent) or those banned by Islam (wines and spirits: 100 per cent).

Exporters are advised to use the irrevocable and confirmed letter of credit, the most widespread means of payment in Qatar, for transactions with local customers.

■ Attitude towards foreign investors

Regulations governing foreign investment were relaxed under a new law passed on 16 October 2000. Foreign investors are now permitted to own 100 per cent of a company in the agricultural, manufacturing, healthcare, education, tourism and energy sectors, subject to the approval of the Ministry of Economic Affairs and Trade. The only condition is that foreign investments comply with the government's development plans.

Sectors falling outside the scope of this legislation include banking, insurance, property and trade. Foreigners investing in these sectors are required to have a majority Qatari partner. Foreign investors may acquire leaseholds for a maximum of 50 years on a renewable lease basis. On the other hand, they are barred from acquiring freehold property.

Disputes between a foreign investor and a local party are referred to local or international arbitration. Foreigners are required to have a Qatari sponsor when applying for a residence permit tied to a work permit.

Plans allowing local investors to access the stock exchange via mutual funds are under review and a decision on this matter is due to be announced by the relevant authorities in due course.

The Ministry of Economic Affairs and Trade grants 100 per cent foreign-funded projects 10-year tax relief and exemption from customs duties for imports of equipment, raw materials and semi-finished goods that are not locally available.

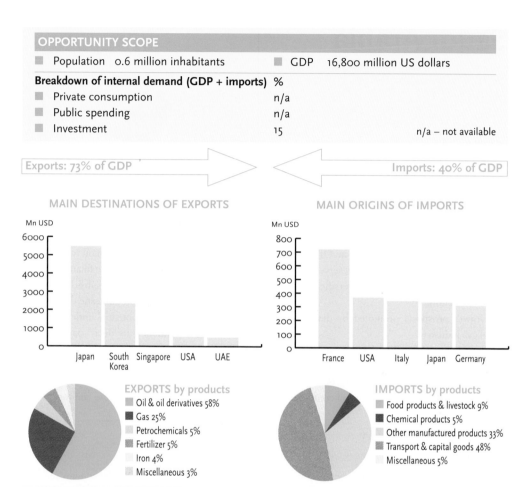

OPPORTUNITY SCOPE

- Population   0.6 million inhabitants
- GDP   16,800 million US dollars

Breakdown of internal demand (GDP + imports) %
- Private consumption   n/a
- Public spending   n/a
- Investment   15   n/a – not available

Exports: 73% of GDP   Imports: 40% of GDP

MAIN DESTINATIONS OF EXPORTS

Mn USD

Japan | South Korea | Singapore | USA | UAE

EXPORTS by products
- Oil & oil derivatives 58%
- Gas 25%
- Petrochemicals 5%
- Fertilizer 5%
- Iron 4%
- Miscellaneous 3%

MAIN ORIGINS OF IMPORTS

Mn USD

France | USA | Italy | Japan | Germany

IMPORTS by products
- Food products & livestock 9%
- Chemical products 5%
- Other manufactured products 33%
- Transport & capital goods 48%
- Miscellaneous 5%

4

STANDARD OF LIVING / PURCHASING POWER

Indicators	Qatar	Regional average	DC average
GNP per capita (PPP dollars)	n/a	7168	6548
GNP per capita	n/a	4625	3565
Human development index	0.803	0.734	0.702
Wealthiest 10% share of national income	n/a	29	32
Urban population percentage	n/a	71	60
Percentage under 15 years old	n/a	36	32
Number of telephones per 1000 inhabitants	n/a	161	157
Number of computers per 1000 inhabitants	n/a	59	64

n/a – not available

Saudi Arabia

Short-term: **A4**

Medium-term:

Coface analysis **Quite low risk**

STRENGTHS

- Main oil producing country in OPEC, with one-quarter of the world's oil reserves.
- Committed to economic diversification and liberalization.
- Growth prospects promoted by development of gas industry.
- Important US ally despite troublesome relationship since 11 September 2001.
- WTO candidacy reassures markets.
- Prince Abdallah ensures political continuity.

WEAKNESSES

- Economy highly dependent on oil revenues.
- Structural imbalances in public finances due to rigid government spending (subsidies, wages and interest payments on domestic debt).
- Private sector growth potential undermined by government tendency to delay payments to suppliers.
- Transfers by foreign workers weaken balance of payments.
- Alarming unemployment rate among Saudi nationals.

RISK ASSESSMENT

After two years of slowdown the economy should pick up in 2003. However the strength of the recovery is subject to uncertainty. It will depend on a recovery in the United States, while implementation of the Gas Initiative, on which the prospects of the diversification of the Saudi economy rely, has been delayed. Regional instability could also affect investment.

The public finances are again in the red, driving an even higher public debt. The country's external financial position, however, remains healthy on account of the low level of foreign debt.

Not very diversified, the Saudi economy remains vulnerable to developments in the oil market. Ultimately, the sustainability of growth and the public accounts balance will depend on economic diversification. The Saudi government is implementing economic reforms, albeit slowly.

The political situation is another risk factor. Regional instability has been exacerbated in the aftermath of 11 September 2001. There are widespread social tensions and the relationship with the United States has become complicated.

MAJOR ECONOMIC INDICATORS

US$ billion	1998	1999	2000	2001	2002(e)	2003(f)
Economic growth(%)	2.8	−0.8	4.9	1.2	0.2	2.5
Inflation (%)	−0.4	−1.6	−0.7	−0.5	0.7	1.5
Public-sector balance/GDP (%)	−10	−6.8	3.3	−3.6	−2.8	−2.8
Exports	38.8	50.7	77.5	72.9	68.4	70.3
Imports	27.5	25.7	27.7	28.6	29	31
Trade balance	11.3	25	49.8	44.3	39.4	39.3
Current account balance/GDP (%)	−8.7	0.3	7.6	7.8	5.5	4.7
Foreign debt/GDP (%)	20.8	20.4	17.2	17.7	18.2	17.7
Debt service/Exports (%)	6.7	6.8	6.2	7.1	7.1	6.6
Reserves (import months)	2.7	3.3	3.3	3.1	3.1	3.1
Public debt/GDP (%)	116	119	87	90	95	100

e = estimated, f = forecast

CONDITIONS OF ACCESS TO THE MARKET

■ Market overview

Saudi households spend the bulk of their income on non-durable goods. As patterns of consumption change there is growing interest in wholesale and discount stores because of the drop in purchasing power. Despite government attempts to get companies to employ more Saudis (employment of locals is up 5 per cent year on year), there is reason to believe that the 2 million least-skilled jobs cannot be quickly filled by locals. Unemployment, which amounts to 15 – 20 per cent of the male working population, has a destabilizing effect on the 200,000 young Saudis who arrive on the job market each year. Consequently the government is giving priority to education and vocational training in the budget.

■ Means of entry

Customs duties are 0 per cent for basic foodstuffs and staple commodities, 5 per cent for 80 per cent of imported goods, 20 per cent for local produce (eg chicken), 25 per cent for some fruit and vegetables, and 100 per cent for milk, wheat and cigarettes.

There is also an import ban on certain items (nutmeg, masks) on religious or other grounds. Variable and reduced rates of duty are applicable to products from Gulf Co-operation Council countries: Jordan, Egypt, Morocco and Syria.

From 1 January 2003 customs duties will be cut to 0 per cent for 53 commodities and 5 per cent for other products under the customs union with GCC countries.

All government procurement contracts are awarded according to the national preference rule (10 per cent for GCC companies and 20 per cent for Saudi companies).

Regulations governing the entry and residence of foreigners are very strict (Saudi sponsor requirement). Industrial drawings and plant varieties are not protected by law.

In general, payments by government agencies are slow (7 to 30 months). Defaults in the oil and petrochemical industries are rare.

■ Attitude towards foreign investors

A new Investment Code was adopted on 10 April 2000. Major improvements include: issue of licences within 30 days, establishment of a one-stop shop for processing applications, ownership of facilities and staff accommodation, abolition of the local sponsor requirement, and access to concessional Saudi financing. However, given the monopoly barring foreigners from holding shares in the country, foreign companies may only set up Saudi law subsidiaries incorporated as private limited liability companies. A negative list of sectors from which foreign investors are barred was published on 11 February 2001. The

4

tax rate applicable to foreign companies has been cut by 15 per cent for profits above 100,000 rials, and losses can now be carried forward over an indefinite number of years.

A reciprocal investment protection and promotion agreement was concluded in June 2002 and is due to come into force shortly.

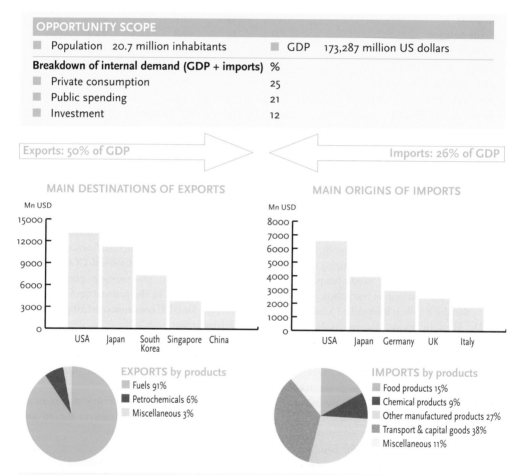

OPPORTUNITY SCOPE

Population 20.7 million inhabitants   GDP 173,287 million US dollars

Breakdown of internal demand (GDP + imports)	%
Private consumption	25
Public spending	21
Investment	12

Exports: 50% of GDP   Imports: 26% of GDP

MAIN DESTINATIONS OF EXPORTS

Mn USD

USA Japan South Korea Singapore China

MAIN ORIGINS OF IMPORTS

Mn USD

USA Japan Germany UK Italy

EXPORTS by products
- Fuels 91%
- Petrochemicals 6%
- Miscellaneous 3%

IMPORTS by products
- Food products 15%
- Chemical products 9%
- Other manufactured products 27%
- Transport & capital goods 38%
- Miscellaneous 11%

STANDARD OF LIVING / PURCHASING POWER

Indicators	Saudi Arabia	Regional average	DC average
GNP per capita (PPP dollars)	11,390	7168	6548
GNP per capita	7230	4625	3565
Human development index	0.759	0.734	0.702
Wealthiest 10% share of national income	n/a	29	32
Urban population percentage	86	71	60
Percentage under 15 years old	43	46	32
Number of telephones per 1000 inhabitants	137	161	157
Number of computers per 1000 inhabitants	60	59	64

n/a – not available

Syria

Coface analysis

Short-term: **C**

Medium-term:
Very high risk

STRENGTHS

- Foreign exchange earnings derived from natural resources (oil and gas).
- Engaged in economic liberalization to encourage investment, create jobs and kick-start growth.
- Tourism has strong growth potential, albeit subject to easing of regional tensions.

WEAKNESSES

- Economy vulnerable to vagaries of agriculture and oil market.
- Still highly indebted.
- Depleting oil reserves.
- Nascent private sector crippled by tight state control of economy, including banks. Slow progress in reforms.
- Continued regional instability.
- Non-transparent economic data.

4

RISK ASSESSMENT

Against a background of stagnant domestic demand the fiscal stimulus package and better agricultural performance should boost growth in 2003. However, the government's expansionary policy continues to widen the budget deficit, while the likely suspension of illicit imports of Iraqi crude should tip the external account into the red this year. Syria remains a highly indebted country, with debt service continuing to use up a third of the country's foreign exchange earnings, despite the relief granted under bilateral rescheduling agreements. The country's financial position could become shaky in the event of a fall in oil prices.

To achieve sustainable economic development in the long term the country needs to undertake structural reforms as economic growth fails to keep pace with population growth or stem the rise in unemployment. But the transition from a planned economy to a market economy is encountering domestic resistance and, coupled with regional tensions, fostering a wait-and-see attitude among investors.

KEY ECONOMIC INDICATORS

US$ billion	1998	1999	2000	2001	2002(e)	2003(f)
Economic growth (%)	7.6	−2	2.5	1.7	1.8	2.3
Inflation (%)	−0.4	−2.1	−0.6	0.4	0.9	1.6
Public-sector balance/GDP (%)	−2.3	−1	−2.4	−5	−5.3	−6
Exports	3.1	3.8	5.1	5	5.8	4.9
Imports	3.3	3.6	3.7	4.2	4.5	4.6
Trade balance	−0.2	0.2	1.4	0.8	1.3	0.2
Current account balance/GDP (%)	−0.2	0.6	5.8	1.2	3.4	−0.9
Foreign debt/GDP (%)	131.4	129.5	118.3	112.8	105.9	109.1
Debt service/Exports (%)	41.1	40.9	36.7	32.3	27.9	31.9
Reserves (import months)	3.9	4.1	4.2	3.9	3.5	3.5

e = estimated, f = forecast

CONDITIONS OF ACCESS TO THE MARKET

■ Means of entry

There are 10 rates of customs duty, from 1 per cent (agricultural or industrial raw materials) to 200 per cent (cars). The weighted average rate of duty is 30 per cent.

In addition to customs duties, there are various taxes (war effort, taxes on consumer and luxury goods) whose rates vary between 5 per cent and 30 per cent of the value of the imported product.

Although export credit organizations are gradually restoring their guarantees for Syria, foreign suppliers use cash payments for ordinary transactions. Private Syrian importers often have funds in foreign banks. Caution is however called for when dealing with public sector procurement agencies, and exporters are advised to check that such agencies have the necessary funds before entering into any deals.

■ Attitude towards foreign investors

In 1991 Syria introduced a series of tax and legal measures collectively known as Law No 10 to encourage investment, regardless of the origin of funds or the nationality of investors.

A Decree Law passed in June 2000 authorizes foreign currency transfers in the event of divestment after a five-year period. It also extends the tax-exemption period for investments in certain locations and sectors.

In accordance with Arab boycott legislation, revived since the Intifada in the Palestinian Territories, the main restrictions concern trade with Israel or with Israeli-held companies.

■ Foreign exchange regulations

The Syrian pound is a non-convertible currency pegged to the dollar. It has four exchange rates:

- the administered rate (11.22 pounds to the dollar) for public sector transactions and imports of raw materials and supervised foodstuffs;
- the customs rate (23 pounds to the dollar) for the calculation of customs duties on a limited number of products;
- the 'neighbouring country' rate (46.5 pounds to the dollar), widely used for trade with foreign countries;
- the market rate (from 49–52 pounds to the dollar) for a number of non-commercial private transactions.

OPPORTUNITY SCOPE

Population 16.2 million inhabitants	GDP 19,200 million US dollars

Breakdown of internal demand (GDP + imports) %

- Private consumption — 47
- Public spending — 10
- Investment — 16

Exports: 38% of GDP   Imports: 35% of GDP

MAIN DESTINATIONS OF EXPORTS   MAIN ORIGINS OF IMPORTS

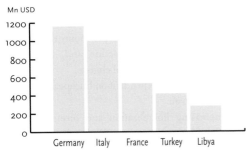

Mn USD — Germany, Italy, France, Turkey, Libya

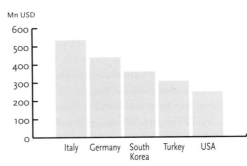

Mn USD — Italy, Germany, South Korea, Turkey, USA

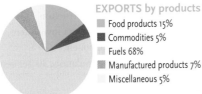

EXPORTS by products
- Food products 15%
- Commodities 5%
- Fuels 68%
- Manufactured products 7%
- Miscellaneous 5%

IMPORTS by products
- Food products 22%
- Chemical products 10%
- Other manufactured products 29%
- Transport & capital goods 20%
- Miscellaneous 19%

4

STANDARD OF LIVING / PURCHASING POWER

Indicators	Syria	Regional average	DC average
GNP per capita (PPP dollars)	3340	7168	6548
GNP per capita	940	4625	3565
Human development index	0.691	0.734	0.702
Wealthiest 10% share of national income	n/a	29	32
Urban population percentage	55	71	60
Percentage under 15 years old	41	36	32
Number of telephones per 1000 inhabitants	103	161	157
Number of computers per 1000 inhabitants	15	59	64

n/a – not available

Tunisia

Coface analysis

Short-term: **A4**

Medium-term:
Quite low risk

ASSETS

- Political stability and forward-looking economic diversification and trade liberalization policies have earned country international political and financial backing.
- Partnership agreement with EU spurs modernization of industry, infrastructure and financial sector.
- Cautious monetary, fiscal and debt policies give country easy access to international capital markets.
- Enhanced access to education and well-developed social services facilitate reduction of inequalities and emergence of vibrant middle class.

WEAKNESSES

- Modest natural resources; economy dependent on agricultural production and, therefore, vulnerable to vagaries of climate.
- Economy also dependent on European demand and tourism.
- Increasing liberalization and termination of multifibre agreement in 2005 call for certain degree of watchfulness and greater efforts to improve industrial competitiveness.
- Uneven implementation of structural reforms programme affects foreign direct investment.
- Chronically high unemployment (15 per cent of working population, 30 per cent youth unemployment).

RISK ASSESSMENT

A fourth year of drought, the drop in tourism and weak European demand badly hit economic growth in 2002. However, despite rigid public spending (about 50 per cent on wages) the government has managed to reduce the budget deficit. Shrinking imports have reined in the country's external financing needs, which were covered by investment related to the privatization of a second GSM licence as well as by a securities issue on the international market.

Against this background the outlook for 2003 remains positive, though dependent on climatic factors and global political developments. The various deficits should remain under control, while there is no likelihood that the increase in foreign debt will cause the country to default. Moreover, political stability and the prospect of further privatizations and structural reforms are likely to attract more foreign investment.

MAJOR ECONOMIC INDICATORS

US$ billion	1998	1999	2000	2001	2002(e)	2003(f)
Economic growth (%)	4.8	6.1	4.7	4.9	1.9	4.5
Inflation (%)	3.1	2.7	3	1.9	2.8	3
Public-sector balance/GDP (%)	−3.1	−3.6	−3.7	−3.5	−2.6	−2.2
Exports	5.7	5.9	5.8	6.6	6.6	6.9
Imports	7.9	8	8.1	9	8.7	9.2
Trade balance	−2.2	−2.1	−2.3	−2.4	−2.2	−2.3
Current account balance/GDP (%)	−3.4	−2.2	−4.2	−4.3	−4.2	−3.7
Foreign debt	11.6	11.8	11.2	11.9	13.1	13.6
Debt service/Exports (%)	17.3	17.7	20.4	14	14.9	15.2
Reserves (import months)	2.2	2.7	2.1	2.1	2.7	2.8

e = estimated, f = forecast

CONDITIONS OF ACCESS TO THE MARKET

■ Market overview

Ninety per cent of products can be freely imported. Authorization must be obtained from the Ministry of Trade for products considered sensitive on grounds of security, public order, health and hygiene, morality, and protection of wild life, plants and cultural heritage. Private vehicles, which have been subject to this measure on a provisional basis, can in theory be freely imported since April 2001.

■ Means of entry

Despite the conclusion of a free trade agreement with the European Union, the average level of tariff protection in Tunisia remains high. Consequently duties on a large number of foodstuffs exceed 100 per cent, as do duties on imported products that compete with local manufacture and so-called luxury goods. Since 1 January 2000 duties on luxury goods have been gradually cut and are due to be abolished by 2008.

Since 1993 payments of ordinary transactions have been made through approved financial institutions (banks) without prior central bank approval.

Disputes over contracts entered into with Tunisian companies are usually brought before Tunisian courts, although the parties may agree to submit to the jurisdiction of a foreign court.

■ Attitude towards foreign investors

Under the Investment Incentive Code of December 1993 foreigners are free to invest in all sectors, except for mining, energy, domestic trade and financial services, all of which are governed by specific regulations. Promoters are only required to notify the relevant government agencies or departments, except for certain activities that are subject to special approval.

Foreign business in the country, however, is specifically governed by the decree law of 1961. Prior authorization must be obtained for certain service activities that are not totally export related and in which the foreign interest exceeds 50 per cent. Tax benefits are granted for investments that are totally export related. Foreigners cannot invest in industries in which the state has a monopoly, unless they are awarded a concession. This area has nevertheless been opened up since the deregulation of electricity

4

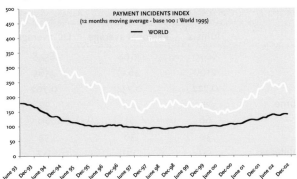

PAYMENT INCIDENTS INDEX
(12 months moving average - base 100 : World 1995)
— WORLD
— Tunisia

generation and mobile telephone services. Foreign investors are barred from owning farm land. They also require the approval of the regional governor to own property.

The country's legislation restricts the employment of foreign staff. However there is very little red tape for offshore banks, totally export-oriented firms and non-profit organizations.

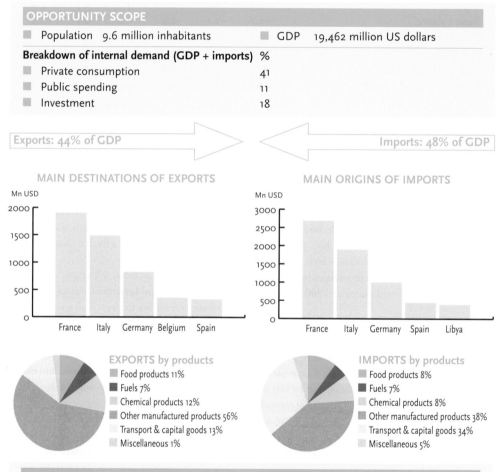

OPPORTUNITY SCOPE

Population 9.6 million inhabitants   GDP 19,462 million US dollars

Breakdown of internal demand (GDP + imports) %
- Private consumption   41
- Public spending   11
- Investment   18

Exports: 44% of GDP   Imports: 48% of GDP

MAIN DESTINATIONS OF EXPORTS
Mn USD

France Italy Germany Belgium Spain

MAIN ORIGINS OF IMPORTS
Mn USD

France Italy Germany Spain Libya

EXPORTS by products
- Food products 11%
- Fuels 7%
- Chemical products 12%
- Other manufactured products 56%
- Transport & capital goods 13%
- Miscellaneous 1%

IMPORTS by products
- Food products 8%
- Fuels 7%
- Chemical products 8%
- Other manufactured products 38%
- Transport & capital goods 34%
- Miscellaneous 5%

STANDARD OF LIVING / PURCHASING POWER

Indicators	Tunisia	Regional average	DC average
GNP per capita (PPP dollars)	6070	7168	6548
GNP per capita	2100	4625	3565
Human development index	0.722	0.734	0.702
Wealthiest 10% share of national income	32	29	32
Urban population percentage	66	71	60
Percentage under 15 years old	30	36	32
Number of telephones per 1000 inhabitants	90	161	157
Number of computers per 1000 inhabitants	23	59	64

Turkey

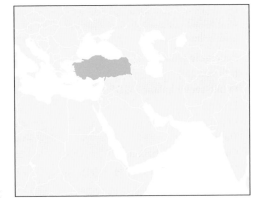

Coface analysis

Short-term: **C**

Medium-term:
High risk

STRENGTHS

- The private sector is diversified and dynamic.
- Several laws voted in 2002 to improve the political framework constitute progress in meeting the political criteria for EU membership.
- Progress made on banking reforms in 2001 and 2002 could provide the basis for sustainable growth and disinflation.
- As a NATO member and European partner, Turkey enjoys international community backing.

WEAKNESSES

- Imbalances in public finances are sustained by debt-linked interest expense depending on financial market confidence. This is a major source of vulnerability.
- Debt and portfolio investments have been financing the internal and external deficits.
- Implementation of public sector privatisation and streamlining measures are slow due to a lack of political will.
- Issues such as the status of Cyprus, Kurdish minority situation, and the army's role in political life continue to weigh on EU membership prospects.

4

RISK ASSESSMENT

The economy is recovering faster than expected and the inflation trend is better than the objectives targeted by the government. The new administration elected in November 2002 enjoys a comfortable majority, which eases political instability risks. A climate of confidence has thus been able to develop as evidenced by the spectacular reduction of spreads and interest rates and strengthening of the lira since November. The resulting feeling of stability is naturally shaky and the AK Party remains under scrutiny on the sensitive secularism issue. Moreover, the international climate remains tense with the possibility of intervention in Iraq. Turkey's financial situation remains very vulnerable to any crisis of confidence on financial markets. IMF aid will likely permit avoiding a new financial crisis in 2003.

Turkish companies are progressively recovering from the crisis, as evidenced by their improved payment record, which nonetheless remains shaky with payments hindered by difficult access to foreign exchange. Meanwhile much is expected from the new government on structural issues. Reforms (privatization, public sector streamlining, banking sector consolidation) are essential to maintain a climate of confidence. Prospects for a firm decision by end-2004 on opening negotiations with the European Union could prove to be a crucial incentive to continue modernizing the economy.

KEY ECONOMIC INDICATORS

US$ billion	1998	1999	2000	2001	2002(e)	2003(f)
Economic growth (%)	3.1	−5	7.2	−7.4	6	4
Inflation (%)	69.7	68.7	39	68.4	33	25
Public-sector balance/GDP (%)	−9.8	−24.2	−19.6	−19	−16.7	−15.2
Exports	31.2	29.3	31.7	35.3	38.6	41.7
Imports	45.4	39.8	54	39.7	47.7	54.1
Trade balance	−14.2	−10.4	−22.4	−4.5	−9.1	−12.4
Current account balance	2	−1.4	−9.8	3.4	−2.7	−3.4
Current balance/GDP (%)	1	−0.7	−5	2.3	−1.5	−1.4
External debt (%)	97.9	103.3	120	115	128	130
wherein short-term debt (%)	23	24.2	24.6	16.3	14.8	15.6
Debt service/Exports (%)	26.3	35.2	37.2	49.4	47	35
Reserves (import months)	3.8	5.1	4	4.2	4.7	4.3

e = estimated, f = forecast

CONDITIONS OF ACCESS TO THE MARKET

■ Means of entry

The Turkish market is by and large open to imports of foreign goods and services. The country's economic mechanisms have largely been harmonized with those in the European Union, except for certain agricultural products. Turkish companies are particularly keen to conclude partnership agreements and joint ventures.

All means of payment are used and accepted. Documentary credit is strongly recommended for initial transactions and during periods of economic instability. It should preferably be obtained with a foreign bank, although Turkish companies generally prefer to work with their own banks. Acceptance credit letters are more widespread, but as they are fairly expensive cash against documents or payment against goods is usually preferred by Turkish importers.

Several audit companies of international standing have offices in Turkey.

■ Attitude towards foreign investors

All foreign investments are subject to the approval of the General-Directorate for Foreign Investment, which reports to the Under-Secretary of State for the Treasury. Start-ups are also subject to the completion of a number of long-winded and complex formalities, which can be handled by a local lawyer.

Persons or companies residing abroad must invest a minimum of US$50,000 to start a company or joint venture or open a branch. Where several foreign partners are involved the minimum investment is calculated by multiplying this sum by the number of partners. Within this amount, the distribution of shares can be freely decided between the partners.

In 2002 the Turkish government set out to amend legislation in order to enhance foreign investment inflows into the country. The changes involved reaffirming the freedom of foreign investment in the

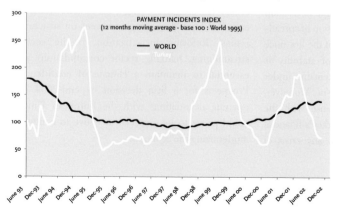

PAYMENT INCIDENTS INDEX
(12 months moving average - base 100 : World 1995)

— WORLD
Turkey

country, reducing administrative reductions and licences, speeding up procedures and facilitating the employment of foreign workers. A foreign investment bill, drawn up along these lines, was submitted to the national assembly in June 2002, where it is still under review.

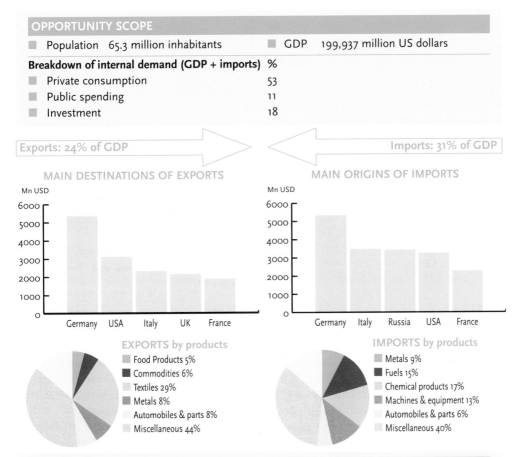

OPPORTUNITY SCOPE

- Population 65.3 million inhabitants
- GDP 199,937 million US dollars

Breakdown of internal demand (GDP + imports) %
- Private consumption 53
- Public spending 11
- Investment 18

Exports: 24% of GDP   Imports: 31% of GDP

MAIN DESTINATIONS OF EXPORTS

Mn USD

Germany USA Italy UK France

MAIN ORIGINS OF IMPORTS

Mn USD

Germany Italy Russia USA France

EXPORTS by products
- Food Products 5%
- Commodities 6%
- Textiles 29%
- Metals 8%
- Automobiles & parts 8%
- Miscellaneous 44%

IMPORTS by products
- Metals 9%
- Fuels 15%
- Chemical products 17%
- Machines & equipment 13%
- Automobiles & parts 6%
- Miscellaneous 40%

STANDARD OF LIVING / PURCHASING POWER

Indicators	Turkey	Regional average	DC average
GNP per capita (PPP dollars)	7030	7168	6548
GNP per capita	3100	4625	3565
Human development index	0.742	0.734	0.702
Wealthiest 10% share of national income	32	29	32
Urban population percentage	75	71	60
Percentage under 15 years old	30	36	32
Number of telephones per 1000 inhabitants	280	161	157
Number of computers per 1000 inhabitants	38	59	64

4

307

United Arab Emirates

Short-term: **A2**

Medium-term:

Coface analysis **Low risk**

STRENGTHS

- Successful economic diversification programme.
- Development of free zones has opened economy to foreign investment.
- Large natural resources (oil and gas).
- Sizeable financial assets held abroad.

WEAKNESSES

- Significant imbalances within Federation, with Abu-Dhabi and Dubai (85 per cent of GDP) effectively subsidising Northern Emirates.
- Structural budget deficit caused by rigid spending. Lack of transparency in public accounting.
- Highly dependent on foreign labour.
- Scarce water resources is matter of strategic importance.
- Unresolved territorial dispute with Iran, which has occupied Abu-Musa and Tomb Islands since 1971.

RISK ASSESSMENT

In the last two years the fall in oil output, against the background of the global economic downturn, has slowed the UAE economy, which has been driven only by the non-oil sector and public spending. In 2003 firmer foreign demand for petroleum products should help the economy to rebound. Economic growth, however, could continue to be affected by regional political uncertainties that are hitting investment and tourism

Despite firm crude prices the performance of the oil market in 2001 and 2002 has caused the current account surplus to shrink and, coupled with higher public spending on large-scale investment projects, the budget deficit to widen. These trends should be reversed in 2003 on the back of a recovery in oil exports and higher budget revenues while crude prices should remain firm. The country's financial situation is not worrying. The debt burden remains modest compared to foreign exchange earnings and reserves and also the country's vast asset holdings abroad.

The government has continued to pursue its policy of economic openness and diversification. In the long term the measures adopted to ease spending (privatizations, franchising of public services, cuts in subsidies, improvements in the tax system) should improve fiscal balance. However, this policy banks on significant foreign direct investment being made in the country at a time when investors could be discouraged by regional political uncertainties.

KEY ECONOMIC INDICATORS

US$ billion	1998	1999	2000	2001	2002(e)	2003(f)
Economic growth (%)	1.4	3.9	7.3	1.9	1.5	3
Inflation (%)	2	2.2	1.4	1.2	1.3	1.3
Public-sector balance/GDP (%)	−17	−15	−2.8	−8	−10	n/a
Exports	31.1	36.5	45.3	41.3	40	41.5
Imports	30.5	31.7	32.5	32.6	32.8	33
Trade balance	0.5	4.8	12.7	8.7	7.2	8.5
Current account balance/GDP (%)	−2.3	6.3	17.5	12	9	10.5
Foreign debt/GDP	57.7	46.2	37.2	37.1	37.8	39.8
Debt service/Exports (%)	8.4	8.4	7.6	8	8.1	8.3
Reserves (import months)	2.4	2.9	3.6	3.8	3.9	3.9

n/a – not available

e = estimated, f = forecast

CONDITIONS OF ACCESS TO THE MARKET

■ Market overview

The UAE market is very open and thus highly competitive.

Under the GCC Customs Union, whose introduction was brought forward to 1 January 2003, the six member states have agreed to apply 5.5 per cent duty on staple commodities and 7.5 per cent on other products.

The UAE is a member of the WTO and, through the GCC, party to talks on a free trade agreement with the European Union.

■ Means of entry

Since August 1994 the standard rate of customs duty on goods entering the country has been set at 4 per cent. However, there are many exceptions (very high taxes on cigarettes and alcohol), together with exemptions for procurements by the government, the ruling families and government agencies. All means of payment are accepted, with the irrevocable and confirmed letter of credit the most widespread and safest means of payment. Payments do not pose any special problems and the country continues to eschew medium- and long-term debt finance. Increasingly strict auditing procedures are now in place, with branches of foreign companies required to undergo an annual audit.

■ Attitude towards foreign investors

UAE's foreign investment policy remains open and liberal. One of the attractions of this market is exemption from corporation and income tax (except for the banking and oil sectors).

Outside the free zones, where a foreign company can hold a 100 per cent stake in a local firm, the rule of the UAE majority joint venture is applicable. In addition foreign companies are required to have a sponsor in order to set up a sales office. New foreign investment legislation is being prepared by the Ministry of Economic Affairs and Trade.

To improve compliance with WTO intellectual property protection rules, in summer 2002 the UAE passed two new laws: one governing copyright (law No 7 – Federal and Related Rights Law of 29 June 2002 amending Law No 40 of 1992), the second governing trademark protection (law No 8 Trademark Law of 31 July 2002, amending Law No 37 of 1992). The Patents and Designs Act No 44 (1992) is also due to be amended shortly.

Ninety per cent of the country's workforce consists of immigrant labour employed under short-term job contracts. Foreign residents are issued residence permits by the Immigration Department. Employers are required to provide welfare cover for their employees by funding an annual healthcare pass that provides access to local hospitals and public health services. For higher quality healthcare, additional welfare cover is required. The federal government is preparing an amendment to the country's health insurance regulations.

4

■ Foreign exchange regulations

The UAE dirham enjoys fixed parity with the dollar (US$1= 3.6725 dirham).

There are no exchange controls or restrictions on obtaining foreign currency. The repatriation of capital and profits is entirely unrestricted.

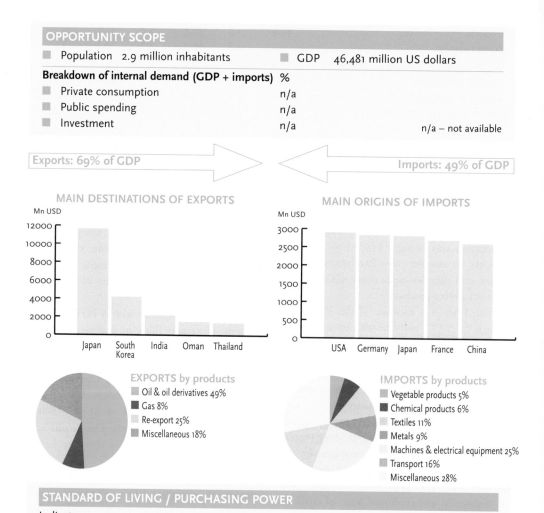

OPPORTUNITY SCOPE

■ Population   2.9 million inhabitants

■ GDP   46,481 million US dollars

Breakdown of internal demand (GDP + imports)	%
■ Private consumption	n/a
■ Public spending	n/a
■ Investment	n/a

n/a – not available

Exports: 69% of GDP

Imports: 49% of GDP

MAIN DESTINATIONS OF EXPORTS

Mn USD

Japan, South Korea, India, Oman, Thailand

MAIN ORIGINS OF IMPORTS

Mn USD

USA, Germany, Japan, France, China

EXPORTS by products
- ■ Oil & oil derivatives 49%
- ■ Gas 8%
- ■ Re-export 25%
- ■ Miscellaneous 18%

IMPORTS by products
- ■ Vegetable products 5%
- ■ Chemical products 6%
- ■ Textiles 11%
- ■ Metals 9%
- ■ Machines & electrical equipment 25%
- ■ Transport 16%
- ■ Miscellaneous 28%

STANDARD OF LIVING / PURCHASING POWER

Indicators	UAE	Regional average	DC average
GNP per capita (PPP dollars)	n/a	7168	6548
GNP per capita	n/a	4625	3565
Human development index	0.812	0.734	0.702
Wealthiest 10% share of national income	n/a	29	32
Urban population percentage	85	71	60
Percentage under 15 years old	26	36	32
Number of telephones per 1000 inhabitants	391	161	157
Number of computers per 1000 inhabitants	154	59	64

n/a – not available

Yemen

Short-term: **C**

Medium-term:

Coface analysis   **Very high risk**

STRENGTHS

- Significant untapped natural gas reserves.
- Foreign debt relief granted by Paris Club.
- Joint ventures with foreign oil companies reduce extraction costs and increase production capacity.
- Border agreement with Saudi Arabia ends territorial dispute and opens way to regional integration.

WEAKNESSES

- Continuing insecurity discourages tourism.
- Economy dependent on oil and emigrant workers' remittances.
- Declining oil reserves (less than 20 years' production).
- Dependent on food imports (70 per cent) as agriculture mainly based on kat.
- Legal environment and security situation discourage investors.
- Poor water management.

4

RISK ASSESSMENT

Lower oil prices in 2003 could slow economic growth and widen the budget deficit. The external account surplus could narrow as oil exports decline while tourism continues to be affected by the climate of insecurity. However, the country's financial situation is manageable thanks to debt relief. Moreover foreign exchange reserves should continue to increase for the fourth consecutive year.

Yemen's economy remains vulnerable to external factors that could affect food imports and oil exports. The structural reform programme aimed at improving and liberalizing the economy, developing the private sector and attracting investment is moving slowly. Insecurity, social unrest and corruption have put a brake on reforms and foreign investment. The IMF has made restoration of its Growth and Poverty Reduction Facility conditional upon progress in reforms.

The strengthening of relations between the Yemeni government and the United States as part of the war on terror is likely to strengthen support for opposition groups.

KEY ECONOMIC INDICATORS

US$ billion	1998	1999	2000	2001	2002(e)	2003(f)
Economic growth (%)	4.9	3.7	5.1	3.3	4.1	3.5
Inflation (%)	11.5	8	10.9	11.9	15.8	9
Public-sector balance/GDP (%)	−6.7	−1.2	7.7	2.8	−1.1	−3.8
Exports	1.5	2.46	3.9	3.3	3.8	3.7
Imports	2.2	2.4	2.8	2.8	2.9	3.1
Trade balance	−0.7	0	1.1	0.5	0.9	0.5
Current account balance/GDP (%)	−4.7	1.5	13.1	5.5	5.2	3
Foreign debt/GDP (%)	85.7	80.7	54.3	56	54.5	53.7
Debt service/Exports (%)	11.6	9.4	5.8	5.8	4.5	4
Reserves (import months)	3.4	4.5	8.5	9.6	10	10.2

e = estimated, f = forecast

CONDITIONS OF ACCESS TO THE MARKET

■ Market overview

The Yemeni market can be considered open, as there are few restrictions and no discrimination between supplier countries.

■ Means of entry

There are several categories of taxes on goods imported into Yemen:

● 'duties and levies' on all authorized imports based on the CIF value: 5 per cent, 10 per cent, 15 per cent and 20 per cent;
● a freight tax calculated on the volume and length of storage;
● 1 per cent tax on net trading profits.

Customs tariff reform is under study. Only irrevocable and confirmed letters of credit should be used, guaranteed by a first rate, preferably foreign bank. Advance payment is also acceptable as some Yemeni traders have financial assets abroad and can use them to pay for transactions in Yemen. If a letter of credit is issued by Crédit Agricole Indosuez (the only Western financial institution with branches in Yemen) it does not need to be confirmed, as long as the seller is prepared to cover the risk of non-transfer.

Certain foreign audit companies (SGS, but not Véritas) are represented in Yemen, but do not have offices there. As a result, caution is called for when handling inspections.

■ Attitude towards foreign investors

Foreign investment is governed by Law No 22 of 2002.

There are also special laws dealing with oil exploration and production and major contracts. Tax breaks and exemptions from customs duty are awarded to investors.

Capital invested and profits can be freely repatriated at the market rate. The law enshrines the principle of equality between Yemenis and foreigners.

Foreigners can hold a majority or even 100 per cent stake in local companies.

Investors are required to give priority to domestic labour. The Labour Code, written in Arabic, covers key issues, but a number of points are open to interpretation. Social protection is poor. Some companies take out private insurance for their employees.

■ Foreign exchange regulations

The dollar serves as the benchmark currency. The rial has been floating against the dollar for a year and in October 2002 the exchange rate was 177 rials to the dollar.

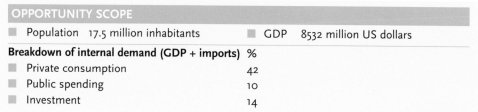

OPPORTUNITY SCOPE

- Population   17.5 million inhabitants
- GDP   8532 million US dollars

Breakdown of internal demand (GDP + imports) %
- Private consumption   42
- Public spending   10
- Investment   14

Exports: 50% of GDP

Imports: 41% of GDP

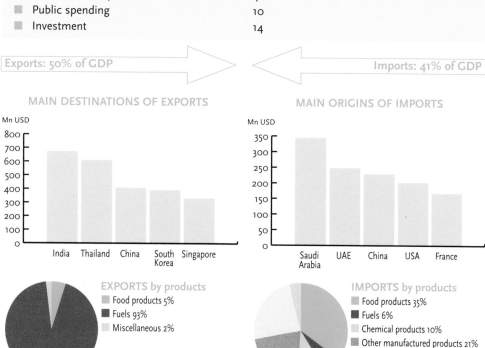

MAIN DESTINATIONS OF EXPORTS

Mn USD

(India, Thailand, China, South Korea, Singapore)

MAIN ORIGINS OF IMPORTS

Mn USD

(Saudi Arabia, UAE, China, USA, France)

EXPORTS by products
- Food products 5%
- Fuels 93%
- Miscellaneous 2%

IMPORTS by products
- Food products 35%
- Fuels 6%
- Chemical products 10%
- Other manufactured products 21%
- Transport & capital goods 24%
- Miscellaneous 4%

4

STANDARD OF LIVING / PURCHASING POWER

Indicators	Yemen	Regional average	DC average
GNP per capita (PPP dollars)	770	7168	6548
GNP per capita	370	4625	3565
Human development index	0.479	0.734	0.702
Wealthiest 10% share of national income	26	29	32
Urban population percentage	25	71	60
Percentage under 15 years old	50	36	32
Number of telephones per 1000 inhabitants	19	161	157
Number of computers per 1000 inhabitants	2	59	64

Sub-Saharan Africa

5

Can Oil Constitute a New Source of Dynamism Capable of Driving Central African (CEMAC) Growth in 2003?

Blaise Leenhardt, Manager

Macroeconomic Analysis Department, French Development Agency

Recent discoveries, the commencement of oil production in Equatorial Guinea, and the start-up in 2004 of the pipeline that will carry oil pumped from the Doba field in Chad to the Cameroonian port of Kribi, are drawing attention to the region. Will this become a new African focal point for oil?

In the absence of new oil discoveries, growth should slacken in 2003.

After the 1999 recession the sharp oil price rise of 2000–01 and successive discoveries in Equatorial Guinea have accelerated overall growth in the region. Moreover, the continuing success in recent years of the programme implemented in Cameroon and, more recently, various agreements with the IMF in virtually all CEMAC countries have fostered a moderate economic recovery, bolstered by very strong oil production growth in Equatorial Guinea. Excluding Equatorial Guinea, the CEMAC region appears to have sustained an estimated 4 per cent growth in 2000 and 2001, with that pace likely to slow in 2003 in the absence of new oil discoveries. Growth should pick up again in 2004 with the effective start-up of the Doba field.

That growth is attributable to the ending of civil strife in the Congo and the resulting recovery of the non-oil economy. Although recent events have doubtless increased operator uncertainty, they serve as a reminder that post-conflict transitions are often long and difficult.

In Equatorial Guinea, discoveries and production start-ups have arrived in rapid succession with oil production (and thus GDP) registering two-digit growth: currently available results for the first quarter of last year indicate an annual production increase of 38 per cent.

Chad has been benefiting concurrently from the return of normal rainfall and the significant impact of work under way in Doba.

Conversely, a worsening oil-extraction outlook has been impeding growth in Gabon, the Congo and, to a lesser extent, in Cameroon. In Gabon and the Congo, implementation of an adjustment and debt reduction policy to bring government spending in line with the country's oil tax revenue potential has led to a slowdown in primary spending and civil service consumption, which fell in volume in both countries last year, by 7 per cent and 10 per cent respectively.

Cameroon is in an intermediate situation. It has been one of the region's engines with the ongoing success of its IMF-sponsored programme, accompanied by an ambitious wage policy and an increase in non-oil revenues. However, growth of public investment has not really lived up to expectations, especially that portion financed with external funds in 2001–02. Effects of oil investments linked to Doba, which have added about a half-point to growth, have begun to wane, and growth should return to a pace closer to 4 per cent than 5 per cent.

For the country to return to that level of growth, current projections suppose increased aid outlays for projects in 2003, which should increase further in 2004 with attainment of the HIPC completion point. The very poor performance in this regard in 2001/02 should thus improve rapidly.

Table 1 shows overall growth estimates based on the 'Jumbo' model and the international environment hypotheses and policies foreseen in the framework of the programmes under way in all regional countries except the Central African Republic. That region enjoyed very strong growth in 2001 and 2002 attributable to Equatorial Guinea, while oil production continued to decline elsewhere.

TABLE 1: CEMAC: GDP VOLUME GROWTH RATE (%)

Main scenario	1999	2000	2001	2002	2003
Total GDP	**-0.6**	**3.4**	**6.4**	**5.8**	**4.6**
wherein GDP excluding oil	-0.1	5.9	6.1	5.3	4.6
wherein GDP from oil alone	-2.0	-4.7	7.5	7.6	4.6
Total GDP except Equatorial Guinea	**-1.0**	**3.0**	**4.0**	**3.8**	**3.1**
wherein GDP excluding oil	-0.9	5.8	5.7	4.0	4.2
wherein GDP from oil alone	-3.4	-6.7	-5.1	-3.6	7.4

Source: Jumbo model (September 2002)

Although the region has been focusing increasingly on oil the remainder of the economy has nonetheless grown strongly – even in countries where oil extraction is diminishing – due to the ripple effect of oil revenues, which has more than offset the production decline. This dynamism should slacken somewhat in 2003.

Since 2001/02, redistribution of oil production assets and the expected appearance of a newcomer in 2004 have notably marked CEMAC's development.

TABLE 2: CEMAC: CRUDE OIL EXPORTS (MILLIONS OF BARRELS PER YEAR)

	1997	1998	1999	2000	2001	2002	2003	2004
Cameroon	38	41	42	41	40	37	35	34
Congo	86	94	98	97	90	92	90	88
Gabon	135	128	114	99	95	88	76	65
Equatorial Guinea(*)	21	33	37	40	71	98	120	120
Chad	0	0	0	0	0	0	0	77
CEMAC	**280**	**296**	**291**	**277**	**296**	**315**	**321**	**384**

(*) Barrels of oil or oil equivalent (methanol)

5

Table 2 shows crude oil exports for countries in the region since 1997 and current forecasts for 2002-04. As of 2004, Chad will join the list of the region's oil producing countries. Moreover, Chad's initial yearly production will be far from negligible since it will be more than double the output expected for Cameroon and exceed Gabon's production, which is likely to decline sharply in the absence of new discoveries. Overall, a profound redistribution of oil production assets is under way in the region.

---

[1]French acronym for *Communauté Economique et Monétaire d'Afrique Centrale*, which includes Cameroon, the Central African Republic, Chad, Congo, Equatorial Guinea and Gabon.

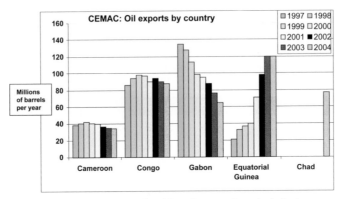

Despite deterioration of the trading terms due to the decline in oil prices early last year and of the dollar exchange rate, African oil producing countries continue to enjoy a favourable situation.

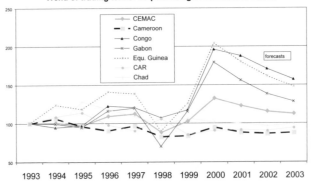

NB: The terms of trade used here represent the quotient of the price index of goods exports expressed in CFA and the price of goods imports also expressed in CFA calculated according to the 'Jumbo' model based on quantities declared to customs (or included by the IMF in the statistical appendices attached to the IMF Article IV reviews) of the main products exported.

CEMAC's average annual terms of change have rarely varied as widely as during the 1997–2000 period, with the price of oil swinging from one extreme to another and remaining at the extremes for years at a time. In recent times the 11 September 2001 attacks have only had a transitory effect and barely accentuated the foreseeable oil price decline. However, they spurred growth forecast revisions and stock market adjustments in the United States, which influenced the euro–dollar exchange rate. Considering the construction of the terms of trade in the 'Jumbo' model – with export and import prices expressed in CFA francs – the continuing high price per barrel has been offsetting the dollar's decline.

The region's oil producing countries have continued to enjoy a very favourable situation compared to the early 1990s. However Cameroon, whose exports are undeniably diversified but on products with not very favourable price trends, seems to be losing some ground due to the terms of trade trend. The country remains nonetheless globally protected from their volatility with price declines of one product offset by increases elsewhere.

In conclusion, the CEMAC landscape has been undergoing a realignment of oil-producing countries manifested by the emergence of new players (Equatorial Guinea, Chad) and an overall production increase in the region. These developments nonetheless do not reflect any emergence of a new African focal point for oil. In fact, by 2004 the region's oil production will be only half that of Angola and one-fifth that of Nigeria.

Country @ratings for Sub-Saharan Africa

Sylvia Greisman and Bernard Lignereux
Coface Country Risk and Economic Studies Department, Paris

The country @rating scale measures the average level of short-term non-payment risk presented by companies in a particular country. It reflects the extent to which a country's economic, financial and political outlook influences financial commitments of local companies. It is thus complementary to @rating Credit Opinions on companies.

Sub-Saharan Africa remains vulnerable to political, ethnic and social tensions as well as to the exogenous shocks that can affect its economic activity.

In 2002, the entire region's growth remained below 3 per cent. Many countries have to contend with falling prices for primary products such as coffee or cotton while surplus resources generated by firm oil prices have not always percolated widely in the economies concerned. Moreover the Ivory Coast, West Africa's second-leading economic hub, has succumbed again to a conflict paralysing the country's northern region.

Implementation of encouraging projects also marked the year 2002. The Organization of African Unity became the African Union with the prospect of eventually evolving along the lines of the European Union. Creation of NEPAD, the New Partnership for Africa's Development, and strengthening of regional economic integration policies have laid the groundwork for an environment more conducive to growth. Moreover, the signature of peace agreements that can put an end to ancient conflicts in Angola, the Great Lakes region, the Democratic Republic of Congo and Burundi constitutes a positive factor. Nonetheless many countries remain faced with public account imbalances and very shaky external financial situations. Although South Africa and some other countries in Southern Africa have not been encountering major problems, recourse to international aid to cover financing needs is commonplace: witness the large number of African countries benefiting from the HIPC initiative.

Those economic and financial weaknesses have been affecting company solvency and are responsible for a payment default rate still above the world average. In consequence, the ratings of countries in the region reflect a relatively high level of risk. With the exception of Botswana, rated A2, Mauritius, Namibia (A3), and South Africa (A4), the ratings of most countries fall into categories B, C, and D. Only one country was upgraded: Mozambique to category C in March 2002. Meanwhile two countries were downgraded in December 2002, Gabon to category C, and the Ivory Coast to D.

PAYMENT INCIDENT INDICES
(12-month moving average; base 100: world in 1995)
— World
— Sub-Saharan Africa

Dec-96 Jun-97 Dec-97 Jun-98 Dec-98 Jun-99 Dec-99 Jun-00 Dec-00 Jun-01 Dec-01 Jun-02 Dec-02

■ Countries rated A4

These countries often present fairly mediocre payment behaviour that could be affected by an economic downturn, although the probability of that causing a large number of payment defaults remains moderate.

South Africa enjoys a favourable macroeconomic framework. The country benefits from moderate external debt and relative political stability. Economic growth has nonetheless been insufficient to combat unemployment, poverty and inequality. Moreover, foreign exchange earnings are still too dependent on raw material price trends. South Africa is also particularly vulnerable to a crisis of confidence in capital markets.

Economic activity remains nonetheless buoyant overall, as evidenced by the satisfactory payment behaviour of companies, which present a level of risk

5

below the world average. However, there are a few difficulties in the electronics sector, which are more a reflection of the worldwide crisis in the sector than of trends in the South African economy. The number of bankruptcies declined sharply in 2002.

■ Countries rated B

A precarious economic environment could affect company payment behaviour, which is often mediocre.

In Senegal, development of the mining and chemical sectors has been driving growth, the farm sector's poor performance notwithstanding. Sustaining buoyant growth will nonetheless depend on the outcome of privatizations in the peanut and electricity sectors and continuation of public accounts consolidation. However, the budgetary cost of assisting rural areas affected by the crisis has been complicating the consolidation process.

The steady economic activity has benefited the company financial situation. Payment incident frequency has nonetheless remained above the world average.

Cameroon, which is enjoying a dynamic economic period, is one of central Africa's economic engines. However, this dynamism is largely attributable to activity linked to construction of the Doba/Kribi pipeline and will have to be sustained by other factors, including acceleration of the structural reforms needed to cope with declining oil production.

■ Countries rated C

A very precarious economic and political environment could worsen payment behaviour that is already often poor.

In Ghana, intensification of the reform process will be necessary to sustain growth and further diversify the economic fabric. Particularly, after years of deterioration that generated heavy debt, consolida-

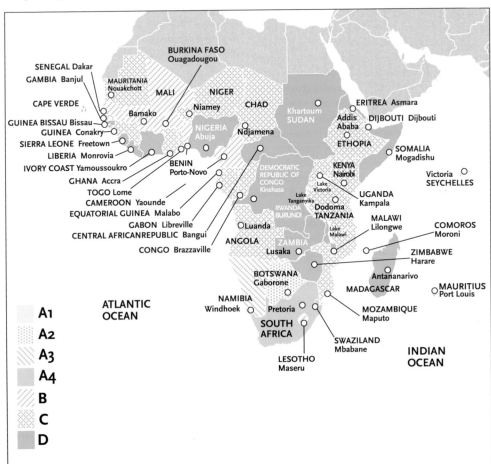

tion of public finances will constitute a major challenge for the authorities who will continue to depend on international community aid.

Mozambique's upgrading from category D to C reflects the substantial improvement in its economic situation resulting from important investments undertaken, progress on reforms, and the debt cancellation that has benefited the country under the HIPC initiative. The situation has nonetheless remained precarious and the country continues to depend on international financial community backing.

■ Countries rated D

The economic and political environment present a very high level of risk that exacerbates generally deplorable payment behaviour.

In the Ivory Coast, the country's de facto partition since September 2002 has severely compromised the economic outlook. In the North transportation and economic activity have been paralysed. The persistent and pervasive climate of insecurity has been jeopardizing the entire cocoa industry and the authorities have had to suspend their investment programme to limit slippage in the public accounts, affected by the drop in fiscal revenues.

The widespread deterioration of the situation has been undermining company solvency even more and could trigger a new wave of payment incidents.

These circumstances led to the downgrading of the Ivory Coast's rating from category C to D at the end of 2002.

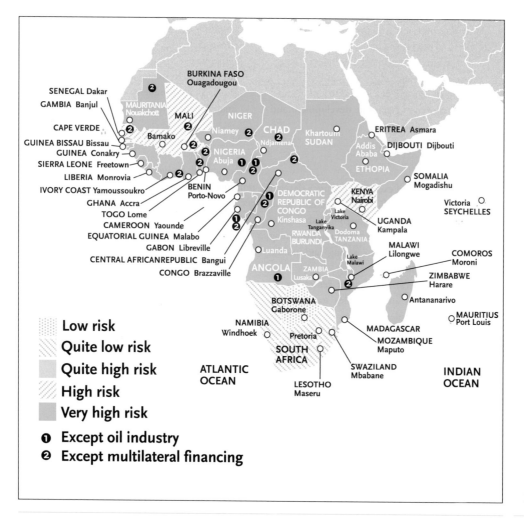

Low risk

Quite low risk

Quite high risk

High risk

Very high risk

❶ Except oil industry
❷ Except multilateral financing

Angola

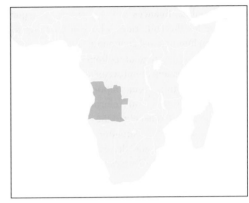

Coface analysis

Short-term: **C**

Medium-term:
Very high risk

STRENGTHS

- Sizeable natural resources (oil and gas, diamonds, hydroelectricity, various ores, agricultural and fishery potential).
- Africa's second largest oil producer (65 per cent of GDP, 75 per cent of budget revenues, 95 per cent of exports). Attracts significant direct foreign investment. Strategically important to West.
- End of civil war will enable country to channel resources towards economic development and poverty alleviation.

WEAKNESSES

- Oil wealth has not filtered through to rest of economy, whose restructuring is bogged down.
- After-effects of civil war seriously undermine country's demographic, economic and financial prospects.
- Opaqueness of public finances detrimental to support of international financial community.
- Business environment, excluding oil and gas, unappealing to foreign investors.

RISK ASSESSMENT

The increase in foreign exchange earnings derived from oil exports and the 25 per cent increase in oil output in 2002 was still not enough to stabilize the country's economic position. Despite the rising growth rate inflation remains strong and public finances remain in the red.

Unsound finances, government reluctance to disclose oil earnings and obstacles to structural reforms prevent implementation of the international financial community's aid programme. But the programme is the key to reducing both domestic and foreign public debt contracted on unfavourable terms and to correcting the external account deficit, widened by rising imports and the highly unfavourable invisible trade balance.

The aid would also enable the country to take advantage of the political situation created by the end of the civil war in April 2002 and channel more resources towards the fight against poverty, infrastructure reconstruction and economic diversification. Nevertheless, there could be renewed political tensions as the 2004 elections draw nearer.

KEY ECONOMIC INDICATORS

US$ million	1998	1999	2000	2001	2002(e)	2003(f)
Economic growth (%)	6.9	3.4	2.1	3.3	9	6
Inflation (%)	107	248	325	115	125	140
Public-sector balance/GDP (%)	−7.6	−16.6	−2	−7	−5.2	−1.7
Exports	3543	5344	7860	6910	8740	8830
Imports	2079	3270	2470	2667	4062	4468
Trade balance	1464	2074	5390	4243	4678	4362
Current account balance/GDP (%)	−33.7	−27.8	−4	−12.3	−1.2	−4
Foreign debt	10,900	10,915	10,312	10,988	9,930	9,910
Debt service/Exports (%)	55.2	32.9	23.3	18.2	12.1	13
Reserves (import months)	0.4	0.8	1.7	1.5	1.2	1.2

e = estimated, f = forecast

CONDITIONS OF ACCESS TO THE MARKET

■ Market overview

The ceasefire agreements that were signed on 4 April 2002 following the death of Jonas Savimbi should considerably alter the country's economic fundamentals and largely mono-sector economy.

Angola has started to open its market to international trade by gradually cutting customs duties, simplifying its international trading arrangements (establishment of a single customs document in May 2002) and revising its direct foreign investment code for the economy as a whole and not just the dominant oil sector.

There is no doubt that three decades or so of war have created a humanitarian disaster and wrecked entire sectors of the country's economy. Even growth sectors such as agriculture and mining (with the exception of diamonds) are on the brink of collapse. Corruption, at first widely bred by arms purchases, has spread throughout the economy and is delaying a fairer distribution of wealth. The privatization programme is making very slow progress and international companies remain unwilling to invest in a country that lacks clear and stable regulations.

■ Means of Entry

Customs duties vary between 0 per cent and 35 per cent. Angola does not apply a preferential customs tariff to member countries of the preferential economic area and the Southern African Development Community (SADC). But two exemptions are due to be introduced for foreign investment-related imports: duty free admission for some products, and 50 per cent reduction in customs duties for imported capital goods and raw materials intended for investment projects undertaken in priority areas.

■ Attitude towards foreign investors

The Foreign Investment Act is expected to undergo root-and-branch changes in the short term. The government plans to liberalize the investment environment and harmonize it with that of other SADC member countries. The Foreign Investment Institute, a one-stop shop, brings together the main economic players. Over the last three years Angola has been the largest recipient of foreign investment in Africa, ahead of Egypt and Algeria, mainly in the off-shore oil sector. While today's legislation lays the foundation for greater openness to direct foreign investment, the situation on the ground is less clear-cut in all sectors, including oil.

Despite the survival of archaic ideological principles, the power of patronage at all levels of the bureaucracy and the economy and the lack of transparency in public accounting and in oil and diamond income statements – all of which slow procedures – a new capitalism-friendly language has emerged since May 2002.

5

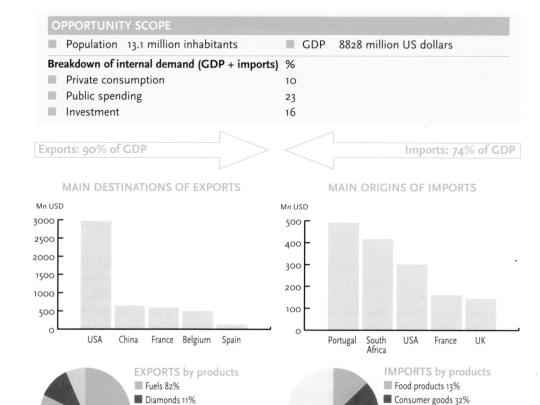

OPPORTUNITY SCOPE

Population 13.1 million inhabitants ▪ GDP 8828 million US dollars

Breakdown of internal demand (GDP + imports) %
▪ Private consumption 10
▪ Public spending 23
▪ Investment 16

Exports: 90% of GDP → ← Imports: 74% of GDP

MAIN DESTINATIONS OF EXPORTS

Mn USD

USA | China | France | Belgium | Spain

MAIN ORIGINS OF IMPORTS

Mn USD

Portugal | South Africa | USA | France | UK

EXPORTS by products
▪ Fuels 82%
▪ Diamonds 11%
▪ Miscellaneous 7%

IMPORTS by products
▪ Food products 13%
▪ Consumer goods 32%
▪ Capital goods 15%
▪ Semi-finished goods 15%
▪ Miscellaneous 25%

STANDARD OF LIVING / PURCHASING POWER

Indicators	Angola	Regional average	DC average
GNP per capita (PPP dollars)	1180	2708	6548
GNP per capita	290	985	3565
Human development index	0.403	0.493	0.702
Wealthiest 10% share of national income	n/a	35	32
Urban population percentage	34	42	60
Percentage under 15 years old	48	43	32
Number of telephones per 1000 inhabitants	5	32	157
Number of computers per 1000 inhabitants	1	15	64

n/a – not available

Benin

Short-term: **B**

Medium-term:

Coface analysis   **Very high risk**

RISK ASSESSMENT

The country's economic position and outlook for 2003 are uncertain. A good cotton harvest, a growing Nigerian economy (a significant proportion of Benin's income is derived from the transit of goods to Nigeria) and strong domestic demand should enable the country to post high growth rates. Moreover, the prospect of debt cancellation in 2003 under the HIPC initiative should release more resources for infrastructure investment (transport, health, education), thus facilitating economic diversification.

Despite delays caused by political bottlenecks structural reforms continue to make progress. Moves towards regional integration under way,

particularly in the field of energy, are likely to consolidate this trend over time.

In the short term, however, major challenges have to be met. Public accounts have been negatively affected due to increased spending on the civil service and on subsidies for cotton producers. The government's ability to raise funds is severely limited by widespread tax evasion and endemic corruption. The external accounts remain in the red and dependent on world cotton prices (45 per cent of export revenues). However, the prospect of continued support from the international community dispels fears of a major crisis.

5

KEY ECONOMIC INDICATORS						
US$ million	1998	1999	2000	2001	2002(e)	2003(f)
Economic growth (%)	4.5	4.7	5.2	5	5.8	6.2
Inflation (%)	5.8	0.3	4.2	4	3.3	3
Public-sector balance/GDP (%)	−1.1	−1.6	−3.5	−4.2	−5.2	−4.5
Exports	239	223	189	210	207	242
Imports	451	474	447	467	479	513
Trade balance	−211	−251	−258	−256	−273	−271
Current account balance/GDP (%)	−5.8	−8.7	−8.1	−7.9	−8.9	−7.1
Foreign debt	1667	1701	1602	1623	1658	1696
Debt service/Exports (%)	13.2	15.2	15.6	14.6	15.4	13
Reserves (import months)	4.8	7	8.4	8	7.7	7.2

e = estimated, f = forecast

Botswana

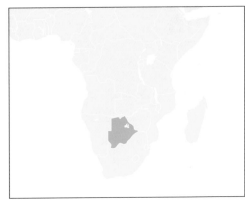

Coface analysis

Short-term: **A2**

Medium-term:
Low risk

STRENGTHS

● Vast natural resources: diamonds (world's second largest producer), copper, nickel.

● Foreign investors attracted by political stability, low level of corruption and well-developed transport and financial infrastructure.

● Progress in economic diversification (textiles, information technologies).

● Low debt and sound foreign exchange reserves give country ample room for manoeuvre in economic crisis.

WEAKNESSES

● Small landlocked market (1.6 million inhabitants). Trade and financial system heavily dependent on South Africa (75 per cent of imports). Tourism hit by crisis in Zimbabwe (2nd largest source of foreign exchange).

● Economy still highly exposed to diamond mining (50 per cent of budget revenues, 80 per cent of export earnings).

● AIDS pandemic (40 per cent of adult population) hinders growth, is responsible for soaring budget expenditure on health and social welfare, and will ultimately create severe demographic and economic imbalances.

RISK ASSESSMENT

In spite of the buoyant manufacturing sector, the levelling off of diamond output and exports has put a damper on economic growth.

The downturn has had a negative impact on the country's finances, which are crippled by the sharp increase in health and social spending associated with the AIDS pandemic. Thanks to the government's tight fiscal policy budget deficits are kept in check and are easily financed.

However the external account surplus has fallen. The low level of foreign debt and the foreign exchange position do not give cause for concern about a balance of payments crisis. Moreover, the country's favourable credit ratings make for easy access to international capital markets.

In the longer term, despite certain assets such as political stability, the country must as a matter of priority deal with the impact of the AIDS pandemic on its economic development and diversification programme.

KEY ECONOMIC INDICATORS						
US$ billion	1998	1999	2000	2001	2002(e)	2003(f)
Economic growth (%)	4.1	8.1	9.2	4.7	3.2	3
Inflation (%)	6.5	7.8	8.5	6.6	5	5
Public-sector balance/GDP (%)	−6.7	5.8	8.9	−2.5	−5.1	−2.8
Exports	2.1	2.7	2.7	2.3	2.4	2.4
Imports	2	1.9	1.8	1.7	1.9	2
Trade balance	0.1	0.8	0.9	0.7	0.4	0.5
Current account balance/GDP (%)	4.1	12.2	10.2	8.2	5.9	3.6
Foreign debt	0.9	0.9	1.1	1	1	0.9
Debt service/Exports (%)	4.9	3.9	4.6	5	4.5	3.9
Reserves (import months)	29.4	31.4	31.9	32.1	25.4	21.4

e = estimated, f = forecast

CONDITIONS OF ACCESS TO THE MARKET

■ Market overview

Botswana is a member of the Southern Africa Customs Union (SACU), which also comprises Lesotho, Swaziland, Namibia and South Africa. Ad valorem common external tariffs and excise duties are applicable to third countries. Under the renewed Lomé Convention and the Generalized System of Preferences Botswanan products have preferential access to European and North American markets (the country qualifies for AGOA). In October 2002 Botswana teamed up with other SACU members to sign a fresh customs protocol establishing a new system for resolving commercial disputes and setting customs duties. Botswana is also an active member of the South African Development Community (14 countries in Southern Africa), headquartered in Gaborone. However, the local market remains narrow, mainly concentrated in towns to the east of the country.

■ Means of entry

Botswana's customs regulations grant duty free admission to raw materials and machinery imported for the manufacture of products intended for export. Other tax measures include exemption from sales tax on raw materials used in exported products.

Sales agents of any nationality are allowed to operate, though local agents and representatives predominate. Public invitations to tender and large-scale works contracts comply with internationally recognized standards.

Imports are usually invoiced in rand, US dollars or pounds sterling. The euro is starting to gain acceptance as legal tender in trade, albeit to a limited degree. Botswana uses similar means of payments to those used in Europe and the United States.

■ Attitude towards foreign investors

Botswana possesses numerous investment-grade assets and is one of the most competitive countries in Africa. It has a liberal economy, no exchange controls, a convertible currency, attractive tax laws (15 per cent corporation tax for manufacturing industry, 25 per cent for others, no VAT, 10 per cent flat-rate sales tax) and peaceful social relations.

The Botswana Export Development and Investment Authority encourages investment in the country, especially through export-related projects and import substitution. The focus is on industrial diversification to reduce the country's dependence on the mining sector (diamonds) and on partnerships between foreign investors and local players with a view to facilitating technology transfers. Priority sectors include manufacturing (glass, leather tanneries, textiles, etc), information and communication technologies, tourism and financial services (international financial centre).

Botswana's legal system is founded on the principles of Common Law and Roman Dutch Law. The arrangements in place are highly liberal and resemble those adopted by developed countries.

The country is a signatory to the World Bank's MIGA Agreement and the OPIC Agreement (United States), and so provides investors with investment safeguards.

5

Foreign exchange regulations

Botswana's foreign exchange reserves enable it to pursue a highly flexible foreign exchange policy. There are no exchange controls and the local currency, the pula, is fully convertible. There are also no restrictions on the repatriation of capital by non-residents. Both dividends and capital can be freely transferred by a foreign investor upon payment of 15 per cent withholding tax.

Burkina Faso

Short-term: **B**

Medium-term:

Coface analysis **High risk**

RISK ASSESSMENT

While the economy grew in 2002 on the back of a good cotton harvest the prospects for 2003 are uncertain. Economic performance will be affected by the impact of exogenous factors on the earnings of the cotton sector and by developments in the Ivory Coast, the country of transit for Burkina Faso's exports and a source of income for many Burkina nationals. Remittances from emigrant workers generate a significant amount of foreign exchange for the country.

Because of the huge external and domestic borrowing requirement, the country will remain dependent on international aid, mainly provided in the form of debt relief since April 2002 when the country reached the 'completion point' under the HIPC programme.

The country should continue to enjoy the support of the international community, subject to the pursuit of structural reforms against a background of rising social and political tensions in the aftermath of the elections of May 2002, won by the thinnest of margins by the outgoing majority.

5

MAJOR ECONOMIC INDICATORS						
US$ million	1998	1999	2000	2001	2002(e)	2003(f)
Economic growth (%)	6.2	6.3	2.2	5.6	5.6	5.7
Inflation (%)	5	−1.1	−0.3	4.9	2	2
Public-sector balance/GDP (%)	−9.8	−13.3	−12.3	−12.6	−13.1	−10.9
Exports	323	254	205	219	258	334
Imports	634.4	580	518	524	546	701
Trade balance	−312	−327	−312	−305	−287	−367
Current account balance/GDP (%)	−10.7	−15.6	−16.9	−15.1	−14.5	−13.3
Foreign debt	1603	1483	1565	1604	1532	1492
Debt service/Exports (%)	11.7	22	24.3	18.9	9.8	8.3
Reserves (import months)	5.7	5.2	4.5	4.9	5.5	5.5

e = estimated, f = forecast

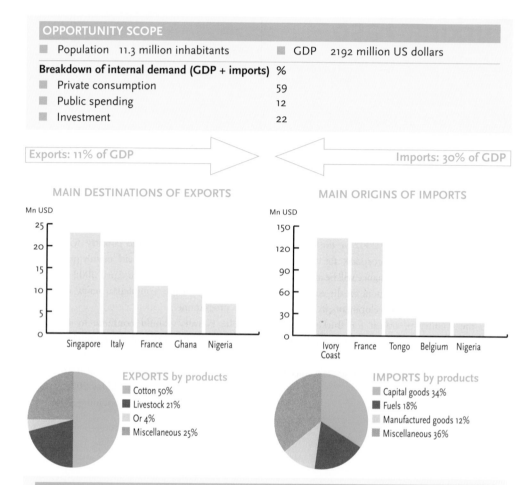

OPPORTUNITY SCOPE

- Population   11.3 million inhabitants
- GDP   2192 million US dollars

Breakdown of internal demand (GDP + imports) %
- Private consumption   59
- Public spending   12
- Investment   22

Exports: 11% of GDP

Imports: 30% of GDP

MAIN DESTINATIONS OF EXPORTS

Mn USD

Singapore   Italy   France   Ghana   Nigeria

MAIN ORIGINS OF IMPORTS

Mn USD

Ivory Coast   France   Tongo   Belgium   Nigeria

EXPORTS by products
- Cotton 50%
- Livestock 21%
- Or 4%
- Miscellaneous 25%

IMPORTS by products
- Capital goods 34%
- Fuels 18%
- Manufactured goods 12%
- Miscellaneous 36%

STANDARD OF LIVING / PURCHASING POWER

Indicators	Burkina Faso	Regional average	DC average
GNP per capita (PPP dollars)	970	2708	n/a
GNP per capita	210	985	n/a
Human development index	0.325	0.493	n/a
Wealthiest 10% share of national income	47	35	n/a
Urban population percentage	19	42	n/a
Percentage under 15 years old	49	43	n/a
Number of telephones per 1000 inhabitants	4	32	n/a
Number of computers per 1000 inhabitants	1	15	n/a

n/a – not available

330

Cameroon

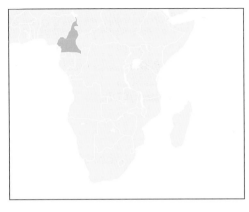

Coface analysis

Short-term: **B**

Medium-term:
Very high risk

STRENGTHS

- One of the most diversified economies on the African continent, with vast agricultural, forestry and energy – oil, gas, hydroelectricity – resources.
- Government's structural reform programme attracts foreign investment and is backed by foreign lenders (debt rescheduling and eventually debt relief).
- Chad–Cameroon oil pipeline should strengthen regional integration and enhance country's growth prospects.
- Membership of CFA franc area and tight fiscal policies make for monetary stability.

WEAKNESSES

- Cameroon remains dependent on exogenous factors such as climate and world commodity prices.
- Country's proven oil reserves are declining.
- Difficult business environment.
- Political instability in neighbouring countries and tensions with Nigeria (oil-rich Bakassi peninsula, smuggling) could have serious repercussions.
- Poverty alleviation remains major challenge for the government.

RISK ASSESSMENT

The Cameroon economy is enjoying something of a boom, making the country one of the growth engines of Central Africa. The upturn, largely a spin-off from the construction of the Doba/Kribi oil pipeline, must be underpinned by other factors, including more vigorous implementation of structural reforms, to offset the fall in oil production.

Falling oil revenues affect the country's domestic and external accounts, already under strain from imports relating to the construction of the oil pipeline. However, international financial assistance under the HIPC initiative, better management of public finances and structural reform should result in cancellation of the country's foreign debt.

Debt relief, by releasing more funds for poverty alleviation, will help ensure greater political stability, as borne out, despite the low turn-out, by the results of the June elections.

5

US$ million	1998	1999	2000	2001	2002(e)	2003(f)
Economic growth (%)	5	4.4	4.2	4.8	4.6	4.9
Inflation (%)	3.9	3.1	0.8	3.4	3.5	2.7
Public-sector balance/GDP (%)	−1.4	1	2	1	0.5	−0.2
Exports	1895	1713	2230	1853	2058	2217
Imports	1452	1413	1693	1679	1902	2175
Trade balance	443	300	537	173	156	42
Current account balance/GDP (%)	−4.3	−1.7	−2.1	−4.5	−4.8	−4.9
Foreign debt	9930	9445	9241	8868	8488	8635
Debt service/Exports (%)	22.5	23	17	18.9	12.1	13.6
Reserves(import months)	0	0	0.9	1.4	1.4	0.8

e = estimated, f = forecast

CONDITIONS OF ACCESS TO THE MARKET

■ Market overview

The Cameroon market is very open to imports and the authorities apply no special protectionist measures or tariff barriers. Customs duties on imports from within the CEMAC area range between 5 per cent for staple commodities and 30 per cent for certain consumer products (10 per cent for raw materials and capital goods, 20 per cent for semi-finished products and miscellaneous items). There is 18.7 per cent VAT from which staple commodities are exempt and an excise duty for so-called luxury products. Nevertheless the entry of goods into the country is hampered by cumbersome, bureaucratic procedures (customs clearance can take several weeks) and lack of security at the port of Douala.

Foreign exporters and investors are strongly advised to check that there are funds available for the project or the materials to be supplied, to ensure that partners are solvent and to respond to invitations to tender only when they are financed by foreign funding agencies. They are also advised to demand cash payment upon confirmation of the order or payment by irrevocable letter of credit confirmed by a first-rate bank.

■ Attitude towards foreign investors

The Investment Code offers a number of incentives, including exemptions from duty and corporation tax. But companies are required to hire Cameroon staff and use natural resources in return for tax breaks. The Investment Code was replaced in 2002 by an Investment Charter offering greater incentives, including a more streamlined tax system, transparency of public tenders, stricter enforcement of international agreements and the setting up of bodies to promote and protect investment. However, enforcement of the charter has made no headway in the last two years.

Under the free point and zone system Cameroon offers foreign investors a range of export incentives. However this system is currently under review and may be abolished. The administrative formalities relating to establishment and the procedures for obtaining the relevant approvals and authorizations are extremely slow. In addition, the inadequacy of the country's transport infrastructure constitutes a major obstacle to the development of the private sector. The problem could be alleviated by privatizing the provision of services, setting up a one-stop shop at the port of Douala, etc. Companies based in the country also have to cope with a heavy tax burden and a largely ineffectual legal and judicial system characterized by circumvention of laws and regulations.

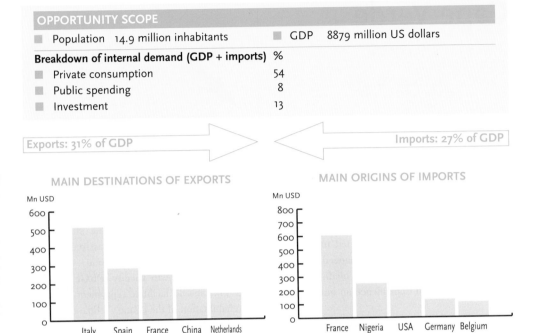

OPPORTUNITY SCOPE

- Population   14.9 million inhabitants
- GDP   8879 million US dollars

Breakdown of internal demand (GDP + imports) %
- Private consumption   54
- Public spending   8
- Investment   13

Exports: 31% of GDP   Imports: 27% of GDP

MAIN DESTINATIONS OF EXPORTS

Mn USD

Italy   Spain   France   China   Netherlands

MAIN ORIGINS OF IMPORTS

Mn USD

France   Nigeria   USA   Germany   Belgium

EXPORTS by products
- Food products 23%
- Commodities 28%
- Fuels 35%
- manufactured goods 5%
- Minerals & metals 6%
- Miscellaneous 3%

IMPORTS by products
- Food products 19%
- Fuels 16%
- Chemical products 13%
- Other manufactured goods 19%
- Transport & capital goods 26%
- Miscellaneous 7%

5

STANDARD OF LIVING / PURCHASING POWER

Indicators	Cameroon	Regional average	DC average
GNP per capita (PPP dollars)	1590	2708	6548
GNP per capita	580	985	3565
Human development index	0.512	0.493	0.702
Wealthiest 10% share of national income	37	35	32
Urban population percentage	49	42	60
Percentage under 15 years old	43	43	32
Number of telephones per 1000 inhabitants	6	32	157
Number of computers per 1000 inhabitants	3	15	64

Cape Verde

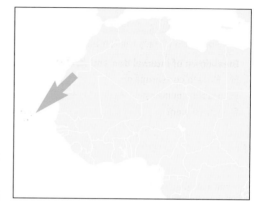

Coface analysis

Short-term: **C**

Medium-term:
Very high risk

RISK ASSESSMENT

The country's economy is hamstrung by a lack of energy and food resources, reflected in a highly unbalanced external account, financed by emigrants' remittances, mounting indebtedness, accumulating arrears and dependence on international aid.

The government has succeeded in sharply reducing the budget deficit and stabilizing the country's sdomestic debt. The implementation of structural reform, while not without repercussions

on economic performance in the short term, enabled the country to qualify for assistance under the IMF's three-year programme – Poverty Reduction and Growth Facility (PRGF) in April 2002. This should facilitate repayment of arrears and rehabilitation of the country's finances. In the longer term Cape Verde could attract more foreign investors by developing its deep-water ports. The stability offered by the currency's peg to the euro should also provide an incentive to investment.

KEY ECONOMIC INDICATORS

US$ million	1998	1999	2000	2001	2002(e)	2003(f)
Economic growth (%)	4.6	8.6	6.8	3	2.5	3.5
Inflation (%)	−1.9	4.4	−2.4	3.7	3	2.5
Public-sector balance/GDP (%)	−17	−18.2	−24.5	−4	−6.6	−5.9
Exports	23	8	24	30	27	30
Imports	208	223	243	218	223	217
Trade balance	−185	−215	−219	−187	−196	−187
Current account balance/GDP (%)	−20.9	−21.1	−20.4	−11	−14.1	−11.1
Foreign debt	255	315	338	502	523	547
Debt service/Exports (%)	6.8	17.9	17.2	12.1	9.9	13
Reserves (import months)	2.3	1.5	1	1.5	1.7	2

e = estimated, f = forecast

Central African Republic

Coface analysis

Short-term: **D**

Medium-term:
Very high risk

RISK ASSESSMENT

The situation of this landlocked country remains alarming. Rising social and political tensions, recurrent coup attempts and border disputes have weakened the country's economic and financial position. Sluggish growth, combined with a growing backlog of arrears, especially of unpaid wages, is making it difficult to draw up an economic recovery programme in co-operation with international financial institutions.

The Central African Republic requires international support to revive its flagging economy and bring its public finances under control.

An improvement in public finances, which are extremely shaky because of the narrow tax base of this poverty-stricken country, would enable the government to obtain new debt rescheduling terms from foreign lenders.

In the long term wide-ranging reforms will have to be implemented so that the country can capitalize on its principal assets: mineral resources (diamonds, gold) and forestry which could attract foreign investment; and vast tracts of arable land that could be farmed to export food to neighbouring countries (Sudan, Chad).

5

KEY ECONOMIC INDICATORS						
US$ million	1998	1999	2000	2001	2002(e)	2003(f)
Economic growth (%)	4.7	3.6	2.3	−0.3	1	1.5
Inflation (%)	−1.9	−1.5	3.1	3.8	2.8	2
Public–sector balance/GDP (%)	−10.7	−10.8	−8.6	−8.7	−9.9	−7
Exports	136	195	166	178	204	191
Imports	159	170	154	139	176	163
Trade balance	−23	25	12	7	8	9
Current account balance/GDP (%)	−8.3	−6.3	−7.9	−4.6	−5.1	−5.8
Foreign debt	919	909	872	868	833	857
Debt service/Exports (%)	19.3	15.6	19.2	17.2	18.4	16.5
Reserves (import months)	6.1	5.6	5.5	5.4	4.6	4.7

e = estimated, f = forecast

Chad

Coface analysis
Very high risk

RISK ASSESSMENT

Growth in 2002 was mainly driven by international investment in Doba oil field operation and financed by foreign funding. From 2004 oil should account for 40 per cent of GDP which, today, is dominated by agriculture. While this would improve the country's economic performance it could create structural problems.

The economic position of this landlocked country, also one of the poorest in the world, remains shaky. Its public finances are extremely unbalanced due to the feeble tax base.

The external account reflects the burden of imports of capital goods for Doba and the drop in cotton earnings. And it has accumulated a large foreign debt, despite being granted rescheduling arrangements.

Against this background, Chad remains reliant on international aid. There is a risk, however, the slow pace of reforms in a difficult political environment and the opaqueness of public finances will lead to lower aid and delays in HIPC-related debt relief.

KEY ECONOMIC INDICATORS

US$ million	1998	1999	2000	2001	2002(e)	2003(f)
Economic growth (%)	6.7	−3.6	0.6	8.9	13.7	8.2
Inflation (%)	4.4	−8	3.8	12.4	6	5.5
Public–sector balance/GDP (%)	−7.6	−10.9	−12.3	−11	−16.2	−11.7
Exports	256	197	177	181	176	196
Imports	267	255	237	547	694	820
Trade balance	−11	−58	−60	−366	−517	−624
Current account balance/GDP (%)	−9	−15	−16	−39	−52	−46
Foreign debt	1103	1142	1116	1329	1483	1624
Debt service/Exports (%)	3.6	10.9	12.7	15.4	19.3	17.9
Reserves (import months)	2.8	2.2	3	1.6	1.4	1.3

e = estimated, f = forecast

Congo

Short-term: **C**

Medium-term:

Coface analysis **Very high risk**

STRENGTHS

- Sizeable natural resources (oil, timber, hydro-electricity, copper, potassium).
- Efforts to restore political stability should facilitate implementation of economic recovery programme.
- Restoration of ties with international financial community enhances prospects (renewed structural reforms, debt relief under HIPC initiative).

WEAKNESSES

- Over-dependent on oil revenues (87 per cent of exports) against a background of depleting reserves.
- Embryonic manufacturing sector. Failure of domestic agricultural sector to feed population generates recurrent imports of food products and consumer goods.
- Extremely high foreign debt secured against oil revenues has led to payment arrears.
- Difficult business environment. Sizeable infra-structure destroyed by three years of civil war (1997–99).

RISK ASSESSMENT

Economic performance faltered as a result of falling oil output and uncertainties surrounding the troubles in the Pool region during spring 2002, which raised fears of a resurgence of civil war.

In 2003 government spending should drive growth by partially offsetting the drop in oil production. However, the financial situation of the country remains shaky, with tax and export revenues vulnerable to oil price fluctuations, high foreign debt, low foreign exchange reserves and recurrent arrears.

The conclusion of an agreement with the IMF and the World Bank on the implementation of a programme to ease the foreign debt burden and generate more resources for poverty alleviation is dependent on faster progress in structural reforms and better management of oil income. The political stability created by the presidential and parliamentary elections in spring 2002 should facilitate moves in that direction.

5

Gabon

Coface analysis

Very high risk

STRENGTHS

- Rich mineral resources mainly of oil and manganese (world's second largest producer) and vast hydroelectric and forestry resources.
- Oil revenues have made Gabon a middle-income country and financed infrastructure development.
- Special policies to diversify the economy and add value to local production.
- Political stability attracts foreign investment.
- Enjoys support of foreign lenders.

WEAKNESSES

- Narrow market (1.2 million inhabitants).
- Heavily dependent on imports as farming satisfies less than 20 per cent of country's food requirements.
- Economy heavily reliant on oil, proven reserves of which are diminishing.
- Inadequate reforms and high restructuring costs place heavy burden on economy and public accounts.
- Heavy foreign debt burden and high borrowing requirement.
- Ineligible for HIPC programme as middle-income country.

RISK ASSESSMENT

The buoyant non-oil sector (timber, manganese, services) helped to drive economic activity, but growth remained modest because of the gradual decline in oil production (70 per cent of tax revenues and 80 per cent of export earnings). In 2003 it may be difficult to keep oil prices at their 2002 second-half levels, which helped partially offset the fall in production and export volumes. This is bound to have an adverse effect on the country's public and external accounts.

To obtain the support of foreign lenders and a fresh rescheduling of its foreign debt in 2003, the Gabonese government must pursue structural reforms, especially the privatization programme, and exercise tighter control on public spending with a view to maintaining sounder public finances.

Social tensions triggered by the reforms and the reduction in purchasing power should not undermine the country's political stability or attractiveness to foreign investors.

KEY ECONOMIC INDICATORS

US$ million	1998	1999	2000	2001	2002(e)	2003(f)
Economic growth (%)	2.1	−6.2	−1.9	1.5	1.9	2.2
Inflation (%)	2.3	−0.7	0.4	2.1	2	2
Public-sector balance/GDP (%)	−14	1.2	11.8	7.6	5	6.1
Exports	1907	2501	3209	2612	2283	2309
Imports	1103	846	924	990	1101	1207
Trade balance	803	1655	2285	1622	1182	1102
Current account balance/GDP (%)	−18.7	−8.8	3.2	−1.1	−4.8	−5.1
Foreign debt	3971	4342	3809	3310	3447	3695
Debt service/Exports (%)	29.4	21.3	16.6	25.5	20.2	19.2
Reserves (import months)	0.1	0.1	0.7	0.1	0.3	0.5

e = estimated, f = forecast

CONDITIONS OF ACCESS TO THE MARKET

■ Market overview

The Gabonese market is very open. The system of customs duties in place is that established by the Economic and Monetary Community of Central Africa (CEMAC). The system's main features include duty free admission of goods from CEMAC (though the volumes of such goods is extremely limited), zero rate of export duty for special products such as medical equipment and stationery, 5 per cent duty for staple commodities, 10 per cent for raw materials and capital goods, 20 per cent for semi-finished goods and miscellaneous items and 30 per cent for consumer goods from third countries.

The most strongly recommended means of payment is the irrevocable and confirmed letter of credit. Documentary collection on presentation of a complete set of bills of lading and bills of exchange should only be used if the customer is well known to the exporter. Bank transfers and cheques, for which the customer is not liable, should be avoided. Exporters should be cautious when dealing with government agencies. For all government orders it is

necessary to obtain a copy of the official purchase order issued by the Budget Expenditure Office at the Ministry of Finance. Orders placed by the government with a foreign supplier have to be countersigned by the Director-General of the Public Accounts Office. Suppliers are advised to check the relevant tax clauses with the departments concerned.

■ Attitude towards foreign investors

The legislative and regulatory environment is extremely liberal and the attitude of government officials generally positive. Investors enjoy freedom of trade through CEMAC, modern instruments of business law through OHADA (Organization for the Harmonization of Business Law), investment security through the Multilateral Investment Guarantee Agency and a guaranteed appeals procedure through the International Centre for the Settlement of International Disputes.

The Investment Charter provides for freedom of enterprise, the right to property (including intellectual property), unrestricted access to foreign currency, free movement of capital, etc. From time to time it is supplemented with special laws (a Forestry Code adopted in December 2001, Investment Code, Mining Act, Oil Act, Labour Code, Competition Act). A one-stop shop, the Private Promotion Investment Agency, was set up in 2002 to provide investors with practical information. The Gabonese Employers Federation gives entrepreneurs proper support and is more proactive than reactive.

Customs duties and VAT are negotiable for large industrial schemes. By 2004 the Mandji Free Zone (Port-Gentil) is due to open its doors to companies

5

engaged in the processing of natural resources, services and the assembly and distribution of finished goods. Companies in these sectors will be eligible for extremely attractive tax incentives and capital transfer provisions (10-year tax exemption, investment- and job-related tax credits, etc).

Wood processing, governed by the new Forestry Code, has tremendous growth potential. Libreville too offers real comparative advantages as a site for the development of services on a regional scale, especially as the regional headquarters of international corporations.

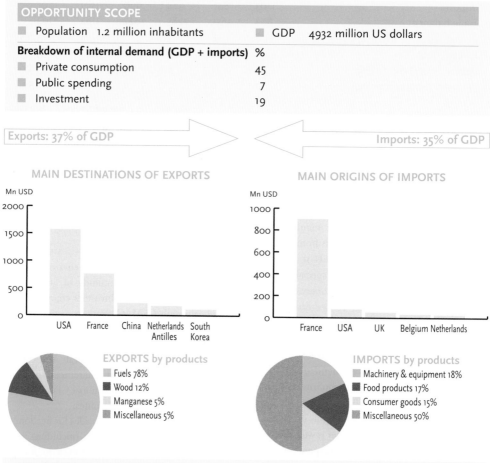

OPPORTUNITY SCOPE

Population 1.2 million inhabitants   GDP   4932 million US dollars

Breakdown of internal demand (GDP + imports) %
- Private consumption — 45
- Public spending — 7
- Investment — 19

Exports: 37% of GDP   Imports: 35% of GDP

MAIN DESTINATIONS OF EXPORTS

Mn USD — USA, France, China, Netherlands Antilles, South Korea

MAIN ORIGINS OF IMPORTS

Mn USD — France, USA, UK, Belgium, Netherlands

EXPORTS by products
- Fuels 78%
- Wood 12%
- Manganese 5%
- Miscellaneous 5%

IMPORTS by products
- Machinery & equipment 18%
- Food products 17%
- Consumer goods 15%
- Miscellaneous 50%

STANDARD OF LIVING / PURCHASING POWER

Indicators	Gabon	Regional average	DC average
GNP per capita (PPP dollars)	5360	2708	6548
GNP per capita	3190	985	3565
Human development index	0.637	0.493	0.702
Wealthiest 10% share of national income	n/a	35	32
Urban population percentage	81	42	60
Percentage under 15 years old	40	43	32
Number of telephones per 1000 inhabitants	32	32	157
Number of computers per 1000 inhabitants	10	15	64

n/a – not available

Ghana

Coface analysis

Short-term: **C**

Medium-term:
Very high risk

STRENGTHS

- Political stability and regional economic and monetary integration in ECOWAS are important assets in the eyes of investors.
- Long-standing structural reform programme backed by foreign lenders.
- Support from foreign lenders should translate into cancellation of foreign debt under HIPC initiative.

WEAKNESSES

- Inadequately diversified economy, with gold and cocoa accounting for two-thirds of export earnings. Vulnerable to external factors (climate, world commodity prices).
- High public debt, substantial arrears and strong inflation.
- Slow pace of privatizations limits much-needed foreign investment for economic diversification.
- Highly dependent on international aid.

RISK ASSESSMENT

Ghana's short-term growth prospects are favourable subject to good climatic conditions. However, structural reform must be stepped up to maintain the country's current growth rate and further diversify its economy.

After years of unsound public finances, which have left Ghana with a huge national debt, improving the country's finances is one of the major challenges facing the government. The country's solvency should remain precarious and will depend on concessional finance and international aid.

Moreover, the external account remains structurally vulnerable to exogenous factors. The country continues to have a large external borrowing requirement and will require international assistance to cover it in the face of weak direct foreign investment.

In 2003 Ghana should reach the 'completion point' under the HIPC initiative, making it eligible for substantial foreign debt relief. It remains to be seen whether the country will subsequently be able to soothe the tensions produced by economic restructuring and take advantage of greater regional integration within ECOWAS.

5

KEY ECONOMIC INDICATORS						
US$ million	1998	1999	2000	2001	2002(e)	2003(f)
Economic growth (%)	4.7	4.4	3.7	4.3	5	5.3
Inflation (%)	14.6	12.4	25.2	32.9	14.1	10
Public-sector balance/GDP (%)	−10.2	−9.8	−10	−9.4	−9.7	−7.3
Exports	2091	2006	1936	1893	2037	2242
Imports	2918	3252	2759	2652	2858	3027
Trade balance	−827	−1246	−823	−759	−821	−785
Current account balance/GDP (%)	−8.8	−13.4	−11.5	−9	−10.2	−8.8
Foreign debt	6883	7214	7020	7332	7473	7715
Debt service/Exports (%)	18.4	17.1	17.9	12.5	12	11.7
Reserves (import months)	1.5	1.4	0.8	1	0.8	0.8

e = estimated, f = forecast

CONDITIONS OF ACCESS TO THE MARKET

■ Market overview

There are no import licences or exchange controls. The country has comprehensive copyright protection laws, though they are not properly enforced. Industrial property is better protected. Trademarks and company logos receive proper and adequate protection, provided they have been registered beforehand. Customs duties vary between 0 per cent and 25 per cent. Some products from the Economic Community of West African States (ECOWAS) are exempt from customs duty. Products from non-ECOWAS countries are subject to 0.5 per cent duty (ECOWAS levy). A new 0.5 per cent tax has also been introduced to provision the Export Development Investment Fund.

Since 1 April 2000 goods inspections at the point of entry have been carried out by GSBV (a Bureau Véritas/Ghana Standards Board joint venture) and by Gateway Services Limited (GSL, a Cotecna/Ghanaian Customs joint venture). GSBV inspects goods at the airport and at land borders, whereas GSL conducts inspections at the ports of Tema and Takoradi.

VAT is applicable at a flat rate of 12.5 per cent on the customs value of goods, in addition to customs duties and levies.

Foreign companies, however, have to come to terms with a stifling bureaucracy, a somewhat arbitrary legal and judicial system subject to outside interference (even if it can be said to be adequate for the job) and poor financing (the banking system is not interested in industrial and business investment).

■ Attitude towards foreign investors

To set up a joint venture with a local partner, a minimum investment of US$10,000 is required. The equity requirement is five times greater for wholly foreign-owned companies. Purchasing and sales groups are required to invest US$300,000 and employ at least 10 Ghanaian staff. These conditions are not applicable to portfolio management firms and companies engaged in the export of Ghanaian products.

OPPORTUNITY SCOPE

■ Population 19 million inhabitants   ■ GDP   5190 million US dollars

Breakdown of internal demand (GDP + imports) %
■ Private consumption 49
■ Public spending 9
■ Investment 15

Exports: 49% of GDP   Imports: 70% of GDP

MAIN DESTINATIONS OF EXPORTS

Mn USD — Netherlands, USA, UK, Germany, Nigeria

MAIN ORIGINS OF IMPORTS

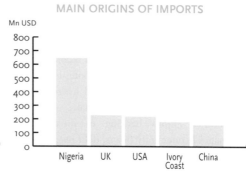

Mn USD — Nigeria, UK, USA, Ivory Coast, China

EXPORTS by products
■ Food products 51%
■ Fuels 4%
■ Commodities 10%
■ Minerals & metals 8%
■ Manufactured goods 19%
■ Miscellaneous 8%

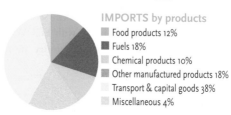

IMPORTS by products
■ Food products 12%
■ Fuels 18%
■ Chemical products 10%
■ Other manufactured products 18%
■ Transport & capital goods 38%
■ Miscellaneous 4%

STANDARD OF LIVING / PURCHASING POWER

Indicators	Ghana	Regional average	DC average
GNP per capita (PPP dollars)	1910	2708	6548
GNP per capita	340	985	3565
Human development index	0.548	0.493	0.702
Wealthiest 10% share of national income	30	35	32
Urban population percentage	38	42	60
Percentage under 15 years old	41	43	32
Number of telephones per 1000 inhabitants	12	32	157
Number of computers per 1000 inhabitants	3	15	64

5

Guinea

Short-term: **C**

Medium-term:

Coface analysis **Very high risk**

STRENGTHS

- Vast mineral resources (world's second largest producer and exporter of bauxite, iron, gold and diamonds) and substantial hydroelectric, agricultural and tourism potential.
- Country enjoys backing of international financial community (loans, debt rescheduling and admission to debt relief under HIPC initiative).
- Steady though slow progress in structural reforms.
- Customs and monetary union with ECOWAS member states should make country more attractive to investors.

WEAKNESSES

- Country's regional environment (Guinea-Bissau, Sierra Leone, Liberia) has generated refugee, guerrilla and smuggling problems. Although stabilizing for now, problems may resurface.
- Above factors plus tense political and financial climate in country discourage foreign investment.
- Inadequate investment limits construction of transport and energy infrastructure, economic diversification and agricultural development (65 per cent of working population) – all essential to poverty alleviation.
- Consequently, country's income overly dependent on bauxite exports.

RISK ASSESSMENT

The country's economic prospects, though encouraging, remain shaky. The easing of border tensions and intensified co-operation with Sierra Leone and Liberia have allowed displaced persons to return, mines to reopen and the economy to pick up, albeit short of its potential. The recovery has also enabled the country to pursue structural reforms and benefit from the continued support of the international financial community, with the prospect of a large write-off of its foreign debt under the HIPC initiative.

However, this trend could be reversed given the Guinean government's lack of room for manoeuvre within a volatile regional environment (Liberia). The public accounts remain imbalanced and the external account continues to deteriorate under the combined impact of mining imports and weak aluminium prices.

Against this background, Guinea's solvency will rest on continued substantial investment inflows into the mining sector and cancellation of its foreign debt.

KEY ECONOMIC INDICATORS

US$ million	1998	1999	2000	2001	2002(e)	2003(f)
Economic growth (%)	4.5	3.9	2.1	3.6	4.2	4.9
Inflation (%)	5.1	4.6	6.8	5.4	3.6	3.5
Public-sector balance/GDP (%)	−3.6	−5.4	−5.6	−7.6	−6.4	−7.5
Exports	717	646	667	731	766	802
Imports	577	582	583	562	643	722
Trade balance	140	64	83	169	123	80
Current account balance/GDP (%)	−6.1	−7.2	−8.2	−5.2	−8.6	−9.2
Foreign debt	3658	3603	3594	3609	3647	3657
Debt service/Exports (%)	46.6	27.1	30	28.7	26.1	25.7
Reserves (import months)	2.9	2.5	1.8	2.5	2.8	2.8

e = estimated, f = forecast

CONDITIONS OF ACCESS TO THE MARKET

■ Market overview

Guinea is a WTO member and the country's market is very open. Average import duty (excluding internal levies, at times high for certain products) is around 16 per cent. The maximum rate of duty is 32 per cent plus 18 per cent VAT.

Import regulations do not pose any special problems, although there is a vast and thriving grey market. The banking sector is active and is made up largely of foreign banks. But its growth is checked by the narrowness of the official currency market and the poor creditworthiness of importers. There are no restrictions on currency transfers, but the shortage of foreign currency on the official market often causes importers to turn to the grey market. The 2 per cent discount at which the local currency trades on this market marks up the price of imported products proportionately.

■ Attitude towards foreign investors

Guinea has adopted and ratified the OHADA treaty (Organization for the Harmonization of Business Law in Africa) and plans to adopt the WAEMU's liberal common external tariff in the medium term. This should enhance investment security. An Arbitration Board and a new Penal Code were established in 1999. While the Investment Code has been amended, in practice the legal system offers few safeguards. Appeals are difficult to obtain and rarely successful. Industrial property protection exists but the system is ineffective in the face of unfair competition from products imported through the grey market.

The legacy of the past and the power wielded by the bureaucracy are everyday obstacles, despite the introduction of incentives encouraging foreign investors to set up businesses alone or with a Guinean partner.

■ Foreign exchange regulations

Guinea is not a member of the CFA franc area, but is one of the IMAO (West Africa Monetary Institute). The Guinean franc is not convertible, though it is de facto pegged to the US dollar and changes in value in response to fluctuations in the value of the dollar. Since 1 September 1999 the Guinean franc's exchange rate has been set by an auction market located at the central bank. Auctions are attended by the country's key financial players as well as international financial institutions and are conducted on the basis of supply and demand.

5

OPPORTUNITY SCOPE

▪ Population	7.4 million inhabitants	▪ GDP	3012 million US dollars

Breakdown of internal demand (GDP + imports) %
- ▪ Private consumption — 59
- ▪ Public spending — 5
- ▪ Investment — 17

Exports: 26% of GDP ➡️ ⬅️ Imports: 31% of GDP

MAIN DESTINATIONS OF EXPORTS

Mn USD

Belgium · USA · Spain · Ireland · France

MAIN ORIGINS OF IMPORTS

Mn USD

France · USA · Ivory Coast · Belgium · China

EXPORTS by products
- ▪ Bauxite 44%
- ▪ Aluminium 15%
- ▪ Gold 18%
- ▪ Diamonds 4%
- ▪ Miscellaneous 19%

IMPORTS by products
- ▪ Semi-finished & capital goods 52%
- ▪ Fuels 13%
- ▪ Food products 19%
- ▪ Miscellaneous 16%

STANDARD OF LIVING / PURCHASING POWER

Indicators	Guinea	Regional average	DC average
GNP per capita (PPP dollars)	1930	2708	6548
GNP per capita	450	985	3565
Human development index	0.414	0.493	0.702
Wealthiest 10% share of national income	32	35	32
Urban population percentage	33	42	60
Percentage under 15 years old	44	43	32
Number of telephones per 1000 inhabitants	8	32	157
Number of computers per 1000 inhabitants	4	15	64

Ivory Coast

Coface analysis

Short-term: **D**

Medium-term:
Very high risk

STRENGTHS

- Strategically located in the heart of West Africa.
- Great economic potential backed by good transport infrastructure.
- Important transit route for Burkina Faso and Mali.
- Membership of West Africa Monetary Union provides monetary stability.

WEAKNESSES

- Dependent on agricultural exports (cocoa – world's largest producer – coffee, cotton) and, therefore, vulnerable to exogenous factors (climate, world commodity prices).
- Public finances and external account weakened by dependence.
- Foreign investors could be put off for a long time by recurrent political, social and ethnic tensions in the country since end-1999.
- Delays in structural reforms.

RISK ASSESSMENT

The de facto division of the country since September 2002 has badly damaged economic prospects, despite encouraging initial forecasts for the year. At the time, the international financial community had restored support, a government of national unity had been formed and foreign exchange earnings were expected to increase on the back of firm world cocoa prices.

The renewal of hostilities has plunged the country into a third year of recession. Transport and economic activity are paralysed in the north. The widespread climate of insecurity threatens the entire cocoa sector. The government has had to interrupt its spending programme to bring under control the country's finances, hit by the slump in tax revenues. Moreover, cancellation of the external public debt under the HIPC initiative has been postponed.

The general deterioration continues to have a negative impact on corporate solvency and could trigger a new series of defaults.

Economic recovery will depend on the restoration of long-lasting political stability. However, this has never seemed further away, because of the sharp escalation in political tensions that have plagued the country for several years.

5

KEY ECONOMIC INDICATORS					
US$ million	1998	1999	2000	2001	2002(e)
Economic growth (%)	5.8	1.6	−2.3	−0.9	−1
Inflation (%)	4.7	0.7	2.5	4.4	4.8
Public-sector balance/GDP (%)	−3	−3.4	−1.7	0.9	−4
Exports	4.1	4.5	3.8	3.7	3.8
Imports	2.8	2.6	2.3	2.2	2.3
Trade balance	1.4	1.8	1.5	1.4	1.5
Current account balance/GDP (%)	−4.1	−2.4	−3.5	−3.1	−2.3
Foreign debt	15.6	14.6	13	13.6	13.8
Debt service/Exports (%)	55	31	37	32	32
Reserves (import months)	1.9	1.4	1.7	2.7	2.6

e = estimated, f = forecast

CONDITIONS OF ACCESS TO THE MARKET

■ Means of Entry

In 2000 and 2001 there were no significant changes to the regulations governing the conditions of access to the Ivory Coast market. Some exemptions from customs duty have been abolished and flat-rate VAT introduced. No progress has been made in the liberalization of the services trade.

The introduction of WAMEU's Common External Tariff (CET) has been accompanied by a reduction in the maximum nominal rate of customs duty vis-à-vis third countries. In 2002 the maximum rate of duty was 20 per cent. There is no way of knowing whether the average protection rate has fallen since that date. The rate today is 10.6 per cent, or 23.4 per cent after VAT. The former customs arrangements and tax laws have been combined since 1 July 1999 in a single law consisting of four rates of duty: 0 per cent, 5 per cent, 10 per cent and 20 per cent (the CET rate applicable since 1 January 2000).

A 1997 study estimated that the CET's introduction on 1 January 2000 would increase the average rate of duty to 13.6 per cent, or 26.8 per cent after VAT. However, this has not been borne out by any recent study. There are import restrictions on 100 per cent cotton fabric, though licences are granted automatically today. Petroleum products are controlled by a sole entity: SIR (Société Ivoirienne de Raffinage).

■ Attitude towards foreign investors

From 1995 Ivory Coast adopted a new Investment Code generally regarded as investment friendly. The Code provides for two different systems according to the size and type of investment. Both systems offer five to eight year tax exemptions. Under the declaration system (applicable to investments in excess of 5 million francs) there is 5 per cent flat-rate import duty on equipment and materials used in approved investment schemes. The Code does not differentiate between origins of investment, and applies to both local and foreign investment. However, legal uncertainty is a major concern for companies.

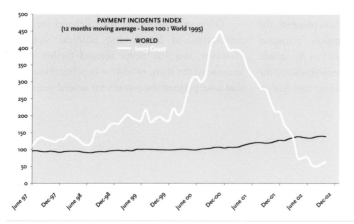

PAYMENT INCIDENTS INDEX
(12 months moving average - base 100 : World 1995)
— WORLD
— Ivory Coast

OPPORTUNITY SCOPE

- Population   16 million inhabitants
- GDP   9370 million US dollars

Breakdown of internal demand (GDP + imports) %
- Private consumption   52
- Public spending   7
- Investment   9

Exports: 46% of GDP   Imports: 39% of GDP

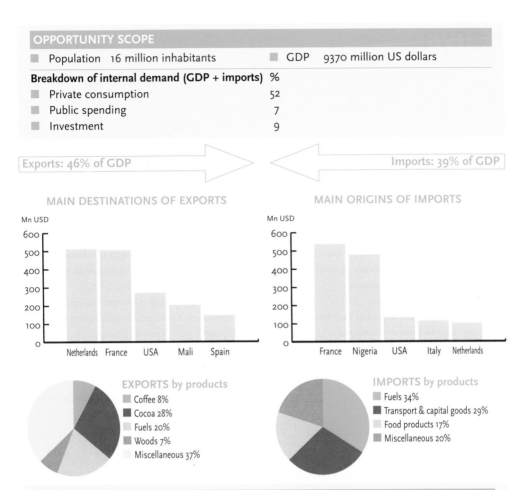

MAIN DESTINATIONS OF EXPORTS

Mn USD

Netherlands   France   USA   Mali   Spain

MAIN ORIGINS OF IMPORTS

Mn USD

France   Nigeria   USA   Italy   Netherlands

EXPORTS by products
- Coffee 8%
- Cocoa 28%
- Fuels 20%
- Woods 7%
- Miscellaneous 37%

IMPORTS by products
- Fuels 34%
- Transport & capital goods 29%
- Food products 17%
- Miscellaneous 20%

5

STANDARD OF LIVING / PURCHASING POWER

Indicators	Ivory Coast	Regional average	DC average
GNP per capita (PPP dollars)	1500	2708	6548
GNP per capita	600	985	3565
Human development index	0.428	0.493	0.702
Wealthiest 10% share of national income	29	35	32
Urban population percentage	46	42	60
Percentage under 15 years old	42	43	32
Number of telephones per 1000 inhabitants	18	32	157
Number of computers per 1000 inhabitants	6	15	64

Kenya

Short-term: **C**

Medium-term:
High risk

Coface analysis

STRENGTHS

- Greater economic diversification than most African countries; significant agricultural (tea, coffee) and tourism resources.
- Economic hub of East Africa (transport, financial services, regional headquarters of many organisations and companies).
- Growing regional integration within COMESA important asset in investors' eyes.

WEAKNESSES

- Economy highly dependent on climatic factors that affect agriculture, hydropower generation and, therefore, industrial activity.
- Erratic relationship with international financial community. Government anti-corruption drive imposed by foreign lenders encountering strong resistance.
- These factors deter investment needed to trigger sustained growth.
- Huge challenges posed by poverty, unemployment and AIDS pandemic.

RISK ASSESSMENT

Despite its assets, Kenya is unable to generate the level of growth required for its economic development partly because of a lack of business confidence and partly because of lack of financing. Its growth prospects for 2003 remain uncertain, depending as they do on the restoration of assistance from foreign lenders as part of a new programme that would lead to the cancellation of the country's debt under the HIPC initiative.

While the conditions for such support (improvement of public finances, real public sector reform and intensification of anti-corruption drive) are gradually being fulfilled, the incoming government formed out of the December 2002 elections, marked by the sweeping victory of Mwai Kibaki and of his supporting coalition, must step up its efforts.

In any event, the support of foreign lenders is essential to improving the country's solvency and reducing its domestic debt.

KEY ECONOMIC INDICATORS						
US$ billion	1998	1999	2000	2001	2002(e)	2003(f)
Economic growth (%)	1.8	1.4	−0.3	1	1	2.5
Inflation (%)	5.8	2.6	6.2	0.8	2	2.2
Public-sector balance/GDP (%)	−0.7	0.1	−5	−3.5	−1.9	−1.8
Exports	2	1.8	1.8	1.8	1.8	1.9
Imports	3	2.7	3	2.9	2.8	2.9
Trade balance	−1	−0.9	−1.2	−1.1	−1	−1.1
Current account balance/GDP (%)	−3.2	−2.2	−3	−3.2	−3.4	−4.3
Foreign debt	6.5	5.6	5.3	5.3	5.2	5.3
Debt service/Exports (%)	21.4	22.3	14.4	14	13.3	11.1
Reserves (import months)	2.4	2.7	2.8	3.4	3.4	3.1

e = estimated, f = forecast

CONDITIONS OF ACCESS TO THE MARKET

Market overview

The Kenyan market is open to various types of investment, especially capital and consumer goods that meet the country's requirements. Only some products (arms, livestock, pesticides, etc) are banned or restricted. A number of protectionist measures exist essentially in connection with foreign ownership of farmland and shareholdings in telecommunications, insurance and the Stock Exchange.

Tariff barriers mainly comprise suspended duties (temporary surcharges) on maize, sugar, wheat, rice and natural fibres, cotton, etc. These duties, which vary between 20 per cent and 80 per cent, apply in addition to other duties and levies. Import duties on certain goods which undergo transformation in Kenya are fairly reasonable. The system of customs duty and VAT has been simplified to facilitate assessment and collection. There are five rates of customs duty: 0 per cent, 3 per cent, 5 per cent, 15 per cent, and 35 per cent. Since the liberalization of trade as well as the currency market, payment difficulties have become rare in the private sector and are usually due to a poor choice of local partner and failure to take elementary precautions.

Means of entry

Some formalities, such as pre-inspection of imports, must be complied with. The US dollar and the pound sterling are the most widely used international units of account, although the euro is also accepted. If there are doubts about a Kenyan partner's financial standing, status enquiries can be carried out by the CFCE (*Chambre français de commerce extérieur*), the PEE (economic desk) of the country concerned, a local credit rating firm or a local bank. At all events, it is advisable to take certain precautions with regard to payments and so to use tested procedures such as presentation of documents against payment, guaranteed bank cheques, transfers and confirmed letters of credit. Intertek Testing Services (for Europe, excluding Great Britain and Ireland) and Cotecna are the two inspection companies operating in Kenya from 2001 until 2003.

Attitude towards foreign investors

The Kenyan government is torn between its desire to attract foreign investment and a desire to Africanize an economy largely in the hands of Kenyans of Indian and British origin. Foreign investment is keenly welcomed by the Kenyan government, especially where it helps to promote exports, technology transfers and jobs.

Growth sectors include agriculture (horticulture), telecommunications, energy (currently undergoing privatization) and some utilities (water supply). There are few restrictive or discriminatory measures, though there are *ad hoc* regulations limiting access to specific sectors.

5

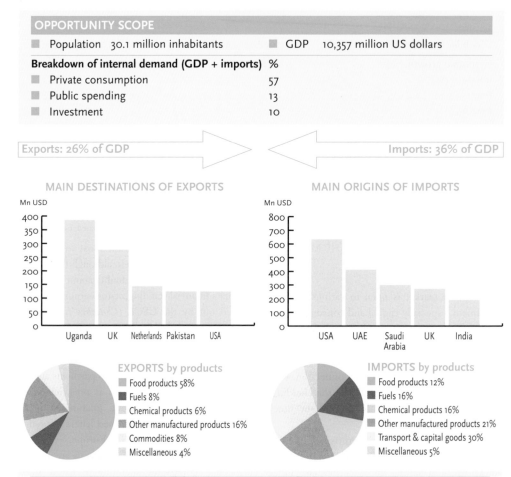

OPPORTUNITY SCOPE

■ Population   30.1 million inhabitants   ■ GDP   10,357 million US dollars

Breakdown of internal demand (GDP + imports) %
■ Private consumption   57
■ Public spending   13
■ Investment   10

Exports: 26% of GDP   Imports: 36% of GDP

MAIN DESTINATIONS OF EXPORTS

Mn USD

Uganda   UK   Netherlands   Pakistan   USA

MAIN ORIGINS OF IMPORTS

Mn USD

USA   UAE   Saudi Arabia   UK   India

EXPORTS by products
■ Food products 58%
■ Fuels 8%
■ Chemical products 6%
■ Other manufactured products 16%
■ Commodities 8%
■ Miscellaneous 4%

IMPORTS by products
■ Food products 12%
■ Fuels 16%
■ Chemical products 16%
■ Other manufactured products 21%
■ Transport & capital goods 30%
■ Miscellaneous 5%

STANDARD OF LIVING / PURCHASING POWER

Indicators	Kenya	Regional average	DC average
GNP per capita (PPP dollars)	1010	2708	6548
GNP per capita	350	985	3565
Human development index	0.513	0.493	0.702
Wealthiest 10% share of national income	36	35	32
Urban population percentage	33	42	60
Percentage under 15 years old	44	43	32
Number of telephones per 1000 inhabitants	10	32	157
Number of computers per 1000 inhabitants	5	15	64

Madagascar

Short-term: **D**

Medium-term:
Coface analysis **Very high risk**

RISK ASSESSMENT

The encouraging economic performance posted by Madagascar, one of the world's poorest countries, was cut short in 2002 by the contested results of the presidential elections held in December 2001. Each of the candidates stood his ground, while attempting to destroy the other's power base and paralysing the country's institutions.

Almost all the sectors of the economy have been affected by the political turmoil. Transport infrastructure has been damaged. The manufacturing activities of the industrial processing zone, which last year accounted for 40 per cent of the country's exports, have ground to a halt. Against this background consumption and investment have fallen, international aid has been suspended, the economy has been plunged into a recession and prices have risen.

The outlook for 2003 depends on restoration of institutional stability. The parliamentary elections held in December 2002, by facilitating the implementation of a reconstruction programme and renewed foreign lending, should help revive the economy.

Still, one of the main challenges facing the new government is improving the country's finances and current account position. But a resurgence of tensions cannot be ruled out as its promises will be difficult to finance.

5

KEY ECONOMIC INDICATORS						
US$ million	1998	1999	2000	2001	2002(e)	2003(f)
Economic growth (%)	3.9	4.7	4.8	6	−11.9	7.8
Inflation (%)	6.2	9.9	11.9	7.4	15.3	6.2
Public–sector balance/GDP (%)	−9.3	−6.4	−6.4	−8.1	−7.7	−7.4
Exports	520	582	839	1011	547	721
Imports	673	749	943	995	670	885
Trade balance	−153	−167	−104	16	−123	−164
Current account balance/GDP (%)	−8	−6.6	−6.5	−2	−5.8	−7.4
Foreign debt	4421	4551	4235	4390	4499	4619
Debt service/Exports (%)	26.2	16.2	10.6	5.6	8.4	7.8
Reserves (import months)	1.7	2.1	2.2	3.1	4.1	3.5

e = estimated, f = forecast

Malawi

Short-term: **D**

Medium-term:
Very high risk

Coface analysis

RISK ASSESSMENT

Landlocked, densely populated and lacking natural resources other than agriculture, Malawi is going through a difficult period marked by a severe food crisis. This makes the tasks and challenges facing the government ever more daunting.

After two years of recession economic recovery remains uncertain. In any event it will be modest. The need to rehabilitate public finances after a period of fiscal laxity and to maintain tight monetary policies aimed at reducing inflation considerably limits the government's scope of action. Its room for

manoeuvre is also restricted by the need to find favour with the international financial community, whose support will be required to cover the country's external financial needs (heavily swollen in 2002 by large-scale imports of foodstuffs).

In the longer term, the government must step up the pace of structural reforms in order to combat poverty and AIDS, diversify the economy and attract foreign investors. However, it will become increasingly difficult to implement the relevant policies as the political climate deteriorates in the run-up to the 2004 elections.

KEY ECONOMIC INDICATORS

US$ million	1998	1999	2000	2001	2002(e)	2003(f)
Economic growth (%)	2	4	1.7	−1.5	−1.3	2.1
Inflation (%)	26.2	44.8	29.6	27.2	17.3	10.7
Public–sector balance/GDP (%)	−11.5	−12.6	−15	−15.9	−13.4	−10.7
Exports	539	447	406	407	421	451
Imports	579	673	563	582	768	657
Trade balance	−40	−226	−157	−175	−347	−206
Current account balance/GDP (%)	−11.6	−17.1	−14.2	−12.9	−26.2	−14.4
Foreign debt	2479	2608	2674	2736	2803	2883
Debt service/Exports (%)	17.6	16.7	20.2	20.5	19.4	19.6
Reserves (import months)	3.9	3.5	4.1	3.5	1.6	3.4

e = estimated, f = forecast

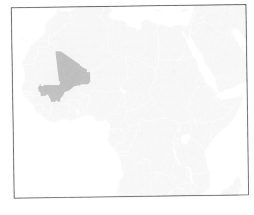

Mali

Short-term: **B**

Medium-term:

Coface analysis **High risk**

RISK ASSESSMENT

Mali's encouraging performance, spurred by a good cotton harvest in 2002 that benefited the textile industry, and growth in gold mining, should not mask the exposure of its little-diversified economy to two exogenous factors: climate and world commodity price fluctuations.

This vulnerability is reflected in the country's high external borrowing requirement and dependence on international aid and remittances from expatriate workers. It is also the driving force behind the country's policy of seeking cancellation

of its foreign debt under the HIPC programme.

The challenge facing the government formed out of the presidential and parliamentary elections of 2002 is to step up the pace of structural reforms, especially in the cotton sector. The fragmentation of the political system (the elections did not produce a majority), electoral apathy (26 per cent turn-out at the parliamentary elections) and trade union opposition may well make it difficult to implement the policies demanded by foreign lenders.

5

KEY ECONOMIC INDICATORS						
US$ million	1998	1999	2000	2001	2002(e)	2003(f)
Economic growth (%)	3.8	6.7	3.7	1.5	9.3	5.3
Inflation (%)	4.1	−1.2	−0.7	5.2	3	2
Public-sector balance/GDP (%)	−8.1	−8.7	−9.7	−11	−10.3	−7.9
Exports	550	571	546	740	787	830
Imports	547	605	594	728	746	791
Trade balance	3	−34	−47	12	40	39
Current account balance/GDP (%)	−9.3	−10.8	−13.0	−14.1	−11.9	−11
Foreign debt	3296	3019	2956	2967	3110	3209
Debt service/Exports (%)	13	14	12	9	13	13
Reserves (import months)	4.5	5	4.9	3.6	3.8	3.8

e = estimated, f = forecast

Mauritania

Coface analysis

Short-term: **C**

Medium-term:
Very high risk

STRENGTHS

- Mineral resources (high quality iron ore, copper, cobalt, gypsum, oil and diamond potential) likely to attract foreign investors.
- Progress in structural reform wins support of international financial community.
- Large debt write-off under HIPC initiative.
- Encouraging signs of greater regional co-operation with Morocco and Senegal.

WEAKNESSES

- Narrow economic base. Small market (2.7 million inhabitants), with iron and fisheries generating almost all foreign exchange earnings.
- Insufficiently diversified economy vulnerable to exogenous factors (climate, world commodity prices).
- Dependent on food imports because of geography (desert) and climate.
- Inadequate infrastructure inhibits development of resources.
- Ongoing inter-community strife.

RISK ASSESSMENT

The high rate of economic growth was bolstered by public as well private sector investment. Despite a slowdown in 2002 due to the impact of poor climate on farming and livestock (and therefore on people's incomes), the debt write-off granted to the country since attainment of the completion point under the HIPC initiative should confirm the economy's upward trend. But these encouraging indicators have done little to reduce poverty levels (50 per cent of the population).

The economy is underpinned by tight budgetary and monetary policies. Continued structural reforms are contributing to economic modernization and diversification.

While the budget balance for 2002 reflected payment by the EU of sizeable royalties under a fisheries agreement, Mauritania remains dependent on foreign capital to cover its borrowing requirement, despite cancellation of its foreign debt. Imports needed to offset the effects of the drought and the currency's depreciation are in fact causing further deterioration in the foreign accounts position and delays in payment by local companies.

KEY ECONOMIC INDICATORS

US$ million	1998	1999	2000	2001	2002(e)	2003(f)
Economic growth (%)	3.7	4.1	5	4.6	4.5	5.5
Inflation (%)	8	4.1	3.3	4.7	4	3.8
Public–sector balance/GDP (%)	2.1	2.2	−4.5	−5.6	−1.4	−2.2
Exports	369	333	359	345	329	348
Imports	358	305	343	357	382	401
Trade balance	11	28	16	−12	−53	−53
Current account balance/GDP (%)	−6.4	−4.3	−6	−10	0	−9.4
Foreign Debt	2589	2528	2474	2471	2440	2417
Debt service/Exports (%)	32.5	22.4	24	19	12.3	11
Reserves (import months)	4.6	5.8	6.2	6.5	7.8	7.6

e = estimated, f = forecast

CONDITIONS OF ACCESS TO THE MARKET

Market overview

The Mauritanian market is totally open to imports, except for certain products banned on grounds of religion (alcohol) or security (arms). The only document required of importers is the Advance Import Notification for transactions in excess of US$5000. EU and African, Carribean and Pacific (ACP) countries pay no customs duties on products listed in the first 21 chapters of the Tariff Nomenclature. ECOWAS countries continue to be exempt from customs duties for local specialities and handicrafts, despite Mauritania's withdrawal from this organisation in January 2000. The average rate of customs duty is about 20 per cent.

Imports can be paid for by letter of credit or documentary credit, but as Mauritanian buyers tend to settle late exporters are advised to use irrevocable letters of credit, preferably confirmed by a French bank. Payments need not involve currency transfers if they are made through legally held foreign accounts funded through a proportion of unrepatriated export earnings, such as income from fishery exports.

The rate of default among private Mauritanian buyers varies.

Foreign exchange regulations

The local currency, the ouguiya, is freely convertible inside Mauritania for business transactions. Over the last two years the government has steadily relaxed exchange controls. Since January 2001 Mauritanian residents have been allowed to open interest-bearing foreign currency accounts. The rate of interest earned depends on the deal struck with the bank.

Attitude towards foreign investors

The lack of impartiality of the Mauritanian judicial system and a certain degree of inequality before the law, especially in matters of taxation, creates an uncertain business environment. Vague property ownership laws add to the uncertainty, although there has been a sharp improvement in this area recently. It remains difficult at times to enforce a ruling against some Mauritanian buyers.

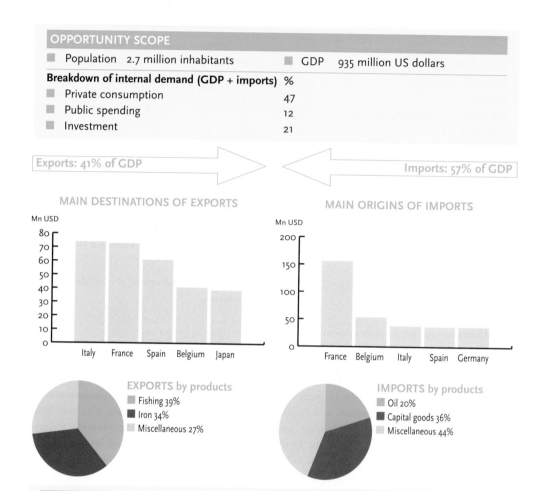

OPPORTUNITY SCOPE

- Population   2.7 million inhabitants
- GDP   935 million US dollars

Breakdown of internal demand (GDP + imports) %
- Private consumption   47
- Public spending   12
- Investment   21

Exports: 41% of GDP

Imports: 57% of GDP

MAIN DESTINATIONS OF EXPORTS

Mn USD

Italy   France   Spain   Belgium   Japan

MAIN ORIGINS OF IMPORTS

Mn USD

France   Belgium   Italy   Spain   Germany

EXPORTS by products
- Fishing 39%
- Iron 34%
- Miscellaneous 27%

IMPORTS by products
- Oil 20%
- Capital goods 36%
- Miscellaneous 44%

STANDARD OF LIVING / PURCHASING POWER

Indicators	Mauritania	Regional average	DC average
GNP per capita (PPP dollars)	1630	2708	6548
GNP per capita	370	985	3565
Human development index	0.438	0.493	0.702
Wealthiest 10% share of national income	28	35	32
Urban population percentage	58	42	60
Percentage under 15 years old	44	43	32
Number of telephones per 1000 inhabitants	7	32	157
Number of computers per 1000 inhabitants	9	15	64

Mauritius

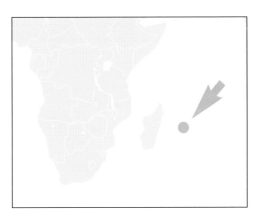

Coface analysis

Short-term: **A3**

Medium-term:
Quite low risk

STRENGTHS

- One of Africa's highest per capita GDP ratios and human development indexes.
- Economic diversification into high added-value activities (new technologies, financial services).
- Export processing zones attract foreign investment and stimulate exports.
- Low external financing needs and, therefore, reasonable level of foreign debt.
- Good economic and financial relations with Western countries and Africa. Promotion of closer ties with India and China.

WEAKNESSES

- Economy highly vulnerable to developments in sugar industry (production, processing, household consumption) and, therefore, to climate (especially cyclones).
- Rising unemployment underlines need to enhance technical skills of workforce.
- Investment in education and vocational training is drain on public finances, already strained by narrow tax base.
- Mounting domestic public debt.

RISK ASSESSMENT

The pace of economic growth slowed in 2002. The cyclone that struck the island in January caused extensive damage to crops as well as tourist and industrial infrastructure. In addition the world economic slowdown has hit export processing zone business (26 per cent of GDP and 66 per cent of exports) and pushed up unemployment.

The projected recovery in 2003 should be moderate. Against a background of uncertainties about the climate and tourism earnings the government is tackling the hole in public finances by reducing investment spending and raising taxes. While such measures may fuel social tensions the country's political stability should facilitate their implementation.

In any event, the government has room for manoeuvre thanks to the healthy external account position and low foreign debt, which carries no risk of default.

5

KEY ECONOMIC INDICATORS

US$ million	1998	1999	2000	2001	2002(e)	2003(f)
Economic growth (%)	6	5.9	7.2	6.1	3.8	4.5
Inflation (%)	5.4	7.9	4.4	6	6.8	6
Public–sector balance/GDP (%)	−3.7	−4.6	−4.3	−7.1	−6.5	−5.6
Exports	1606	1680	1525	1633	1625	1670
Imports	2016	2046	2006	1913	1917	2012
Trade balance	−411	−366	−480.6	−280	−292	−342
Current account balance/GDP (%)	−2.8	−1.5	−1.6	1.8	1.5	0.2
Foreign debt	2482	2464	2374	2442	2420	2554
Debt service/Exports (%)	7	7.6	7.9	9.8	6	9.7
Reserves (import months)	3.6	3.5	4	4.7	5.1	5.3

e = estimated, f = forecast

CONDITIONS OF ACCESS TO THE MARKET

■ Market overview

Mauritius has been a full member of the WTO since the 1994 Marrakesh Summit. It signed the New York Convention on International Arbitration in June 1996 and ratified it in October 2002. It has dismantled tariff barriers under a series of regional trade agreements and in 1998 introduced 10 per cent flat-rate VAT, which was raised to 15 per cent in the 2002–03 budget.

Import licences remain in force for only three product categories: prohibited (dangerous items such as arms and explosives; vehicle spare parts); supervised or subject to government approval (foodstuffs, energy and pharmaceuticals); unrestricted or formality free.

Tariff barriers include:
- The system of customs duties, adopted in 1994, which differentiates between exporting countries benefiting from a preferential tariff (European Union, the United States, COMESA, SADC) and the 25 or so countries subject to a general tariff. Import duties under this system vary between 0 per cent and 80 per cent;
- Reduced rates of duty on certain products under regional agreements seeking to promote free trade areas;
- Excise duties on four broad categories of imported and/or locally manufactured products (wines and spirits, cigarettes, petrol and motor vehicles). Ranging from 15 per cent to 400 per cent ad valorem for imported products, excise duties can be as high as 255 per cent for locally manufactured products (cigarettes).
- VAT-free access for some products (staples and pharmaceuticals) and services (education, transport, electricity and water).
- Customs duties of between 0 per cent and 80 per cent are applied to all imported products. Since 1998 duties have been cut significantly.

Non-tariff barriers include:
- Import licences and price controls for staples, 30 of which are also subject to administered pricing or profit control;
- Government monopolies with exclusive powers to import so-called 'strategic' products.

The two largest monopolies are:
- The STC (State Trading Corporation), which imports almost all the rice, wheat flour, petroleum products and cement (up to 50 per cent of requirements). Rice also enjoys a subsidy.
- The AMB (Agricultural Marketing Board), which holds an import monopoly for onions, garlic, maize, certain seeds, soya, cotton seeds and certain animal feeds. However, since 1998, approved private agents have been allowed to import potatoes subject to certain conditions but no price controls. The purpose of the AMB is to regulate markets and protect local producers.

OPPORTUNITY SCOPE

■ Population 1.2 million inhabitants   ■ GDP   4381 million US dollars

Breakdown of internal demand (GDP + imports) %
■ Private consumption   41
■ Public spending   7
■ Investment   16

Exports: 64% of GDP   Imports: 67% of GDP

MAIN DESTINATIONS OF EXPORTS

Mn USD

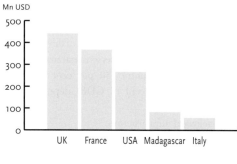

UK   France   USA   Madagascar   Italy

MAIN ORIGINS OF IMPORTS

Mn USD

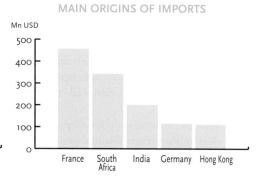

France   South Africa   India   Germany   Hong Kong

EXPORTS by products
■ Food products 24%
■ Manufactured goods 75%
■ Miscellaneous 1%

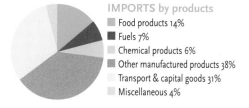

IMPORTS by products
■ Food products 14%
■ Fuels 7%
■ Chemical products 6%
■ Other manufactured products 38%
■ Transport & capital goods 31%
■ Miscellaneous 4%

5

STANDARD OF LIVING / PURCHASING POWER

Indicators	Mauritius	Regional average	DC average
GNP per capita (PPP dollars)	9940	2708	6548
GNP per capita	3750	985	3565
Human development index	0.772	0.493	0.702
Wealthiest 10% share of national income	n/a	35	32
Urban population percentage	41	42	60
Percentage under 15 years old	26	43	32
Number of telephones per 1000 inhabitants	235	32	157
Number of computers per 1000 inhabitants	101	15	64

n/a – not available

Mozambique

Coface analysis

Short-term: **C**

Medium-term:
Very high risk

STRENGTHS

- Natural resources (coal, hydroelectricity, gas) and tourism potential attractive to foreign investors.
- Strong economic and financial ties with South Africa.
- Ambitious structural reform programme backed by international financial community.
- Benefited from huge debt relief; one of the first countries admitted to HIPC initiative.

WEAKNESSES

- Economy still marked by legacy of thirty years of war (refugees, displaced persons, extreme poverty).
- Agricultural country (80 per cent of population, 34 per cent of GDP) dependent on climatic factors.
- Backward infrastructure.
- Structurally unfavourable trade balance makes country highly dependent on international aid.
- Development concentrated in Maputo region. Regional inequalities could inflame underlying political tensions that remain since end of civil war (1994).

RISK ASSESSMENT

Mozambique's high economic growth rate is driven by foreign investment. However, economic activity is too concentrated geographically and dependent on large-scale projects. The country's longer-term development prospects are marred by poor infrastructure and inadequate financing due to the country's low savings ratio.

For this reason Mozambique continues to rely on international backing to remain solvent. Public finances, overburdened by support for the banking sector that has swollen the national debt, remain in a precarious state. Capital goods imports for large-scale projects under way have increased the external borrowing requirement, which debt relief under the HIPC initiative (Mozambique was one of the first countries to reach the 'completion point') will help reduce.

The country's political stability and increasing economic integration with Southern Africa are seen as major assets by investors.

KEY ECONOMIC INDICATORS						
US$ million	1998	1999	2000	2001	2002(e)	2003(f)
Economic growth (%)	12.6	7.5	1.6	13.9	9	8
Inflation (%)	0.6	2.9	12.7	9	16.6	6.5
Public-sector balance/GDP (%)	−10.5	−13.2	−16.1	−17.8	−16.9	−13.5
Exports	244.6	284	364	704	711	759
Imports	817	1200	1162	1117	1769	1738
Trade balance	−573	−916	−798	−413	−1058	−979
Current account balance/GDP (%)	−18.9	−28.2	−27.8	−23.5	−40.2	−34.4
Foreign debt	7845	6581	7157	4219	4906	5567
Debt service/Exports (%)	20	15.3	9.1	3.5	4.1	4.3
Reserves (import months)	5.5	4.5	4.9	4.6	3.3	3.8

e = estimated, f = forecast

CONDITIONS OF ACCESS TO THE MARKET

■ Market overview

Customs duties currently range from 0 per cent for pharmaceuticals, 2.5 per cent for commodities and 7.5 per cent for semi-finished goods to 30 per cent for luxury products. According to foreign companies based in Mozambique the country's strong grey market, which is not subject to import duties and levies or VAT, creates unfair competition and hampers exports of their products.

■ Means of entry

Customs procedures are so long-winded and complex that it is essential to hire the services of a special Mozambican agent, who marks up and slows imports. For payments, other than credit from international lenders, the irrevocable and confirmed documentary letter of credit is strongly recommended.

Even after central bank and Ministry of Finance approval has been obtained foreign capital may be repatriated only if the investment project had been authorized beforehand by the Investment Promotion Centre. Customs management has been sub contracted until 2003 to the UK firm Intertek

Testing Services. International firms have been invited to tender for the new customs management contract, but the outcome is not yet known. On the whole, ITS is judged to have performed efficiently.

■ Attitude towards foreign investors

The CPI was set up to co-ordinate procedures and promote investment. While there is no legal requirement to consult this body, foreign investors are strongly recommended to do so. The government guarantees the protection of property and other rights under the law. The tax benefits code and industrial free zone legislation offer foreign investors many incentives. As free zones are still at an embryonic stage their development should be greatly boosted by the new regulations adopted in September 1999.

The minimum level of direct foreign investment is US$50,000 in the form of equity. While the country's legislation does not prohibit the establishment of wholly foreign-owned businesses, joint ventures with local partners are encouraged by the government.

Living conditions for expatriates are suitable. However, hygiene is still far from satisfactory.

5

■ Foreign exchange regulations
An inter-bank currency market regulating purchases and sales of foreign currency has been set up. This market is closed to everyone but the central bank and approved financial institutions. The value of the local currency, the metical, is determined daily on the basis of supply and demand. Foreigners are strongly advised to carry out all foreign exchange transactions via approved banks and bureaux de change. Banks may carry out currency transactions up to the value of their hard currency cash holdings. There are no restrictions on capital transactions.

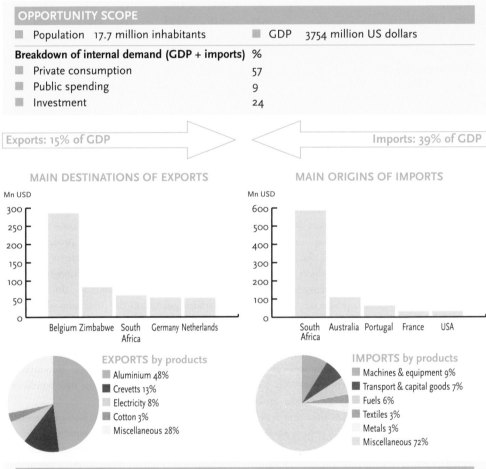

OPPORTUNITY SCOPE

■ Population   17.7 million inhabitants   ■ GDP   3754 million US dollars

Breakdown of internal demand (GDP + imports)	%
■ Private consumption	57
■ Public spending	9
■ Investment	24

Exports: 15% of GDP   Imports: 39% of GDP

MAIN DESTINATIONS OF EXPORTS

Mn USD — Belgium, Zimbabwe, South Africa, Germany, Netherlands

MAIN ORIGINS OF IMPORTS

Mn USD — South Africa, Australia, Portugal, France, USA

EXPORTS by products
- ■ Aluminium 48%
- ■ Crevetts 13%
- ■ Electricity 8%
- ■ Cotton 3%
- ■ Miscellaneous 28%

IMPORTS by products
- ■ Machines & equipment 9%
- ■ Transport & capital goods 7%
- ■ Fuels 6%
- ■ Textiles 3%
- ■ Metals 3%
- ■ Miscellaneous 72%

STANDARD OF LIVING / PURCHASING POWER

Indicators	Nigeria	Regional average	DC average
GNP per capita (PPP dollars)	800	2708	6548
GNP per capita	210	985	3565
Human development index	0.322	0.493	0.702
Wealthiest 10% share of national income	32	35	32
Urban population percentage	40	42	60
Percentage under 15 years old	44	43	32
Number of telephones per 1000 inhabitants	4	32	157
Number of computers per 1000 inhabitants	3	15	64

Namibia

Short-term: **A3**

Medium-term:
Quite low risk

Coface analysis

RISK ASSESSMENT

Namibia remains highly exposed to external shocks. The bulk of its income is still derived from agriculture, fisheries and mining (diamonds). Its market is narrow and the country is heavily reliant on South Africa for its imports, direct foreign investment, currency (pegged to the rand) and economic growth.

The economy's failure to meet the population's needs may exacerbate the country's underlying weaknesses: demographic pressure, poverty, land distribution difficulties, poor water supply, the AIDS epidemic and continued regional instability despite the end of the civil war in Angola. Moreover, progress in structural reforms is inadequate.

The outlook is, however, encouraging thanks to the country's economic and political stability. Namibia's external solvency is comfortable, despite the deterioration in public accounts and the increase in domestic debt. Furthermore, efforts are under way to diversify the economy and exports (metalworking, textiles, tourism), underpinned by investment in communications, transport and energy infrastructure.

5

KEY ECONOMIC INDICATORS						
US$ million	1998	1999	2000	2001	2002(e)	2003(f)
Economic growth (%)	2.4	2.9	3.3	2	3.2	5
Inflation (%)	8.7	7.9	8.3	9.3	10.5	9.5
Public-sector balance/GDP (%)	−4	−4.2	−3.2	−5.2	−4.4	−5.3
Exports	1278	1288	1400	1213	1282	1467
Imports	1451	1564	1611	1386	1403	1519
Trade balance	−173	−276	−211	−173	−121	−52
Current account balance/GDP (%)	4.7	1.7	2.4	3.2	3	6.1
Foreign debt	128	158	160	390	437	471
Debt service/Exports (%)	1.9	1.1	1.1	2.9	3.2	3.2
Reserves (import months)	1.5	1.7	1.4	1.4	1.9	1.8

e = estimated, f = forecast

Niger

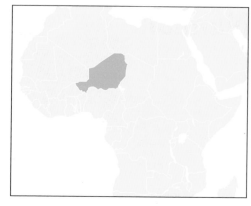

Short-term: **C**

Medium-term:
Very high risk

RISK ASSESSMENT

Niger, one of the world's poorest countries, remains dependent on the performance of its agricultural sector, especially livestock farming (second largest export earner after uranium) and on the support of the international financial community. Moreover, the country's grey economy is thriving due to the level of activity in neighbouring Nigeria.

In the circumstances, Niger's economic performance was mixed. The government has struggled to improve the public finances or eliminate arrears. The privatization programme is behind schedule. Wage cuts have created strong social tensions that could trigger military uprisings of the kind seen in August 2002 and undermine the current IMF programme.

Niger requires IMF support to cover its large external financing needs and to reach the 'completion point' set by the HIPC programme that would make it eligible for substantial debt relief.

KEY ECONOMIC INDICATORS						
US$ million	1998	1999	2000	2001	2002(e)	2003(f)
Economic growth (%)	10.4	−0.6	0.1	7.6	2.5	4
Inflation (%)	4.5	−2.3	2.9	4	3	3
Public–sector balance/GDP (%)	−8.1	−9.7	−16.3	−8.6	−9	−9.7
Exports	327	300	306	280	303	356
Imports	388	331	350	344	390	457
Trade balance	−61	−31	−44	−64	−87	−101
Current account balance/GDP (%)	−10	−7.7	−7.5	−7.5	−8.6	−9.5
Foreign debt	1613	1685	1696	1668	1728	1841
Debt service/Exports (%)	25	19.5	22.7	27	32.1	23.3
Reserves (import months)	1	1	2	3	2	2

e = estimated, f = forecast

Nigeria

Coface analysis

Short-term: **D**

Medium-term:
Very high risk

STRENGTHS

- Accounts for half the population of West Africa. Vast oil and gas resources attract foreign investment; strong agricultural potential.
- Expected to act, for this reason, as a political and economic engine of both region and entire African continent.
- Integration within ECOWAS additional asset in investors' eyes.

WEAKNESSES

- Highly dependent on oil and gas revenues (98 per cent of exports, 82 per cent of budget revenues).
- Constitutional and political climate obstructs implementation of reforms required by foreign lenders.
- Heavy foreign debt contributes to ongoing fiscal imbalance.
- Investors discouraged by business climate.
- Continued tensions created by ethnic and religious antagonisms, inequalities between North and South, poverty and unemployment.

RISK ASSESSMENT

The performance of the Nigerian economy will continue to be disappointing. Growth, largely driven by public spending, has only partially benefited from the increase in oil and gas prices. Inflation remains high. Defaults have grown despite the fact that the oil sector generates significant foreign exchange earnings, attracts foreign investors and facilitates coverage of the country's external financing needs.

Given the lack of consensus, the pace of structural reforms has been slow and is not expected to pick up in the highly charged atmosphere surrounding the run-up to the presidential elections in March 2003. Against this background the government has called off negotiations with the IMF on the implementation of a three-year programme. But Nigeria will have to return to the international financial community's fold to obtain new finance and reschedule afresh its foreign debt.

In the longer term the country needs to encourage non-oil investments in order to diversify its economy and reduce its dependence on oil and gas.

5

KEY ECONOMIC INDICATORS

US$ billion	1998	1999	2000	2001	2002(e)	2003(f)
Economic growth (%)	1.8	2.8	3.8	3.9	2.3	3.9
Inflation (%)	10.3	6.7	6.9	18.9	16.9	14
Public-sector balance/GDP (%)	−9.3	−7.5	2.2	−5.3	−6.8	−5
Exports	10.1	11.9	20.4	20.3	17.1	20
Imports	9.3	10.5	12.4	13.7	14	14.3
Trade balance	0.8	1.4	8.1	6.5	3.1	5.7
Current account balance/GDP (%)	−9.3	−10	5	3	−2.9	7.4
Foreign debt	30.3	29.2	34.1	33.7	33.9	34.2
Debt service/Exports (%)	33.6	28.6	14.8	18.5	14.6	11.8
Reserves (import months)	5.3	3.6	5.5	5.7	4.4	5.1

CONDITIONS OF ACCESS TO THE MARKET

■ Market overview

The Nigerian market is very open to foreign trade. Imports account for over 30 per cent of GDP and exports for over 50 per cent. Imports are extremely varied and liable to customs duty ranging from 5 per cent to 100 per cent of the CIF value. Many products are prohibited, including re-treaded and second-hand tyres, second-hand clothes, cars that are more than five years old and frozen foods.

The Nigerian government has adopted a growing number of protectionist measures in favour of local products and announced a forthcoming ban on cement, fabric, etc. Labour is very cheap. At an estimated 14 per cent in 2002, the rate of inflation has not been offset by wage increases.

The increase in the price of consumer goods has been partly counterbalanced by a fall in the value of the naira following the setting up of a new exchange rate system. A skilled worker earns about 150 nairas a month, whereas an English-speaking local secretary earns 245 nairas. Employees usually receive an extra month's pay.

■ Attitude towards foreign investors

The Nigerian Investment Promotion Commission, a government agency based in Abuja, regularly publishes a list of priority investment sectors and incentives (financial, tax, etc) granted by the government to companies. The repatriation of capital, dividends and profit is unrestricted, though extremely slow.

Nigeria encourages oil companies to develop their exploration and production activities. The country's long-term objective is to produce 4 million barrels of oil daily. The year 2003 should see the development especially of deep-sea oil fields as well as a substantial increase in gas production capacity. The majors support the growth of the gas group NLNG, which is setting up new production facilities.

■ Foreign exchange regulations

The Central Bank of Nigeria (CBN) uses the Dutch auction system to supply the local market with currency. The inter-bank currency market, which brought commercial banks face to face with the CBN and matched currency demand with supply, has given way to a procedure under which twice a week the CBN announces the volume of currency (dollars) it is prepared to sell against nairas and invites importers and foreign currency end-users to put in, through their banks, purchase bids for nairas. In October 2002 the exchange rate was 128 nairas to the dollar. On the grey market, the naira now trades only at a 5 per cent discount.

Exporters are strongly advised to obtain payment for all orders before shipment either by irrevocable and confirmed letter of credit or by cash in a hard currency. French banks no longer operate in the country.

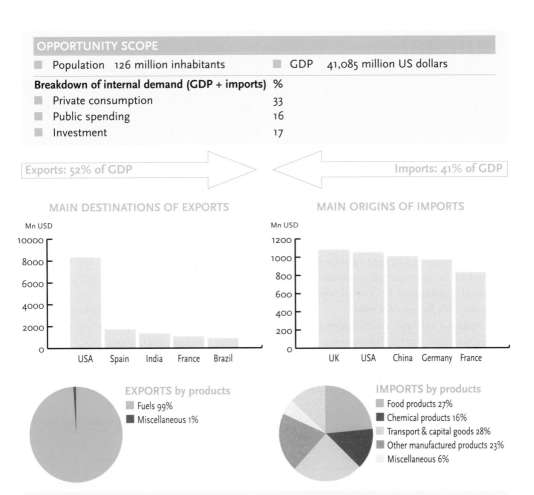

OPPORTUNITY SCOPE

Population   126 million inhabitants   GDP   41,085 million US dollars

Breakdown of internal demand (GDP + imports)	%
Private consumption	33
Public spending	16
Investment	17

Exports: 52% of GDP   Imports: 41% of GDP

MAIN DESTINATIONS OF EXPORTS

Mn USD

USA   Spain   India   France   Brazil

MAIN ORIGINS OF IMPORTS

Mn USD

UK   USA   China   Germany   France

EXPORTS by products
- Fuels 99%
- Miscellaneous 1%

IMPORTS by products
- Food products 27%
- Chemical products 16%
- Transport & capital goods 28%
- Other manufactured products 23%
- Miscellaneous 6%

5

STANDARD OF LIVING / PURCHASING POWER

Indicators	Nigeria	Regional average	DC average
GNP per capita (PPP dollars)	800	2708	6548
GNP per capita	260	985	3565
Human development index	0.462	0.493	0.702
Wealthiest 10% share of national income	41	35	32
Urban population percentage	44	42	60
Percentage under 15 years old	45	43	32
Number of telephones per 1000 inhabitants	4	32	157
Number of computers per 1000 inhabitants	7	15	64

Senegal

Short-term: **B**

Medium-term:
High risk

Coface analysis

STRENGTHS

- Enjoys political stability and a good public image.
- Backed by international community (multilateral organizations, EU, United States), which assists with foreign debt relief.
- Continued economic diversification (fish farming, chemicals, tourism, information technology) and, since 1995, high economic growth.
- Greater regional integration (energy, transport) is an additional factor in making country more attractive to foreign investors.

WEAKNESSES

- 60 per cent of working population dependent on agriculture (20 per cent of GDP), and hence on climate vagaries.
- Population explosion, unemployment and poverty (65 per cent of population) exacerbate social problems and tensions.
- Delays in restructuring of highly indebted public sector companies.
- Dependent on international community to cover borrowing requirement.
- Unresolved Casamance separatist issue bad for tourism.

RISK ASSESSMENT

Expansion of the mining and chemicals sector should drive growth in 2003. Nevertheless the pace of growth will be conditioned by the outcome of privatizations in the groundnut and electricity industries and progress in the consolidation of public accounts. However, restructuring of public-sector companies is dogged by delays, and the cost of providing assistance for the rural population, hit by the crisis, will make their reorganization much more difficult.

At the same time the external accounts continue to be marked by high deficits that will only level off when the country's debt is cancelled under the HIPC initiative.

While the present government is assured a long tenure before the next elections in 2006, the confidence it enjoys among the people seems to be eroding. None of the priorities of the new government – the resolution of the Casamance issue and job creation – have made real headway, while the expected stepping up of structural reforms could heighten social tensions.

KEY ECONOMIC INDICATORS						
US$ million	1998	1999	2000	2001	2002(e)	2003(f)
Economic growth (%)	5.7	5	5.6	5.8	4.5	5.8
Inflation (%)	1.1	0.8	0.7	3.1	2.5	2.5
Public–sector balance/GDP (%)	−3.3	−3.5	−2	−3.9	−2.6	−2.2
Exports	968	1026	920	959	1111	1326
Imports	1281	1372	1337	1339	1516	1820
Trade balance	−313	−346	−417	−381	−405	−494
Current account balance/GDP (%)	−7.8	−7.9	−9	−6.4	−6.7	−7.1
Foreign debt	3833	3639	3626	3641	3692	3742
Debt service/Exports (%)	16.3	12	11.7	9.9	9.9	9.4
Reserves (import months)	2.8	2.4	2.4	2.8	2.9	2.4

e = estimated, f = forecast

CONDITIONS OF ACCESS TO THE MARKET

■ Market overview

The customs union established by the member states of WAEMU (West African Economic and Monetary Union) is simple and inexpensive. Customs duties vary between 0 per cent and 20 per cent according to product category. Imports are also liable to some token surtaxes and 18 per cent flat-rate VAT. All importers and exporters must be registered with the Foreign Trade Department (Comex). The main restrictions concern arms and drugs.

The Senegalese government has appointed Cotecna Inspection to carry out goods inspections under the Import Verification Programme. An Advance Import Notification must be submitted for all imported goods with a CIF value of FCFA 1 million or more. From 15 October 2001 imports with a CIF value of FCFA 3 million or more are subject to pre-shipment inspection.

■ Attitude towards foreign investors

To make faster progress in its policy of offering improved terms of access to investors, Senegal is

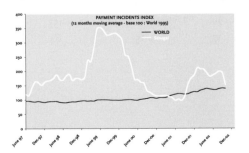

PAYMENT INCIDENTS INDEX
(12 months moving average - base 100 : World 1995)
— WORLD

banking on a number of factors, including a sharp improvement in production facilities primarily through wider availability of electricity (power supply from Mali, emergency plan for Sénélec), land transport (railways, roads, motorways) and cement for construction purposes (commissioning of a new cement works in 2002); better penetration of European and US markets by means of the preferential benefits it receives along with other African countries (especially LDCs); rapid expansion of West African financial markets and the regional stock market BRVN (38 listed companies, including Sonatel, which accounts for 25 per cent of the market's 1 billion-plus euro capitalization); and WAEMU's continued role as guarantor of economic and monetary stability and economic openness (Community Investment Code under preparation).

■ Foreign exchange regulations

There are no restrictions on business-related transfers within the franc area, provided they are handled by approved intermediaries such as banks. Fund transfers in excess of CFA 300,000 outside the franc area are subject to presentation of either an invoice, a pro forma, a contract or a documentary letter of credit. Dividend transfers are permitted, but must be handled by approved intermediaries (banks) and supported by proof of payment. Companies incorporated under local law are free to hold foreign currency accounts subject to the approval of the Ministry of Finance. From 8 October 2001, the Central Bank for West African States is in charge of euro account opening applications.

OPPORTUNITY SCOPE

- Population 9.5 million inhabitants
- GDP 4371 million US dollars

Breakdown of internal demand (GDP + imports)	%
Private consumption	57
Public spending	7
Investment	14

Exports: 31% of GDP

Imports: 40% of GDP

MAIN DESTINATIONS OF EXPORTS

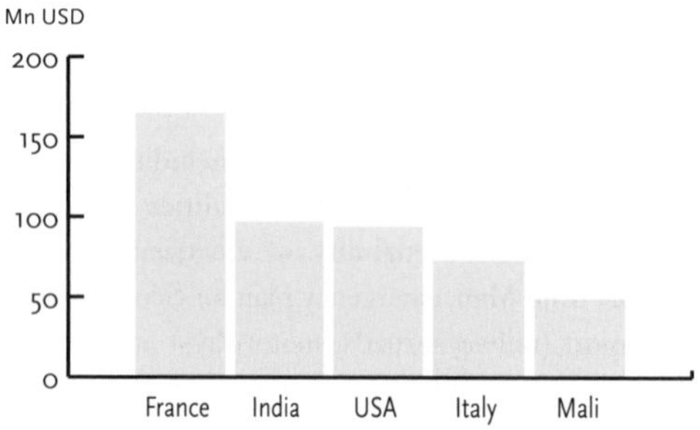

Mn USD
200
150
100
50
0
France
India
USA
Italy
Mali

MAIN ORIGINS OF IMPORTS

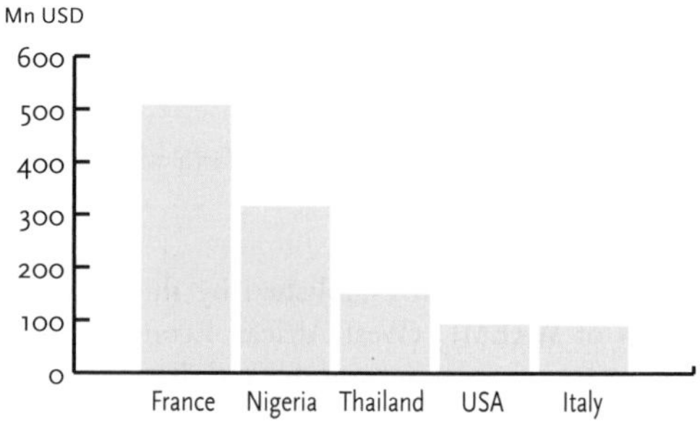

Mn USD
600
500
400
300
200
100
0
France
Nigeria
Thailand
USA
Italy

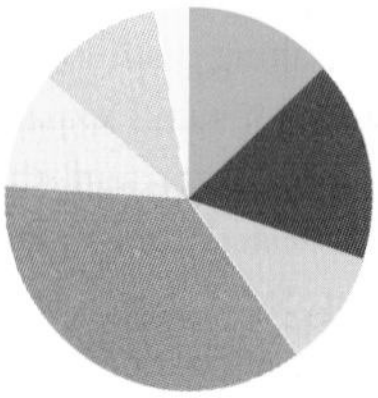

EXPORTS by products

- Food products 13%
- Fuels 17%
- Minerals & metals 10%
- Chemical products 36%
- Other manufactured products 10%
- Transport & capital goods 11%
- Miscellaneous 3%

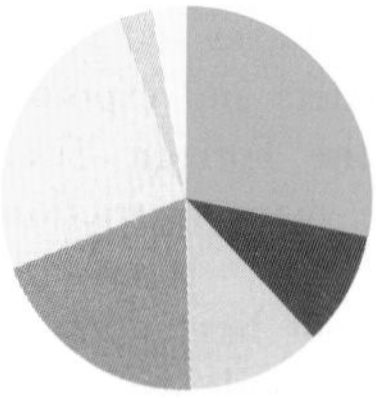

IMPORTS by products

- Food products 29%
- Fuels 10%
- Chemical products 12%
- Other manufactured products 20%
- Transport & capital goods 26%
- Miscellaneous 3%

STANDARD OF LIVING / PURCHASING POWER

Indicators	Senegal	Regional average	DC average
GNP per capita (PPP dollars)	1480	2708	6548
GNP per capita	490	985	3565
Human development index	0.431	0.493	0.702
Wealthiest 10% share of national income	34	35	32
Urban population percentage	47	42	60
Percentage under 15 years old	44	43	32
Number of telephones per 1000 inhabitants	22	32	157
Number of computers per 1000 inhabitants	17	15	64

South Africa

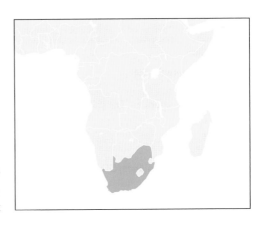

Short-term: **A4**

Medium-term:
Coface analysis **Quite low risk**

STRENGTHS

- Accounts for 40 per cent of Africa's GDP and plays ever-bigger role on regional, political and economic stage.
- Vast mineral resources, diversified industry and booming service sector (banks, telecommunications, transport).
- Public finances under control – favourable trade balance and low foreign debt.
- Current macroeconomic stability policy not at risk despite domestic tensions.

WEAKNESSES

- Lacks resources to finance development. Low savings and investment levels.
- Consequently, dependent on foreign funding, which is volatile due to domestic and regional environment.
- Vulnerable to crisis of confidence in capital markets.
- Economy not growing quickly enough to meet social demands or development needs. This could spark off social and political tensions.
- Aids pandemic major challenge in coming years.

RISK ASSESSMENT

Continued economic growth is subject to many constraints. The sharp depreciation of the rand, which stimulated exports, switched to an appreciation that has reduced the competitiveness of South African products. Inflation has forced the monetary authorities to raise interest rates. The uncertain regional environment (Zimbabwe) has a negative impact on foreign investment which, together with weak foreign exchange reserves, makes the country highly vulnerable to a fall in confidence on international capital markets.

However, sound management of public finances and low domestic and public debt give the government plenty of scope to support economic activity. Similarly, the country's level of development, political stability and influence in Southern Africa, which makes it a springboard for penetrating neighbouring markets, should help dispel uncertainties.

5

KEY ECONOMIC INDICATORS

US$ billion	1998	1999	2000	2001	2002(e)	2003(f)
Economic growth (%)	0.8	2.1	3.5	2.9	3	3.1
Inflation (%)	6.9	5	5.3	5.7	9.6	7.2
Public-sector balance/GDP (%)	−2.3	−2	−2	−1.5	−2.1	−2.1
Exports	29.1	28.6	31.7	30.4	31.8	35.1
Imports	27.3	24.6	27.4	25.5	26.6	30.1
Trade balance	1.9	4.1	4.4	4.9	5.2	4.9
Current account balance/GDP (%)	−1.6	−0.5	−0.4	−0.2	0.2	−0.4
Foreign debt	37.5	38.9	36.9	31.5	34.3	35.2
Debt service/Exports (%)	15.6	15.5	13.8	14.6	13.6	8.4
Reserves (import months)	1.4	2.1	1.9	2	2.4	2

e = estimated, f = forecast

CONDITIONS OF ACCESS TO THE MARKET

■ Market overview

South Africa's trade liberalization programme, which began in 1990, has come a long way since the country's membership of the WTO in 1995.

South Africa uses the World Customs Organization's harmonized international nomenclature. Customs duties have been significantly reduced in the last five years and tariff reforms completed in late 1999.

■ Means of entry

Under the free trade agreement signed with the European Union in October 1999 some 86 per cent of products imported from the European Union will be exempt from customs duty by 2012. South Africa is not a signatory to the WTO Agreement on the award of government procurement contracts. Up until now tenders have been overseen at the central level by the State Tender Board and at the local level by one of nine Provincial Tender Boards. In the near future a common service provider is due to replace the tender boards for the purposes of putting in place a uniform policy in the field of government procurement. The Preferential Procurement Policy Framework Act, in force since February 2000, creates a points system that favours companies whose shareholders or managers comprise 'historically underprivileged people' (blacks, mixed race, Indian), women and the disabled. South African public tender legislation consequently favours South African or foreign companies that team up with black partners (Black Empowerment). Where a public tender exceeds US$10 million, foreign companies are required to pay 30 per cent compensation on the total value of imports under the National Participation Programme.

The South African Bureau of Standards co-operates with a large number of similar international bodies to harmonize technical standards and regulations. International standards such as IEC and ISO are recognized by the bureau, but still have to be cleared with it.

■ Attitude towards foreign investors

Foreign companies are required to observe the various statutory requirements under the Black Empowerment and Affirmative Action Programmes. This limits their decision-making powers, as does the lack of transparency and unpredictability of the administrative environment for privatizations and public tenders. Invoicing of imported goods is generally done in US dollars. The other currencies used are the euro, the pound sterling, the Japanese yen and the South African rand. The means of payment used in South Africa are similar to those used in Europe and the United States.

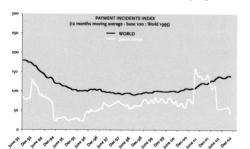

PAYMENT INCIDENTS INDEX
(12 months moving average - base 100 : World 1995)
— WORLD
— South Africa

Foreign exchange regulations

Exchange controls, which are governed by the 1961 Act and its manifold subsequent amendments, have been considerably relaxed in the last few years. The provisions governing transfers of capital related to ordinary business transactions have been liberalized. Currency traders believe that there are no more de facto exchange controls for non-residents, with a few notable exceptions (borrowings in local currency, loans from a parent company to a South African subsidiary, etc).

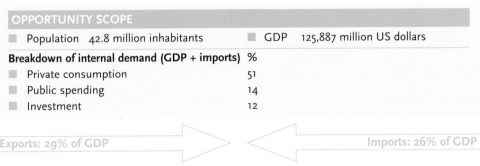

OPPORTUNITY SCOPE

- Population 42.8 million inhabitants
- GDP 125,887 million US dollars

Breakdown of internal demand (GDP + imports) %
- Private consumption 51
- Public spending 14
- Investment 12

Exports: 29% of GDP   Imports: 26% of GDP

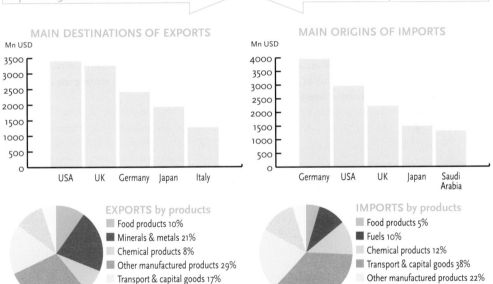

MAIN DESTINATIONS OF EXPORTS (Mn USD)

USA, UK, Germany, Japan, Italy

MAIN ORIGINS OF IMPORTS (Mn USD)

Germany, USA, UK, Japan, Saudi Arabia

EXPORTS by products
- Food products 10%
- Minerals & metals 21%
- Chemical products 8%
- Other manufactured products 29%
- Transport & capital goods 17%
- Fuels 10%
- Miscellaneous 5%

IMPORTS by products
- Food products 5%
- Fuels 10%
- Chemical products 12%
- Transport & capital goods 38%
- Other manufactured products 22%
- Miscellaneous 13%

5

STANDARD OF LIVING / PURCHASING POWER

Indicators	South Africa	Regional average	DC average
GNP per capita (PPP dollars)	9160	2708	6548
GNP per capita	3020	985	3565
Human development index	0.695	0.493	0.702
Wealthiest 10% share of national income	46	35	32
Urban population percentage	55	42	60
Percentage under 15 years old	34	43	32
Number of telephones per 1000 inhabitants	114	32	157
Number of computers per 1000 inhabitants	62	15	64

Sudan

Short-term: **D**

Medium-term:
Very high risk

Coface analysis

RISK ASSESSMENT

The Sudanese economy has several positive features: strong growth driven by rising oil output, oil exports and oil-related investment; tight fiscal and monetary policies; and a wide-ranging structural reform programme since 1997 which has helped improve the business climate.

In addition, the conclusion of an agreement with rebels in the south of the country in July 2002 could strengthen foreign investor interest, which could induce much needed economic diversification.

The upturn, however, should not mask the country's weaknesses: external account still in the red, high debt and behind in payments. Moreover, its prospects remain heavily dependent on the oil sector and on the outcome of the current negotiations to reach a settlement over the secession of the South, wealth sharing and a lasting peace.

KEY ECONOMIC INDICATORS						
US$ million	1998	1999	2000	2001	2002(e)	2003(f)
Economic growth (%)	6.1	6.9	6.9	5.3	5	5.6
Inflation (%)	17.1	16	8	4.9	6	5
Public–sector balance/GDP (%)	−12.2	−0.9	−0.8	−1	−0.5	−1
Exports	596	780	1864	1688	1934	2269
Imports	1925	1412	1553	1585	1892	1605
Trade balance	592	−632	311	103	42	664
Current account balance/GDP (%)	−22.8	−15.4	−14.3	−10.6	−11.2	−11.9
Foreign debt	23,523	24,505	21,163	22,263	23,463	25,226
Debt service/Exports (%)	120.9	108.9	64.5	66.9	58	69.9
Reserves (import months)	0	0	0.1	0	0.1	0.1

e = estimated, f = forecast

Tanzania

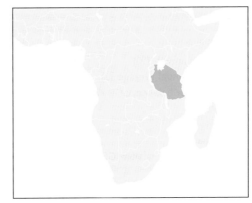

Coface analysis

Short-term: **C**

Medium-term:
Very high risk

STRENGTHS

- Large economic potential (arable land, mineral riches, tourism) capable of attracting more foreign investment.
- Political stability has facilitated significant structural reforms.
- Support of foreign lenders instrumental in cancellation of the country's foreign debt under HIPC programme.
- Greater regional integration (EAC, SADC) asset to country's economy.

WEAKNESSES

- Insufficiently diversified economy (agricultural products, gold) extremely vulnerable to external crises.
- Half the population lives in poverty.
- Highly dependent on international aid.
- Lack of funding of public infrastructures affects their operation and supplies to companies, and delays their privatization.
- Difficult business environment.
- Volatile relations with Zanzibar, whose economy is in very bad shape.

RISK ASSESSMENT

The progress made by Tanzania, reflected in strong growth, implementation of structural reforms and the boom in mining, especially of gold, falls short of what is required to meet the numerous challenges facing the country: poverty, unemployment, AIDS and infrastructure development.

These challenges place a heavy burden on the country's limited finances, which are heavily dependent on international aid. Foreign aid is also essential to cover the country's foreign borrowing requirement.

While the external account has benefited from cancellation of the country's foreign debt under the HIPC programme, it is expected to deteriorate in the short term due to capital goods imports related to new mining investment. In the longer term, the projected increase in gold exports and tourism revenues should help to correct the external account deficit.

5

KEY ECONOMIC INDICATORS						
US$ million	1998	1999	2000	2001	2002(e)	2003(f)
Economic growth (%)	4	4.7	4.9	5.6	5.9	6
Inflation (annual average %)	12.8	7.9	5.9	5.2	4.6	4.2
Public-sector balance/GDP (%)	−3.5	−7.8	−5.3	−5.6	−9.8	−8.5
Exports	577	543	663	776	850	910
Imports	1518	1573	1337	1492	1504	1678
Trade balance	−941	−1030	−674	−716	−654	−768
Current account balance/GDP (%)	−14.6	−12.9	−9.4	−9.3	−8.9	−9.3
Foreign debt	6094	6622	6956	7113	6564	5798
Debt service/Exports (%)	36.6	33.4	22.5	6.2	6.3	7.7
Reserves (import months)	3	3.9	5.2	5.8	7.4	7.8

e = estimated, f = forecast

CONDITIONS OF ACCESS TO THE MARKET

■ Market overview

The open general licence system or the system of import licensing administered by the Republic of Tanzania has been abolished since 1994. As a rule there are no import controls other than pre-shipment inspection under customs supervision.

On 1 March 1999 the Tanzania Revenue Authority appointed Cotecna Inspection SA to carry out pre-shipment inspections. Commercial imports with an FOB value in excess of US$5000 are subject to inspection, as are goods shipped in containers, whatever their FOB value.

The Customs and Excise Department is responsible for collecting international trade levies. Import duties have been cut since 1996 and the ceiling rate lowered from 40 per cent to 25 per cent. Tariff categories have been gradually reduced from seven to four. Import duties are calculated on the CIF value of goods imported into the country. A number of priority products are admitted duty free.

All exchange controls have been abolished in Tanzania. There are no restrictions on the availability of hard currency. However, the notification requirement for large transactions remains in place.

The means of payment are decided by the contracting parties. SWIFT transfers are the most widespread means of payment for trade transactions with countries having this facility. However, transactions are still carried out by telex, letter of credit and guaranteed bank cheques.

Transactions are usually denominated in Tanzanian shillings or US dollars, although the euro is slowly gaining acceptance.

■ Attitude towards Foreign Investors

As well as its economic liberalization and privatization programme, Tanzania has adopted a strategy to promote direct foreign investment spearheaded by the Tanzania Investment Act 1997. This Act sets up a national investment promotion agency, the Tanzania Investment Centre (TIC), which serves as a one-stop shop for both foreign and domestic investors whose investments are above the thresholds set under the Act (US$300,000 for foreign investors). The TIC issues an acknowledgement certificate or certificate of incentives to investors who meet the legal requirements. This certificate entitles them to statutory tax breaks, including exemption from import duties, VAT and corporation tax during the first five years of business.

In 2002 the Tanzanian government set up free zones. While the legislation governing these zones offers additional incentives, it also imposes an export requirement in respect of finished goods.

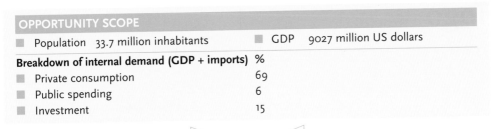

OPPORTUNITY SCOPE

■ Population 33.7 million inhabitants ■ GDP 9027 million US dollars

Breakdown of internal demand (GDP + imports) %
■ Private consumption 69
■ Public spending 6
■ Investment 15

Exports:15% of GDP   Imports: 23% of GDP

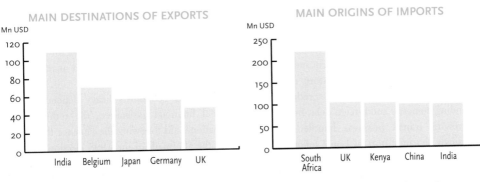

MAIN DESTINATIONS OF EXPORTS

Mn USD

India Belgium Japan Germany UK

MAIN ORIGINS OF IMPORTS

Mn USD

South Africa   UK   Kenya   China   India

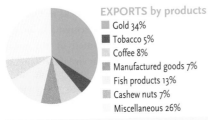

EXPORTS by products
■ Gold 34%
■ Tobacco 5%
■ Coffee 8%
■ Manufactured goods 7%
■ Fish products 13%
■ Cashew nuts 7%
■ Miscellaneous 26%

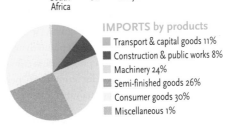

IMPORTS by products
■ Transport & capital goods 11%
■ Construction & public works 8%
■ Machinery 24%
■ Semi-finished goods 26%
■ Consumer goods 30%
■ Miscellaneous 1%

5

STANDARD OF LIVING / PURCHASING POWER

Indicators	Tanzania	Regional average	DC average
GNP per capita (PPP dollars)	520	2708	6548
GNP per capita	270	985	3565
Human development index	0.44	0.493	0.702
Wealthiest 10% share of national income	30	35	32
Urban population percentage	28	42	60
Percentage under 15 years old	45	43	32
Number of telephones per 1000 inhabitants	5	32	157
Number of computers per 1000 inhabitants	3	15	64

Togo

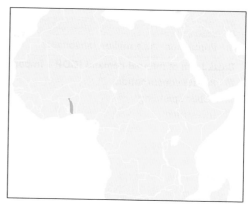

Short-term: **C**

Coface analysis

Medium-term:
Very high risk

RISK ASSESSMENT

The adoption of stringent adjustment measures is helping the country slowly to restore the main macroeconomic balances and reduce its outstanding domestic and foreign debt. Because of the growing transit business handled by the increasingly dynamic port of Lomé following the setting up of an export processing zone and the restructuring of the phosphate industry, Togo could benefit from an upturn in foreign investment.

Prospects however remain dependent on developments in the cotton and phosphate sectors, which between them account for around 66 per cent of the country's exports. Analysts foresee that the development of these two sectors will be exposed to fluctuations in world markets and climatic conditions.

Given the economy's heavy dependence on external financial assistance, the reduction in international aid following the violence that flared up in the aftermath of the 1998 elections marred economic performance. It is far from certain whether the results of the oft-postponed parliamentary elections that were held in October 2002, in which the ruling party scored a landslide victory but which were boycotted by the main opposition parties, will rapidly revive the economy.

KEY ECONOMIC INDICATORS

US$ million	1998	1999	2000	2001	2002(e)	2003(f)
Economic growth (%)	−2.1	2.7	−0.5	1.1	3	3.2
Inflation (%)	1	−0.1	1.9	3.9	5.7	3.7
Public-sector balance/GDP (%)	−7.4	−3.9	−11.5	−0.1	−4.5	−3
Exports	398	392	331	319	348	354
Imports	557	490	452	448	464	526
Trade balance	−158	−98	−121	−128	−115	−173
Current account balance/GDP (%)	−16.1	−12.5	−14.8	−15.1	−14.4	−13.1
Foreign debt	1610	1561	1498	1453	1429	1423
Debt service/Exports (%)	17	20	20	20	21	18
Reserves (import months)	2.5	3	4	3.4	4.9	4.3

e = estimated, f = forecast

Uganda

Short-term: **C**

Medium-term:
High risk

Coface analysis

STRENGTHS

- Vast economic potential backed by progress in economic diversification.
- Moves towards closer regional integration enhance country's attractiveness.
- Strongly supported by international financial community thanks to government's structural reform policy.
- International support has enabled country to benefit from HIPC initiative.
- Encouraging progress in education, poverty alleviation and public health.

WEAKNESSES

- Highly dependent on agriculture (40 per cent of GDP, with coffee accounting for 30 per cent of exports) and, therefore, on climatic factors and food prices.
- Continued dependence on international aid to cover borrowing requirement.
- Investment and implementation of poverty alleviation and AIDS control programme hampered by poor administrative resources and business climate.
- Country's image tarnished by continued regional and domestic tensions.

RISK ASSESSMENT

Uganda continues to enjoy strong growth and low inflation on the back of a tight economic policy, despite the drop in export earnings in 2002 as a result of falling coffee prices and a sluggish global economic environment.

While the prospects for 2003 are favourable the imbalance in public finances and the deteriorating external account give cause for alarm. The country's finances are crippled by security spending and the difficulty the government is having in expanding the country's tax base. The

drifting postion of external accounts is more worrying, especially as the country's foreign debt burden has been significantly reduced.

Against this background, characterized by lower than expected direct foreign investment, the country will continue to depend on international assistance to cover its borrowing requirement. However, support will be conditional on moves to bring calm to the region (especially in the Democratic Republic of Congo) and political liberalization.

5

KEY ECONOMIC INDICATORS						
US$ billion	1998	1999	2000	2001	2002(e)	2003(f)
Economic growth (%)	5.4	7.5	5.5	5.4	5.5	6
Inflation (%)	−0.2	6.3	5	2.4	−1	2.4
Public-sector balance/GDP (%)	−6.4	−6.3	−13.9	−9.3	−11.5	−9.9
Exports	459	549	454	442	456	540
Imports	966	1039	978	973	1085	1209
Trade balance	−507	−490	−524	−531	−629	−669
Current account balance/GDP (%)	−8.5	−9.1	−10.7	−13.1	−14.9	−16
Foreign debt	3893	3708	3591	3826	4292	4407
Debt service/Exports (%)	26.3	18.3	12.1	7.7	8	7.6
Reserves (import months)	6	5.9	5.7	5.7	5.9	5.8

e = estimated, f = forecast

CONDITIONS OF ACCESS TO THE MARKET

■ Market overview

Piecemeal customs and VAT management pose major problems for importers and investors. However, Ugandan customs have made great strides in not only speeding up customs clearance procedures but also improving tax collection and the procedure for refunding import duties on goods used in export-related manufacture.

Ugandan customs duties are among the lowest in East Africa, with three rates of duty in force: 0 per cent, 7 per cent and 15 per cent. Zero rate of duty is applied to manufacturing equipment and staples.

■ Attitude towards foreign investors

Foreign investment in Uganda is governed by the outdated 1991 Investment Code. In a pragmatic move, the government has given the Ugandan Investment Authority (UIA), the body responsible for issuing licences and promoting investment, wide powers of initiative to reduce discrimination between foreigners and nationals pending introduction of a more liberal-minded code.

To obtain a licence foreign investors must submit to the UIA a business plan along with a detailed financial statement of their company's operations. The accounts do not have to be prepared with the utmost precision as licences for a minimum period of five years are automatically granted if the investment complies with the Code.

The UIA is responsible for preparing a report on each investment application within 30 days and for reaching a decision within an additional 14 days. The Ugandan Investment Code does not guarantee foreign investors equal treatment with local ones. Foreign investors are subject to a number of requirements not applicable to domestic investors, including a minimum investment threshold of US$100,000, the opening of a local branch, staff training, purchase of locally manufactured goods and environmental protection. Moreover, foreign investors have restricted access to local credit, although this measure is not enforced in practice. The ban on farming by foreigners has been lifted.

For the vast majority of foreign investors, the main post-start-up problems, in descending order, are the slowness of the legal system, government corruption and tax maladministration (unequal treatment by the Uganda Revenue Authority).

The Investment Code provides for international arbitration of disputes in a form mutually acceptable to both parties. Uganda has ratified the New York Convention on International Arbitration and the International Centre for Settlement of Investment Disputes Convention. It has also signed reciprocal investment protection agreements with the United Kingdom, Italy, Egypt and Mauritius. Talks are under way on the conclusion of similar agreements with South Africa, Belgium, Canada and the Netherlands.

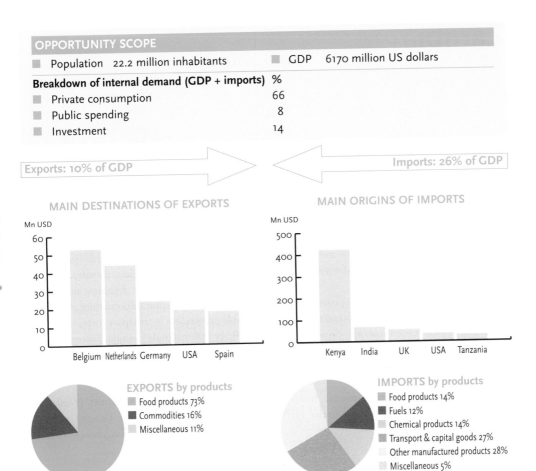

OPPORTUNITY SCOPE

Population   22.2 million inhabitants   GDP   6170 million US dollars

Breakdown of internal demand (GDP + imports) %
- Private consumption   66
- Public spending   8
- Investment   14

Exports: 10% of GDP   Imports: 26% of GDP

MAIN DESTINATIONS OF EXPORTS

Mn USD

Belgium Netherlands Germany USA Spain

MAIN ORIGINS OF IMPORTS

Mn USD

Kenya India UK USA Tanzania

EXPORTS by products
- Food products 73%
- Commodities 16%
- Miscellaneous 11%

IMPORTS by products
- Food products 14%
- Fuels 12%
- Chemical products 14%
- Transport & capital goods 27%
- Other manufactured products 28%
- Miscellaneous 5%

STANDARD OF LIVING / PURCHASING POWER

Indicators	Uganda	Regional average	DC average
GNP per capita (PPP dollars)	1210	2708	6548
GNP per capita	300	985	3565
Human development index	0.444	0.493	0.702
Wealthiest 10% share of national income	30	35	32
Urban population percentage	14	42	60
Percentage under 15 years old	49	43	32
Number of telephones per 1000 inhabitants	3	32	157
Number of computers per 1000 inhabitants	3	15	64

5

Zambia

Coface analysis

Short-term: **D**

Medium-term:
Very high risk

STRENGTHS

- Significant mineral resources (world's leading producer of cobalt, and Africa's leading producer of copper).
- Government policy of exploiting country's vast agricultural and tourism potential should facilitate much-needed economic diversification.
- These assets, along with implementation of structural reforms, potentially attractive to foreign investors.
- Enjoys support of international financial community (foreign debt relief under HIPC programme).

WEAKNESSES

- Economy extremely vulnerable to external crises (world copper prices, climate).
- Land-locked country. Exports suffer from inadequate transport infrastructure and vulnerable to increases in transport costs.
- Shaky external trade position. Extremely heavy foreign debt and low foreign exchange reserves.
- Large sections of population live in poverty and infected by AIDS virus.
- Unstable regional environment (Zimbabwe, Democratic Republic of Congo) potential source of tensions (smuggling, refugees).

RISK ASSESSMENT

Zambia is going through troubled times and prospects for 2003 will be affected by the consequences of Anglo-American's withdrawal from KCM (Konkola Copper Mine), which accounts for two-thirds of the country's copper exports, and drought. Growth will be insufficient to meet the challenges of poverty alleviation and infrastructure modernization.

Moreover, as the government can no longer count on a stable majority in parliament, it will be that much more difficult to correct the public accounts, whose recurrent deficit is fuelling high inflation.

Against this background the borrowing requirement will remain high, even if the projected increase in copper prices will help to offset the country's growing food imports. Zambia will remain dependent on the support of the international financial community.

KEY ECONOMIC INDICATORS						
US$ million	1998	1999	2000	2001	2002(e)	2003(f)
Economic growth (%)	−1.9	2.4	3.6	4	2.8	2.6
Inflation (%)	24.5	26.8	26.1	21.4	22	22.5
Public-sector balance/GDP (%)	−10.8	−11.6	−11.6	−13	−13.7	−12.9
Exports	816	756	746	884	945	1122
Imports	971	922	978	1253	1308	1436
Trade balance	−155	−166	−232	−369	−363	−314
Current account balance/GDP (%)	−17.7	−17	−18.8	−20.2	−18.6	−18
Foreign debt	6982	6237	6404	6114	6226	4959
Debt service/Exports (%)	16	14.9	17.2	14.5	14.1	12.5
Reserves (import months)	0.4	0.4	0.9	0.8	1.5	1.8

e = estimated, f = forecast

CONDITIONS OF ACCESS TO THE MARKET

■ Market overview

Zambia's level of development is lower than the African average. The rural population is engaged in subsistence farming, often living on the edge of organized economic areas and enjoying only limited access to healthcare and education. The country has considerable resources in the form of minerals (copper and gems), hydro electric power, agriculture (export-led horticulture) and tourism (Victoria Falls, Lake Tanganyika, national parks). The tapping of these resources, however, necessitates large-scale investment.

Because of the government's commitment to maintaining a free trade policy backed by the absence of exchange controls, business confidence has been partially restored and private investment projects look set to continue. The government is likely to persist with the privatization of a dozen large companies in keeping with its commitments to the Bretton Woods institutions. In the circumstances there is little medium-term risk of lending institutions withdrawing their assistance.

■ Means of entry

The liberalization of the economy has reached an advanced stage, with the breaking up of a number of monopolies, privatization of state-run enterprises, tax reform and greater freedom of trade.

In addition, customs duties have been more than halved over the past four years, and even abolished for capital goods in export sectors and raw materials. SGS carries out goods inspections through its local branch to ensure that imports comply with standards.

The financial solvency of private businesses is still fairly poor. Great caution is thus called for when dealing with local businesses. Exporters are advised to obtain maximum guarantees and work with international, British or South African banks based in the country.

■ Attitude towards foreign investors

The subsidiary of a foreign company is treated as a local company and may therefore acquire a majority interest in a Zambian company and transfer capital and dividends on payment of 10 per cent withholding tax. Expatriates must cope with the typical problems of a poor country: lack of infrastructure, under-stocked shops (although the situation has clearly improved), poor hygiene, etc. Foreign workers are subject to stringent restrictions and must obtain both work and residence permits.

■ Foreign exchange regulations

The exchange rate of the Zambian kwacha is set by the market. There are no exchange controls, but the country's foreign exchange reserves are low.

5

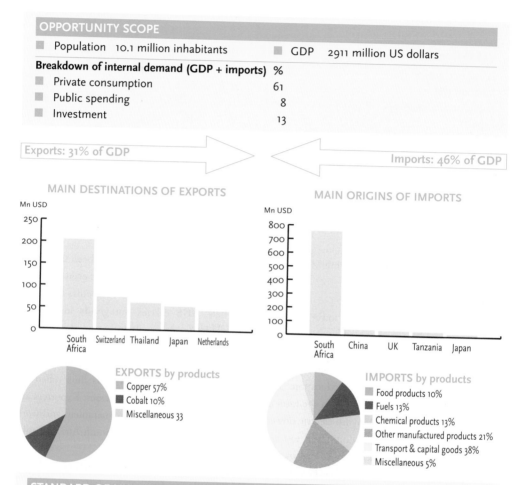

OPPORTUNITY SCOPE

■ Population   10.1 million inhabitants   ■ GDP   2911 million US dollars

Breakdown of internal demand (GDP + imports) %
■ Private consumption   61
■ Public spending   8
■ Investment   13

Exports: 31% of GDP   Imports: 46% of GDP

MAIN DESTINATIONS OF EXPORTS

Mn USD

South Africa · Switzerland · Thailand · Japan · Netherlands

MAIN ORIGINS OF IMPORTS

Mn USD

South Africa · China · UK · Tanzania · Japan

EXPORTS by products
■ Copper 57%
■ Cobalt 10%
■ Miscellaneous 33

IMPORTS by products
■ Food products 10%
■ Fuels 13%
  Chemical products 13%
  Other manufactured products 21%
  Transport & capital goods 38%
  Miscellaneous 5%

STANDARD OF LIVING / PURCHASING POWER

Indicators	Zambia	Regional average	DC average
GNP per capita (PPP dollars)	750	2708	6548
GNP per capita	300	985	3565
Human development index	0.433	0.493	0.702
Wealthiest 10% share of national income	41	35	32
Urban population percentage	45	42	60
Percentage under 15 years old	47	43	32
Number of telephones per 1000 inhabitants	8	32	157
Number of computers per 1000 inhabitants	7	15	64

Zimbabwe

Coface analysis

Short-term: **D**

Medium-term:
Very high risk

STRENGTHS

- Enormous economic potential underpinned by abundant mineral and agricultural resources, diversified industry and well-trained workforce.
- Good transport and financial infrastructure will provide platform for future recovery.
- Could exercise economic and political leadership in Southern Africa alongside South Africa.

WEAKNESSES

- Terrible economic and financial position. Effects of crisis will take long to surmount.
- Country has defaulted on payments to international financial institutions and creditors.
- Increasingly isolated in international community.
- Strong social and political unrest fuelled by economic crisis.
- AIDS contamination rate one of the highest in Africa and the world.

RISK ASSESSMENT

Zimbabwe sank deeper into crisis as the drought took its toll on agricultural ouput, which fell by over 20 per cent in 2002, causing food shortages. In spite of price controls the budget deficit has led to soaring inflation. The drying up of credit has prevented businesses from acquiring energy and semi-finished goods. The country has not honoured its international commitments because of a shortage of foreign exchange and is treated as a pariah by the International Monetary Fund and international financial community.

Against this background the outlook for 2003 is bleak. Not only is the political and social situation extremely tense, but also the current economic situation is unlikely to improve following President Mugabe's re-election in spring 2002.

If an upturn were to occur it will take Zimbabwe a long time to put its house in order. The country should therefore remain dependent on international aid for several years to come.

5

KEY ECONOMIC INDICATORS						
US$ million	1998	1999	2000	2001	2002(e)	2003(f)
Economic growth (%)	4.1	−1.2	−4.9	−7.3	−12.1	−8.8
Inflation (%)	31.7	59	58	75	132	282
Public-sector balance/GDP (%)	−4.6	−11.5	−22.8	−12	−17.8	−11.5
Exports	1925	1924	1801	1280	1400	1.3
Imports	2020	1675	1520	1000	1780	1.4
Trade balance	−95	249	281	280	−380	1.8
Current account balance/GDP (%)	−4.6	2.3	−2.5	−6.2	−4.1	−6
Foreign debt	4510	5122	4800	4166	3677	4.1
Debt service/Exports (%)	33.2	21.9	28.6	44.9	46.2	39
Reserves (import months)	0.5	1.2	0.7	0.5	0	0.6

e = estimated, f = forecast

CONDITIONS OF ACCESS TO THE MARKET

■ Attitude towards foreign investors

An investment protection agreement was concluded in 1999. Government policy still aims to 'indigenize' the economy. In some sectors of activity, there is a 70 per cent, 35 per cent or 30 per cent ceiling on foreign shareholdings. Living conditions for expatriates are good.

■ Foreign exchange regulations

The shortage of foreign currency is the result of the monetary policy pursued since early 1999. The Zimbabwe dollar has been artificially maintained at the rate of 38 to the US dollar. This totally unsustainable rate has led rapidly to the creation of an unofficial currency market, accounting for 75 per cent of all currency transactions. The grey market rate lies somewhere between 55 and 65 Zimbabwe dollars to the US dollar. The fixed exchange rate policy has resulted in the erosion of competitiveness in the agricultural, industrial and mining sectors, which are the pillars of the country's economy. At the end of September 2001, one US dollar fetched 300 Zimbabwe dollars on the grey market.

The IMF welcomes the role of the grey market as it helps to stem the decline in business activity. It has even asked the government to support this market until conditions are ripe for a unification of rates.

OPPORTUNITY SCOPE

■ Population   12.6 million inhabitants   ■ GDP   7392 million us dollars

Breakdown of internal demand (GDP + imports) %
■ Private consumption   50
■ Public spending   19
■ Investment   10

Exports: 30% of GDP   Imports: 31% of GDP

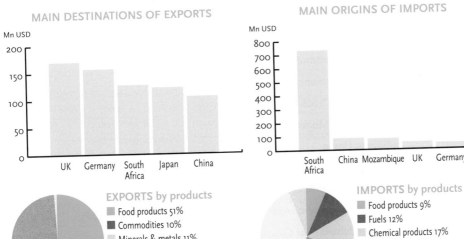

MAIN DESTINATIONS OF EXPORTS

Mn USD

UK | Germany | South Africa | Japan | China

EXPORTS by products
■ Food products 51%
■ Commodities 10%
■ Minerals & metals 11%
■ Manufactured goods 27%
■ Miscellaneous 1%

MAIN ORIGINS OF IMPORTS

Mn USD

South Africa | China | Mozambique | UK | Germany

IMPORTS by products
■ Food products 9%
■ Fuels 12%
■ Chemical products 17%
■ Other manufactured products 23%
■ Transport & capital goods 35%
■ Miscellaneous 4%

5

STANDARD OF LIVING / PURCHASING POWER

Indicators	Zimbabwe	Regional average	DC average
GNP per capita (PPP dollars)	2550	2708	6548
GNP per capita	460	985	3565
Human development index	0.551	0.493	0.702
Wealthiest 10% share of national income	40	35	32
Urban population percentage	35	42	60
Percentage under 15 years old	45	43	32
Number of telephones per 1000 inhabitants	18	32	157
Number of computers per 1000 inhabitants	12	15	64

ACRONYM TABLE AND LEXICON

AFTA	ASEAN Free Trade Area
ASEAN:	Association of South-east Asian Nations
CEE:	central and eastern european
CEFTA:	Central European Free Trade Agreement
CEMAC:	Central Africa Economic and Monetary Community
CIF:	cost, insurance and freight
CIS:	Community of Independent States
COMESA:	Common Market for Eastern and Southern Africa
DFI:	direct foreign investment
EAC:	East African Community
ECOWAS:	Economic Community of West African States
EFTA:	European Free Trade Association
EMU:	Economic and Monetary Union
EU:	European Union
GCC:	Gulf Co-operation Council
GDP:	gross domestic product
HDI:	Human Development Index (0 to 1 range measured by the UNDP)
HIPC:	Heavily Indebted Poor Countries (programme/initiative)
ILSA:	Iran–Libya Sanctions Act — voted by the US Congress in August 1996 to penalize Iran and Libya, notably via trade sanctions
IMF:	International Monetary Fund
NAFTA:	North American Free Trade Agreement
NEPAD:	New Partnership for Africa's Development
NICT:	New information and communication technologies (also ICT without new)
OHADA:	Organization for the Harmonization of Business Law
OPEC:	Organization of Petroleum Exporting Countries
PRGF:	Poverty Reduction and Growth Facility
SACU:	Southern Africa Customs Union
SADC:	Southern African Development Community
SMES:	small and medium sized enterprises
UNDP:	United Nations Development Programme
WAEMU:	West African Economic and Monetary Union
WMD:	weapons of mass destruction
WTO:	World Trade Organisation

Cairns Group: WTO group of 18 agricultural exporting countries including Argentina, Australia, Bolivia, Brazil, Canada, Chile, Colombia, Costa Rica, Fiji Islands, Guatemala, Indonesia, Malaysia, New Zealand, Paraguay, Philippines, South Africa, Thailand and Uruguay.

Chapter XI: US commercial law procedure affording ailing companies temporary protection from creditors.

Currency Board: a system whereby a country pegs its currency to a foreign currency (generally the US dollar or euro) with a currency board replacing the central bank.

European Commission: the executive arm of European Union institutions, the commission drafts EU laws and policies and implements them as adopted by the EU Council and Parliament.

European Stability and Growth Pact: adopted during the European Council meeting in Amsterdam (1997), this pact commits states belonging to the monetary union to comply with strict fiscal rules, notably on control of public deficits.

Greenfield investments/ventures: new investments starting from scratch, unrelated to privatizations or asset acquisitions.

Paris Club: an informal group of official creditors of developing nations.

Real-effective exchange rate: nominal exchange rate adjusted for a country's internal inflation rate and the price differential with respect to its main trading partners.

SWIFT network (Society for Worldwide Interbank Financial Telecommunication): an organization equipped with an electronic system for transferring funds between member banks in Europe and North America.

5